T0360815

The Foundations of Economic Method, Second Edition

Methodology is often viewed as a bit-part player within economics. Too tied down with debating past disputes, methodology has been viewed by many within economics as an irrelevance.

This book attempts to change the sidelining of economic methodology by focusing on current neoclassical research programs, which are beginning to provide a sound theoretical basis for the evolution of economics, game theory, institutions and the market-based system. The book provides a clear analysis of the fundamentals of economic methodology and goes on to show how Karl Popper's theory of science has not been widely adopted by economists, how his philosophy has been misunderstood by methodologists and how Popperian theory can be incorporated into current neoclassical theory to change it for the better.

Many consider *Foundations of Economic Method* to be Boland's best work. This updated edition is radically changed from the original and will be much appreciated by not only students and researchers within economic methodology and philosophy, but also all those involved in neoclassical economics today.

Lawrence A. Boland is Professor of Economics at Simon Fraser University, Canada. He has published widely within economic methodology and is a Fellow of the Royal Society of Canada.

Routledge INEM Advances in Economic Methodology

The field of economic methodology has expanded rapidly during the last few decades. This expansion has occurred in part because of changes within the discipline of economics, in part because of changes in the prevailing philosophical conception of scientific knowledge, and also because of various transformations within the wider society. Research in economic methodology now reflects not only developments in contemporary economic theory, the history of economic thought, and the philosophy of science; but it also reflects developments in science studies, historical epistemology, and social theorizing more generally. The field of economic methodology still involves the search for rules for the proper conduct of economic science, but it also covers a vast array of other subjects and accommodates a variety of different approaches to those subjects.

The objective of this series is to provide a forum for the publication of significant works in the growing field economic methodology. Since the series defines methodology quite broadly, it will publish books on a wide range of different methodological subjects. The series is also open to a variety of different types of works: original research monographs, edited collections, as well as republication of significant earlier contributions to the methodological literature. The International Network for Economic Methodology (INEM) is proud to sponsor this important series of contributions to the methodological literature.

The Foundations of Economic Method, Second Edition

A Popperian Perspective

Lawrence A. Boland, FRSC

Routledge
Taylor & Francis Group

LONDON AND NEW YORK

First edition published 1982
by George Allen and Unwin

Second edition published 2003
by Routledge
2 Park Square, Milton Park, Abingdon, Oxon, OX14 4RN
Simultaneously published in the USA and Canada
by Routledge
605 Third Avenue, New York, NY 10017

British Library Cataloging in Publication Data
A catalogue record for this book is available from the British Library

Library of Congress Cataloging in Publication Data
Boland, Lawrence A.
    The foundations of economic method: a Popperian perspective / Lawrence A. Boland
    – 2nd ed.
        p. cm. – (Routledge INEM advances in economic methodology; 1)
Includes bibliographical references and index.
1. Economics–methodology. I. Title. II. Series.

HB131.B64 2003
330'.07'2–dc21

200204598

ISBN 13: 978–0–415–77114–6 (pbk)
ISBN 13: 978–0–415–26774–8 (hbk)

Dedication: To Reenie

Contents

Part II:
THE VISIBLE AGENDA OF NEOCLASSICAL ECONOMICS

Part V:
PUTTING POPPER ON THE AGENDA

Preface to the Second Edition

Anyone familiar with the first edition of this book will immediately notice that this edition is at least seventy percent larger. There are two key reasons for this. The most obvious is that the field of economic methodology has grown by leaps and bounds over the last two decades. But the more important reason is that, unlike other methodology books about economics, both versions of this one are devoted to what has become known as 'small-m' methodology. Small-m methodology is applied methodology. Small-m methodology is distinguished from big-M Methodology because the latter is more concerned with just the timeless questions that have bothered philosophers of science for decades or centuries. Small-m methodology is about issues that affect the decisions economic model builders make everyday. And those decisions differ year-by-year, decade-by-decade. Consequently, the various applied topics of concern in this edition will be those found in today's economic literature.

As with the first edition, I have endeavored to apply some core methodological considerations to a set of model-building decisions that face mainstream, neoclassical economists. In the first edition, the primary issues addressed were those facing neoclassical model builders in the early 1980s such as the limitations of the then popular Rational Expectations Hypothesis, the urgency of dealing with the problems of disequilibrium analysis, the questions posed by the alleged need for microfoundations of macroeconomics and the on-going concern for the problems created by the extent to which neoclassical economics seems incapable of dealing with the element of time in a satisfactory manner.

In this edition, the field of application is very different – partly because the methodological questions currently facing model builders are different and partly because I have expanded the field of application to include some generic methodological problems that I failed to address in the first edition. Specifically, the new questions are those raised by the consideration particularly of New Institutional Economics, game theory and evolutionary economics. Thus, to expand the field, I will also address methodological problems such as those presented by so-called 'bounded rationality', ideal-type methodology, Bayesian decision theory and the economics of information – some of these directly involve issues of learning methodology and epistemology.

The core methodology that I applied in the first edition is fundamentally the same here – I still call its manifestation the 'hidden agenda' of neoclassical economics. The discussion of this core has been expanded and I have added an extensive discussion of what I call the 'visible agenda', which involves how rationality is treated in neoclassical economics today and in particular with its use in game-theoretical models.

In this edition, as signaled with the added sub-title, the methodological perspective is entirely devoted to that provided by Karl Popper's theory of science. In particular, it should be noted, up front, that it is a perspective grounded in Popper's 'Critical Rationalism' as distinguished from what I think is a mistaken view, the one others call 'falsificationism'. Popper explicitly rejects so-called falsificationism and for good reasons. In this edition, several chapters are devoted to explaining why it is important to see why falsificationism is a false representation of Popper's theory of science.

In the first edition, I was satisfied just to outline the essential ingredients of any Popper-oriented research program that would address the important methodological problems of neoclassical economics. In this edition, I am going further to offer some examples where my version of a Popperian program can be applied. They are all examples where small-m methodology has a direct application. The application is direct since neoclassical models must be able to explain how an individual makes decisions and thus how he or she deals with information and disappointments. Thus, I argue, the individual decision maker's methodology and epistemology must explicitly be recognized in neoclassical models.

While the first edition of this book sold well under the circumstances – the limited market for economic methodology books – and it continues to be cited, those methodologists interested in the big-M Methodology questions found little of interest in my various books about small-m methodology. But, judging by recent conferences in Vancouver of the History of Economics Society and the International Network for Economic Methodology, the infatuation with big-M Methodology seems to be coming to an end. There were even multiple sessions about model building! Whether this amounts to a belated endorsement of my advocacy of small-m methodology remains an open question. It is to urge such a movement that motivates this revised edition of my 1982 book.

L.A.B.
Burnaby, British Columbia
15 September 2002

Preface to the First Edition

Given that most textbooks on neoclassical economic theory begin with a chapter about methodology, one might easily conclude that most economists think that the methodology of economics is absolutely fundamental. This is an illusion. The view that the appropriate methodology must be in hand *before* we begin our analysis of the facts is an artifact of an old-fashioned philosophy of science (viz., Inductivism) that was long ago discarded. According to the currently accepted philosophy of science (viz., Conventionalism), the nature of neoclassical theory is supposed to be quite independent of any individual economist's opinion of the appropriate methodology of economics. Today, we are supposed to believe that there is no need to discuss methodology simply because it does not matter. I shall endeavor to show that it does matter – and that, furthermore, methodology cannot be easily detached so as to be simply dispatched in an introductory chapter. The pressing theoretical problems that continue to challenge neoclassical theorists today are direct consequences of implicitly accepted views of the appropriate methodology for neoclassical economics.

Although I have written this book for economists – it has not been tailored to the tastes of philosophers – it is presumed that the reader is aware of the more elementary views of methodology found in standard textbooks and books on the history of economic thought. Since I cannot see how one can understand economic methodology without understanding economic theory, I shall presume that the reader has successfully negotiated a course through intermediate micro- and macroeconomic theory.

My argument in this book is rather straightforward. I shall argue that every neoclassical research program is designed (1) to be consistent with acceptable ways of dealing with the Problem of Induction, and (2) to provide a methodological individualist explanation of economic behavior of the economy, that is, one which is based on the methodological prescription that allows only individuals to be posited as the locus of decision-making. With this in mind, I shall argue that neoclassical economists have thereby made their research program an impossible task because the Problem of Induction cannot, and need not, be solved. They compound this difficulty with psychologism, that is, by erroneously identifying individuals with psychological states. I will not press the additional point that the Conventionalist view of methodology (viz., that an individual's view of methodology does not matter) is inconsistent with a neoclassical theory which is supposed to see the individual as the center of everything – but this point does show that usual reluctance to discuss methodology might lead to certain inconsistencies.

If my argument concerning the design of neoclassical economics and its reliance on psychologism is correct, then it will be seen that most of the leading *theoretical* problems are impossible to solve. However, I shall also attempt to show that the essential individualist spirit of neoclassical economics can be preserved if the Problem of Induction is rejected and the concept of individualism is freed of its usual psychologism. All of this is a matter of fundamental methodology and thus for theoretical reasons we need to examine the foundations of economic method.

L.A.B.
Burnaby, British Columbia
8 October 1981

Acknowledgments

I wish to thank the editors and publishers of *The Canadian Journal of Economics*, *The Journal of Economic Literature* and *The South African Journal of Economics* for again giving me permission to reuse copyright material that I used in the first edition. I particularly wish to thank Sage Publications for permission to use material from 'Situational analysis beyond neoclassical economics' that appeared in *The Philosophy of the Social Sciences* (1998, pp. 515–21) and the *Universidad de Ciencias Empresariales y Sociales* for permission to use material from 'Recognizing knowledge in economic models' that appeared in Ενεργεια: *International Journal of Philosophy and Methodology of Economics* (2002, pp. 22–31).

As well, I wish to take this opportunity to thank Irene M. Gordon and David L. Hammes who read the entire manuscript, providing many extremely useful comments and criticisms. And I wish to thank Max Albert, Atsu (James) Amegashie, Rafe Champion, Phil Curry, Ruth Forsdyke, Anita Gantner, Dorian Hajno, Kenneth Allen von Hopf, Mike Maschek, and Johann Scharler for reading and criticizing particular parts; also John Finch, Phil Mirowski and Roy Weintraub for help on some needed research material.

Prologue

Understanding the methodology
of economics

It has often been said, and certainly not without justification, that the man of science is a poor philosopher. Why then should it not be the right thing for the physicist to let the philosopher do the philosophizing? Such might indeed be the right thing at a time when the physicist believes he has at his disposal a rigid system of fundamental concepts and fundamental laws which are so well established that waves of doubt cannot reach them; but, it cannot be right at a time when the very foundations of physics itself have become problematic as they are now. At a time like the present, when experience forces us to seek a newer and more solid foundation, the physicist cannot simply surrender to the philosopher the critical contemplation of the theoretical foundations; for, he himself knows best, and feels more surely where the shoe pinches.

Albert Einstein [1936, pp. 58–9]

This book examines the methodology of modern economics. By the term 'methodology' I mean the economists' view of the relationship between their theories and their methods of reaching conclusions about the nature of the real world using those theories. To many this endeavor may seem to be an easy task. But I will argue that the methodology of economics is not as obvious as it might first appear because the actual practice of methodology is taken for granted. I will argue that, until the late 1990s, what was usually discussed under the topic of 'economic methodology' was more concerned with the interests of philosophers of science than with the interests of economic theorists. I will advance the view that a proper study of methodology should be concerned with the actual role of methodology as manifested in the nature of neoclassical theories, models and research agenda.

By 'modern economics' I mean primarily the economics taught today in the first-year economic principles courses and textbooks found in almost all universities and colleges in North America and most of Britain and continental Europe. The so-called heterodox alternatives such as institutional, Austrian or Marxist are regrettably marginal. Modern economics is instead dominated by neoclassical economics, which is based on a view that the economy being explained is the result of decisions made by people acting individually in the pursuit of their own interest. As we will see, even this simple statement of neoclassical economics embodies a lot of hidden methodology and thus this hidden methodology will be the primary focus of the discussion in this book. It should also be noted that, as a result of the overwhelming dominance, even referring to 'neoclassical' economics presents problems for discussion since mainstream economists seldom refer to their own economics as being 'neoclassical'. It is simply taken for granted that modern economics is inherently neoclassical economics – and, as I will argue, things taken for granted are always a rich source of problems for methodology discussions.

Since the mid-1960s, few economists have found it necessary to question what they call their 'methodology'; most seem quite convinced that they can survive without ever examining their methods of analysis. As fads go, methodology is still not considered to be a 'mainstream' research topic. Where actually offered in an economics curriculum, methodology has been more an intellectual 'luxury' item for which there is little demand. Why, then, would anyone want to increase the supply of such studies?

While over the last twenty years there has been a growing interest in developing methodology as a sub-discipline of economics, methodology continues to be ignored by mainstream economists. The absence of a demand for new methodology among mainstream economists does not preclude there being an old methodology that is still being used like a set of old tools. The prevailing views of methodology in mainstream, neoclassical economics still are, in effect, part of our intellectual capital. The reason why there has been no market for new methodology is that the potential demanders continue to be quite satisfied with the productivity of their old methodology and they cannot see any potential for improvement. However, it is still necessary to examine one's tools occasionally to see if they are doing their job. My central concern here will be that what is often taken for granted in methodology by mainstream economists is exactly what is most important to examine.

Before I assess the productivity of the prevailing views of methodology, I will examine the role of methodology in neoclassical theory. I will argue that, although our methodological capital is often taken for granted, the prevailing methodology of economics plays an essential role in *theoretical* questions considered quite topical today. Methodology plays a role both by affecting the nature of the theoretical questions that have the highest priority and then by affecting the viability of the solutions to those problems.

How to study the methodology of neoclassical economics

Since neoclassical economics is a discipline that is primarily concerned with the consequences of 'rational' decision-making, methodology – as a study of methods of assessing information and of changing knowledge – cannot be considered irrelevant. Any decision-maker must have some knowledge from which to determine, and by which to assess, the options available. What do we presume about the individual decision-maker's knowledge? Or, better still, what do we presume about the individual decision-maker's methodology that allows for 'rational' choices? If neoclassical economics is supposed to explain, or even just to describe, the process of making decisions, surely the methods utilized by the decision-maker must play a central role in the *process* and thereby in the outcome of the process.

If it is granted for the moment that decision-makers do depend on some sort of methodology in their decision-making process, is there any relationship between the neoclassical economist's conception of that practical methodology and the methodology utilized in forming explanations of that process? I will argue that there is. And moreover, I will argue that this rarely explored relationship is the major obstacle in the further development of a successful neoclassical theory of an economy as envisaged by Adam Smith, Alfred Marshall or Leon Walras – that is, one which consists only of individual decision-makers. But if methodology is so important, why is it not a high-priority research topic? The answer to this question is that most economists think either that there is only one possible methodology or that all other approaches are irrational.

This study of the methodology of neoclassical economics will involve the recognition of an uncommon distinction – one between how methodology is practiced by economic theorists and model builders and the methodology they presume is practiced by the typical economic agent whose behavior they wish to explain. Specifically, I will distinguish between two different perspectives on the role of methodology in neoclassical economics. First, I will examine the methodology embodied in every neoclassical theory or analysis. That is, I will examine various alternative views of how neoclassical economists explain the behavior of the decision-makers in the economy. Although I will discuss the various views, I nevertheless will argue that just one view dominates the economists' explanation of their own behavior with respect to methodology. Second, I will explore the methodological consequences of this dominance on the economic theorist's conception of the methodology of the individual decision-maker who is the object of economic studies.

What is important about this distinction is that there is always the possibility that the methodology *practiced* by neoclassical economists is inconsistent with the methodology *presumed* to be the basis of the individual decision-making process. What is interesting is that even without an explicit discussion of methodology by mainstream economists, there is, nevertheless, a remarkable consistency between these two perspectives. However, I shall also argue that this is one of the major shortcomings of neoclassical economics. The view that dominates neoclassical theory, both in practice and in its conception of rational decision-making, is based on an inadequate theory of knowledge. Although at first this may seem to be a criticism of neoclassical theory, I shall also argue that the dominant view is not only unnecessary for the neoclassical conception of rational decision-making but it limits that conception. Hence neoclassical theory can be easily improved by a broader view of methodology.

The second perspective, the neoclassical conception of the rational decision-maker's methodology, will be a primary topic of this book because it is here that the study of methodology can have a profound impact on the nature of specific neoclassical theories. Before the theoretical issues of the appropriate conception of the decision-maker's methodology can be examined, a clear idea about the mainstream methodology embodied in neoclassical economics needs to be developed. To begin, a little detective work is necessary because the embodied methodology is not very visible. On the one hand, as I have noted, few economists discuss methodology while they are using it because they take it for granted; and on the other hand, when it is discussed, few neoclassical economists practice what they preach.

The failures of the 'new methodologists' and their 'big-M' methodology

I have been careful so far to focus on the discussion of methodology among *mainstream* economists. The reason is that since 1982 there has been the establishment of a small, non-mainstream group of would-be methodologists who do openly discuss economic methodology. This group has been impressively successful in developing a methodology-oriented sub-discipline – complete with conferences, journals and at least one Ph.D. program. Unfortunately, mainstream economists mostly ignore this group. The reason is simple: mainstream economists reject the interests of these new methodologists. From the beginning, the new methodologists thought that to be successful they should be able to fit in with the activities and interests of philosophers. However, as has been observed [McCloskey 1985], mainstream economists are not interested in 'big-M' Methodology with its concerns for big philosophical questions. Instead, mainstream economists are more likely to be interested in 'small-m' methodology that focuses on useful methodological ideas that help them make practical decisions when building their models.

The promise of 'small-m' methodology

Mainstream economists do not feel any need to consult philosopher-kings or philosopher-priests. Instead, mainstream economic model builders need 'methodological plumbers'. While there was a brief period when the new methodologists urged the study of the actual practice of economics, their success continued to be hampered by the presumption that such a study must be done in accordance with the goals and objectives of philosophers and philosophers of science. Not much was accomplished and hardly anyone in the mainstream took notice. But the mainstream does seem to be interested in 'small-m' methodology whenever the issues are focused on econometric methodology. Recently, the new methodologists have taken notice of the methodology of economic model building (prompted by the publication of a book about models and model building [viz. Morgan and Morrison 1999]). If the new methodologists follow through with their recognition of a practical role for methodologists in the process of developing economic models, then there is hope for 'small-m' methodology as a useful sub-discipline of mainstream economics.

Textbook rituals and relics

Despite the mainstream economist's professed disinterest in both big-M and small-m methodology, there still are explicit discussions of methodology that appear at the beginning of almost all undergraduate economics textbooks. Unfortunately, these discussions are poor reflections of the actual methods embodied in the economics theories presented later in those textbooks. The textbook discussions are nothing more than ritual exercises. They serve no other purpose and they have virtually no bearing on the nature of the theories that are presented.

In principle, the textbook methodology chapters should be a good guide to an understanding of the methodology actually used in economics. The ritual they serve would have us believe that by following the correct methodology we are guaranteed the avoidance of virtually all mistakes. We are told that economic theory is based on some principles of methodology, such as the recognition of the importance of distinguishing between 'normative' and 'positive' statements. The latter are supposedly scientifically superior to the former and are sometimes distinguished from 'tautologies'. Again, positive statements are to be preferred. We are sometimes told that economists agree that only 'testable' statements are scientifically important. Recent textbooks also urge us to recognize that all 'facts' are 'theory-laden' and thus that economic theory can never 'prove' anything.

Any textbook chapter on methodology that consists of such a collection of observations is useless because it is an *ad hoc* hodgepodge of relics from ancient methodological disputes. The difficulty with historical relics living in current practice is not that they are old but that they are taken for granted and thereby put beyond criticism. Methodological problems can be fundamental. And to that extent it is rather dangerous to take them for granted. But worse than this, the items in the collection very often are contradictory. Not only are the textbook principles of methodology relics from old debates over the appropriate methodology to use in economics, but also often both sides of any given debate are advocated.

Methodology vs. techniques

Anyone interested in studying the methodology of economics will have to look somewhere other than introductory chapters of textbooks. The only other apparent sources are the explicit mainstream discussions of methodology that appear in econometrics articles. For my purposes these simply misuse the term 'methodology'. Presentations of methodology in typical econometrics articles are really nothing more than reports about the mechanical procedures used, without any hint of the more philosophical questions one would expect to find in a book on methodology. So-called 'methodological critiques' turn out, upon examination, to be critiques of the statistical definitions or statistical tests used in the study in question. Similarly, 'methodological issues' turn out to be questions of whether to use 'comparative statics' or whether to use a 'moving average' or discrete observations, etc.

Of course, everyone is free to use the word 'methodology' in any way he or she wishes. All that is important here is to recognize that questions about appropriate research techniques are of little interest to those interested in the more traditional philosophical questions of epistemology or methodology; that is, questions about the relationship between our theoretical knowledge and our conceptions of the world around us. Specifically, studies of research techniques will yield virtually no clues about the objectives of a particular line of research or theoretical investigation. And above all, there is nothing involved in the questions of research techniques that could be identified as being 'neoclassical'.

Methodology vs. the philosophy of economics

The few mainstream economists who might have an interest in studying the methodology of economics also think we should always begin by consulting philosophers of economics. Unfortunately, philosophers of economics are too often concerned with the philosophical question of whether economics is a science, that is, a science like physics or chemistry. But, of course, the rest of the mainstream economists will not usually be interested in such a question. I say usually because there are times, like after-dinner speeches, where the question might be addressed. Of course, after-dinner speeches are entertainment. Moreover, while philosophers should not be discouraged from studying economics, so far, philosophers have been unable to produce much that might interest the mainstream model builder. And above all, the philosophers of economics so far have not provided anything that will help those of us interested in understanding 'small-m' methodology.

Methods of understanding methodology

If we cannot be guided either by textbook methodology chapters, the philosophy of economics, or by econometrics 'methodology', how can we hope to understand economic methodology? Perhaps the answer can be found in the practice of the economics profession. But how can we bring to light the actual methodology practiced by neoclassical economists?

Traditionally, there has been only one approach to an understanding of economics methodology – one would study methodology by reviewing all of the famous past debates about methodology [Albert 1979/99; Blaug 1980/92; Caldwell 1982/94]. This popular approach has its shortcomings primarily in that it contributes new life to old relics and skeletons that would better be left to rest in peace. The major shortcoming is that historians tend to focus on high-profile exceptions to the rule rather than on the more mundane, everyday methods that are tacitly employed by practicing economists.

At first blush one might consider the history of economic methodology as a special case of the history of scientific methodology. This approach begs the methodological question of whether there really is a unity of method in all sciences [Agassi 1969b; see also Hands 2001]. Those economists who do not ascribe to the unity-of-method philosophy are lost in the shuffle. And probably worst of all, few of the economics writers who ascribe to the unity-of-method approach are likely to be sufficiently competent in matters of physics or chemistry to draw meaningful parallels with economics and to avoid giving life to relics from the history of the physical sciences.

Note that the traditional approach is serial in nature, as is evident in the usual classification of methodology as a branch of the study of the history of economic thought (see, for example, the *Journal of Economic Literature* classifications and the discussion of them in Boland [2001]). If we think of the history of thought approach to economic methodology as a 'time-series' explanation of current practice, the obvious alternative would be a 'cross-sectional' explanation.

The major disadvantage of the time-series approach is that it presumes a certain continuity of the nature of economics and the concept of continuity begs certain questions that need to be examined. For example, why do economists continue to use one particular methodology or take one particular methodological perspective when there are alternatives available? Such a continuity perspective does not always explain *why* economists adhere to their practiced methodology. One of the advantages of a cross-sectional study of current methodology is that it immediately requires consideration of the reason for consciously perpetuating a particular methodology or consideration of why it is taken for granted. This is important, as I wish to examine those problems that are 'hidden' because they are taken for granted and which are the foundation of most methodological strategies pursued by economic theorists and model builders.

Obviously, even if one looked only at the current practice of economists, it would be impossible to avoid making references to philosophical relics, since much of everyday thought can be traced back to antiquity. One difficulty with the historical, or time-series, approach to methodology is that it gives life to all relics regardless of their relevance to current practice. There is no doubt that some relics do still live in the body of economic analysis today (for example, some philosophers of economics think John Stuart Mill's methodology lurks in the halls of modern economics [see Hausman 1992]). But if the relics are still alive, their reason for existence must be found in current practice and not just in the fact that they were popular many years ago.

The cross-sectional approach used in this book will be very different from the usual discussions of economics methodology. Rather than attempting to explain which philosophical problems troubled Sir Isaac Newton, I will be more concerned with the philosophical problems that directly or indirectly impinge on the theoretical and practical concerns of today's neoclassical economic model builders.

Methodology as agenda

The study of neoclassical methodology presented here will focus on the *research agenda* of every neoclassical theory, model, analysis, article, etc. The idea of an 'agenda' is not novel. It is rather standard in theories of organizations [e.g., Arrow 1974; Jarvie 2001]. The idea of an agenda is also appreciated by anyone familiar with parliamentary procedures. The chair of a committee, for example, runs a meeting according to an agenda. The agenda of a meeting is a list of items to be handled and their relative position on the list indicates their priority, in the sense that they are handled in the order of their appearance on the list.

The idea of an agenda will be employed as an ordered list of items to be handled in any research program. Specifically, a research agenda is an ordered list of theoretical or philosophical problems that either are to be solved by the research conducted or are problems whose solutions play a necessary role in the solutions of the other problems to be considered.

Paradigms and research programs

Every essay, research report, article, book, etc., is written according to a specific 'agenda'. The agenda may be different for each, although many will have common items. The objective of a cross-sectional study of current practice in neoclassical economics is to identify those items that appear on every agenda.

A reader familiar with the view of science advocated by Thomas Kuhn or Imre Lakatos will likely consider the common agenda items to be the 'paradigm' or 'research program'. While such a consideration is quite compatible with what will be presented here, it can be a bit misleading, since their view of science is based on an historical or continuity view of natural science. Most applications of their view of science tend to identify the explicit assumptions traditionally used by neoclassical economists as the essence of the neoclassical paradigm. The most common example of a paradigm is the visible use of the maximization hypothesis in neoclassical analysis. I will argue that such *explicit* assumptions are not enough to specify the agenda.

The cross-sectional approach utilized here will go beyond the Kuhn-Lakatos view by considering any particular neoclassical research program or paradigm to be only one specific *implementation* of the neoclassical agenda. That is, I will be concerned with the agenda which is the common foundation of many diverse research programs from Alchian [1950], Clower and Leijonhufvud [1973], Stigler and Becker [1977], Lucas and Sargent [1978], Solow [1979], to Williamson [1985], Kreps [1990], Laibson [1997] and Pessendorfer [1995] and including, perhaps more surprising, that of Leibenstein [1979] or Simon [1986]. It will be apparent that what the followers of Kuhn (or Lakatos) commonly consider the 'paradigm' of neoclassical economic theory represents only a small subset of the items on any particular research agenda – usually they identify only the maximization hypothesis. For the purposes of this study of methodology, the concept of a research program will have to be expanded to require a complete specification of the research agenda by identifying the implicit as well as the explicit agenda items. The cross-sectional approach presented here will be distinguished primarily because the items on the agenda are considered as specific problems to be dealt with in every article or research project.

An example of a neoclassical methodology agenda

Before this prologue becomes any more abstract, let us consider a typical neoclassical agenda, the one that is at the core of every mainstream textbook. For more than thirty years, the Ordinal Demand Theory of Hicks and Allen [1934] was the subject of extensive analysis [e.g., Chipman, *et al.* 1971]. The purpose of the analysis was to identify a specific set of assumptions that together would be just sufficient to yield a traditional set of results. Stating the purpose this way immediately begs two questions. What is the traditional set of results? And, what assumptions are admissible into the set?

To keep this example straightforward let us follow the lead of the 1970 Nobel prize-winner, Paul Samuelson, and require that any given theory of demand at least be able to yield his 'Fundamental Theorem of Consumption Theory', namely the proposition that the slope of the demand curve for any normal good be negative [1953, p. 2]. The only limitations on admissible assumptions are that they must include (a) an assumption that an individual's utility function exists, and (b) an assumption that utility is being maximized subject only to the constraints of given prices and a given income. Beyond these simple requirements, virtually anything goes.

The problem that any particular neoclassical analysis of demand must solve continues to be: how can the utility function be specified so as to yield the 'Fundamental Theorem'? For example, should we assume cardinal or ordinal utility or is it enough to assume diminishing marginal rates of substitution? These problems form the visible agenda of neoclassical demand theory; and its specification is the task of a broader methodological agenda, which is usually hidden because it is taken for granted.

The broader methodological hidden agenda is concerned with questions about why one would ever bother with individual utility functions, maximization hypotheses, etc. To discover the nature of a given methodological agenda, we need to ask questions such as 'What problem is solved by treating the individual as the sole possessor of a specific utility function?', 'What problem is solved by assuming the demander is a maximizer rather than, say, a "satisficer"?', 'What problem is solved by establishing that demand curves are usually downward sloping?', and so on.

Foundations as problems on the 'hidden agenda'

It will be argued here that the foundations of neoclassical economic methodology, the hidden agenda, consist of two related but autonomous methodological problems. The first is the much-discussed 'Problem of Induction'. The other is the less discussed but more pervasive 'Explanatory Problem of Individualism'. The nature and significance of these two methodological problems will be explained in Part I. How they are manifested in the visible agenda of neoclassical economics is discussed in Part II. How the foundations influence the research programs in neoclassical economics will be critically examined in Part III. Part IV will critically examine two related questions about the methodology of neoclassical economists: How is methodology practiced in mainstream neoclassical economics? And, how have the new methodologists of the 1980s and 1990s viewed the actual practice of methodology in the process of mainstream neoclassical economic model building? Part V will suggest how neoclassical economics can be improved by explicitly considering Karl Popper's theory of science. And, Part VI will discuss explicit applications of the 'small-m' methodology promoted in this book.

The strategy employed throughout this book is the following. Every essay, article, research report, etc., will be considered to be an offered solution to a specific problem or set of problems. To understand an essay (or article, etc.) is to understand the problem-situation [Popper 1945/66, 1963/94]. The problem-situation or 'situational logic' approach to understanding is easy for trained economists to appreciate, since it is also the methodological basis for most neoclassical economics analyses. Again, for example, we can see that Ordinal Demand Theory is based on an analysis of a specific problem-situation. Namely, the problem faced is how to achieve the demander's aim of maximizing utility given his or her objective and the constraints formed by the givenness of the prices and income.

My approach then is to presume that in every problem situation we need to recognize the *aim* of the decision-maker and the *constraints* faced. Usually, it is the task of the theorist to *conjecture* both the problem including the aim and a set of one or more constraints that impede the attainment of the objectives. And thus the theorist's claim is that the behavior being explained does solve the conjectured problem. However, one must be careful here to distinguish between two different problem situations. One is the situation facing the individual demander or supplier as hypothesized by the theorist; the other is the situation facing the theorist as hypothesized by the methodologist. The latter methodological problem-situation will be the primary focus of the analysis of this book.

Part I
THE 'HIDDEN AGENDA' OF NEOCLASSICAL ECONOMICS

1 The Problem *of* Induction vs. the Problem *with* Induction

Hume's objective doctrine … has two parts: … (1) in causation there is no indefinable relation except conjunction or succession; (2) induction by simple enumeration is not a valid form of argument. Empiricists in general have accepted the first of these theses and rejected the second. When I say they have rejected the second, I mean that they have believed that, given a sufficiently vast accumulation of instances of a conjunction, the likelihood of the conjunction being found in the next instance will exceed a half; or, if they have not held exactly this, they have maintained some doctrine having similar consequences.

Bertrand Russell [1945, p. 667]

Hume showed that inductive arguments could not be justified, even in part, but he did not think that they were thereby incorrect. Most later writers have agreed.

David Miller [1994, p. 13]

Scientists never 'explain' any behavior, by theory or by any other hook. Every description that is superseded by a 'deeper explanation' turns out upon careful examination to have been replaced by still another description, albeit possibly a more useful description that covers and illuminates a wider area. I can illustrate by what everyone will agree is the single most successful 'theory' of all time. I refer to Newton's theory of universal gravitation.

Paul Samuelson [1964, p. 737]

Since the time when Adam Smith's friend David Hume observed that there was no logical justification for the common belief that much of our empirical knowledge was based on inductive proofs [Hume 1739; Russell 1945], methodologists and philosophers have been plagued with what they call the 'Problem of Induction'. The paradigmatic instance of the Problem of Induction is the realization that we cannot provide an inductive proof that 'the sun will rise tomorrow'. This leads many of us to ask, 'So *how* do we know that the sun will rise tomorrow?' If it is impossible to provide a proof, then presumably we would have to admit that we do not know! Several writers have claimed to have solved this famous problem [Popper 1972; Hollis and Nell 1975; see Miller 2002] – which is quite surprising, since it is impossible to solve. Nevertheless, what it is and how it is either 'solved' or circumvented is fundamental to understanding all contemporary methodological discussions.

The Problem *of* Induction

> It is clear, Hume felt, that sense experience is the primary matter of all knowledge; ideas, general concepts, theories, universals, and all such things are secondary or derivative. This contention, that all knowledge is derivative from sense experience, leads directly to the 'problem of induction'. No matter how many swans I have seen, nor how many have been seen by others, there is no justification for asserting the general proposition that 'all swans are white'.
>
> Scott Gordon [1991, p. 127]

Since the Problem of Induction is fundamental, a clear statement of it is needed. Before attempting this, let me clarify some of its elementary parts. First, there is the implicit presumption that empirical knowledge requires logical justification. I will call this 'Justificationism'. Justificationism probably needs little explanation at this stage, since it is widely presumed or accepted, but for future reference, let me be specific.

> *Justificationism* is the methodological doctrine that asserts that nobody can claim to possess knowledge unless he or she can also demonstrate (with a proof) that his or her knowledge is true; that is, everyone must justify his or her knowledge claims.

Crudely stated, this requirement says, 'knowledge' is not Knowledge unless it is (proven) *true* knowledge. Second, there is the further requirement that the justification of empirical knowledge requires an inductive, as opposed to a deductive, proof. This additional requirement will be called 'Inductivism'. Although Inductivism has been around for several hundred years, the operative view of it will be the following:

> *Inductivism* is the methodological doctrine that asserts that any justification of one's knowledge must be logically based *only* on experiential evidence consisting of particular or singular observation statements; that is, one must justify his or her knowledge using only verifiable observations that have been verified by experience.

Given Inductivism, any straightforward solution to the Problem of Induction requires an 'Inductive logic', that is, there must be a form of logic which permits arguments consisting of only 'singular statements' (e.g., 'The sun rose in Vancouver at 7:03am on November the 2nd, 2002'), while the conclusions that validly follow may be 'general statements' (e.g., 'The sun will rise every day'). Now I can state the famous problem:

> The *Problem of Induction* is that of finding a general *method* of providing an inductive proof for anyone's claim to empirical knowledge.

In other words, this is the problem of finding a form of logical argument in which (a) the conclusion is a *general* statement, such as one of the true 'laws' of economics, or the conclusion is the choice of the true theory or model from among various competitors; and (b) the assumptions include *only* singular statements of *particulars* (such as simple observation reports). With an argument of this form one is said to be arguing inductively from the truth of particulars to the truth of generals. (In contrast, a deductive form of argument supposedly proceeds from the truth of generals to the truth of particulars.) If one could solve the Problem of Induction, the true 'laws' or general theories of economics (i.e., economic knowledge) could then be said to be induced logically from particular observations (and thereby justified).

For very many, many years virtually everyone believed that science and its 'scientific method' represented a solution to the Problem of Induction [see Agassi 1963]. This belief was based on the commonly accepted view that Newtonian physics represented *true* knowledge, since there were many reports of the existence of inductive proofs of that knowledge. Late in the nineteenth century, when doubts were raised concerning the absolute truth of Newtonian physics, a more moderate claim for science was developed [e.g., Poincaré 1905/52; Duhem 1906/62; Eddington 1928].

The Problem of Induction in economics

> All theory depends on assumptions which are not quite true. That is what makes it theory.
>
> Robert Solow [1956, 65]

It is interesting to note that except for some earlier books explicitly about methodology [e.g., Hollis and Nell 1975; Stewart 1979; Blaug 1980/92], economics writers have rarely been concerned with this allegedly fundamental problem. There is a very simple reason for this. For most of the nineteenth century, economists simply believed that the Problem of Induction had been solved; thus it did not need any further consideration. After all, Newton seems to claim to have arrived at the laws of physics from scientific observation using inductive methods [e.g., Newton 1704/1952]. In Adam Smith's time, inductive generalization was the paradigm of rational thinking; Newton's physics was the paradigm of inductive generalization.

Unfortunately, Hume's critical examinations of logical justifications for the acceptance of inductive proofs were largely ignored [Russell, 1945 pp. 659ff.]. Consequently, most thinkers continued to believe that there was an inductive logic. Thus there was no apparent reason to doubt the claims made for the 'scientific' basis of Newton's physics. And there was no reason to doubt the possibility of rational (i.e., inductive) decision-making. Supposedly, whenever one had all the facts, one needed only to be inductively rational to arrive without doubt at correct decisions. Moreover, whenever one made an error in judgment, it would have had to be due to either an irrational moment or a failure to gather all the facts.

Although economic theory has been deeply affected by the eighteenth-century beliefs about rational decision-making, the rationalism of economic theory is not obviously inductivist – with the possible exception of the textbook distinction between 'positive' and 'normative' economics. At least, very little of the faith in rationalism *appears* to have survived as explicit Inductivism. The reason for the absence of explicit Inductivism in mainstream economics today is that neoclassical economics reflects the concerns of late nineteenth-century and early twentieth-century philosophers, who were becoming aware of the possibility that Newton's physics might not actually be true and, more important, that Inductivism might not be able to live up to its promises.

It can be argued that anyone who believed that Newton's physical laws were true because they had been inductively proven must have been in some way mistaken. Such an argument would lead to two questions: (1) Did Newton fail to prove his theory true because he was mistaken about the objective *quality* of his 'facts'? (2) Was Hume correct about the absence of an adequate inductive logic, so no *quantity* of 'facts' could ever prove Newton's theory true? In response to such questions modern economic methodology falls generally into one of two opposing methodological camps depending on the answers given (what methodology is actually *practiced* by economists is a wholly separate question to be discussed later in this chapter). On the one hand (for want of a better name), there are the 'conservative' methodologists who would give an affirmative answer to (1) and a negative one to (2) and would promote the importance of the distinction between 'positive' and 'normative' economics. On the other hand, there are the 'liberal' methodologists who would give a negative answer to (1) and an affirmative one to (2) and would find the views of Solow and Samuelson, quoted above, more to their liking.

The Problem *with* Induction

The major point to be stressed here is that both positions taken by methodologists are based on Justificationism as well as on some form of Inductivism. And thus, both methodological positions accept the Problem of Induction. They differ only in regard to how the Problem *with* Induction is recognized.

The 'conservative' methodologists in economics say that there is nothing fundamentally wrong with inductive arguments, with the one possible exception that we must be very careful in the collection of 'facts'. For the 'conservative' methodologists, if there should be a problem with the application of induction in economics or other social sciences, then it is that there are not enough 'hard facts' [e.g., Leontief 1971]. Specifically, before beginning an inductive proof one must assure quality and thus be careful to eliminate subjective or 'normative' opinions about what are the 'facts'. The 'conservative' methodologists thus stress that for economics to be scientific it must be based on 'positive' rather than 'normative' statements.

The 'liberal' methodologists in economics take a position which is less optimistic but more devious. Rather than simply admitting that some theories which were once thought to be true are actually false, the 'liberals' obfuscate the methodological questions by denying that (non-tautological) theories could ever be true. For example, they might argue that only a tautology can be true and only a self-contradiction can be false [Quine 1965].

Theories, according to the 'liberal' methodologists, are to be considered 'better' or 'worse', rather than true or false. The reason for this switch is that the 'liberal' methodologists still think that the Problem of Induction must be solved before one can discuss 'truth' but, to their credit, they recognize that there is a problem with inductive logic. Specifically, they realize that no *finite* quantity of true singular statements could ever prove that any given general statement is true. In short, they admit that there is no inductive logic, and *that* is the Problem *with* Induction.

The retreat to Conventionalism

> This doctrine [Conventionalism] contends that a scientific theory is, like a descriptive language, a device for ordering and communicating information which works because the members of a community know the rules and obey them. Thus, for example, in a telephone book all names are arranged in order according to the rules of the alphabet. This is purely a matter of convention. Any other ordering system could work equally well if it were generally accepted. The concepts of science, according to this view, are, similarly, only conventions that scientists have created. They are used to order empirical data but they cannot be construed to satisfy the positivist insistence that concepts should be representations of the real world.
>
> This view of science has some merits. It emphasizes that science is a human creation and a *social* phenomenon, and it focuses on the utility of scientific concepts rather than their brute descriptive realism. But its defects greatly exceed its virtues. Like the contention that empirical observations are 'theory-laden', it considers only the nature of *concepts,* and neglects the role of *explanatory hypotheses* in scientific investigation.
>
> Scott Gordon [1991, p. 610]

Despite the generous nods given to the positive/normative distinction in many economics textbooks, this popular distinction is nothing but a relic left over from late nineteenth-century attempts to save Inductivism (see J.N. Keynes [1917]). Since almost all economic methodologists have by now accepted that there is a Problem *with* Induction, one has to wonder why economics textbooks continue to promote the positive/normative distinction. The reason appears to be quite simple: For methodologists in economics, the Problem of Induction is still not dead!

The most openly adopted methodological position, in effect, puts Inductivism on a 'back-burner' for the present and temporarily puts a different position, 'Conventionalism', in its place along with Justificationism. I will argue here that, despite the attendant smoke, noise and celebration, the methodological controversies of the early 1960s, were merely family squabbles. That is to say, virtually all economic methodologists bow to the Problem of Induction (possible recent exceptions are Latsis [1972], Wong [1973], Newman [1976], Coddington [1979], Caldwell [1991a], Hands [1996] and Hoover [2001]). Since this problem is insolvable without an inductive logic, most methodological arguments in economics today are about the appropriate way to circumvent the Problem of Induction.

Given Conventionalism, it would appear that economists as methodologists do not attempt to solve the Problem of Induction itself but instead try to solve a weaker form of the Problem of Induction. For the purpose of discussing methodology, the problem-shift is unfortunate because the modified form of the Problem of Induction, which will be called the 'Problem of Conventions', is a bit more complicated than the original problem. The aim of the original Problem of Induction was a straightforward, objective, inductive proof of the (absolute) truth of any true theory. Contrarily, as I shall show, the aim of the Problem of Conventions is a choice of the 'best' theory according to current conventional measures of acceptable 'truth'. Without an inductive logic, the solution to the Problem of Conventions can get rather complicated (in exactly the same way welfare economics has difficulties with social choices [see Boland 1989, chap. 5]). To add to the complications, there are many different measures to choose from (e.g., simplicity, generality, testability, etc.), and the measure used may or may not involve 'inductive' evidence.

The Problem of Conventions

Let me now state the problem which still dominates economic methodology.

> The *Problem of Conventions* is the problem of finding generally acceptable criteria upon which to base any contingent, *deductive* proof of any claim to empirical 'knowledge'.

Note that although the Problem of Induction and Problem of Conventions differ regarding the nature of the proof required for justification, they are the same in regard to the requirement of Justificationism. The word 'knowledge' has been specifically enclosed in quotation marks because one of the consequences of the presumed Justificationism is that 'knowledge' is not Knowledge unless it has been proven absolutely true, and deductive proofs always depend on given assumptions.

Where pure Inductivism requires a final (absolute) inductive proof for any true theory, Conventionalism requires only a *conditional* deductive argument for why the chosen theory is the 'best' available. This poses a new problem. On the one hand, we assume because we do not know and, on the other, deductive arguments always have assumptions. Thus, the choice of any theory is always open to question. That is, one can always question the criteria used to define 'best' or 'better'. Thus, there is always the danger of an infinite regress – for example, by what meta-criteria would we choose the criteria of 'best'? There is also the danger of circular arguments – for example, the operative criteria are deemed appropriate because they are sufficient to justify our choice. Ultimately, the Problem of Conventions becomes one of providing a justification while at the same time avoiding an infinite regress and a circular justification – and all this is to be done without an inductive logic!

Conventionalism as fideism rather than skepticism

Behind Inductivism and Conventionalism is the worry surrounding Hume's rejections of any logic of induction. Specifically, those who abided by Justificationism in the eighteenth century feared that without an inductive logic, we would be left with skepticism, that is, left with the view that there could never be knowledge of any kind, since without a sufficient logical basis consisting of observable facts, any proof would lead to an infinite regress. In response, religious philosophers chose to stop the infinite regress with a foundation of presuppositions that are accepted as a matter of faith. Doing so is called 'fideism'. About this, the philosopher Joseph Agassi [1985, p. 88] notes:

> Most twentieth-century philosophers are fideists. Usually, since fideism is based on the pragmatic argument that we need faith for practical purposes, fideists tend to be pragmatists. They recommend those presuppositions that are most conducive to survival, namely the presuppositions of science.

While some fideists may be motivated by such practical concerns, here I am only concerned with recognizing that, in general, fideism is just one example of Conventionalism. And as such, fideism as Conventionalism is just the most common way to overcome the Problem *with* Induction and does so without claiming that one's knowledge is true. Instead, it is only claimed that in science knowledge is considered acceptable by presuppositions or criteria that are the current scientific conventions. Pragmatism, in general, usually makes a stronger claim along the lines that practical success is a sufficient condition to prove the truth of one's knowledge and thereby worthy of one's unshakable faith. But, in this case Pragmatism goes beyond Conventionalism. For now, I will postpone the discussion of Pragmatism in general until Chapter 11 – except to note here that Pragmatism is just another 'liberal' way to solve the Problem of Conventions.

Conventionalism vs. Inductivism

The 'conservative' methodologists (those who still do not wish to abandon Inductivism completely) might say that the Problem of Conventions is too precarious and tentative and that we would be better off trying to solve the original Problem of Induction – for example, by finding a way to establish objective facts [e.g., Rotwein 1980]. The 'liberal' methodologists (who deny the possibility of inductive logic) can counter by arguing that any claimed solution to the Problem of Induction is an illusion and that the 'solution' is but another instance of the Problem of Conventions. Their reasoning is simple. There are no 'objective facts' because all 'facts' are 'theory-laden' [e.g., Hanson 1965; Samuelson, Nordhaus and McCallum 1988] – that is, any claimed 'facts' must have been based on the acceptance of one or more theories. Thus, according to the 'liberal' view, any inductive 'proof' cannot be complete because every reported 'fact' will require a proof too. Hence, we will begin an infinite regress unless we have already accepted 'conventions' concerning the 'truth' of the 'facts'. In other words, the most we could ever expect to achieve is a logically consistent, deductive proof based on the prior acceptance of a set of 'conventions'. In this manner, the 'liberal' methodologists can claim that our concern is not whether a theory is *true*, but only whether our argument in its favor is logically *valid* – that is, logically consistent with the accepted conventions.

The 'conservative' methodologists still need not concede defeat. If all facts are theory-laden, our being concerned only with logical validity might mean that our ultimate goal can only be the creation of tautologies. The 'liberal' methodologists have handled this possibility with the *ad hoc* prescription that all economic theories and models must at the very least be 'falsifiable' or 'testable'. This prescription does avoid tautologies – but it does so only at the expense of leaving room for the 'conservative' methodologists to argue that empirical (i.e., inductive) evidence must play a role. Even though empirical evidence cannot provide a final proof, incomplete induction may be employed in the creation of competing theories or models, leaving deductive argument for the justification of the choice between them. This view also allows inductive evidence to be involved in the choice criteria used.

One can easily see that this is indeed a family dispute between 'liberal' and 'conservative' methodologists and that it could probably go on forever, since there never will be the allegedly needed and decisive arbiter of final (inductive) proofs. Both positions advocate a form of Conventionalism. Where the 'liberals' argue for a pure Conventionalism without any necessary role for inductive evidence (the so-called Hypothetical-Deductive model), the 'conservatives' advocate a more modest form of Conventionalism which does not completely abandon Inductivism or the need for some inductive evidence. As long as the necessity of logical justification (i.e., Justificationism) continues to be presumed while still admitting the impossibility of inductive proofs of general statements, some form of Conventionalism will always be seen to be a 'better' methodological position than pure Inductivism (that is, the strict requirement of final inductive proof). But perversely and more significantly, it must be observed that it is seen to be 'better' only if dealing with the Problem of Induction is still considered an important objective.

In some sense the only difference between the 'liberal' and 'conservative' positions is that only the latter holds out for a long-run solution to the Problem of Induction. In the short run – that is, for day-to-day methodological concerns – the positions are identical. Both positions require that the Problem of Conventions be solved in the short run. The 'conservative' methodologists thus have two viewpoints. They adopt Conventionalism in the short run and hold out for Inductivism in the long run. Given their ambivalence, discussing methodology in economics is often rather difficult because it is not always clear which viewpoint is operative. For the remainder of the book, except where specifically noted, Conventionalism will be identified with the short-run viewpoint so that there will be no need to distinguish between the 'conservative' and 'liberal' positions.

Conventionalism in economics

> From the very beginning the theory of consumer's choice has marched steadily towards greater generality, sloughing off at successive stages unnecessarily restrictive conditions.
>
> Paul Samuelson [1938, p. 61]

For my purposes it is unfortunate that the term 'Conventionalism' has been promoted as a pejorative one by the philosopher Karl Popper and his followers. Many can rightfully object to the apparent name-calling that is implied by the use of such terms as 'Conventionalist', 'Inductivist', 'Instrumentalist', and the like.

Few philosophers today would promote themselves as Conventionalists. But more important, in economics it is very difficult to find anyone who exactly fits one of the molds delineated by Popper. Nevertheless, Popper's methodological categorization does serve a heuristic purpose. However, despite its possible entertainment value, I do not wish to label individuals with peculiar philosophical tastes. My only concern here will be the identification of impersonal items on the impersonal hidden agenda of neoclassical economics.

The effects of Conventionalism

My argument here is that the first item on the hidden agenda of any neoclassical article is the Problem of Induction. The agenda item usually appears, however, in its weaker, modified form, as the Problem of Conventions.

When I say that any particular problem is on the hidden agenda of a given article I am saying either that one of the objectives of the article is to solve that problem or that it is presumed to have been solved already and that what appears in any given neoclassical article will be consistent with the presumed solution. Since the solution of the Problem of Conventions (and, hence, a circumvention of the Problem of Induction) is taken for granted, it might be difficult to find direct evidence of its presence. However, two clues to its presence can be identified.

First and foremost is the absence of references to any theory being true or false. The reason for this lacuna is that, *given Conventionalism*, if one were to refer to a theory being true, then it would imply that one has solved the Problem of Induction and thus has the ability to prove the theory's truth. But this would be inconsistent, as Conventionalism is predicated on a denial of the possibility of solving the Problem of Induction. So, strictly speaking, Conventionalism precludes any references to truth or falsity.

The Conventionalist ban on the use of the terms 'true' and 'false' would present obvious difficulties even for simple discussions. It would also complicate the use of other terms such as 'knowing' and 'knowledge', as well as 'explaining' and 'explanation'. The long-standing ban on the use of the words 'knowledge' and 'explanation' is somewhat compromised today with the game-theorists recognition that when one game player confronts another game player, there seems to be a necessity for some sort of assumption concerning what each knows about the other player as well as the rules of the game. I will discuss the problems of how game theory treats the decision-maker's knowledge in Chapter 4. For those economists who still think 'to know' means to possess 'true knowledge' and 'to explain' must mean to provide a true explanation, the prohibition still needs to be explained. To the extent that the prohibition continues, it seems to be due to a variation of the presumption of Justificationism, that to know is to have obtained provably 'true knowledge' and, similarly, 'to explain' is to give a provably 'true explanation'.

Although the ban on using the terms 'true' and 'false' in their literal sense is rather complete [e.g., Aumann 1985], the terms 'knowledge' and 'explanation' do appear often in the literature. What needs to be understood, however, is that there is a presumption that whenever the term 'explanation' is used one never means literally true explanation. Instead, an 'explanation' only means a 'true' explanation *relative* to some accepted conventional measures of 'approximation' [Samuelson 1952, 1964; Simon 1979].

Consider, for example, the old debates over the theory of imperfect competition [Archibald 1961; Stigler 1963] – where the truth status of the theory never seemed to be at issue. Instead, some argued that the concept of imperfect competition is either empty or arbitrary and unduly complex. Simplicity would be served by merely applying perfect competition or monopoly where appropriate [Friedman 1953]. The dispute thus became one of 'which is a better approximation' – a simplifying approximation which gives more positive results, or a generalizing approximation which allows for a better description of what firms actually do? This dispute will not be resolved without an accepted criterion of approximation.

The second clue to the presence of Conventionalism is the methodologists' apparent concern for making a choice among competing theories or models. As mentioned above, most methodological articles and debates have been about the criteria to be used in any 'theory choice'. There is virtually no discussion of *why* one should ever be required to choose *one* theory! The reason for the lack of discussion of the motivation for 'theory choice' is that the Problem of Conventions is simply taken for granted [e.g., Tarascio and Caldwell 1979]. A direct consequence of accepting the need to solve the Problem of Conventions is the presumption that any article or essay must represent a revealed choice of a theory and that any such choice *can* be justified. The only question of methodological interest in this case concerns how to reveal the criteria used to justify the theory choice.

Conventionalism and 'theory choice' criteria

Given the Problem of Conventions, most questions of methodology reduce to what amount to exercises in economic analysis. Specifically, any choice of a theory or model can be 'explained' as being the result of a maximization process in which the objective function is an accepted measure of 'truthlikeness' and the constraint is the set of available alternative theories or models. To choose the best theory is to choose the one which maximizes some desired attribute. Over the last sixty years, several different criteria or objective functions have been mentioned. The most well defined have been 'simplicity', 'generality', 'verifiability', 'falsifiability', 'confirmability', 'and 'testability'. Less well-defined are 'empirical relevance', 'plausibility' and 'reasonableness'.

Each of these criteria has its advocates and its critics. Those advocates who wish to remain consistent with the dictates of Conventionalism will not claim that their explanation of the choice of any particular theory in any way constitutes a proof that the theory is actually true. If by chance the chosen theory is 'best' by all criteria, there could never be an argument. But usually competing theories are best by one criterion and not by another, and in such cases critics, who may also wish to remain consistent with Conventionalism, are thus forced to quibble over a choice between criteria [e.g., Samuelson 1967; Lucas 1980; Aumann 1985; Debreu 1991].

Limitations of choice criteria

Those critics who are not bound by the dictates of Conventionalism can take a different approach. One line of criticism is to reject Conventionalism by arguing that each criterion is based on an allegedly absolutely *true* theory of the nature of any true theory of the phenomena in question. For example, choosing a theory which is the 'most simple' presumes that the real world is inherently simple, thus any true theory of the real world must also be simple, and that furthermore, although the truth of one's theory may not be provable, the simplicity of competing theories can be established if the measure of simplicity is well defined. A similar argument can be raised against the version of Conventionalism which judges theories on the basis of the criterion of generality.

Advocates of any Conventionalist criterion might wish to deny that they have assumed that their theory of the world is true, since such an assumption violates the requirements of Conventionalism. But, if the advocacy of a particular criterion is not based on the presumed true theory of the essential nature of the world which the theory 'explains', then the use of the criterion either leads to an infinite regress or opens the choice to a charge of arbitrariness. Specifically, one can always question the choice of the choice criterion. If a true theory of the world is not presumed, then we are right back at the doorstep of the Problem of Induction.

Conventionalist criteria other than simplicity or generality would seem to be less vulnerable. Unfortunately, there still are problems. One of the first Conventionalist criteria was verifiability, but that criterion is no longer taken seriously, as it has not fared well against the logical criticism of Popper and others who argue that all informative, non-tautological theories are inherently unverifiable. For Popper, theories are informative only if they are falsifiable. He seems successfully to have destroyed the belief in verification, as falsifiability and testability are now widely accepted as a minimum condition for the acceptability of any theory or model in economics. This is unfortunate, as 'theory choice' criteria, falsifiability and testability are still quite arbitrary. But worse, those critics *not* bound by Conventionalism can also argue that the true theory may *not* be the most falsifiable or the most testable of the available alternative theories [Wisdom 1963; Bartley 1968].

Validation, confirmations and disconfirmations

For some purists, the acceptance of the criteria of verifiability or falsifiability might seem a little inconsistent if one still accepts Conventionalism and its denial of a (non-tautological and non-self-contradictory) theory being either true or false. If a theory cannot be false, what does 'falsifiable' mean? These purists find refuge in a set of weaker criteria for the lesser purpose of 'validation' [Stewart 1979] or 'appraisal' [Weintraub 1985, 1988]. In between, the most widely used criterion is 'confirmability', and rather than seeking to verify a theory or model we are said to be only seeking its confirmation. For example, the universal statement 'All swans are white' may be said to be confirmed (but not proven) when a very large number of 'white swans' have been observed in the absence of any 'non-white swans'. Those who accept Popper's criticism of the purpose for verification may opt for the criterion of 'testability' where the objective is to select only theories which in principle could be 'disconfirmed' [Hempel 1966, chap. 4].

Unfortunately, such validation criteria have their limitations, too. For example, a highly confirmed theory may still be false. But purists can counter with the observation that this is not a problem, since any theory which does not violate the axioms of logic (i.e., one which is logically consistent) cannot be considered false even in the presence of a reported refutation (an observed counter-example) because any refuting fact is itself theory-laden – that is, any proponent of the 'refuted' theory can defend it by questioning the alleged truth of the observed counter-example [cf. Agassi 1966a]. This example highlights one of the prominent features of logically consistent Conventionalism. In place of the concepts of 'true' and 'false', Conventionalism uses 'valid' and 'invalid'. And furthermore, the only *objective* and non-arbitrary test to be applied to theories or models is that of logical consistency and validity. Even if we cannot prove a theory or model is true, at the very minimum to be true it must be logically consistent.

The concept of confirmation is not without its logical problems, too. In its simple form it equates a probability of truth with a degree of confirmation. Following Hume, some might claim that although objective inductive proofs may be impossible, it is still possible to argue inductively, and the outcome of such an argument will be a 'degree of probability of truth'. Such a 'degree' concept presumes that a greater quantity of positive evidence implies a higher degree of probability of truth. Unfortunately, with this simple concept one has merely assumed what one wished to establish.

Recall that an inductive argument proceeds from particular positive statements – e.g., observation reports such as 'A white swan was observed in British Columbia today' – to general statements such as 'All swans in BC today are white.' In the absence of refuting observations, the general statement's probability of truth is measured by the ratio of the number of confirming observations to the unknown but finite number of possible observations – such as the ratio of observed white swans (without double-counting) to the number of all swans in BC today. So long as we specify which day 'today' is, this general statement is both verifiable and refutable. (Note that what Popper objected to was the verification of strictly universal statements where the quantity of possible observations were not finite.)

For the purposes of this discussion, let the number of swans in BC today be N_s and the number of observed white swans be N_{ws}, thus the ratio in question is $(N_{ws})/(N_s)$. So, when the next white swan is observed, the numerator of the ratio increases by 1 and thus the ratio becomes $(N_{ws}+1)/(N_s)$; this higher ratio supposedly represents a reason to be more confident that the next swan that comes by will also be white.

Now, the only question of empirical significance here is whether subsequent observations of confirming evidence (e.g., more white swans) *necessarily* increase the degree of confidence in the general statement *as opposed to its denial* (e.g., the statement that there is at least one non-white swan in BC today). Based on the quantity of evidence available, what degree of confidence does one have that the *next* swan observed will be white? Advocates of the confirmability criterion would have us believe that each past observation of a white swan necessarily increases the probability that all future swans observed will be white. This alleged necessity is actually based on a prior, and unsupported, assumption that the general statement is true (or that its ultimate probability is 1.00).

Since the criterion of confirmability is so widely used in econometrics, perhaps I should offer an explanation for my claim. If I think the general statement 'All swans in BC today are white' is *false*, my confidence in the *denial* will *also* be increased by the observation of each *white* swan. In other words, the probability that the next swan observed will be non-white (hence proving the falsity of the general statement in question) will *increase* as each white swan is observed (and tagged to avoid double-counting) – that is, the relevant ratio to represent the probability and thus a measure of my confidence that the next observed swan will be non-white (thereby refuting the general statement) is $(1)/(N_s - N_{ws})$. With each subsequently observed *white* swan my confidence that the next swan observed will be the refuting non-white swan increases, too. That is, when the next white swan is observed, my ratio becomes $(1)/(N_s - (N_{ws}+1))$ which is also higher simply because now the denominator is smaller as a result of the *same* evidence. So, observing each white swan causes both anyone who presumes the general statement is true and anyone who presumes the statement is false to think they have more confirming evidence to support their presumptions. Thus, I think we can conclude that the significance of one's confirmations is based solely on one's *prior* assumptions. You can see confirming evidence for your empirical generalizations only because you have already assumed that they are true!

It must be realized that not all advocates of confirmation rely on a probability construct. But avoiding any reliance on probability will not circumvent the more well-known logical problems of confirmation. All conceptions of a logical connection between positive evidence and degrees of confirmation suffer from a profound logical problem called, by some philosophers, the 'paradox of confirmation' [cf. Sainsbury 1995].

The philosopher's paradox of confirmation merely points out that any evidence which does not refute a theory consisting of a simple universal statement (for example, 'All swans are white') must increase the degree of confirmation. The paradox is based on the observation that, *in terms of what evidence would count*, this example of a simple universal statement is equivalent to its 'contra-positive' statement 'All non-white things are non-swans.' Any observation that is consistent with one statement is consistent with the other, equivalent statement. Moreover, positive evidence consistent with the contra-positive statement would have to include red shoes as well as black ravens, since in both cases we have non-white things which are not swans. That is, the set of all confirming instances must include all things which are not non-white swans. This merely divides the contents of the universe into non-white swans and everything else [Agassi 1966b; Hempel 1966].

The remnants of Inductivism

For the most part neoclassical economics has ignored the alleged problems with conventional choice criteria. Today, among methodologists there is still considerable discussion of falsifiability as a minimum condition for the acceptability of any theory or model. So, one might wish to conclude that Conventionalism has completely supplanted Inductivism in economics. Such a conclusion would be somewhat mistaken, as there still remain many remnants of the vanquished Inductivism!

The most popular remnant is the alleged hierarchy which consists of 'hypotheses', 'theories' and 'laws'. In the tradition of Inductivism, every science was developed in stages. Each supposedly begins with an 'hypothesis' which has been formed only after collecting and examining empirical data. The next step is the submission of the hypothesis to experimental testing. If the hypothesis survives the test, it is to be elevated in status to a 'theory'. Eventually, if it somehow survives tests performed independently by other researchers, it reaches the ultimate status: it is crowned a 'law'. It is difficult to take such a view seriously these days. Nevertheless, one still finds distinctions being made as if there were some significant difference between hypotheses, theories and laws. And related to this is a ban on speculations – 'one must not jump to conclusions until the facts are examined'. If Inductivism were actually completely abandoned, it would be difficult to see any reason for the continued promotion of the hierarchy or for a ban on conjectures and speculations.

Even if methodologists today avoid promoting the hierarchical distinctions of Inductivism, the dominant methodological perspective is that the fundamental problem facing all economists is one of choosing the one 'best' theory or model. While it might be understandable for historians of economic thought to be concerned with this choice problem, it is less so for methodologists. Methodologists should move on to more interesting philosophical problems, particularly those problems involved in any application of methodology to economic model building. Nevertheless, it is this choice problem that is the primary remnant of Inductivism and the related presumption that we must deal with the Problem of Induction.

The practice of methodology in economics: Conventionalism vs. Instrumentalism

> In [Bishop] Berkeley's time the Copernican System of the World had developed into Newton's Theory of gravity, and Berkeley saw in it a serious competitor to religion. He saw that a decline of religious faith and religious authority would result from the new science unless its interpretation by the 'free-thinkers' could be refuted; for they saw in its success a proof of *the power of the human intellect, unaided by divine revelation, to uncover the secrets of our world* – the reality hidden behind its appearance.

This, Berkeley felt, was to misinterpret the new science. He analysed Newton's theory with complete candour and great philosophical acumen; and a critical survey of Newton's concepts convinced him that this theory could not possibly be anything but a 'mathematical hypothesis', that is, a convenient *instrument* for the calculation and prediction of phenomena or appearances; that it could not possibly be taken as a true description of anything real.

Karl Popper [1963/89, pp. 98–9]

in my view, scientific theories are not to be considered 'true' or 'false'. In constructing such a theory, we are not trying to get at the truth, or even to approximate to it: rather, we are trying to organize our thoughts and observations in a useful manner.

One rough analogy is to a filing system in an office operation, or to some kind of complex computer program. We do not refer to such a system as being 'true' or 'untrue'; rather, we talk about whether it 'works' or not, or, better yet, how well it works...

Some philosophies deny altogether the existence of objective truth, but for my purposes this is not necessary, and I do not wish to insist on it. The concept of truth applies to *observations;* one can say that such and such were truly the observations. It also applies to all kinds of everyday events, like whether or not one had hamburger for dinner yesterday. It does not, however, apply to *theories.*

Robert Aumann [1985, pp. 31–2, 34]

With the possible exception of Aumann's 1985 apology – which is simply a statement of conservative Conventionalism – today few practicing economists or economic model builders would dare engage in a public discussion of methodology, Conventionalist or otherwise. But, obviously, they have to have some sort of methodology. All too often, it is difficult to see a consistency between what economic theorists and model builders say about their view of methodology and what they actually practice. Certainly, today, there are few who would think that economics involves constructing verifiable theories or models. But, in the 1940s, critics of neoclassical economics frequently employed Conventionalist methodology in an attempt to discredit neoclassical theory. Critics (presumably knowing that most economists of the day took verifiability for granted) challenged the realism of the assumption of maximization in accordance with the Conventionalism of the 1930s – that is, any claims to realism would require verifiability. Presumably, then, the methodological issue was that, if decision-makers could not or would not actually calculate the marginal cost in order to fulfill the necessary condition for profit maximization in accordance with the requirements of ordinary calculus, then one could never verify the behavioral assumptions of neoclassical theory.

With the mathematics of calculus being raised as a point of criticism, one is reminded of Bishop Berkeley's relegating theorizing to being mere instruments that are incapable of making a claim to a realistic representation of Nature. (See the quotation from Popper above.) Was the assumption of maximization merely a 'mathematical hypothesis', that is, a mere instrument? Milton Friedman (with his [1953] version of Instrumentalism) is famous in methodology circles for, in effect, agreeing with Berkeley and willingly accepting the view that economic theories and models are merely instruments. Many philosophers and methodologists rebel at the notion that theories and models are mere instruments. Instead, they think theories and models can be 'true' – but, of course, not absolutely true but only 'true' to the extent allowed by Conventionalism.

Today, practicing economists – particularly those who wish to enhance their claims to scientific credibility – will likely proclaim the tenants of Conventionalism, but, whenever pressed, economic model builders will equivocate and vacillate between Conventionalism and Instrumentalism. In Chapter 5, I will discuss how some model builders explicitly recognize that they are merely building instruments – instruments that may be useful for policy makers if properly used [e.g., Kydland and Prescott 1991, 1996].

The hallmark of Instrumentalism, as practiced by model builders, is the methodological position that theories or models are not claimed to be true or even 'true' by one of the many Conventionalist criteria used to solve the Problem of Conventions. Instead, the truth status of a theory or model does not matter. All that matters when evaluating a theory or model is whether the theory or model is *useful* or whether a theory or model 'works'.

When economists do dare to talk about methodology, they very often present a confused view. A typical example is Aumann's heroic attempt to explain the methodology of game theory. Part of this is quoted above and reveals some language that sounds like straightforward Conventionalism when he talks about *not* trying to construct theories that are true. Note he is not saying that truth or falsity does not matter, as would be the case with straightforward Instrumentalism. He is saying that he is not seeking theories that are absolutely true and thus they should not be judged on this basis. He goes on to say that we should instead view a theory as a tool to organize thoughts and observations. This sounds like Instrumentalism, particularly when he adds that as a tool of organization, a 'filing system', should be judged only on 'how well it works'. But since this is a judgment of how well it works as a filing system, this view is not the concern of Instrumentalism. Instrumentalism proper is about questions of applying economic theories to practical problems. Presumably, Aumann's fear is that if we demand true theories and models in the short run, we may prematurely reject potentially fruitful theoretical research projects that can be developed further. So, when Aumann says that we should recognize that, unlike theories, observations can be true or false, we see that he is just espousing his version of conservative Conventionalism – which opts for Conventionalism as a short-run strategy but hopes for more in the long run. All this said, it is still not clear what Aumann is advocating. Perhaps he is just being inconsistent since he seems to be arguing at the (research) methodology level that we should be Conventionalists but at a (philosophical) meta-level, he is advocating an Instrumentalist position to justify his choice of Conventionalism. This contrasts with Friedman's famous essay which (as I argued in Boland [1979a and 1997, chap. 2]) is at least consistent as he gives an Instrumentalist argument in favor of Instrumentalism.

One wonders at times about the sincerity of those who openly espouse Instrumentalism (or even Aumann's type of conservative Conventionalism). Do they think that by repeatedly showing that neoclassical theory is useful that they are thereby, in the long run, inductively proving the truth of neoclassical economics? Are they merely saying that since in the long run one wants theories or models that work, Conventionalist theory-choice criteria are useless? Are they merely trying to avoid premature rejection of a model before there has been time to develop its ideas and make them amenable to empirical evaluation? The answers to these questions are not easy to obtain – the reason is simply that today economists are very reluctant to put their views of methodology on record. Whenever one is successful getting economists who practice Instrumentalism to address questions about the truth status of their theories or models, almost always they will fall back to the tenets of Conventionalism [e.g., Aumann 1985]. That is, since we cannot prove the truth of our assumptions, we cannot claim that theories or models based on them are absolutely true.

The key question is what is the purpose for our theorizing at all? Is it just to construct useful tools? Or, is it part of an effort to understand reality? Can theories or models ever be the basis of understanding reality if, following Conventionalism, they are not considered literally true but only 'true' according to the currently accepted Conventionalist criteria? These questions will be lurking behind almost all of the discussion in all of the following chapters. And, in particular, how Instrumentalism or Conventionalism is manifested in explicit methodological discussion in economics will be the central concern of Part IV.

2 The Explanatory Problem of Individualism

At the outset it is useful to emphasize the individualistic character of the methods of pure theory. Almost every modern writer starts with wants and their satisfaction, and takes utility more or less exclusively as the basis of his analysis... I wish to point out that ... it unavoidably implies considering individuals as independent units or agencies. For only individuals can feel wants...

For theory it is irrelevant *why* people demand certain goods: the only important point is that all things are demanded, produced, and paid for because individuals want them. Every demand on the market is therefore an individualistic one, altho, from another point of view, it often is an altruistic or a social one.

The only wants which for the purpose of economic theory should be called strictly social are *those which are consciously asserted by the whole community...*

Many writers call production, distribution, and exchange social processes, meaning thereby that nobody can perform them – at least the two last named – by himself. In this sense, prices are obviously social phenomena...

the term 'methodological individualism' describes a mode of scientific procedure which naturally leads to no misconception of economic phenomena.

Joseph Schumpeter [1909, pp. 214, 216–17, 231]

A Schumpeterian innovation which was fully successful in the sense that it has been explicitly accepted by some and implicitly by practically all modern economists is the distinction between political and methodological individualism.

The distinction is essential because political and methodological individualism are often mistakenly considered to be the same... Some people may, of course, endorse both political and methodological individualism; but it is equally possible that a socialist finds methodological individualism preferable for use in his analysis, or that a political individualist chooses to employ 'social categories' [collectives] in his. The significance of the conceptual separation is, to Schumpeter, that economic theory may employ a sound individualistic or 'atomistic' method without burdening itself with a political program such as *laissez faire.*

Schumpeter rejects methodological collectivism... He does not deny strong social influences upon the conduct of the individual, the close ties between the members of the social group, or the importance which social entities may have for sociological analysis. But he is concerned with pure economic analysis, and for it methodological individualism – although not preferable on any *a priori* grounds – has proved most useful.

Fritz Machlup [1951, pp. 150]

Methodological individualism, the research program outlined by Schumpeter, has been identified as the 'view that social theories must be grounded in the attitudes and behavior of individuals, as opposed to "methodological holism", which asserts that social theories must be grounded in the behavior of irreducible groups of individuals' [Blaug 1980/92, p. 250]. The view that neoclassical economics is firmly grounded on a research program of 'methodological individualism' is today rather commonplace [see Arrow 1994]. Methodological individualism is the second main item on the hidden agenda of neoclassical economics. For future reference, here is my specification:

> *Methodological individualism* is the view that allows *only* individuals to be the decision-makers in any explanation of social phenomena.

In other words, 'things' do not decide, only individuals do. Thus, explanations involving non-individualist decision-makers, such as institutions, weather or even historical destiny, are not allowed.

Individualism as a research program

From the viewpoint of methodology, we need to examine the reasons why methodological individualism is a main item on the neoclassical agenda. Unfortunately, the reasons are difficult to find, as there is little methodological discussion of why economics *should* involve only explanations that can be reduced to the decision-making of individuals – except, perhaps, for Schumpeter's [1909] commonsense argument and Hayek's [1937/48; 1945/48] arguments for the informational simplicity of methodological individualism [cf. Hoover 2001, chap. 3]. The task in this chapter is to provide a rudimentary examination of the nature and purpose of methodological individualism in neoclassical theory. Along the way I will review some developments in the understanding of this agenda item.

Individualism vs. holism

An examination of the reasons for the presence of methodological individualism on the agenda is more complicated than it might at first appear. Supposedly, there is a built-in dichotomy which allows only two options – methodological individualism vs. methodological holism [e.g., Schumpeter 1909; Blaug 1980/92]. Given the individualism-holism dichotomy, the reasons for promoting methodological individualism may be rather negative. The social-philosophical basis of neoclassical economics is dominated by the eighteenth-century anti-authoritarian rationalism that puts the individual decision-maker at the center of the social universe. A rejection of individualism would be tantamount to the advocacy of a denial of intellectual freedom. For intellectual reasons, we would need to promote the view that individuals are free to decide their own fate in order to avoid endorsing authoritarianism. For political reasons, it would seem we have to favor individualism in order to avoid inadvertently advocating any ideology based on 'holism' – such as communism, Marxism, etc.

Adding to the confusions caused by the acceptance of the (possibly false) dichotomy between individualism and holism, there is the confusion raised by the alternative view of individualism promoted by Popper in his *Open Society*. Specifically, there is his version of 'methodological individualism' [Popper 1945/66, vol. 2, p. 91], which does not accept the individualism-holism dichotomy and thus is apparently more general than the individualism defined by Schumpeter (and Blaug). In Popper's terms, Schumpeter's 'methodological individualism' should be called 'psychologistic individualism' and Blaug's 'methodological holism' should be called 'institutional holism', while Popper's 'methodological individualism' should be called 'institutional individualism' [Agassi 1960; 1975; 1987]. Unfortunately, this approach only adds a second dichotomy – psychologism vs. institutionalism. It does not automatically give us an explanation for the advocacy of individualism.

In order to explain why neoclassical economics is based on methodological individualism, one can, of course, point to obvious questions of ideology [Weisskopf 1979] but as an explanation this only begs the question at a different level. If the decision to adopt methodological individualism is based on ideological considerations, how do individual economists choose their ideologies? Must our explanation of the choice of ideologies be constrained by the prescriptions of methodological individualism? To what must the explanation of the choice of ideologies be reduced? To avoid an infinite regress, it cannot be an ideology.

Individualism and explanations

> All human conduct is psychological and, from that standpoint, not only the study of economics but the study of every other branch of human activity is a psychological study and the facts of all such branches are psychological facts... The principles of an economic psychology ... can be *deduced* only from facts... A very general view of common well-known facts gave English writers the concept of a 'final degree of utility,' and Walras the concept of 'rarity'... From the examination of the facts we were led, by induction, to formulate those notions...
> Vilfredo Pareto [1916/63, sec. 2078]

Pareto's candid comments (quoted above) suggest a very different approach: one that connects psychology with induction. This approach will be examined in the remainder of this chapter. I shall argue that there is a close connection between the Problem of Induction and the research program of methodological individualism. Specifically, for neoclassical economics, methodological individualism is a research program that is designed to facilitate a *long-run* solution to the Problem of Induction.

To examine the relationship between Inductivism and individualism in neoclassical theory, we need to consider another aspect of Pareto's comments. What Pareto, and John Stuart Mill before him, presumed was that there are rules of explanation that prescribe the existence of an irreducible set of acceptable 'primitives'. Since the time of Mill, most economists have accepted the view that for individualism to be the basis of all explanations in social theory, the irreducible minimum must be the given psychological states of the decision-makers [see also Scitovsky 1976; Earl 1988]. Today we might simply say that the psychological states of all individuals are *exogenous*, but Popper sees something more in the view of Mill, which he calls 'psychologism' [Popper 1945/66, chap. 14]. We must be careful here to distinguish psychologism from individualism, as it is possible to form a psychologistic methodology which is 'holistic' and with which, for example, explanations are reduced to 'mob psychology' or 'class interest'. For reference I shall define the more general methodological principle as follows:

> *Psychologism* is the methodological prescription that psychological states are the *only* exogenous variables permitted beyond natural givens (e.g., weather, contents of the Universe, etc.)

And I shall always use Agassi's term 'psychologistic individualism' to identify the Mill-Pareto prescription as a special form of methodological individualism. Specifically,

> *Psychologistic individualism* is the (narrow) version of individualism which identifies the individual with his or her psychological state.

I should note immediately that the implications of adhering to a psychologistic-individualist version of neoclassical theory means that everything or every variable which cannot be reduced either to someone's psychological state or to a natural given must be explained somewhere in the theory. It should also be noted that a theory can conform to methodological individualism without conforming to psychologistic individualism only if the requirements of psychologism are abandoned [Boland 1992a, chap. 10].

Reductive individualism

> The metaphysical difference between institutionalism and psychologism somewhat resembles the difference between a drawing and a pointillist painting which contains only coloured dots but looks *as if* it contains lines. Psychologism admits institutions into the picture of society in the same manner in which the pointillist admits lines into his painting – as mere illusions created by oversight of details.
>
> Joseph Agassi [1987, p. 133]

In light of the proscription of non-individualist and non-natural exogenous variables, the key methodological obstacle for neoclassical theories of economic behavior is the specification of an appropriate conception of the relationship between institutions and individuals. On the one hand, social institutions are consequences of decisions made by one or more individuals. On the other hand, individual decision-makers are constrained by existing institutions. If any given institution is the result of actions of individuals, can it ever be an exogenous variable? That is, can institutions really be constraints? If institutions limit the range of choices facing any individual, are the individual's choices really free? If any institution is a creation of groups of individuals, can it have aims of its own or must it merely be a reflection of the aims of the individuals who created it?

These questions are not often discussed in the economics literature because the psychologism of Mill or Pareto is simply taken for granted. Thus, whenever anyone feels bound by methodological individualism, he or she is immediately bound also by the psychologistic individualism. As a result, in any economics explanation in which institutions are recognized, they are always to be treated as mere epiphenomena, analogous to lines in Agassi's pointillist paintings. In more common terms, institutions are to be analogous to pictures printed in the newspaper. What appears in any newspaper picture as a person's face is actually only a collection of black and white dots. One can explain the appearance of a face by explaining why the dots are where they are.

Methodological individualism in general

The explanatory obstacle posed by the existence of institutions exists regardless of the prescriptions of psychologism. Methodological individualism alone leads to two primary methodological requirements. First, no institution can be left unexplained and, moreover, every institution must be explained in individualist terms. Second, any conceived institution must be responsive to the choices of every individual. The first requirement begs a fundamental methodological question about what constitutes a successful explanation. Is there a set of automatically acceptable givens? The second raises the thorny question considered in Kenneth Arrow's (Im)Possibility Theorem. Can the choice of an institution be rationalized in the same manner as we rationalize an individual's choice of a bundle of goods? If it can, then the social utility (welfare) function used to make the social choice must also be a social institution – one which, like the picture on the newspaper page and a line in a pointillist painting, must be an epiphenomenon. Either the social choice is nothing more than the logical consequence of individual choices, or the social utility function must be perfectly responsive to changes in any individual's utility function.

Now, it is commonly accepted that all explanations require some givens – i.e., some exogenous variables. In a fundamental way, specification of the exogenous variables is probably the most informative theoretical assertion in any theoretical model [see Boland 1989, chap. 6]. The various competing schools of economics might easily be characterized on the basis of which variables are considered exogenous. Marxian models take 'class interest' and 'rates of accumulation' as exogenous givens. Some institutional models take the evolution of social institutions as a given and use it to explain the history of economics. Many neoclassical models would instead attempt to explain 'rates of accumulation' and 'institutions', and it is conceivable that some might even try to explain 'class interest' as an outcome of rational decision-making. Whatever the case, no one model can explain everything; there must be some givens. For neoclassical economics today what the presumption of psychologism does is conveniently to restrict the list of acceptable givens. Given psychologistic individualism, the psychological states of the individuals in society are the irreducible givens.

The methodological view that there is but one permissible set of exogenous variables to which all successful explanations must be reduced is called 'reductionism'. Supposedly, theorists who are bound by reductive methodological individualism are obligated to explain away any non-individualistic variable which might appear to be exogenous, or any 'macroeconomic propositions that cannot be reduced to microeconomic ones' [Blaug 1980/92, p. 46]. Blaug recommends giving up methodological individualism rather than macroeconomics. I suspect that he has only psychologistic individualism in mind, since, contrary to what Blaug says, Popper's methodological individualism does not have to be a narrow reductionist program; only the special version, psychologistic individualism, does. In Popper's version of methodological individualism – now called 'institutional individualism' – individuals are not identified with psychological states but rather with their unique problem-situations. With Popper's institutional individualism, the decision-maker is considered a problem-solver with specific aims which may not be psychologically motivated [Agassi 1960, 1975; Popper 1994, chap. 8]. I will discuss Popper's problem-solver more generally in the next chapter.

Towards individualism without psychologism

The conception of methodological individualism as a reductionist program can be somewhat misleading. It might not always be clear what constitutes a permissible individualistic exogenous variable. In any psychologistic-individualist version of neoclassical theory, what constitutes the individualistic variable is easy to see: it is the individuals' psychological states. Specifically, individuals are always identified with their utility functions (as firms are often implicitly identified with their production functions [cf. Oi 1983]).

Viewing psychology as the foundation of all economics explanations raises some subtle questions and dilemmas. Would a psychological basis for all economics explanations imply that everyone will make the same choice when facing the same given price-income situation, or will there never be two individuals doing the same thing? The first option seems to deny individuality and free will, and the second is rather unrealistic. (Some may argue that the latter is not unrealistic since in the real world there is only a finite set of choice options which eliminates the possibility of complete individuality.)

In order to understand the methodological role of individualism we need to consider a key question: is it possible to construct an individualistic explanation which is not psychologistic? Or, similarly, is it possible to be in favor of individualism while at the same time being against psychologism? To answer these questions we need first to examine the nature of psychologism, then we will be able to consider Popper's alternative form of methodological individualism which denies psychologism.

Psychologism

Psychologism is primarily a basis for explaining the behavior of both individuals and social institutions and as such it can too easily be made a part of a specification of the second main item on the neoclassical hidden agenda. Along these lines, psychologism might be considered a mere arbitrary reductionist program in that it may only provide the minimum conditions for the acceptability of any given theory. Although it does make methodological individualism a reductionist program and it does specify an acceptable set of exogenous variables – only psychological states and natural constraints are to be allowed – this narrow conception of psychologism as a convenient methodological tool would seem to me to be a bit superficial. Reliance on psychologism is more than a methodological ploy to solve the Problem of Conventions because psychologism implicitly involves a specific theory of society and the individual.

The basis of psychologism is a theory that there is something which all individuals have in common. The common element is sometimes called 'Human Nature'. The accepted view of what constitutes Human Nature has changed considerably over the last two hundred years. Today, it is merely asserted that all individuals are governed by the same 'laws' of psychology. In its simplest form psychologism would have us believe that any two individuals facing exactly the same situation would behave in exactly the same way. With simple psychologism, whenever two people are behaving differently, they must be facing different situations. In this light it would appear that, as a program of explanation, simple psychologism is very versatile; it can serve as the basis for Freudian psychoanalysis [see Popper 1945/66, chap. 25], for anthropological explanations of the differences between primitive tribes [see Jarvie 1964], and even for economics [e.g., Stigler and Becker 1977].

Although psychologism would seem to be a straightforward specification of methodological individualism, in its simple form, surprisingly, it actually precludes individuality! Methodologically speaking, simple psychologism allows differences between the choices of individuals to be explained only in terms of the differences between the nature-given situations facing the two individuals. All individuals are, in effect, identical. Obviously, simple psychologism does beg an important philosophical question. If everyone were governed by the same psychological 'laws', what would be the basis of individuality?

It is interesting to note that even though neoclassical theories are usually based on psychologism, they seem to have overcome this last question by being able to have it both ways. (However, they do so by stopping short of complete reduction.) Consider demand theory. Saying that individuals can have any utility function they wish preserves individuality. However, saying that all individuals' utility functions do have one common feature also preserves psychologism. Specifically, it is said that every utility function exhibits a negatively sloped marginal utility curve (at the place where utility is being maximized – assuming calculus concepts always apply). Although the slopes of their respective marginal curves must all be negative, the individual utility functions differ in that there are an unlimited number of possible (negative) magnitudes for the slopes of their marginal curves. Thus it would seem that there is wide scope for individuality, yet the essential commonality for the purposes of psychologistic economic theory is still provided. Again, it is the combination of universal constraints (natural givens) and psychological differences that is the basis of neoclassical explanations constructed in accordance with psychologism. However, one might wonder whether psychologism is actually a necessary element in neoclassical theory. I shall argue that it is not.

Psychologism is very versatile. In the short run it satisfies the needs of Conventionalism in that it provides at least one criterion for the acceptability of alternative theories or models in terms of the prescription of acceptable exogenous variables. In the longer-run perspective of Pareto or Mill it also focuses on one source of atomistic facts in order to imitate inductive science. It is unlikely that anyone ascribes to this long-run perspective anymore. Instead, I shall argue that psychologism is retained because it is a part of the Conventionalist program to deal with the Problem of Induction.

Sophisticated psychologism

As I will explain, so long as neoclassical economics is based on a reductive methodological individualism, some form of psychologism must be retained to stop a possible infinite regress. But, as explained above, there is a problem with simple psychologism, as it seems to deny individuality in order to satisfy the methodological needs of reductionism. That neoclassical economics is an intellectually impressive solution to the problem of simple psychologism is not widely recognized. Instead, those who recognize that there is a problem with simple psychologism can opt for a more sophisticated form of psychologism.

The most common sophisticated alternative to simple psychologism merely denies the uniformity of Human Nature and instead claims that there are different types of people. Thus, when two individuals face the same situation but respond differently, one could explain the difference as the result of the two individuals being of different psychological types. Sometimes people will be said to have different 'mentalities', which amounts to the same thing.

This form of psychologism is probably the most widely accepted today. It is used to explain all sorts of happenings. There are supposedly many different types of individuals. For example, there are 'criminal mentalities', 'extroverts', 'introverts', 'artistic types', 'mathematical minds', 'risk averse types', and so on. The methodological basis of Thomas Kuhn's famous book *The Structure of Scientific Revolutions* relies on a form of sophisticated psychologism. Kuhn presumes that the reason why the structure of science is different from other disciplines is that scientists have a different mentality [1971, pp. 143ff.].

Unfortunately, sophisticated psychologism, while allowing for individuality, opens the door to an infinite regress. Instead of asserting the existence of a Human Nature consisting of a uniform psychological type (e.g., a set of needs shared by everyone), sophisticated psychologism asserts a set of possible categories of types. One of the more sophisticated forms says that there is a hierarchy of needs and that people differ only because they rank them differently [e.g., Maslow 1954]. Given a finite number of needs, there would then be a finite (but larger) number of possible rankings to use to explain differences between individuals. For example, if there were three human needs, then there would be six possible rankings and hence six different types of individuals.

The key issue concerning the existence of Human Nature is whether or not there is something uniformly attributable to all individuals. If we try to avoid simple psychologism by saying there are many different psychological types, then to complete a reductive use of psychologism we would have to explain why any given individual is one psychological type rather than another. This immediately leads to an infinite regress which can be stopped only by asserting the existence of some deeper uniform attribute of Human Nature. In other words, a reductive methodological individualism based on psychologism can only lead to some form of simple psychologism. Otherwise, it is completely arbitrary.

Institutional individualism

Earlier I mentioned that the key question for the explanatory problem of methodological individualism is the explanatory relationship between institutions and individual decision-makers. This is also the key question for distinguishing the individualism usually presumed in neoclassical theory from the version which Popper offered in his book *The Open Society and its Enemies*. The relationship between Popper's version of individualism and other forms, as well as the relationship between individualism and holism, was developed by his student Joseph Agassi [1960, 1975, 1987]. In order to understand the nature and shortcomings of psychologism, the Popper-Agassi alternative view will be presented next.

Institutions and the aims of individuals

The central feature of psychologistic individualism is its insistence that only individuals can have aims and that aims are considered psychological states. Popper and Agassi reject the identification of aims with psychological states. Individuals do have aims, but they need not be psychologically given. Aims may be changed, yet *at any point in time* they may still be givens. If any individual treats an institution as a constraint, then institutions must be included in the set of permissible exogenous variables. Thus, Popper and Agassi reject the limitation on acceptable exogenous variables. Institutions are to be included among the explanatory variables along with the aims of individuals. It is for this reason that Popper's alternative is called 'institutional individualism'. Unlike psychologistic individualism, institutional individualism is not necessarily a reductionist research program. The existence of given institutions in any explanation is not a threat to its individualism. Institutions are still the creations of individuals – e.g., creations of past decisions of individuals – yet, for the purpose of real-time decision-making, some institutions have to be considered as given [Newman 1976, 1981].

To some observers, institutional individualism may appear to be either a paradox or an impossibility. But such a perception might only betray their belief in the reductionist version of individualism. Nevertheless, there is something missing. How can a minimally satisfactory Popper-Agassi explanation consider institutions as givens and yet consider them to be creations of individual decision-makers? As far as I know, neither Popper nor Agassi has explicitly addressed this question.

For students of Marshall's neoclassical economics, however, the answer to this question is rather simple. The overlooked element is 'time'. In any particular real-time situation, institutions are included in the list of 'givens' simply because any one individual decision-maker cannot change all of them [Newman 1981]. In fact, in many cases it is easier for individuals to change their aims than to alter some of their givens. In some cases it is simply not possible to change some of the givens. In other cases, the individuals have chosen not to change some of them. In other words, the exogeneity of some givens may be a matter of the *decision-maker's* choice. No two individuals may choose to face the same situation. Even if they did, they may choose to have different aims. Stating this in terms more consistent with neoclassical economics, there is no reason to consider psychological states as givens, since sometimes they, too, may be a matter of choice.

Individualism as an explanatory problem

Institutional individualism is an interesting perspective for the study of neoclassical research programs for the following reasons. On the one hand, institutional individualism can be a way of dealing with the explanatory problem of methodological individualism without having to endorse psychologism. On the other hand, psychologism is not a *necessary* attribute of neoclassical theory. Specifically, if we strip away the psychologism that is traditionally presumed in neoclassical economics, we will find an approach to explanation that comes very close to that promoted by Alfred Marshall in his *Principles*. In Marshall's short run, virtually all variables but the quantities of labor and output are fixed and given. In the longer run, more things are variable (and, thus, subject to choice), but there are still some things, such as 'social conditions' or the 'character' of some individuals, that take generations to change [Marshall 1920/49, p. 315, and Book VI] – we might even say that things that are 'fixed' are merely things which take an infinity of time to change [Hicks 1979]. It is unfortunate that Marshall's optimistic Victorian view that even personal character was not immutable was lost somewhere along the way. This raises an interesting methodological question: why has psychologism – which has its origins in Hume's Romantic accommodation of the Problem of Induction – been able to survive even the overwhelming dominance of Marshall's Victorian economics?

Explanation and rational decision-making

The reason why psychologism survives is that it is supported by the common presumption that rationality is a psychological process. This presumption, in turn, has a tradition based on a belief that Hume was able to overcome the Problem of Induction [see Popper 1972, chap. 1]. It is also supported by the older view that rational decision-making must in some way involve inductive rationality.

As Popper explains, Hume's 'solution' to the Problem of Induction (and the Problem *with* Induction) is to say that although there is no objective inductive rationality, there is a subjective one which allows people to think inductively. In other words, people do things in their heads which they cannot do on paper. This psychologistic view of rationality led to a long history of attempts to understand the psychological processes of knowing and learning.

Surprisingly, this psychologistic view of rationality is even accepted by the many critics of the use of the assumption of rational decision-making in economics [e.g., Shackle 1972; Simon 1979]. These critics do not deny the psychologistic view of rationality; instead they deny the possibility of collecting sufficient facts to acquire inductively the knowledge necessary to make a rational decision. In other words, they do not deny Inductivism, only the feasibility of inductive knowledge. This leads them to argue that neoclassical economics is wrong in assuming that individuals are maximizers, since the supposedly needed inductive knowledge of the successful decision-maker is a practical impossibility. If one were to deny any need to satisfy Inductivism, then their critiques lose their force. Rationality as maximization will be discussed further in the next chapter.

How can one explain behavior on the basis of rational decision-making without endorsing or presuming Inductivism or a psychologistic view of rationality? This is a problem which has not been dealt with in economics, but it will have to be if economists are going to avoid the criticisms of Simon and Shackle or give Popper's views more than a superficial gloss.

The view that rationality is a psychological process is a relic of the late eighteenth century. Even today, it is still commonplace to distinguish humans from other animals on the basis that humans can be rational. Thus any criticism of a psychologistic view of rationality might be considered dangerous. Nevertheless, the psychologistic view is based on a simple mistake. It confuses one's *argument* in favor of an individual's decision with the *process* of making the decision. It also confuses being rational with being reasonable – the latter only implies the willingness to provide reasons for one's actions. The reasons may not always be adequate.

As will be discussed in the next chapter, the case against psychologistic rationality is rather straightforward. Simply stated, humans cannot be rational – only arguments can be rational. An argument is rational only if it is not logically inconsistent (i.e., only if it does not violate the axioms of logic). But, most important, whether an argument is rational can be decided independently of the process of its creation or the psychological state of its creator. Since there is no inductive logic, our knowledge of the process of creating a theoretical argument cannot provide the argument with logical validity if it is one which is nevertheless devoid of contradictions. Popper puts it quite simply, 'what is true in logic is true in psychology' [Popper 1972, p. 6]. Psychologistic rationality cannot be more than what is provided by logical arguments. Thus, any discussion of rational decision-making need not involve psychology. So I ask again, why is psychologism still commonly accepted?

Psychologism and induction in the long run

There is one important reason why the adherence to both psychologism and Inductivism never presents a problem in neoclassical economics. It is simply that neoclassical models liberally use long-run analysis. A reductive psychologistic-individualist explanation is successful *only if* all non-individualistic exogenous variables can be made endogenous (i.e., explained), leaving only natural constraints or psychological states (i.e., individuals). In neoclassical economics, a variable is endogenous only if it can be shown to be the consequence of a maximizing choice. If a variable is an externally fixed constraint, it cannot be a matter of choice. Thus, a minimum requirement for maximization is that the object of choice be representable as a variable point on some sort of continuum – Marshall called this requirement the 'Principle of Continuity'. This in turn would require that all short-run *constraints* which are neither natural nor psychological givens must eventually be explained as objects of choice. If one allows sufficient time, everything can be changed. Thus, it is easy to see that in the long run – when everything (except the permitted exogenous variables) is variable and thus subject to maximizing choice decisions – reductive psychologistic individualism is at least possible (for more on the limits of long-run reductive psychologism, see Chapter 1 of Boland [1986a]).

The same claim could have been made for induction. If we allow a sufficiently long time, perhaps all the facts needed for an inductive proof might be found. In other words, in the long run the Problem of Induction is non-existent. It must be remembered, though, that whenever 'a sufficiently long time' really means an infinity of time, we are dealing with an impossibility. One way to say some task is impossible is to say that it would take an infinity of time to complete it. Conversely, if we do not mean an infinity of time, then it is an open question whether all the facts have been provided or whether no counter-facts exist anywhere.

Individualism as an agenda item

> individualistic atoms of the rare gas in my balloon are not isolated from the other atoms. Adam Smith, who is almost as well known for his discussion of the division of labor and the resulting efficiency purchased at the price of interdependence, was well aware of that. What he would have stressed was that the contacts between the atoms were *organized* by the use of markets and prices.
>
> Paul Samuelson [1963/66, p. 1411]

Now I will attempt to explain why individualism is an item on the hidden agenda of neoclassical economics. The explanation I will give is that individualism is on the agenda because it has been viewed as a means of providing the basis for a long-run inductive research program. Perhaps it may be possible to identify other reasons for being in favor of an individualist theory of society but, it will be argued, they only add support. This is to say, it is possible to be in favor of an individualist society without advocating an Inductivist view of explanations – but without Inductivism the individualist view may seem rather weak.

It would appear, then, that Blaug [1980/92, pp. 229 and 250] was correct in identifying the methodological individualism of neoclassical economics as a reductionist research program. However, reductive methodological individualism is inherent not in neoclassical theory but only in the aims of individual neoclassical theorists. In effect, neoclassical theory is an institution which has its own aims – namely, to demonstrate that it is possible to view society as the consequence of decisions made only by individuals. It does not necessarily have the same aims of some neoclassical theorists – for example, of those who wish to show that society is the consequence of decisions which logically follow only from the psychological states of individual decision-makers and that there is no need for holistic ideologies.

Attempting to explain the nature of neoclassical theory as that of an institution raises all of the questions I have been discussing in this chapter. For my explanation of neoclassical economics to be correct, must one argue that neoclassical economics is an epiphenomenon reflecting only what individual economists do, or is one allowed to argue that neoclassical economics has a life of its own, which is independent of what particular economists do? We see immediately, then, that the explanation I am offering still may not satisfy those who only accept reductive (i.e., psychologistic) individualist explanations.

Individualism as Inductivism

When explaining why individualism is on the agenda of neoclassical economics, one must be careful to distinguish between the general research program of any neoclassical theory and the specific research program of individual neoclassical theorists. Since the primary concern in this book is to understand the methodology of neoclassical economics, we should only be concerned with the specification of neoclassical research programs. So how do we accommodate the specific aims of individual economists? Was Jacob Viner correct when he (supposedly) said, 'Economics is what economists do'?

Can economics be something other than exactly what contemporary economists do? If we are limited to a reductive individualist explanation of the institution of neoclassical economics, then we would have to agree with Viner. Furthermore, it would seem, if we wish to learn anything about neoclassical economics we will have to form our conclusions only from specific examples of what economists do. That is to say, reductive individualist explanations can only be inductive explanations.

A reductive individualist explanation of the nature of neoclassical economics (such as Viner's) raises certain questions. If we find some 'economist' who is not behaving as other economists do, must we question whether that person really is an economist? How do we decide? Which came first, the nature of neoclassical economics or the behavior of individual neoclassical economists? Such questions arise whenever one is bound by the reductive individualist research program. One could instead choose to explain institutions according to that which is allowed by a non-reductive program such as institutional individualism. Given that neoclassical economics existed before most of today's neoclassical economists were born, it would be possible to argue that neoclassical economics continues to follow reductive individualism only because today's economists choose to accept such a hidden agenda as their exogenous guide. (Perhaps this is because no individual neoclassical economist could ever hope to change the *hidden* agenda in his or her lifetime.) In this sense, neoclassical economics is an exogenous element whenever the individual economist is choosing a specific research program.

The only thing at issue, then, is whether reductive individualism is an *essential* element of neoclassical methodology. To decide this one would need to determine whether or not the conclusions of today's neoclassical economics require reductive individualism. If the conclusion of any neoclassical article can be shown to be independent of any reductive individualism – e.g., it may presume the existence of exogenous non-individualistic variables other than natural constraints – then it will have to be concluded that reductive individualism is not essential. For now I will leave this question open (alternatively, see Newman [1981]).

Now I assert, perhaps perversely, that the methodological individualist agenda item of neoclassical economics is, as Blaug claims, a reductionist version. However – and this is where I am being perverse – the reason why it is a reductionist version is not because neoclassical economists or neoclassical economics are essentially Inductivist but only because economists have not endeavored to purge the unnecessary Inductivist and reductionist elements in neoclassical economics. In other words, neoclassical economics is based on reductive methodological individualism by default.

This view only raises another question. Why have economists not purged the reductive individualism and instead adopted the more modest individualism which Marshall was promoting (which simply accepts short-run non-individualist and non-natural constraints such as the amount of physical capital)? The answer to this question is the key to my argument here. Reductive individualism has not been purged because it is thought to be the means of providing the 'atoms' or minimal facts from which one is to 'induce' the 'laws of economics'. Supposedly, if one knew the utility functions of all individual consumers in society and the production functions of all individual firms in society then, given only the natural constraints (e.g., resource endowments), we could derive (and thus explain) all prices, quantities, and institutions. Few neoclassical economists would disagree with such a supposition. However, they might admit that obtaining all the necessary knowledge is a virtual impossibility. But again, this admission may only reflect a belief in the necessity of induction. In short, neoclassical economics today is based on reductive individualism because economists have not yet chosen to reject the need to deal with the Problem of Induction.

Psychologism and Conventionalism

As I argued above, economists not only accept the reductive individualist research program, but they compound this when they also accept psychologism by the identification of individuals with their respective utility functions, that is, with their respective psychological states. I argue that since individualism is too often presumed only for the philosophical purposes of dealing with the Problem of Induction, the role psychologism plays in the individualist agenda item needs to be examined.

Again I have to be perverse. On the one hand, psychologism is accepted because it facilitates a reductive individualist research program to deal with the Problem of Induction. On the other hand, psychologism is also accepted as an arbitrary means of solving the Problem of Conventions that was discussed in Chapter 1. It may seem that psychologism is being used to solve contradictory problems, since Conventionalism is considered an alternative to Inductivism. But there is no contradiction here. Conventionalism is based on Inductivism in the following sense. Conventionalism accepts the impossibility of an inductive proof of the truth of any theory. Another way of stating this is that Conventionalism accepts that an inductive proof would require an infinity of time to complete. Thus, in the short run, Conventionalism attempts to establish rules of acceptance for choosing between competing theories. Invoking psychologism provides one of the rules of acceptance, namely, that the allowable exogenous variables in any acceptable theory must not include any givens other than the natural givens and the psychological states of the individuals. Other variables may be temporarily fixed (e.g., institutional constraints) but not exogenous. That is, it must be possible to explain them, in principle, by allowing for an artificial passage of time. But true to Conventionalist principles, any choice based on an hypothetical passage of time cannot be construed as a proof.

This point needs to be stressed in order to understand the role of psychologism. As explained in the last section, if we were to allow for an infinity of time, induction might not be impossible. If we were to allow for an infinity of time, then all artificial, non-individualist constraints could be relaxed so that the only exogenous givens would be individualist variables. In other words, in the very long run both Inductivism and psychologism would be feasible. However, no one could claim that a long-run argument constitutes an *inductive* proof. Rather, what is provided by long-run arguments (which are consistent with psychologism) is only a demonstration of the hypothetical possibility of an inductive proof and a complete reduction to psychological states. In other words, fixed non-individualist constraints are allowable in the short run only if it can be demonstrated that it is the *natural* shortness of the run which alone explains their fixity. Every long-run model provides such a demonstration.

To a great extent, then, given that Conventionalism does not allow proofs of absolute truth, psychologism would seem to be a successful, albeit arbitrary, means of solving the Problem of Conventions. By legislating psychological states as the only accepted set of non-natural exogenous variables, we are allowing conditional explanations to avoid the infinite regression that would seem to be required of an absolutely true explanation. By taking psychologism and Conventionalism as methodological givens, we are never expected to explain the individual's psychological state.

So, if we reject any need to solve the Problem of Induction or the Conventionalist Problem *with* Induction, it would seem that we can dispense with any need to require the reductive version of methodological individualism. Of course, to do this we will have to dispense with the ideological motivation to suppress *at all cost* any chance of encouraging methodological holism. As well, we may have to avoid relying exclusively on long-run explanations and recognize that in the real world, there will always be givens in a situation facing any decision-maker – givens that cannot be changed simply because they are the results of irreversible past decisions. Institutional individualism allows for this. Every decision-maker in neoclassical economics faces a situation defined by the givens and thus must decide which to take as exogenously fixed and which to consider changing. For example, in elementary neoclassical economics a consumer is assumed to be a utility maximizer when choosing an amount of a good to purchase but facing a fixed budget and fixed price. Of course, the fixity of the givens is open to question. The budget may be the consequence of institutional arrangements between the consumer and his or her employer. The fixity of the price may be the result of the institutional nature of the market. But, in neoclassical explanations, the consumer is assumed to just accept both the budget and the price as fixed even though in the real world the consumer could offer a different price or go about changing the budget since, after all, neither is a natural given. Thus, in effect, the neoclassical consumer must be choosing to treat the budget and the price as fixed and so these choices are also part of the explanation of the consumer's choice of the amount of good in question. While institutional individualism does not deny the typical neoclassical explanation, it does allow the neoclassical theorist to go beyond the limits of psychologistic individualism. In the next chapter, I will turn to examine the typical neoclassical explanation to reveal the visible agenda of neoclassical economics. Inductivism and methodological individualism will be on prominent display.

Part II
THE VISIBLE AGENDA OF NEOCLASSICAL ECONOMICS

3 Rationality vs. Maximization

Economics sometimes uses the term 'irrationality' rather broadly ... and the term 'rationality' correspondingly narrowly, so as to exclude from the domain of the rational many phenomena that psychology would include in it.
Herbert Simon [1986, p. S209]

rationality is not in principle essential to a theory of the economy, and, in fact, theories with direct application usually use assumptions of a different nature.
Kenneth Arrow [1986, p. S387]

utility analysis rests on the fundamental assumption that the individual confronted with given prices and confined to a given total expenditure selects that combination of goods which is highest on his preference scale. This does not require (a) that the individual behave rationally in any other sense; (b) that he be deliberate and self-conscious in his purchasing; (c) that there exist any *intensive* magnitude which he feels or consults.
Paul Samuelson [1947/65, pp. 97–8]

The main points in the further development of the utility theory of the consumer are well-known. (1) Rational behavior is an ordinal property. (2) The assumption that an individual is behaving rationally has indeed some observable implications ... but without further assumptions, they are not very strong. (3) In the aggregate, the hypothesis of rational behavior has in general no implications.
Kenneth Arrow [1986, p. S388]

The assumption of rationality has been a visible part of all versions of economics and economic theory since Adam Smith's eighteenth century. An explicit maximization hypothesis has been the hallmark of neoclassical economics since the end of the nineteenth century and might easily be seen to be the one major departure that distinguishes neoclassical from classical economics. It can be further noted that today the assumption of rationality is usually invoked to represent a presumed psychological process whereas maximization seems only to be a convenient assumption used to 'close' a model (e.g., make it possible to logically derive and thereby explain the existence of a set of prices that would clear all markets).

As noted in Chapter 2, critics of neoclassical economics have often focused on the knowledge requirements of the maximization hypothesis to claim that it is a weak link in any explanation of social events. The claims and counter-claims concerning the nature and role of rationality or maximization can be very confusing. In this chapter I will try to clear up some issues by discussing the methodology of constructing a neoclassical explanation of economic phenomena. I will also continue my argument that if one wishes to abandon psychologism while maintaining methodological individualism, the presumption that rationality is a psychological process must also be abandoned. Stated another way – and going beyond the observations of both Arrow and Samuelson, as quoted above – it will be argued that presuming rationality to be a psychological process is not only unnecessary, it is misleading.

Rationality as logic vs. rationality as psychology

> The analysis of situations, the situational logic, plays a very important part in social life as well as in the social sciences. It is, in fact, the method of economic analysis... The method of applying a situational logic to the social sciences is not based on any psychological assumption concerning the rationality (or otherwise) of 'human nature'. On the contrary: when we speak of 'rational behaviour' or of 'irrational behaviour' then we mean behaviour which is, or which is not, in accordance with the logic of that situation.
>
> Karl Popper [1945/66, vol. 2, p. 97]

At that time in the eighteenth century when Adam Smith's friend David Hume was recognizing the Problem of Induction, most thinkers seemed to believe that the rationality of science was based on inductive logic. But by recognizing that there is no logic (formal or otherwise) with which one could 'justify' (i.e., prove) the truth of a general statement using only particular statements (that is, one cannot prove all swans are white just by listing all of the past observations of white swans), Hume seemed to adopt the view that rationality would have to be seen as a psychological process (or otherwise we would have to take a skeptical view of scientific knowledge). I think most economists today still take Hume's view for granted. And beyond what I explained in Chapter 1 – namely, that economists opt for some form of either Conventionalism or Instrumentalism to overcome the Problem of Induction – here I want to focus on the methodological consequences of accepting Hume's view that rationality must be seen as a psychological process. I will argue that there is no need for economic theorists to do so and the reason is simply that Hume's view does not solve any essential problem in economics.

Rationality as logic

As noted in Chapter 2, it is important to recognize that rationality is a property of arguments; it is not a psychological disposition. In economics, this recognition is important because we are trying to explain events and phenomena of the social world we see outside our windows. Of course, every explanation is fundamentally an argument. And an argument is a set of reasons (each claimed or presumed to be true) which together are claimed to be logically sufficient to prove the truth of the statement of the event or phenomenon in question. A logically sufficient argument is usually called a valid argument. But we must always keep in mind that claiming an argument to be valid is not the same as claiming that all of its constituent reasons are thereby true.

Some readers will wish to note that while rationality may not be a psychological disposition, being reasonable surely is. In response, I would say that neoclassical economists rarely make use of any individual's reasonableness. When we ask people to be reasonable, we are merely asking them to be willing to give reasons for their actions or for their claims of knowledge. That is, we are asking them to provide a valid argument. If we wish to challenge the validity of their argument, we can challenge either whether the set of reasons offered is logically sufficient for their claims to the truth of their knowledge or whether their actions are logically consistent with the reasons they give. Following Aristotle's view of ordinary logic, reasons are (simple) statements that are either true or false. Since the reasons given are all claimed to be true, we know that a set of reasons will not be logically sufficient if some of the reasons are contradictory (i.e., if the truth of one implies the falsity of another). While, like being reasonable, being consistent can be viewed as a psychological attribute, it need not be. Instead, both could be seen as sociological attributes.

Note that all the given reasons are claimed to be true because this is the only direct way to use the validity of an argument in favor of the truth of the statement in question. In general, every argument in favor of the truth of one statement is a claim that 'since every reason I give is a true statement, and since taken together the reasons form a valid argument, then the statement in question must be true'. Logic textbooks sometimes refer to this use of the validity of an argument as arguing *modus ponens*. Simply stated, it says for a logically valid argument, whenever *all* of the reasons are true, *all* of the statements that the argument can be used to explain must be true as well. It immediately follows that there is another way to use the validity of an argument. It is called *modus tollens*, and says, 'your argument may be valid but I have found a statement that your argument would explain that is false and thus at least one of your reasons must be false'. This is so because if it were a valid argument and all the reasons were true then there could not be an explainable statement that is false. And all this is simply because this is what we mean by claiming or showing that an argument is logically valid.

What does rationality as logic do for economic theorists?

An argument is rational only if it is logically valid. When a reasonable person provides a valid argument to explain his or her situation and actions, doing so says that *anyone* who would accept the truth of each and every reason that is used to form the argument, as well as the logical validity of the argument, would engage in the exact *same* action whenever facing the same situation and sharing the reasons given. In other words, everyone who accepts (as true) the reasons of a valid argument will necessarily reach the same conclusions. If they do not reach the same conclusions (concerning the truth of the explained statements), then the argument must not be logically sufficient. A rational argument, then, is both *universal* and provides *unique* conclusions. This is what rationality provides that is most useful for economic theorists. When we offer a theory to explain the behavior of an individual (e.g., as a part of demand theory), we put forth a set of reasons that together form an argument for why the consumer's behavior is what it is. When we ask consumers why they did what they did, if they are reasonable they answer by giving us their reasons. The reasons provided by the theorist may be very different. In the 1940s there was a celebrated debate between Fritz Machlup [1946; 1947] and Richard Lester [1946; 1947] over the realism (i.e., truth) of the typical reasons provided by neoclassical theorists to explain the behavior of profit maximizing firms. Specifically, as I noted near the end of Chapter 1, the issue was whether one would actually do the marginal calculations necessary to determine that profit is being maximized as assumed by the theorists. In 1950 Armen Alchian argued in a social-Darwinist fashion that the truth of the maximization assumption did not actually matter. That is, the profit maximizer need not be consciously calculating marginal profit (the difference between marginal revenue and marginal cost) to make sure that it is zero. The reason is simply that in a long-run equilibrium (i.e., where competition leads to the maximum total profit being zero), any firm not maximizing profit will go out of business. Moreover, the survivors will be maximizing profit whether they think so or not. So, the reasons given by a survivor for its actions (price charged, quantity produced) may not correspond to the reasons provided by the theorists to explain the surviving firm's actions.

Does rationality as a psychological process matter?

From the standpoint of a theorist, the rationality of the offered explanation is what matters. If one agrees with Alchian's dismissal of the need for realistic theoretical reasons (subsequently argued more generally by Milton Friedman [1953] with his de facto promotion of Instrumentalism), then there would be no room for viewing rationality as a psychological process of the decision-maker in question. Nevertheless, even without arguing over the 'realism of assumptions', some may still think that rationality must be considered a psychological process [e.g., Scitovsky 1976 and Earl 1988].

To consider the relevance of rationality as a psychological process, the key issue is whether or not we are explaining behavior in the context of an equilibrium. Behavior in an equilibrium context requires only the consistency discussed above. If rationality as a psychological process is ever to matter, it will be when the question is raised as to *how* the equilibrium is reached or when one asks how decision-makers know what they need to know to achieve the equilibrium. Actually, learning is involved in both questions. Surely, it will be argued, learning must be something addressable with psychological considerations. Perhaps; but for those favorably disposed to consider rationality as a psychological process, there is little evidence that much has been accomplished within neoclassical economics that might be credited to such a psychologically oriented research program. That is, as far as neoclassical economics is concerned, rationality as a psychological process does not seem to matter.

In Part VI, I will return to the matter of how we can deal with the question of the decision-maker's learning process and offer there an alternative that considers these questions about learning in a non-psychological context. For now, further considerations of rationality as a process will be postponed until the next chapter where I turn to look at how game theorists are addressing and using the concept of rationality.

The role of maximization in neoclassical economics

Since Alfred Marshall's time, economists have tended to use 'rationality' and 'maximization' interchangeably. This tendency has been very misleading for students of economics. Of course, maximization can be seen as a psychological process, too, but in neoclassical economics it does not need to be. Instead, the assumption of maximization by the decision-maker in question captures the two essential properties provided by a rational argument that explains the decision-maker's actions – namely, the universality and uniqueness that I discussed above.

Maximization vs. eighteenth-century rationality

Rationality in the eighteenth century was more a matter of prescription than explanation. That is, those promoting rationality when talking about social policy were often recommending that people be rational or at least saying that if people were rational they would always avoid making mistakes. One could easily argue that the French Revolution was a direct outcome of the belief in the power of rational thought. Specifically, many 'rationalists' of the eighteenth century were in effect saying 'kill the king and get rid of the priests'. And the basis for this advocacy was that it was the rational thing to do.

Since Marshall's time, economists consider rationality to be an essential ingredient in the explanation of the economy. The change from eighteenth-century prescriptive rationality to today's explanatory rationality is probably reflected in the change from the disciplinary names of 'political economy' of the nineteenth century to 'economic science' or 'economics' of the twentieth century. In most of the nineteenth century, political economy was supposedly a discipline primarily concerned with social policy. The changeover was complete by the time Marshall was able to say on the first page of the preface to the seventh edition (1916) of his *Principles of Economics*, that it was 'a general introduction to the study of economic science'.

As noted above, explanatory rationality relies on the universality of rational explanations, that is, of rational arguments; and it relies on the uniqueness of deductions from rational arguments. To restate, anyone who accepts (as true) all of the reasons that together constitute a logically valid rational argument will also have to accept (as true) all statements that logically follow from that argument. Moreover, to be an explanation of a particular act – that is, an individual's particular choice between multiple options – an argument must be sufficient. That is, it must also explain why none of the alternative actions (i.e., options) were chosen. Without this, a question would be begged as to why the one rather than any other non-excluded option was chosen. Earlier, I referred to this as the uniqueness of the explanatory conclusion (i.e., deduction) from a rational argument. For the neoclassical theorist, maximization, as an achievement (rather than a process), provides everything useful that rationality as logic can provide –

namely, by providing both universality and uniqueness. For future reference, let me illustrate this with a simple diagram, Figure 3.1. This diagram is to represent the choice made by an individual and the criterion used to make the choice. Specifically, the individual faces a continuous range of options (represented by the points along the horizontal axis) and chooses one of them, represented by point E. The neoclassical explanation is that the choice was made because something was maximized – in this illustration, the 'something' is satisfaction. The curved line represents the graphical profile of the respective levels of satisfaction obtained for the options along the continuum. When the neoclassical theorist (explaining the individual's choice) says that the individual chose the point E because it was the one that yielded the highest level of satisfaction, one particular idea is implied. That is, to be a true explanation, all other options must yield lower levels of satisfaction. And this is what is illustrated in Figure 3.1.

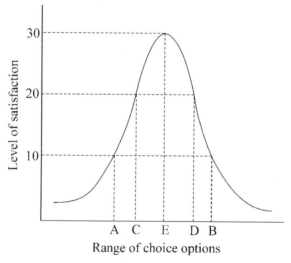

Figure 3.1 Maximization and choice

This figure also illustrates that *anyone* facing the same continuum of options and has the same profile of the levels of satisfaction associated with all of these options will choose the *same* point, namely, E. The explanation is thus both universal (it applies to anyone) and unique (all such individuals will choose the exact same point).

Maximization and the methodology of neoclassical economics

In order to explain a choice made by the consumer, as Paul Samuelson said, we do not have to assume rational behavior beyond maximization – the consumer selects 'that combination of goods which is highest on his preference scale'. That is, we say that the consumer makes a choice that is logically consistent with the consumer's preferences and constraints (prices and income). As far as neoclassical economics goes, there is no attempt to explain how the consumer determines what is 'highest on his preference scale'. There is no attempt to predict a choice, either. Instead, neoclassical explanations come after the fact of a choice. So, the question addressed by neoclassical theory is why *did* the consumer choose that combination of goods? Or, why *did* the firm produce the level of output that it did? And the answer in neoclassical economics is always that every choice made has maximized something – utility, profit, wealth, etc. It will be important to keep in mind that when we explain a consumer's choice, we are not necessarily predicting that choice – as some methodologists used to say (see the discussion of the 'symmetry thesis' in Blaug [1980/92, pp. 5–10]).

Popper's situational analysis and neoclassical economics

> *the logic of the situation*, … besides the initial conditions describing personal interests, aims, and other situational factors, such as the information available to the person concerned, … tacitly assumes, as a kind of first approximation, the trivial general law that sane persons as a rule act more or less rationally.
>
> Karl Popper [1945/66, vol. 2, p. 265]

> My views on the methodology of the social sciences are the result of my admiration for economic theory: I began to develop them, some twenty-five years ago, by trying to generalize the method of theoretical economics.
>
> Karl Popper [1963/94, p. 154]

In 1963, Popper attempted to explain his view of how economists explain social behavior to a meeting of Harvard's economics department [Popper 1963/94]. As is evident above, during his talk he claimed that situational analysis (using what he sometimes calls 'situational logic' and other times the 'logic of the situation') is the foundation of both his view of methodology and what all (neoclassical) economists do.

Maximization and the logic of the situation

In neoclassical economics, what Popper called 'personal interests' or 'aims' is simply what we call utility maximization, profit maximization, wealth maximization, etc. – nothing more. The 'situation' is what neoclassical textbooks identify as the 'givens' including constraints. For example, for the typical textbook consumer, it includes the utility function (or preferences) used to model the 'aims' and the given budget and prices that are used to model the constraints. The only 'information available' is that concerning relevant prices.

Popper often refers to his 'logic of the situation' interchangeably as the 'problem situation'. If we are to explain the choice made by a consumer, we are to see the consumer facing a problem: 'How do I achieve my aims given the constraints I face?' Interestingly, stated this way, the 'How' suggests a process but, just like all neoclassical economists, Popper never means this. Nor by 'act more or less rationally' does he mean anything more than the choice made is logically consistent with the aims and the situation.

When Popper applies his 'situational analysis' as a research program for social science, he really is just extending the method used by neoclassical economists to explain the actions of a decision-maker whether they are economic, political or sociological. In effect, we can say every neoclassical explanation or model is a rational reconstruction; that is, it is a specification of the decision-maker's 'aims' and the 'situation', nothing more, nothing less.

Maximization and metaphysics

For now, I am mentioning Popper's situational analysis only to demonstrate an explicitly non-psychologistic view of neoclassical economics. Later (Chapter 15), I will go further to work backward from this to show why it might be easier for neoclassical economists to understand Popper's theory of science in general than try to swallow the traditional analytical philosopher's view of science (viz., Conventionalism). But here, I want to focus only on the neoclassical economic theorists' problem situation.

The central problem facing every neoclassical economic theorist is: 'How can I explain the actions of the decision-maker in question as being those which can be shown to be logically based on successful constrained maximization?' Many neoclassical theorists, those who are motivated by their ideology, go further by limiting constraints to situations involving market determined prices. Such a limitation is not necessary for situational analysis.

Every model offered by a neoclassical economist (whether ideologically limited or not) is a solution to the central problem I have just identified. But constrained maximization is not just any assumption. If one were to actually test the offered model and find that it did not fit observed data, the last thing a neoclassical theorist will do is question the veracity of the maximization assumption. Instead, it will be presumed that there must be some other way to model the decision-maker's actions – one that still assumes successful maximization. One might then think that the model-building process is primarily a matter of the model builder's cleverness.

Putting maximization beyond question merely demonstrates that maximization is the neoclassical economist's metaphysics. To some this might seem to be a criticism. Today, this would be a mistaken view, but there was a time in the 1930s when any mention of metaphysics could only be part of ridicule. Then, most philosophers of science believed that one must choose between science and metaphysics. Hopefully, today, we see that every science has its metaphysics.

More generally, every research program has its metaphysics. In fact, it would be difficult to define one's research program without identifying one's metaphysics. Many sociologists take the existence of a power structure to be beyond question. Many psychologists consider the existence of emotions beyond question. And so on. It is easy to say that every science can be defined by what it puts beyond question – that is, its metaphysics.

There was a time when metaphysical statements were seen as tautologies [e.g., Hutchison 1938]. Some economists, such as Harvey Leibenstein [1979], further claimed that assuming maximization turned neoclassical economics into a tautology. This confusion of metaphysical statements with tautologies is a common mistake. The error is due to not recognizing that a tautology is a statement which is true regardless of the meaning of the non-logical words used (e.g., the tautological statement 'I am here or I am not here' is true regardless of who 'I' am or where 'here' is). A tautological statement is one for which we could never conceive of a counter-example. That is, a tautology is not conceivably false. This is not true of a metaphysical statement. A metaphysical statement is not a tautology and this is so simply because a metaphysical statement can be false (which is why it is put beyond question). Clearly, the assumption that all decision-makers are maximizers is conceivably false – particularly whenever one also specifies what is supposedly being maximized.

Maximization as an implementation of methodological individualism

Alfred Marshall was very explicit in his version of neoclassical economics. His version is still the staple of undergraduate textbooks. Following his version we would offer a form of explanation that is to apply universally to any individual decision-maker. Following Marshall, if we are theoretically successful, we will be able to infer that we have thereby explained the whole economy. In Marshall's approach, we are to see each individual decision-maker as a maximizer. His method is sometimes called 'partial equilibrium' analysis to distinguish it from Leon Walras' 'general equilibrium' analysis. Marshall's partial equilibrium method is the paradigm of methodological individualism in neoclassical economics.

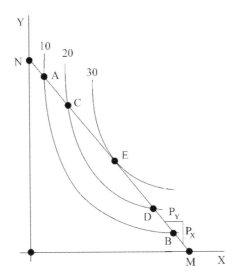

Figure 3.2. Maximizing individual consumer

The modern textbook's version of partial equilibrium analysis of a consumer's choice, for example, is illustrated in Figure 3.2. As usual, each point in this diagram represents a 'bundle' of quantities of the goods X and Y that the consumer may consider purchasing. In this figure, the consumer is thought to be facing a constraint formed by a fixed budget and fixed prices such that if the consumer spent all of his or her budget on good X, the maximum affordable quantity that may be chosen is represented by point M. Similarly, point N represents the maximum affordable quantity of good Y. Since Marshall assumes that the individual must take the prices as fixed givens (no bargaining), the affordability constraint is a straight line between points M and N. The curved lines represent a topographical 'map' of the levels of satisfaction that would be obtained by consuming the various bundles represented by points in the diagram. For readers unfamiliar with economics textbooks, think of the map as analogous to a topographical map that indicates altitudes on a map of a mountain. That is, each line represents one of the levels of satisfaction that we were considering in Figure 3.1 and is labeled with the corresponding level of satisfaction (i.e., 10, 20 or 30). In effect, one can think of Figure 3.1 as simply recording what the level of satisfaction would be when the consumer considers just the continuum of the points along the line representing the budget line. As with Figure 3.1, the individual maximizes satisfaction by choosing point E since this would have the consumer choosing the point which is on the highest level of satisfaction represented by the iso-satisfaction level curve that is tangent to the budget constraint line at point E. A modern follower of Marshall would assume that the consumer has considered points on the budget constraint and made substitutions until point E is reached. Marshall called this his Principle of Substitution; today we call it the maximization hypothesis.

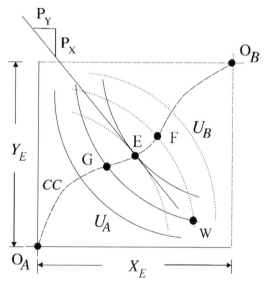

Figure 3.3. Equilibrium in an Edgeworth-Bowley Box

The major limitation of Marshall's method is that, by assuming prices are unchangeable fixed givens, it applies only to individuals who are participating in an economy's state of equilibrium. Nevertheless, within this limitation, one can explain the decision-maker's choices in accordance with methodological individualism. And, as I have already noted, in a long-run equilibrium, psychologistic individualism can easily be accommodated. With Marshall's method, once an equilibrium is reached it should always be possible to pick *any* individual participating in the equilibrium and find that he or she is making a unique choice that is maximizing his or her utility, profit, etc. for the given equilibrium prices.

Walras' general equilibrium approach is only slightly different. In a state of general equilibrium, by definition, everyone is maximizing subject to Nature-given constraints. Walras' general equilibrium approach is usually employed to illustrate the equilibrium between individuals rather than just one individual's personal equilibrium (i.e., maximization status). Specifically, it says that we can pick any two individuals (and any two produced goods) and it will be the case that there is no way either person could gain without the other person losing (by exchanging the goods shared between them). This is often referred to as a state of Pareto optimality and usually extended to recognize all possible pairs of individuals in all possible markets or competitions. For future reference, Figure 3.3 provides the typical illustration of a pair of competing consumers.

This figure would be used to represent the competing aims of two individuals – here we have individual A's preference map U_A represented by the solid lines and individual B's map U_B represented by dotted lines. (For readers unfamiliar with such diagrams, note that B's map has been rotated 180 degrees so that any point in the box represents a complete allocation of the goods shared between person A and person B.) The common situation faced by these two individuals is that there are fixed amounts of goods X and Y (determined by the total amounts of X_E and Y_E available between the two individuals as a consequence of the state of general equilibrium) and equilibrium prices (P_X and P_Y) for those two goods. The two individuals are in their exchange equilibrium at point E and so each is choosing point E along their respective budget lines (with the negative slope P_X/P_Y). Point E is also a point on the so-called Contract Curve (represented by the dashed line, *CC*) that connects all points in the box where the two preference maps are tangent (thus *CC* is the locus of all possible Pareto optima – that is, points where in any further exchange one person can gain some satisfaction only if the other loses some). At point E, both individuals can be seen to be at their respective Marshallian partial equilibria and thus Walrasian analysis also accommodates methodological individualism.

An interesting issue is raised by such an elementary illustration. As noted before, as long as we are only explaining an individual's behavior in the state of equilibrium, rationality or maximization can easily be viewed as a matter of logic rather than a matter of process. But in the 1960s, theorists were concerned with the question of which point along *CC* would be a possible equilibrium consistent with the choice made by any other individual in the economy. To consider this question, the individuals in Figure 3.3 would be put at a point like W where both individuals could gain in an exchange without the other individual losing. But which point along the *CC*? Clearly, it will have to be a point between points F and G. Much printer's ink was spent trying to specify assumptions about the nature of the preference maps that would answer this question. That is, could we specify the situation sufficiently that the answer is a simple matter of mathematical mechanics? Had they been successful, it would seem that there would be no room for autonomous choice for individuals – even more so, given that prices were assumed to be fixed givens in equilibrium situations. Dropping this assumption allowed us to see the question of which point the individuals would reach as a matter of game theory, particularly, bargaining theory. But game theory then seemed to be just another mechanical exercise that left no room for individuality or autonomy. In particular, game theory offered solutions to economic problems that formally seemed to be nothing more than a version of linear programming's simplex method [see Vajda 1956]. I will return to the issues raised by game theory in the next chapter. But for now, let me continue examining equilibria as states of universal maximization.

Maximization and equilibrium theory

To some degree, it is possible to claim that the notion of equilibrium is redundant once we assume every decision-maker participating in the economy is maximizing. This is obviously the case with Walrasian general equilibrium theory since the definition of such an equilibrium requires universal maximization. It is also the case with Marshallian long-run equilibrium analysis if we define the demand curve to be the locus of price-quantity points where every demander is maximizing his or her utility and we define the supply curve similarly for every supplier maximizing its profit. But, is universal maximization merely a different expression used to describe an equilibrium?

Economists are particularly sloppy when discussing the notion of equilibrium. Usually what is called an equilibrium is merely a balance. That is, when demand equals supply, this is a balance and not necessarily an equilibrium. A simple equality (e.g., between demand and supply) is a static notion but the idea of an equilibrium implies a dynamic notion. To understand this distinction, consider a coin balanced on its edge. If it is tilted slightly to either side, its physical position will completely change. That is, it falls over and there is no reason for the coin to bring itself back into the original upright balance. Textbooks would say that this is an 'unstable equilibrium', but the concept of an unstable equilibrium is self-contradictory. Similarly, textbooks would say that an equality between supply and demand is an equilibrium when actually it is only a balance. For an equilibrium, more is required. Specifically, for a balance to be an equilibrium, there must be some reason for why, if the balance is upset, the balance will always be restored. Such reasoning will then show that we not only have a balance but also a stable balance. Thus, when textbooks talk about an 'unstable equilibrium', they are talking about an oxymoron. They really mean an unstable balance.

The importance of this distinction is that the point of balance can represent a state of universal maximization. But, a balance between demand and supply may not be relevant for an explanation of the set of observed prices unless there are some reasons for why the balance must exist. Furthermore, that balance must be the only one if it is to be used to explain the observed set of prices since, otherwise, the question is begged as to why the observed balance was reached instead of one of the other logically possible points of balance. One obvious form of reasoning would be that while the other points of balance might logically allow for universal maximization, only the observed one is a stable balance. That is, we would need some 'stability analysis'. But, it is not inconceivable that there might be multiple stable balances (which textbooks would call multiple equilibria). In this case, our explanation of prices is at best incomplete. We would need some reasoning to show that the observed equilibrium is the only one to which the economy moves. Showing this has not been easy and thus most neoclassical model builders focus on settings where there is only one possible equilibrium. The problems raised by multiple equilibria will be discussed further in Chapters 7 and 9.

Maximization and 'ideal-type' methodology

Rather than raising a question of how an economy moves toward an equilibrium (thereby raising many methodological problems such as those involving learning and knowledge), the equilibrium model – the model where everyone is maximizing and thus there is no reason to change anything – is employed by neoclassical economists as an ideal-type. Ideal-type methodology (usually attributed to Max von Weber) says that we can explain the real world as being some explainable 'distance' from the ideal model, that is, from an ideal state obtained in the long-run or general equilibrium model.

The paradigm notion of an ideal-model is that used in physics when discussing movement of a block along an inclined plane. In the absence of friction, the block would almost instantly slide down the plane as a result of gravity. In the real world, the block does not do this because there is friction slowing down or stopping the slide. By analogy, in economics, inability to reach an equilibrium might be due to imperfections concerning competition, divisibility of goods being chosen, or other exogenous constraints. So, the explanations of the choices or decisions being made always involve two elements. First is the ideal model's situation and the second is the reasons given for the inability to fulfill the conditions of the ideal situation.

The only methodological question raised here is whether the reasons given for the inability to fulfill the conditions of the ideal situation violate methodological individualism. Of course, if the reasons given involve only Nature-given constraints, then there is no problem. If one opts for something like Herbert Simon's bounded rationality (based on the notion that maximization would require more Nature-given brain power than is realistic to presume along the lines of Lester's criticism of neoclassical economics), it, too, might be seen as a Nature-given constraint. But if we have to explain the extent of the distortion from the ideal in this manner, it would seem that we are begging questions that require recognition either that rationality (and maximization) is a psychological process or that the psychologistic version of methodological individualism is being violated. Recent game-theoretical versions of neoclassical economics do not seem to be plowing the familiar fields of ideal-type methodology but, as we shall see, the same dilemma is present. In the next chapter I will discuss how game theory manifests the visible agenda of maximization, after which, I will return in Chapter 5 to discuss how ideal-type methodology is employed in neoclassical economics.

4 Maximization and Game Theory

in so far as individuals are modelled as Humean agents, game theory is well placed to help assess the claims of [psychologistic] individualists. After all, game theory purports to analyse social interaction between individuals who, as Hume argued, have passions and a reason to serve them. Thus game theory should enable us to examine the claim that, beginning from a situation with no institutions..., the self-interested behaviour of these ... rational agents will either bring about institutions or fuel their evolution. An examination of the explanatory power of game theory in such settings is one way of testing the individualist claims.

... the recurring difficulty with the analysis of many games is that there are too many potential plausible outcomes. There are a variety of disparate outcomes which are consistent with ... individuals *qua* individuals interacting. Which one of a set of potential outcomes should we expect to materialise? We simply do not know. Such pluralism might seem a strength. On the other hand, however, it may be taken to signify that the selection of one historical outcome is not simply a matter of ... rational individuals interacting. There must be something more to it outside the individuals' preferences, their constraints and their capacity to maximise utility. The question is: what? It seems to us that either the conception of the 'individual' will have to be amended to take account of this extra source of influence (whatever it is) or it will have to be admitted that there are non-individualistic ... elements which are part of the explanation of what happens when people interact.

Shaun Hargreaves Heap and Yanis Varoufakis [1995, p. 33]

Game theory *by itself* is not meant to improve anyone's understanding of economic phenomena. Game theory ... is a tool of economic analysis, and the proper test is whether economic analyses that use the concepts and language of game theory have improved our understanding. Of course, there is an identification problem here. Without the concepts and language of game theory, essentially the same economic analyses may well have been carried out; game theory may be nothing more than window-dressing. Hence improvements in understanding that I may attribute in part to game theory may in fact have little or nothing to do with the theory.

David Kreps [1990, p. 6]

Game theory is very popular today and thus needs to be critically examined in terms of the hidden agenda as well as the visible agenda of neoclassical economics. I will discuss the visible agenda first. Specifically, I will discuss game theory methodology as an alternative to the typical calculus-based, partial-equilibrium conception of maximization and then examine how maximization is employed within game theory.

Neoclassical vs. non-calculus maximization

To begin, consider Figure 4.1, which might be a typical diagram associated with calculus-based methodology. This diagram can be used to illustrate the selection by a single revenue-maximizing decision-maker of one point located anywhere within the area bounded by the curve drawn from point C to point B passing through point D and E plus the horizontal line between points A and B as well as the vertical line between points A and C. The points in or on the boundary of this area are considered feasible points and points outside are not feasible. The presumed aim or purpose of the selection, subject to feasibility, is to maximize revenue in accordance with the given price line P–P which indicates both the relative value of goods Y and X and the level of revenue (revenue goes up in the direction of the arrow). To determine which point will provide the maximum revenue, the calculus-based methodology would have us provide a continuous mathematical function that would tell us the revenue level at each point along the continuous curve between points C and B. All feasible points below or to the left of any point on the curve will be ruled out as obviously inferior – that is, 'dominated' – if both goods have positive values (or prices). In other words, for any point in the interior of the area it is always possible to increase one good without reducing the other by definition of feasibility. By this consideration, all but the points on the curve are eliminated from consideration.

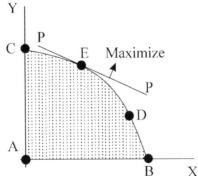

Figure 4.1. Calculus-based maximization

Now, what is most important is that for all points *on the curve*, restricting our consideration to feasible points means that increasing the amount of good Y would require the reduction of the amount of good X. Thus if there is a revenue maximum, it will be on the curve. Once the curve has been represented by this continuous function, elementary calculus would be applied (in a manner similar to Figure 3.1) to straightforwardly identify point E as the only revenue-maximizing point and then the maximum revenue obtainable is calculated. (That is, to find the maximizing point, the continuous function would be differentiated and by then setting the value of the differentiated function to zero – a necessary condition of maximization – and using the undifferentiated function to express good Y as a function of good X, the resulting differentiated function is used to solve for the amount of good X at the maximizing point. The corresponding amount of Y is then determined using the undifferentiated function.)

Until the late 1940s, maximization might commonly be seen this way and the individual's choice of point E facing the feasible set and the revenue function illustrated would be explained as having maximized revenue. But, as a by-product of research done during the Second World War (and inspired by earlier work of John von Neumann [1928]), continuous functions seemed either unrealistic or impractical considerations. A practical view would be to approximate the curve with a small set of straight lines that can in turn be used to approximate the bounded area. By doing so, the maximization problem can be transformed into a simple linear algebra problem – that is, into a matter of finding the point that simultaneously satisfies a set of linear inequalities and has the highest revenue as indicated by the linear revenue function. Note two things. We have to use inequalities only because the bounding lines are linear and some of the points in the feasible set are below or to the left of these bounding lines. The revenue function is linear simply because in neoclassical economics it is assumed that the individual decision-maker must take the prices as fixed and given (which is unproblematic as long as this modeling is limited to prices that are equilibrium prices in the fashion of Marshallian partial equilibrium analysis). This way of characterizing the maximization problem (as one of maximizing while facing linear constraints) is called linear programming.

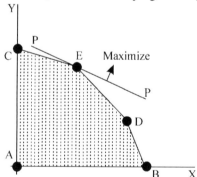

Figure 4.2. Non-calculus maximization

Now, consider Figure 4.2 which might be a typical diagram associated with linear-programming methodology. This diagram would be used to illustrate the selection of one point located anywhere in or on the polygon formed by the points A, B, C, D and E. This polygon also represents the feasible set of options. Again, the selection in question is to maximize revenue in accordance with the given price line P–P which indicates both the relative value (i.e., relative prices) of goods Y and X and the level of revenue (revenue goes up in the direction of the arrow). Calculus cannot be used here since we do not have a well-behaved continuous curve to which calculus can be applied (a well-behaved curve would not have any sharp corners). George Dantzig [1949/51] is usually credited with the development of a multi-step algorithm which is used to determine the maximizing point without using calculus. His algorithm is called the 'simplex method'. The first step involves identifying the 'extreme points'. In Figure 4.2, these would be points A, B, C, D and E. Then for step two, one of the points is selected and evaluated in accordance with the price line P–P. The next step involves moving to an adjacent extreme point to see if revenue goes up or down. If up, continue in that direction to the next extreme point. The process stops when the revenue goes down after going up and the immediately previous point is selected. It is obvious in the simple two-dimensional illustration, but when there are many dimensions, simplex method is not so obvious but is nevertheless effective.

Game theory and non-calculus-based maximization

This simplex methodology is being examined here because by the 1950s, as noted in Chapter 3, it was recognized that solutions to most game theory problems of the day were interchangeable with solutions to linear programming problems [Dantzig 1949/51; Vajda 1956]. As also noted in Chapter 3, game theory can be seen to be a way of dealing with the interaction between any two individuals not in the general equilibrium situation (see the discussion of Figure 3.3). That is, consider two individuals who are thought to be (for whatever reason) at a point like W in Figure 3.3 (which is not at a point of Pareto optimum) but they are considering how they might mutually reallocate or exchange the two goods between them. At some point, one needs to explain the movement from point W to one of the equilibrium points along the Contract Curve between points G and F in that figure. If the path of the movement were explicitly explained as a game-theoretic solution to how the equilibrium point is reached, it would appear that game theory might be explaining maximization as a process. In the 1950s this possibility was encouraged by seeing the game as a two-person, zero-sum non-cooperative game which led to seeing that the game's solution was analytically the same as the solution to a linear-programming problem [Vajda 1956, p. 89]. The details of this observed identity are not important here. The textbooks of the day simply noted that both solutions were 'minimax' solutions in the sense that the optimum could be seen as choosing the point where one player is maximizing the minimum that he or she could have and the value of that point would be the same as the other person's who is minimizing the maximum attainable [see Chiang 1984, p. 671]. In linear programming, this situation was also characterized as the 'duality theorem' [Vajda 1956, p. 75].

Game theory analysis typically does take something like the linear-programming approach in one fundamental way that does not involve any analytical complexities. Specifically, we saw with linear-programming that maximization was reduced from considering a continuous sequence of an infinity of points along a curve (such as the curve in Figure 4.1 or the horizontal line in Figure 3.1) to choosing one among a small finite set of 'extreme' points such as the points at each corner of a multisided polygon (such as the one illustrated in Figure 4.2). In game theory, the situation is similarly set up by first identifying a small set of representative options that each player is said to choose between and then setting out the combinations in the form of a logic box – such as Figure 4.3. (I say 'representative' only to recognize that a game can involve choices along a continuum – such as would be the case in Figure 3.3 where there might be a movement along a continuous path from point W to one of the infinity of points somewhere on the Contract Curve between points G and F.)

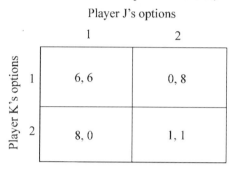

Figure 4.3. Payoff table as logic box

To illustrate typical game theory analysis, consider two players, J and K who have just two alternative options ('moves' or 'plays') to choose between, namely, options 1 and 2. The logic box would then be such that each cell of the box contains the outcome of the respective choices (the first number is K's revenue or payoff and the second is J's). Here each player is engaging in a choice problem while facing a small number of options. This is just as it was for the individual decision-makers in the linear programming case – the only difference being that unlike facing a fixed revenue function or line, the revenue each player gets depends on the option chosen by the other player. So, typical game theory analysis combines both the limited options of linear programming's simplex method with the intention of dropping the fixed revenue function and replacing it with interactively contingent revenue.

Game theory, maximization and predicting behavior

Let the game described in Figure 4.3 be one where the two players choose simultaneously and do so without any way to communicate between them. Let us also consider how we might use maximization with such a game by considering two possible questions of methodological interest. Can we use a game-based analysis to explain choices that have been observed? And, can we use game-based analysis to predict the players' choices? Let us ignore for a while the matter of explaining observed behavior and instead limit our concern to predicting which cell of our logic box represents our prediction. Such a cell prediction is usually called the solution of the game presented. There are two techniques that can be employed to answer this question of prediction. One does so by elimination; that is, by eliminating options that the player would not choose because that option is 'dominated' by another option, particularly when one does not know what the other player will do. In many games, this technique does not identify any solution. The other technique used to find a solution is predicated on the players knowing the payoff table and knowing that once one player chooses an option, the other player will choose the best option available as a consequence. Specifically, if one player chooses option 2 in Figure 4.3, the other player will also choose option 2 (since a payoff of 1 is always better than one of zero). If one player chooses option 1, the other player will still choose option 2 (since 8 is always better than 6). Given this knowledge, both will choose option 2 even though both would be better off by both choosing option 1. Our prediction is nevertheless that both will choose option 2. The knowledge that the players need for this technique includes both the knowledge of the game and the knowledge that the other player knows the game and that the other player will choose the best available option. Game theorists, equating such maximizing with rationality, call this combination of assumptions: 'Common Knowledge of Rationality' or simply 'Common Knowledge'.

The 1994 Nobel laureate, John Nash [1951], discussed a key condition that must be met for such a solution to be predicted. Namely, for the predicted cell, neither player would want to change their choice. Unfortunately, by meeting his condition it is said we have an 'equilibrium' even though we are speaking of a very static situation. This common misuse of the term 'equilibrium' need not be a problem so long as we limit our use of the so-called Nash equilibrium notion to predicting choices. As noted in Chapter 3, if we are to use maximization to explain behavior or choices, we also need to employ an equilibrium rather than a balance (i.e., rather than just a mutual consistency of choices made by all players or market participants). That is, just how did we arrive at the state of balanced choices? But since at this stage we are discussing predictions, no problem.

Game theory's use of rationality and the hidden agenda

> we cannot expect game and economic theory to be descriptive in the same sense that physics or astronomy are. Rationality is only one of several factors affecting human behavior; no theory based on this one factor alone can be expected to yield reliable predictions...
> We strive to make statements that, while perhaps not falsifiable, do have some universality, do express some insight of a general nature; we discipline our minds through the medium of the mathematical model; and at their best, our disciplines do have beauty, simplicity, force and relevance.
> Robert Aumann [1985, pp. 36 and 42]

Game theory as a process of explicit maximization

Some game theorists are now concerned that many predictions based on game theory analysis have failed when subjected to experiments with real people (e.g., Binmore 1997; Samuelson 1997; Camerer 1997). In the long history of game theory, much of the analysis was done in the manner of Instrumentalism since it was seen to be a concern for formal mathematical analysis. That is, many times, notions have been introduced to solve mathematical problems rather than worry about whether such notions can be presumed to apply or exist in the real world. Examples include such things as the 'Common Knowledge of Rationality' assumption and 'backward induction' (which I will examine later) that merely assume away some essential impossibilities. Professional mathematicians may think nothing of assuming whatever they want since very often their primary concern is with working out the logic of their analysis (sometimes their ultimate concern is limited to the esthetics of their analysis). But some theorists today are finding little that is useful in models built with assumptions that could never represent real-world behavior.

Game theory and rationality: 'Procedural', 'Substantive', 'Epistemic', 'Communicative' or 'Instrumental'?

Game theory literature is filled with references to rationality. Most of it uses Herbert Simon's distinction between what he called 'substantive' and 'procedural' rationality. These correspond to what I have called 'rationality as logic' and 'rationality as psychology'. Some game theorists, who may be more interested in pleasing philosophers, distinguish between 'practical' and 'epistemic' [e.g., Bicchieri 1993]. Practical rationality seems to be merely Simon's substantive rationality. Epistemic rationality is closely associated with procedural rationality by questioning how one knows what one needs to know in order to make a rational decision. In this sense, epistemic is just another way of looking at Simon's procedural rationality.

A distinction not common to game theory is between 'communicative' and 'instrumental'. This distinction is attributed to a German philosopher (Jürgen Habermas). Few neoclassical economists would go down this road. Communicative rationality does have some similarities with the psychological version, but only to the extent that it goes beyond what is possible with rationality of logic. So-called instrumental rationality seems to be like Simon's substantive rationality but also seems to presume that logic-based rationality is a version of Instrumentalism. Few economic model builders seem to find this distinction useful.

Game theory and the Common Knowledge of Rationality: The problem of (backward) induction

> The common knowledge assumption underlies all of game theory and much of economic theory. Whatever be the model under discussion, whether complete or incomplete information, consistent or inconsistent, repeated or one-shot, cooperative or non-cooperative, the model itself must be assumed common knowledge; otherwise the model is insufficiently specified, and the analysis incoherent.
>
> Robert Aumann [1987, p. 473]

> Without intending any disrespect to the authors, I believe that there is little of genuine significance to be learned from any of the literature that applies various formal methods to backward-induction problems – even when the authors find their way to conclusions that I believe to be correct. It seems to me that all the *analytical* issues relating to backward induction lie entirely on the surface. Inventing fancy formalisms serves only to confuse matters…
> Formalists will object, saying that an argument is open to serious evaluation only after it has been properly formalized.
>
> Ken Binmore [1997, pp. 23–4]

Before critically examining the notions of 'Common Knowledge' and so-called 'backward induction', we need to consider a game where these are commonly used. The game illustrated in Figure 4.4 considers the players to be making moves in turns as opposed to the simultaneous moves presumed in Figure 4.3. At each 'node' of this so-called centipede game in Figure 4.4 (the game's name comes from the appearance of the figure when there are very many nodes but for my purposes a tripede will do), the player chooses between two options, option *a* (across) which continues the game one more turn and option *d* (down) which promptly ends the game. At each J node, the player J considers what the other player, K, will do if J chooses 'across'. To consider this, J assumes both that K knows the game (namely, its sequence of options and corresponding payoffs) and that K is 'rational', that is, K will always choose the best option available.

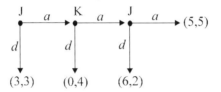

Figure 4.4. A centipede game

The common way to determine the equilibrium solution is to use 'backward induction' which has nothing to do with the induction discussed in Chapter 1. Instead, it is a variation on what mathematicians call induction. For example, in mathematics, we would assess a sequence of values determined by a given function for a series 1, 2, 3, 4 ... N, N+1. Mathematical induction assumes 'if the function gives a true value for 1 and gives a true value for N, then it must give a true value for N+1'. In this way, mathematicians simply assume induction works. It is not a proof, just an assumption. Backward induction works in a similar way by ignoring matters of realism – in other words, backward induction is just another Instrumentalist tool.

Parenthetically, game theorists sometimes invoke an assumption they call 'forward induction'. This, too, has nothing to do with the induction discussed in Chapter 1. How game theorists arrive at the names they give their tools is curious since it is often misleading. Backward induction is actually about possible future moves. Forward induction is about the past moves made by the other player when analyzing games in the extensive form. The question addressed by forward induction is when looking back at the moves made by the other player, what should be concluded from an observed deviation from 'rationality'? Forward induction says that you should not consider the deviation to be a mistake but instead some sort of rational signal. As such, forward induction is just a straightforward application of neoclassical economics.

In the centipede game backward induction begins by considering what K would do at the next-to-last node. Given the pervasive assumption of Common Knowledge of Rationality, game theorists can simply ignore the Problem of Induction and say that K knows that J will choose the best available option at the last J node (which here is down since 6 is better than 5). When J does choose down, K would get only 2 but at this node if K instead plays down, K gets 4. Being 'rational', as game theorists assume, K will choose down at the K node. With this in mind, J at the first node considers what K would do at the second node – and we just saw that K would choose down. If K chooses down then J would get 0 but if J at the first node chooses down, J gets 3. So, by this backward method of analysis, it follows that J would end the game at the first opportunity.

Until recently, game theorists have openly accepted this way of solving for the equilibrium of this game situation. But, as Ken Binmore [1997] argues, if players are 'rational' as the assumption of Common Knowledge of Rationality claims, the second and third nodes in the centipede game would never be reached and thus the technique of backward induction does not make sense or is at least inapplicable since the condition presumed for application (reaching the second node) is false.

In 1985 Robert Aumann, a major leader in developing the mathematics of game theory and its primary defender, published his musings about game theory and its methodology. Recall from the quotation near the end of Chapter 1, his expressed view was that

> scientific theories are not to be considered 'true' or 'false.' In constructing such a theory, we are not trying to get at the truth, or even to approximate to it: rather, we are trying to organize our thoughts and observations in a useful manner.
>   One rough analogy is to a filing system in an office operation, or to some kind of complex computer program. We do not refer to such a system as being 'true' or 'untrue'; rather, we talk about whether it 'works' or not, or, better yet, how well it works. [1985, pp. 31–2]

While Aumann's view is a somewhat confused combination of Instrumentalism and Conventionalism, it does make it clear that an assumption being false would not be considered an important obstacle. Binmore and others are now openly challenging the usefulness of Aumann's version of Instrumentalism.

Aumann [1995; 1996] argues that common knowledge of rationality is consistent with backward induction and thus sees no need to abandon the assumption of common knowledge. But, there seems to be little, if any, discussion of how the players know what they need to know – let alone how it becomes so common. Sometimes, particularly with extensive form games (i.e., games where moves can be seen to be alternating in sequence), players are allowed to remember the other player's past moves and thereby engage in 'forward induction'. Presumably, they inductively learn that the other player is 'rational'. Even if we were to ignore the Problem of Induction (which here would challenge how the player knows that the other player's moves will be consistent with past moves), few formalist game theorists seem to be concerned with how the players know the rules of the game before it is played or know the other player's payoffs. At best the assumption of common knowledge simply assumes away the Problem of Induction. And the game theorist more interested in the formalism of mathematical model building simply follows Aumann by invoking some version of Instrumentalism or Conventionalism to deflect any criticism of the realism of their assumptions.

Game theory and methodological individualism

> The attempt to view social life as strategic interaction is proving immensely fertile yet disturbingly prone to paradox. Game theory provides an elegant, universal logic of practical reason, offering much to anyone whose notion of rationality is instrumental and whose view of the social world is individualist. Yet paradoxes beset its account even of coordination, trust and the keeping of promises.
>
> Martin Hollis and Robert Sugden [1993, p. 32]

At a basic level, game theory separates games into two groups determined by whether prior commitments (including agreements, promises, threats) are enforceable. In a non-cooperative game each player has to make his or her decision based solely on the knowledge of the game. There is either no communication with the other player or no way to enforce any prior agreements. Non-cooperative games are fully compatible with methodological individualism but not necessarily with the more narrow psychologistic individualism.

Cooperative games present an interesting dilemma for game theorists. If the commitments are enforceable, then the commitments should be treated as a fixed part of the game and its rules. Alternatively, since commitments involve conscious involvement of the players, should the commitments be explained as something chosen by the players, that is, something for which each player is maximizing in an individualist manner? This latter alternative is nothing more than the one that haunts the psychologistic-individualist version of neoclassical economics, itself. Neither socially created commitments and enforcement rules nor rules of the game itself are nature given – hence, all of game theory violates psychologistic individualism. Yet, there does not seem to be any effort on the part of the formalist game theorists to explain where the rules and commitments come from. If we were to be able and willing to purge psychological views of rationality from the view of 'rational' decision-making in games, then the way is open to adopt the Popper-Agassi approach to methodological individualism – discussed in Chapter 2. The only obstacle to going this way is that many formalist game theorists who wish to recognize the knowledge of the maximizing decision-maker too often opt for what they call 'Bayesian rationality'. Bayesian rationality is the basis of maximizing 'expected utility' based on a subjective probability assessment. But, for the purposes here, it is enough to recognize that Bayesian rationality is just the sophisticated, modern form of Hume's psychology-based rationality. As such, the individual is supposed to mysteriously make a probability assessment of the truth status of his or her knowledge of the game and the other players.

Game theory, uncertainty and rationality as psychology

> [I am] reluctant to believe that our decisions are made at random. [I] prefer to be able to point to a reason for each action we take. Outside of Las Vegas we do not spin roulettes.
>
> Ariel Rubinstein [1991, p. 913]

The notion that one should be able to place a probability assessment on the truth of a statement or theory is characteristic of 1930s attempts to operationalize

Conventionalism. Again, according to this sophisticated version of Conventionalism, theories are not to be considered true or false, but only better or worse. Moreover, the theory that is considered better is one with the highest probability assessment.

As noted in Chapter 1, Conventionalism is one way of dealing with the Problem of Induction. Unmodified Conventionalism appeals to objective criteria to determine which theory is best (significance test, measures of simplicity or generality, etc.). Sophisticated Conventionalism allows a subjective assessment that can be measured, usually, as a probability. Where did economists get such an idea that probabilities could be substituted for 'true' or 'false' truth status? It was apparently due to the clever move made by a young philosopher in the late 1920s, namely, Frank Ramsey. In a 1926 paper (published in 1931) titled 'Truth and probability', Ramsey showed that choices expressed as being between gambles can be made to yield measures of one's preferences (subjective utilities) and one's 'beliefs' (subjective probabilities). While some Cambridge economists were aware of Ramsey's demonstration, not much was done with it. Using gambles to measure subjective assessments of probabilities was resurrected in the 1940s [see von Neumann and Morgenstern 1944] and is the major source for arguments of this type among game theorists. Statisticians credit Leonard Savage [1954] for resurrecting Ramsey's demonstration to make it part of decision-making under uncertainty. What is methodologically interesting here is that Ramsey's and Savage's objective seems to be to purge psychology from decision-making under uncertainty.

Purging psychology from decision-making in general was one of the first problems that Paul Samuelson [1938] addressed in his long career. Today, we know his solution as 'revealed preference' analysis. The basic idea is that we can infer from choices made by consumers what their preferences are – at least to the point that we can derive any consumer's demand function. Samuelson's methodological objective was to avoid assuming we know the consumers' preferences (i.e., their utility functions) in order to derive demand curves from an assumption of utility maximization. The previous analysis of John Hicks and Roy Allen [1934] identified a set of conditions on preferences and utility functions that would allow the logical derivation of demand curves (later this led to much mathematical analysis involving assumptions about the necessary shape of the preference map – indifference curves are convex, preferences are transitive, satiation is impossible, etc. – as displayed in Figure 3.2 above). Samuelson's solution was to posit a different set of necessary conditions to derive the demand curve, conditions that did not involve reading consumers' minds. Utility for Samuelson was a complicated psychological attribute that could not be observed let alone measured. His alternative conditions were very simple. The consumer need only be able to make a unique choice and to be consistent this must be the same unique choice whenever facing the same situation. Specifically, consistency was assured in a simple way: whenever a person could afford two bundles of goods, A and B, and the consumer chooses A, then to be consistent the consumer will be observed to choose B only when he or she faces constraints where A was unaffordable. Implicit is the view that whenever considering the choice between two bundles, the preferred bundle is chosen. Unfortunately, Samuelson's solution was an illusion since being consistent presumed preferences never change which implied that Samuelson was still smuggling utility in through the back door and this was revealed and accepted by Samuelson in 1950 (for a detailed explanation of Samuelson's failure, see Wong, [1978]).

Interestingly, Savage also wished to avoid making assumptions about desires and beliefs (both deemed to be psychological attributes) and instead, like Samuelson, posited a set of conditions which if met allows the utility-maximization basis for the explanation of a decision-maker's choices to be 'bleached of all psychological content' [Hollis and Sugden 1993, p. 7]. Savage only requires that the choices made be consistent with his posited conditions. One of his conditions is that whenever the decision-maker considers one event subjectively more probable than a second event, the decision-maker prefers to bet on it rather than the second. Making such a bet would thereby reveal the preference.

The result of all of this type of analysis (both Samuelson's and Savage's) is that, by seeing choice as a matter of ranking options and then choosing the best, knowing the decision-maker's preferences would not tell us anything we *need* to know. Clearly, with this approach to explaining 'rational' choices in mind, there is no role for any notion of rationality as a psychological process. To users of Savage's approach to dealing with decisions made facing uncertainty, rationality *appears* to be only a matter of logical consistency. But like Samuelson's revealed failure, there is a lot of mysterious psychology lurking behind the scenes, in this case, it is in the essential notion of *subjective* probability assessments.

The notion that begs to be critically examined is why – with few exceptions [see Davidson 1991 and Lawson 1988] – economic theorists in general, and game theorists in particular, see no reason to question the presumption that, when facing uncertainty, every decision-maker will treat a decision as a gamble and thereby presume uncertainty always requires the assessment of probabilities. Given the pervasive absence of critical examination, one smells a whiff of the emperor's new clothes in the closet. In Chapter 8, I will return to the methodology of probability assessment and of using randomization to address strategic problems of making decision when facing so-called 'incomplete knowledge'.

The boundedness of 'bounded rationality'

Those theorists who continue to presume that rationality must be considered a psychological process were challenged by Herbert Simon, the 1978 Nobel prize-winner, to recognize that maximization as a process of applied calculus might require the maximizer to go beyond what is psychologically possible for any human being. Simon suggested that, rather than maximize, decision-makers actually just try to 'satisfice'. To illustrate this notion, consider Figure 4.5 which represents the choice among the available options by a profit maximizing firm.

If we were to take the profit-maximization explanation that is typical for neoclassical economics, then we would say that the firm has chosen option E because, at that option, profit is maximized at 30 (and thus marginal profit – the slope of the curve – is zero). But how does the firm know its profit is maximum or that its marginal profit is zero? More specifically, how does the firm know what its level of profit is for each of the possibly infinite number of options which the theorist represents with the curve profile? Satisficing would instead say that the firm would be satisfied by being close to the maximum of 30 – that is, the level of at least S (for now, about 28) would be satisfactory.

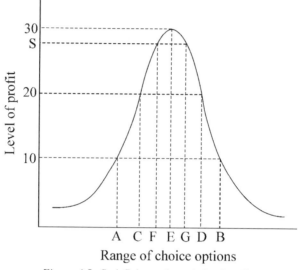

Range of choice options

Figure 4.5. Satisficing as bounded rationality

As I have been stressing, maximization is just the modern version of the eighteenth-century rationality. Satisficing would obviously challenge that notion of rationality, too. If we were to follow Simon's suggestion and assume the firm is a 'satisficer' rather than a maximizer, the corresponding view of rationality would be what Simon originally called 'approximate' rationality [1955, p. 114] and what everyone now calls 'bounded rationality'. Specifically, rather than say the firm chooses the 'rational' option E, in the process of satisficing, instead, the firm is assumed to narrow the rational options to any point between F and G – since for any of the points between F and G the minimum satisfactory level of profit will be obtained or exceeded. So, by assuming that the decision-maker is only boundedly rational, we could not conclude that the firm will choose option E (except by accident).

By assuming satisficing behavior and thereby bounded rationality, the theorist gives up uniqueness and limits the usefulness of universality in the process of explaining the behavior of the decision-makers that populate neoclassical theory. While bounded rationality might be a satisfactory alternative for those theorists who think rationality must represent a realistic psychological process, it is not clear what such an explanation accomplishes. Moreover, how would we know that such an explanation is false? While, in the case of Figure 4.5 (where it is reasonable to presume that the level of profit is observable in some way), we would be able to say that if the firm chose an option to the left of point F or to the right of point G, then we would be able to conclude that the explanation is false. But, what part of the explanation is false? Does the firm do something other than satisfice? Perhaps the firm has a lower standard of a satisfactory level of profits. While the choice of option C might refute an explanation that presumes that S is the minimum acceptable level of profit, it would not refute an explanation that allows 20 to be the minimum acceptable. Thus the choice of option C does not refute the assumption of bounded rationality. Unless the explanation is explicit in what is assumed to be the minimum level of satisfactory profit, it is not clear what bounded rationality is presuming. Simon [1955] goes so far as to suggest that one obstacle to maximization is that it is costly to collect all of the information necessary to be able to be sure profit is maximized. But justifying less than exact maximization on the grounds of cost minimization seems to be inconsistent. How does the firm know its costs of information have been minimized? Of course, the firm could be satisficing when accepting a cost that does not exceed a maximum acceptable level of costs. Again, how do we know when this explanation of cost minimization is false? How does the firm decide what is a maximum level of information costs? Remember, all of this mess is the result of trying to maintain the assumption that rationality must be a psychological process. If we drop that assumption, perhaps we can drop the messy bounded rationality, too.

Game theory as Instrumentalist mathematics

> The ambitious claim that game theory will provide a unified foundation for all social science seems misplaced to us. There is a variety of problems with such a claim... Some are associated with the assumptions of the theory..., some come from the inferences which are often drawn from these assumptions ... and yet others come from the failure ... to generate determinate predictions of what 'rational' agents would, or should, do in important social interactions.
>
> At root we suspect that the major problem is ... that people appear to be more complexly motivated than game theory's instrumental model allows and that a part of that greater complexity comes from their social location.
>
> Shaun Hargreaves Heap and Yanis Varoufakis [1995, p. 260]

Game theorists are unlikely to follow my advice to give up psychologism or bounded rationality since few would find any need to consider questions of methodology. The primary reason for this is that game theory is nothing more than a mathematical tool of analysis and thus firmly planted in the domain of Instrumentalism. With the possible exceptions of Robert Aumann's [1985] musings and Cristina Bicchieri's [1993] struggles with what she calls the 'paradoxes of rationality', no serious attempts have been made by game theorists to address the methodological problems of explanation. While some game theorists recognize that historically game theory has been directed at prescriptions and thus offer what might be useful considerations (particularly during war time situations), when game theory is put to test as a mode of either explanation or description of observed behavior, few game theorists have been satisfied with the results. In Chapter 9, I will return to consider a new use for game theory, one where the consideration of only singular individuals each in partial equilibrium seems inappropriate, namely, game theory will be viewed as an alternative to the perspective of macroeconomics. For now, I will close this chapter with some relevant critical observations and suggestions for game theory by a leading game theorist that point to many of the issues to be discussed in the next four chapters as well as the central topic that I will take up in Part VI:

> Overall, game theory accomplishes only two tasks: It builds models based on intuition and uses deductive arguments based on mathematical knowledge. Deductive arguments cannot by themselves be used to discover truths about the world. Missing are data describing the processes of reasoning adopted by the players when they analyze a game. Thus, if a game in the formal sense has any coherent interpretation, it has to be understood to include explicit data on the player's reasoning processes. Alternatively, we should add more detail to the description of these reasoning procedures.
>
> Ariel Rubinstein [1991, p. 923]

Part III
CRITICAL APPLIED METHODOLOGY

5 Ideal-type Methodology and Instrumentalism

there are quite defensible reasons for a reluctance to abandon theories of rationality in favor of psychological theories. In particular, I think most economists view the rational model as a useful approximation, rather than as a precise description of human behavior. Experimental demonstrations that people deviate from the model do not strike at the heart of the belief that the approximation is a useful one, since all approximations are false at some level of detail. In view of this, some kinds of evidence, and alternative models, are likely to be more successful than others in attacking the central role of rationality assumptions in the economic literature.

Alvin Roth [1996, p. 198]

It must be admitted that in many areas of mathematical economics very substantial abstractions are being used, so that one can hardly speak of a good approximation to reality. But it should be remembered that, on the one hand, mathematical economics is a very young science and, on the other, that economic phenomena are of such a complicated, involved nature that far-reaching abstractions must be used at the start merely to be able to survey the problem, and that the transition to more realistic assumptions must be carried out step by step.

Abraham Wald [1936/51, p. 369]

So, this is where we stand. In addition to the visible agenda that is based on a presumption that every decision involves maximization, I have been arguing that all neoclassical research programs are also based on a hidden agenda consisting of two main items. One is the acceptance of the need to deal with the so-called Problem of Induction either directly or, what is more common, indirectly by dealing with its variant, the Problem of Conventions. The other item is the requirement of methodological individualism – that every explanation must assume that only individuals make decisions. However, it was pointed out that, at present, neoclassical theory is based on a narrow version of methodological individualism – specifically, one which identifies the individuals with their exogenous psychological states (such as their given utility functions). The strict reliance on the reductive narrow version – that is, on psychologistic individualism – always presents a general problem of explanation which I have called the problem of simple psychologism: if everyone is governed by the same laws of psychology, then there is no psychological basis for individuality. It was noted that neoclassical theory provides a solution to this problem by restricting the laws of psychology to only that which specifies that everyone faces diminishing marginal utility (or its equivalent). This solution allows people to have different utility functions; hence it provides a means of allowing for individualism as well as solving the Problem of Conventions. The latter problem is solved in current neoclassical economics by relying on the narrow psychologistic version of methodological individualism which accepts only models which exclude all exogenous variables except psychological states and natural givens. But, relying on psychologistic individualism is problematic since, in solving the Problem of Conventions, it can easily lead to an infinite regress.

Note well, then, that the two hidden agenda items are not completely independent, as the latter one is sustained partly because it supports the former. That is, it would be difficult for most neoclassical economists to give up their reliance on psychologistic individualism and their solution to the problem of simple psychologism because that would entail the lack of a means of dealing with the Problem of Conventions. Furthermore, this difficulty is compounded by the fact that most neoclassical economists take the Problem of Conventions for granted; hence it is difficult for most to see that there may not be a need to deal with any of these problems.

The visible research program of neoclassical economics is rather straightforward. It is to explain observable socio-economic events as the consequences of maximizing decisions made by individuals. So stated, the program is easily compatible with methodological individualism. The question that will be considered is whether the psychologistic version of individualism is still considered essential by practicing neoclassical theorists and model builders in a consistent manner.

It is not the methodologist's job to form a final judgment or methodological 'appraisal' of the existing neoclassical research program, as some might wish [e.g., Blaug, 1980/92, p. 137]. Instead, I think we should try to establish a clear understanding of what neoclassical economics is rather than to determine what some philosophers think it should be. We also need to examine what practicing economists think economics should be while recognizing that they may not all share the same view. Although some of what I shall argue is critical of certain aspects of some neoclassical models, I do not intend to present a destructive criticism of neoclassical economics. If one did intend a destructive criticism at this stage, one would immediately set about eliminating the current items on the hidden agenda – either the Problem of Induction or the Problem of Conventions and its reliance on the narrow psychologistic individualism – which would appear to eliminate the more impressive aspects of neoclassical theory. But my purpose is quite different. In particular I wish to understand the methodological nature and purpose of existing neoclassical research programs which accept the items on the current hidden agenda as well as the visible agenda, and thus for my purposes I shall take the two hidden items as givens. Besides, as I shall argue, *although the current hidden agenda is necessary for the explanation of neoclassical methodology, it is not necessary for neoclassical economic theories.*

In this and the next five chapters, I will critically examine how the current hidden agenda is manifested in the methodology of current research programs of neoclassical economics. I begin with the pervasive ideal-type methodology.

The dominance of ideal-type methodology: Is it Conventionalist or Instrumentalist?

> Knowledge is useful if it helps to make the best decisions.
> To illustrate useful knowledge we shall take ... examples [that] are admittedly crude ... compared with the complex actual world since their very purpose is to isolate the essentials of a problem by 'idealizing reality'...
>
> Jacob Marschak [1953, p. 1]

The notion of 'idealized reality' and the associated ideal-type methodology have been around for a century or more. The basic idea concerns a specific strategy for explaining what we see out our windows, namely, the real world. As noted in Chapter 3, the strategy is adopted from the physics textbook's explanation of a block sliding down an inclined plane which ideally in the absence of friction says that the block would slide to the bottom instantly (or at least the maximum speed as dictated by the force of gravity and the angular slope of the plane). The same strategy is involved when physicists assuming an ideal vacuum say that if two different objects such as a feather and a cannon ball were dropped simultaneously from the Tower of Pisa they would (in the vacuum) reach the ground at the same instant. But when we try to observe these ideals in the real world, the block does not slide or does so slowly and the feather lands much later than the cannon ball. The second step in this explanatory strategy is to invoke the existence of friction or air pressure to explain why we do not observe the ideal results. Friction is used to explain why the block slides at the particular speed that it does and air pressure explains the discrepancy between the times of landing. One might wonder which came first, friction or the ideal frictionless world, air pressure or the ideal vacuum? Stated another way, why do physicists not simply declare that their ideal models are false as Bishop Berkeley argued they should? The reason is that by using this two-step manner they wish to use their ideal models as instruments to explain away what we see and thereby be able to maintain their unobservable laws of physics. Nevertheless, we all feel that we understand what we see by using this two-step method of explanation.

Ideal-type methodology in economics

> Transaction costs are the economic equivalent of friction in physical systems. The manifold successes of physics in ascertaining the attributes of complex systems by assuming the absence of friction scarcely require recounting here. Such a strategy has had obvious appeal to the social sciences.
>
> Oliver Williamson [1985, p. 19]

> we look upon economic theory as a sequence of conceptual models that seek to express in simplified form different aspects of an always more complicated reality. At first these aspects are formalized as much as feasible in isolation, then in combinations of increasing realism. ... The study of the simpler models is protected from the reproach of unreality by the consideration that these models may be prototypes of more realistic, but also more complicated, subsequent models.
>
> Tjalling Koopmans [1957, p. 142]

Ideal-type methodology was not openly and enthusiastically promoted in economics until the 1950s after a major promotion of formal mathematical model building was commenced. Those economists who are only interested in developing theoretical models without regard to policy applications will not be seen to be promoting ideal-type-methodology. If they openly promote any methodology it will be some form of Conventionalism. However, they commonly invoke ideal-type-methodology when defending their preoccupation with mathematics and formalism.

The 'sequence of models' approach promoted by the 1975 Nobel prize-winner, Tjalling Koopmans, has been the standard methodology since mathematical model building became such a conscious process in the early 1950s. The basic strategy is to begin the sequence with a simple model, one made simple by overly strong assumptions that rule out almost all complexities. Examples of such strong assumptions might include assuming all consumers are alike, assuming all firms in any industry are identical, assuming all decision-makers possess complete and perfect knowledge, assuming all decision-makers are successful maximizers, assuming that there is a market for every conceivable good, assuming 'perfect competition' (i.e., every decision-maker is a 'price-taker'), assuming all transactions are costless, assuming that there are only two goods produced, two consumers and two factors used in the production process, etc. There are many more detailed assumptions such as assuming all production functions exhibit constant returns to scale (doubling inputs always doubles output), all consumer goods are 'normal' goods (increased income always leads to increasing demand for *all* goods), assuming there is 'free enterprise' (i.e., there are no barriers to trade or to entry into any industry), assuming there is no government and hence no unexplained institutions, and so on.

Each of the 'simplifying' assumptions excludes some sort of conceivable phenomena. Obviously, not all people are alike. Surely, it will be said, no one individual can know everything (that is, can have an *a priori* true theory of the economy – both today's and the future's). If everyone knew everything, there would be no need for markets or the study of economics. Obviously then, these assumptions are all like the physicist's initial assumptions of the existence of a perfect vacuum and a frictionless inclined plane. To continue with the analogy, which of these assumptions allows for some measurable distance from the real world in the manner of measurements of friction?

The most common assumptions to be subjected to friction-type measurements are the assumptions of perfect competition, perfect knowledge and costless transactions. Since perfect competition among producers is usually represented by their facing perfectly elastic demand curves (or equivalently, that they are price takers who are unable to affect their price by producing more or less), the extent to which the actual elasticity of demand differs from this is a measure of how far the idealized perfectly competitive model differs from the real world [see Boland 1992a, chap. 5]. The idea of imperfect knowledge has been dealt with in many ways but usually by expressing the imperfection as a probability less than one (see Chapter 4). Recognizing that assuming costless transactions is a significant simplification has led to 'transaction cost analysis' and the development of 'New Institutional Economics' [e.g., Williamson 1985, chap. 1]. I will return to each of these in the following chapters.

Ideal-type methodology vs. Conventionalism

All sciences have the common task of describing and summarizing empirical reality. Economics is no exception.

Paul Samuelson [1952, p. 61]

The theory of value is treated here with the standards of rigor of the contemporary formalist school of mathematics. The effort toward rigor substitutes correct reasonings and results for incorrect ones, but it offers other rewards too. It usually leads to a deeper understanding of the problems to which it is applied... It may also lead to a radical change of mathematical tools. In the area under discussion it has been essentially a change from the calculus to convexity and topological properties, a transformation which has resulted in notable gains in the generality and in the simplicity of the theory.

Allegiance to rigor dictates the axiomatic form of the analysis where the theory, in the strict sense, is logically entirely disconnected from its interpretations.

Gerard Debreu [1959, p. viii]

Many of the obviously simplifying assumptions are usually considered to be just the first step in the sequence of models that Koopmans advocated. One might start with a theory or model of the consumer's choice of a combination of quantities of two goods (e.g., Figure 3.2) and proceed to 'generalize' the theory or model so as to explain a choice involving many goods simultaneously. The implicit methodological choice criterion of generality is evident in the early development of mathematical model building. The 1983 Nobel prize-winner Gerard Debreu's famous but thin 1959 monograph, *Theory of Value*, has always been the paradigm of generality. He claims mathematical formalism also yields elegant simplicity but the simplicity of such a formal model is due solely to its being 'disconnected from its interpretations'. Mathematical formalists typically stress the elegance achieved by developing formal, axiomatized mathematical models of economic theories, but I think the elegance achieved may only be in the eyes of the beholder. (Note that Debreu uses the term 'theory' in a way that differs from ordinary use – I will discuss his type of 'theory' in Chapter 12.)

Ideal-type methodology as an exercise in Instrumentalism

Marshall took the world as it is; he sought to construct an 'engine' to analyze it, not a photographic reproduction of it.

In analyzing the world as it is, Marshall constructed the hypothesis that, for many problems, firms could be grouped into 'industries'...

The abstract model corresponding to this hypothesis contains two 'ideal' types of firms: atomistically competitive firms, grouped into industries, and monopolistic firms... The ideal types are not intended to be descriptive; they are designed to isolate the features that are crucial for a particular problem ... Marshall's apparatus turned out to be most useful for problems in which a group of firms is affected by common stimuli, and in which the firms can be treated *as if* they were perfect competitors.

Milton Friedman [1953, pp. 35–8]

Milton Friedman is the 1976 Nobel prize-winner. As noted in Chapter 1, his [1953] self-conscious methodology is now famous for being an explicit form of Instrumentalism. Economists usually characterize Instrumentalism as the 'as-if methodology' but too often confuse Instrumentalism with the sequence-of-models version of Conventionalism. Both do begin with simplifying assumptions. In the sequence-of-models version of Conventionalism, there are many steps to follow whereby the simplifying assumptions are replaced with more complex ones that are hoped to make the models 'more realistic'. Instrumentalism, instead, would see no need to replace them although sometimes there are two or more simple assumptions to choose from. For example, Friedman advocates explaining imperfect competition by mixing or choosing between an ideal perfect competitor (i.e., a firm too small to affect its market-given price) and a perfect monopolist (i.e., a firm that is the only producer in the 'industry'). Alfred Marshall, approvingly quoted by Friedman [pp. 34–5], said that:

> At one extreme are world markets in which competition acts directly from all parts of the globe; and at the other those secluded markets in which all direct competition from afar is shut out, though indirect and transmitted competition may make itself felt even in these; and about midway between these extremes lie the great majority of the markets which the economist and the business man have to study.

But for Friedman, that these ideal types were descriptively false is of no concern and we are encouraged to consider them to be the first and last tools needed to explain the real world. No sequence of models is necessary. Elsewhere in his methodology essay Friedman [p. 18] explicitly invokes one of the physicist's ideal types, the assumption of a vacuum, to demonstrate that its lack of realism does not matter:

> The formula $s = \frac{1}{2}gt^2$ is valid for bodies falling in a vacuum and can be derived by analyzing the behavior of such bodies. It can therefore be stated: under a wide range of circumstances, bodies that fall in the actual atmosphere behave *as if* they were falling in a vacuum... Yet ... [the] hypothesis can readily be rephrased to omit all mention of a vacuum... The formula is accepted because it works, not because we live in an approximate vacuum – whatever that means.

Friedman appears here to be trying to avoid admitting that the first step of an explanation might be based on a false assumption by simply declaring that the assumption of a vacuum made solely to justify using the formula is an unnecessary assumption. Just assume the formula works since that is all that will be needed to calculate the speed of a falling object.

One could adopt the same strategy by just assuming decision-makers in economic models are price takers and make no mention of possibly false assumptions that one might use to justify this assumption. To invoke the price-taker assumption would normally require the assumption of perfect competition or of the existence of a long-run equilibrium (where every producer is just covering costs with its price and would thus lose money by lowering its price or go out of business by charging a higher price). This hiding of a needed assumption is a strategic trick and is the same trick used by Alchian [1950] to avoid requiring the possibly false assumption of conscious profit maximizing (see Chapter 3). Again, any strategy such as this is thought to be justified solely because it is claimed that 'it works'.

Ideal-types vs. impossible types

It is all too easy for critics of Friedman's Instrumentalism to question who gets to decide whether someone's model or prediction 'works'. But, I think that his methodology is criticized mostly for ideological reasons. As I have discussed elsewhere [Boland 1997, pp. 283–4], some criticisms of his methodology *per se* are hypocritical. In particular, there are econometricians and mathematical model builders who claim to disagree with Friedman's economics but nevertheless commonly (but tacitly) invoke the key elements of Friedman's Instrumentalism.

What Friedman means by 'works' or 'useful' contrasts with what the mathematical model builders such as Aumann mean by these terms. When Friedman talks about whether a formula or hypothesis works, he is talking about whether it is useful in the process of forming economic policy or predictions. As I noted in my 1980 reply to one of the critics of my 1979 article which criticized the standard critiques of Friedman's 1953 methodology essay:

> In the short run or for most practical problems, one's theories do not have to be true to be successful... When we take our television to a repairman, we do not usually think it necessary to quiz the repairman about his understanding of electromagnetics or quantum physics. For our purposes, it is usually quite adequate for him to believe there are little green men in those tubes or transistors and that the only problem was that one of the little green men died. So long as the tube or transistor with the little green dead man is replaced *and* our television subsequently works, all is well. [1980, p. 1556]

This is the essence of Friedman's Instrumentalism. Presuming the existence of 'little green men' is logically no different from assuming the formula '$s = \frac{1}{2}gt^2$' alone is useful.

A question seldom asked by proponents of ideal-type-methodology is whether there are sensible limits on assumptions. Is it sensible to assume the existence of ideal 'little green men'? Probably not. Those who advocate the sequence-of-models version of Conventionalism might allow such implausible ideal types but only if in the sequence they soon lead to models that no longer require such assumptions. The problem with Friedman's Instrumentalism is, as noted above, that its proponents willingly stop with the initial ideal-type assumption. But in either case, is it sensible to assume the possibility of some event or process that is in fact an impossible event or process?

The problem I have in mind here is whether it is sensible to assume the possibility of induction when modeling the knowledge and learning needed by a decision-maker. While Friedman did not bother with explaining the knowledge that a successful decision-maker would have to have to guarantee success, many theorists and model builders today are seeing that something must be assumed. We saw in Chapter 4 that game theorists readily assume common knowledge of rationality. What is rarely explained is how this knowledge is acquired or arrived at. That is, how do the players in a game learn what they need to know to play the game as the theorists prescribe? Too often, it is just presumed that such knowledge is acquired by means of induction – that is, simply by making observations.

While a frictionless world or a perfect vacuum might be conceivable, induction as a process of learning requires an inductive logic to demonstrate that the process is conceivable. As noted in Chapter 1, there is no such logic. But there the discussion was about whether scientific knowledge was acquired through induction. The issue at hand here is about what we assume about the humble decision-maker whose behavior we are trying to explain. This issue, however, is not much different since anyone's knowledge is also open to question. That is, we can always ask how the decision-maker came to know what he or she thinks needs to be known in order to make a decision. In other words, what is the decision-maker's theory of the situation he or she faces? Or, how would he or she explain their decision? At root, all knowledge (of the individual or the scientific community) consists of explanations – thus, if one takes Justificationism for granted, the Problem of Induction must always be faced.

Every explanation to be a sufficient argument must include at least one assumption in the logical form of a strictly universal statement and at least one in the logical form of a singular statement that is usually seen to be the assertion of an 'initial condition' [Popper 1934/59]. For a classic example, when we ask 'why did Socrates die?', the logically simple explanation involves two statements: (1) 'all men are mortal' and (2) 'Socrates was a man'. The first statement is a strictly universal statement since it refers to all men and is unlimited in both time and space. It does not say 'some men' (which would beg the question why Socrates was included in that group) nor does it say 'all men in the fifth century BC' (which would beg the question of whether this would be true today). The second statement is not controversial so long as it has a meaning that is independent from the fact that Socrates died.

If one thinks that the strictly universal statement is true because it was successfully 'induced' with repeated observations (e.g., noting all the men that have died so far), then such knowledge would be open to question. Namely, how does one know that there does not (or will not) exist a counter-example? Of course, one can claim to know this by positing another theory. For example, a biological theory that explains why biological entities must eventually die or in the case of why the sun will rise tomorrow, a theory of celestial mechanics. But doing so only requires yet more strictly universal statements that in turn would have to be inductively proven.

Specifically, there is no way to prove the non-existence of a counter-example of the 'induced' knowledge and thereby avoid an infinite regress. Thus, for knowledge to be the basis for explaining phenomena of any type, that knowledge must be based on the *presumption* of at least one true 'strictly universal' statement (e.g., '*all* decision-makers *are* maximizers', '*all* men *are* mortal').

Now, by definition, an inductive proof would involve only singular, particular observation statements – that is, without any strictly universal statements – hence it is always conceivable and possible that a refuting observation might be subsequently observed. Of course, every explanation (induction-based or otherwise) is open to question. As noted in Chapter 1, asking for explanations that are beyond question is the demand of Justificationism which itself would beg for justification [see also, Popper 1934/59, chap. 3; 1972, chap. 5]. Instead, one's claim of knowledge requires only that one's knowledge, as an argument in favor of the phenomena being explained, must be without contradictions, must not include any empirically false statement and must be logically sufficient in the sense of *modus ponens*. That is, *if* all of the assumptions of one's explanation are true, *then* the statement of the phenomena in question which is being explained *must* be true. But, in the case of induction, *even if* all of the observations are true, one still may not claim that the strictly universal statement, that is supposed to inductively follow from them, must be true.

While it is easy, of course, to assume that the decision-maker acquires true knowledge by simply making sufficient observations, doing so would merely assume an impossibility. And this is the crux of the problem I am raising here. While a perfect vacuum is not inconceivable, as it may be possible with the right technology, no technology can ever overcome the Problem of Induction. So, when a model builder explicitly or implicitly presumes that a decision-maker's knowledge is true because there were sufficient opportunities to make the necessary observations and does so to move on with some Instrumentalist research program, questions need to be raised. The main question is why would anyone accept any presumption involving an impossibility? I think that not only are contradictions not acceptable in logical arguments, impossibly true statements are equally unacceptable.

As we saw in Chapter 4, Binmore explicitly showed how any application of backward induction in the centipede game contradicts the assumption of common knowledge of rationality. Forward induction, if it is supposed to be the basis for true common knowledge (no game theorist would assume that the common knowledge is false), is an impossibility. This is at the heart of the methodological problem with mathematical formalists who think they have no limits on what they can assume to build their models. For mathematicians, anything goes (other than contradictions). Mathematicians will assume a variable can achieve an infinite or infinitesimal value in order to provide some logically necessary conclusion. But infinities and infinitesimals in the real world are impossible *by definition*. But if mathematical formalists such as Aumann cheerfully accept that their ideal models are necessarily false, impossibilities will not seem to matter.

Ideal-type methodology and calibration

> One of the functions of theoretical economics is to provide fully articulated, artificial economic systems that can serve as laboratories in which policies that would be prohibitively expensive to experiment with in actual economies can be tested out at much lower cost. To serve this function well, it is essential that the artificial 'model' economy be distinguished as sharply as possible in discussion from actual economies... Any model that is well enough articulated to give clear answers to the questions we put to it will necessarily be artificial, abstract, patently 'unreal'...
>
> On this general view of the nature of economic theory then, a 'theory' is not

a collection of assertions about the behavior of the actual economy but rather an explicit set of instructions for building a parallel or analogue system – a mechanical, imitation economy.

Robert Lucas [1980, pp. 696–7]

General equilibrium models have people or agents who have preferences and technologies, and who use some allocation mechanism. The crucial difference between the general equilibrium and the system-of-equations approaches [viz., traditional econometrics] is that which is assumed invariant and about which we organize our empirical knowledge. With the system-of-equations approach, it is behavioral equations which are invariant and are measured. With the general equilibrium approach, on the other hand, it is the willingness and ability of people to substitute that is measured...

To address a specific question one typically needs a suitable model economy for addressing the specified question... Model-economy selection depends on the question being asked... Unlike the system-of-equations approach, no attempt is made to determine the true model. All model economies are abstractions and are by definition false.

The model has to be calibrated. The necessary information can sometimes be obtained from data on individuals or households. An example of such information is the average fraction of discretionary time household members who are, or who potentially are, labor market participants actually spent in market activity. In many other cases, the required information easily can be obtained from aggregate nonbusiness-cycle information. The task often involves merely computing some simple averages, such as growth relations between aggregates. This is the case for inventory-output and capital-output ratios, and long-run fractions of the various GNP components to total output, among others...

Once the model is calibrated, the next step is to carry out a set of computational experiments. If all the parameters can be calibrated with a great deal of accuracy, then only a few experiments are needed... The final step is to report the findings.

Finn Kydland and Edward Prescott [1991, pp. 163, 170–1]

The notion of calibration is an artifact of engineering physics methodology in particular and ideal-type methodology in general. The physicist starts by building an ideal model that assumes a frictionless system motivated only by the force of gravity and then lets the block made of a particular substance slide down the inclined plane (also made of some particular substance). The next step is to measure the actual speed of the sliding block. The physicist then posits the existence of a 'coefficient of friction' to correct for the discrepancy between the almost instantaneous speed predicted by the ideal model and observed speed. When the physicist uses blocks made of different substances, different coefficients will be needed to correct for the observed discrepancies. Once all of the possible coefficients of friction have been measured in this manner, the physicist has a system consisting of the ideal model and the list of coefficients that can be used to predict physical phenomena including the forces involved in gear action, for example, the forces needed to insert screws into wood or tighten nuts on bolts.

As an alternative to the formalists' prospect of a progressive sequence of models that unfolds by relaxing simplified model-building assumptions, the 'real business cycle' methodology of Kydland and Prescott is not so quick to relax assumptions. Instead, it begins with a simplified version of a formalist general equilibrium model that will be used to explain the real world in the manner of the physicist's ideal models that are made to 'fit' the observations available. Kydland and Prescott distinguish this approach from what they call the 'system-of-equations' way of dealing with the real world. In the system-of-equations approach (which is typical of many econometrics models of macroeconomics), one would make a series of many observations to deduce (i.e., 'estimate') what the value of parameters of the model would have to be for the model to fit the observed data. Such general equilibrium models are frequently very large – that is, they have very many variables and thus very many parameters to be estimated. The issue of 'fit' is usually a matter of statistical criteria found in econometrics textbooks. And usually, the larger the model is, the weaker the fit.

When choosing a model to begin with, Kydland and Prescott say that 'In addition to having a clear bearing on the question, tractability and computability are essential in determining whether the model is suitable' [1991, p. 170]. But critics will immediately say that Kydland and Prescott are putting the convenience of their model-building technique ahead of the realism of their model. Inspired by the 1995 Nobel prize-winner Robert Lucas' version of Instrumentalism (see the quotation above), they prefer dealing with any claim about the limited degree of 'realism' that such intentionally simple models yield by using calibration – rather than the more elaborate econometric estimation of parameters which would be pointless with simple general equilibrium models. One would suspect that general-equilibrium econometricians would not so eagerly give up their statistical criteria that embody an acceptable degree of descriptive realism if it means a lesser realism.

It is not the job of an applied methodologist to judge the ideal-type Instrumentalist methodology advocated by Kydland and Prescott; the job is to understand the methodology. But, as with all forms of Instrumentalism, when made part of a policy-oriented program, a lot of ideology can be smuggled in through the back methodology door. So long as the practice of this methodology does not expect us to assume something is possible on the part of any decision-maker that is logically impossible (e.g., an inductive foundation for the decision-maker's needed knowledge), not much more needs to be said.

6 Psychologistic Individualism and the Methodology of New Institutional Economics

> The conditions under which the price system might not achieve optimal resource allocation have gradually been refined... The basic thesis is that the optimal resource allocation will not be achieved by a competitive market system if there are technological externalities. These are goods (or bads) for which no market can be formed.
>
> Kenneth Arrow [1979/84, p. 216]

> I contend that market failure is a more general category than externality...
>
> Current writing has helped bring out the point that market failure is not absolute; it is better to consider a broader category, that of transaction costs, which in general impede and in particular cases completely block the formation of markets. It is usually though not always emphasized that transaction costs are costs of running the economic system...
>
> Kenneth Arrow [1969/83, p. 134]

> transaction cost economizing figures prominently in explaining ... major features of the business environment.
>
> Oliver Williamson [1981, p. 1538]

> Transaction cost economics is part of the New Institutional Economics research tradition.
>
> Oliver Williamson [1985, p. 16]

> The economics of institutions has become one of the liveliest areas in our discipline... A body of thinking has evolved based on two propositions: (i) institutions do matter, (ii) the determinants of institutions are susceptible to analysis by the tools of economic theory.
>
> R.C.O. Matthews [1986, p. 903]

The ideal-model versions of neoclassical economics usually assume away transaction costs as well as the services provided by social institutions (including those of markets and legal institutions). And, as argued in Chapter 2, the psychologistic version of methodological individualism requires that only Nature-given exogenous (viz., unexplained) variables are allowed. All constraining institutions must ultimately be explained. Such institutions might be allowed in short-run models, but if one is going to base one's explanation on long-run results, the constraining institutions must be explained away as the consequences of the decisions made by the participating individuals. Some proponents of so-called New Institutional Economics have begun to question the need to explain institutions away. Instead, they think institutions matter because institutions can be seen to solve a perceived problem of reducing transaction costs. But, how do they get from the existence of transaction costs and the need to consider constraining institutions without violating psychologistic individualism?

Consideration of an essential role for institutions in the understanding of economics is not a new idea. The notion that social institutions matter was at the center of the so-called institutionalist school of economic thought that dominated American academic economics during the first half of the twentieth century [Rutherford 1997, 2001]. But this 'old' institutionalism was often uncomfortable with neoclassical economics. Many of these institutionalists simply rejected both the idea of an independently 'rational' decision-maker and the associated (psychologistic) individualist methodology. Instead, decision-makers are to be considered creatures of habit and cultural trends. Institutions are thus seen to be a result of cultural traditions rather than deliberative thought and social policy [Hodgson 1998]. Other institutionalists (including some of the proponents of New Institutional Economics) have set about trying to accommodate institutions within a neoclassical framework [see Rutherford 2001]. On the surface it would seem that such an accommodation is possible only by restricting the neoclassical framework to the short run, but doing so would require abandoning narrow psychologistic individualism – though not necessarily methodological individualism in general.

So, just what is 'New Institutional Economics'?

After World War II and the rise of mathematical economics which was financed by governmental agencies during that war – because it was thought that many logistical problems could be solved with a combination of mathematics and economics – academic economics became dominated by neoclassical economics. If for no other reason, this was because neoclassical economics is easier to model with mathematics than was the old institutionalists' explanations of the economy. Except for some of the notions of primitive behavior that the earliest American institutionalist economist, Thorstein Veblen, identified at the beginning of the twentieth century, there was rarely anything approaching the universality that neoclassical economic theorists think they are providing with their narrow psychologistic-individualist methodology. Moreover, neoclassical economists typically dismiss (old) institutional economics as a sub-discipline of academic sociology.

Eventually, economic historians became uncomfortable with a methodology that seemed to ignore institutions. It is difficult even to conceive how one might study economic history and not see a role for institutions. Thus some economic historians (led by 1993 Nobel laureate Douglass North [1978]) began to address this methodological problem and thus 'New' Institutional Economics was born.

New Institutional Economics is the neoclassical economists' attempt to deal with the observed fact that institutions matter. New Institutional Economics is now alleged by some to have begun with the famous paper by the 1991 Nobel prize-winner Ronald Coase [1937] where the methodological issue was, if we are to maintain psychologistic individualism, how can there be an entity such as the firm (which by definition is something other than an individual)? From his perspective, we are to think of the firm as a conglomeration of individuals who, if they so choose, could operate as individuals who first produce their specific part of the final product and then they would engage in a barter exchange. This would mean that individually, they would have to negotiate with the other individuals to coordinate their achievement of the ultimate product. Such a negotiation involves, at best, significant transaction costs. In other words, as Williamson suggests, the institution of the firm is a solution to the problem of minimizing or at least reducing transactions costs. Within a firm, a manager solves the problem of coordination that would have existed alternatively with costly inter-individualist negotiation.

New Institutional Economics as short-run neoclassical economics

In effect, New Institutional Economics can be seen to be merely a short-run version of neoclassical economics. Let me explain.

If one were going to explain the firm's choice of its level of output (and thereby, its supply), one would surely have to explain both the amount of labor hired *and* the amount of productive capital acquired which together are thought to determine the level of output. According to Alfred Marshall [1920/49, p. 315], for a 'scientific' explanation of the firm (i.e., as a maximizer), distinguishing between long and short runs is necessary. Marshall explicitly recognized that some things can be changed faster than other things and this made it possible in the short run to say that some things that might be explained in the long run can be temporarily considered to be exogenously given and thus allowed to be unexplained. For example, in the neoclassical theory of the firm this would simply be the amount of capital (viz., the machines and production facilities) in the short run. (His temporal ordering is easy to understand since in his day, it was easier to hire more workers than adding more machinery since the latter would take more time to obtain. Specifically, machinery would first have to be produced before it can be used to increase the firm's productive capacity.)

To manifest his view of scientific explanation, Marshall proposed a methodology that has three stages. The first stage corresponds to a day or week during which neither labor nor capital can be changed (his 'very short run period'). Within this stage we can explain only the price – specifically, the price is the one that would clear the market for the fixed supply. In this stage, the supply is fixed because the firm does not have enough time to change its ability to produce or in the case of a perishable farm good, because the tomatoes have already been picked. His main methodological point here was that one cannot explain a choice made unless there has been enough time to vary the choice. So, one can explain the level of output or supply as a result of making a (profit) maximizing choice only if it is possible to vary the level of output. In his second stage – the short run – he allows the firm to change the level of output by varying the level of labor hired. Interestingly, Marshall was explicit in specifying that the short run corresponds to 'several months' [p. 314] such as a harvest period: the more workers one can hire, the more produce that can be planted and picked.

Presumably, in his day, producing new capital machinery would have to take a longer period of time. So, if one is to explain the choice of the amount of capital available for use, one needs to recognize a longer period of time where the amount of capital available is variable. Thus, in his third stage – the long run – we can explain the choice of the amount of capital available if we take a long-run view – that is, allow for more than several months. The long run in Marshall's time was 'several years' [p. 315] because supposedly that is how long it would have taken for technology to change. In his *Principles*, there is little or no attempt to explain technology and thus it is just accepted as an exogenous constraint in his 'scientific' explanations of the firm. That is, 'secular' or generational changes over a period of time longer than 'several years' are also ruled out of consideration [p. 315].

Parenthetically, it should be pointed out that most economists misread Marshall's references to time periods. He explicitly refers to the long run as the 'long period' [pp. 305–15]. Modern textbooks mistakenly lead students to think that the long run refers to some point of time in the future. Marshall, instead, is merely taking the neoclassical approaching of saying that *only if there has been enough time to change a chosen variable can we then assume that the decision-maker has made the maximizing choice*. If the period of time allowed for consideration is not enough then we cannot be sure the chosen amount is *currently* the optimum possible. In other words, Marshall's long and short runs are central matters of his methodology of explanation and it is for this reason that he calls their use in his methodology his 'Principle of Continuity' [see the Preface to his first edition, p. vi]. And, as I noted in Chapter 3, he calls the 'scientific' use of the assumption of maximization his 'Principle of Substitution' [p. 284]. (For a more elaborate discussion of Marshall's 'Principles' and his methodological use of time, see Boland [1992a, chap. 3].)

For New Institutional Economics, a broader view is offered to recognize that social institutions – which the economy depends on or is constrained by – are like capital and thus also take time to be changed. By analogy, perhaps Marshall's methodology is just being extended to address those constraints assumed to be constant during the long run but changeable over what we might call the *super long run*. Thus, we could say that in the short run, not only is capital fixed but the relevant social institutions are also fixed. In Marshall's long run, we could say both labor and capital are variable and thus endogenous but institutions are still fixed and exogenous. So, we can see why neoclassical economic historians talk today of the evolution of institutions [e.g., North 1991]. But, the question remains whether by this analogy institutions are like capital and thus subject to matters of 'rational' choice in this super long run just as the chosen amount of capital made available is a matter of choice in the long run.

Is New Institutional Economics a rejection of neoclassical economics?

> The two behavioral assumptions on which transaction-cost analysis relies ... are bounded rationality and opportunism...
> The term bounded rationality was coined ... to reflect the fact that economic actors, who may be presumed to be 'intendedly rational,' are not hyper-

> rational... Opportunism effectively extends the usual assumption of self-interest seeking to make allowance for self-interest seeking with guile...
> but for bounded rationality, all economic exchange could be effectively organized by contract. Indeed, the economic theory of comprehensive contracting has been fully worked out. Given bounded rationality, however, it is impossible to deal with complexity in all contractually relevant respects... As a consequence, incomplete contracting is the best that can be achieved.
>
> Oliver Williamson [1981, pp. 1545]

While Oliver Williamson talks about *the economics of* transaction costs, it would appear at times that he is rejecting neoclassical economics. Rather than assuming outright 'rationality' or maximization, he advocates assuming 'bounded rationality' [1981, p. 1545]. While it is tempting to see a direct analogy between transportation costs and transaction costs (since they might both represent reasons for prices exceeding the costs of labor and capital used) and thereby talk about 'minimizing transaction costs' [see Hennart, *et al.* 1993], doing so would preclude invoking Simon's satisficing or bounded rationality as it would mean explaining the nature of firms and corporations as that of *minimizing* transaction costs at the same time as denying the 'rationality' that would be necessary to determine whether the transaction costs are in fact minimized. So, it is not surprising that while avoiding an outright rejection of neoclassical economics and the essential role it gives to the maximization of profit by minimizing costs, Williamson seems reluctant to refer to minimization [e.g., 1981, p. 1551]. At minimum this raises the question of what he means by 'the economics of'. Usually, this involves neoclassical economics and thus has something to do with maximization or minimization and the resulting methodology of explanation that I discussed in the previous two chapters (and elsewhere [Boland 2000]). And so it is still not clear what an economics explanation based on bounded rationality can ever accomplish.

Is bounded rationality falsifiable?

Recall from Chapter 4 that 'bounded rationality' is just another way of describing what Simon offered as an alternative to assuming maximization, one which he called 'satisficing'. It was also pointed out that assuming satisficing fails to provide the necessities of explanation. Even when explaining observable behavior such as that of a firm and its profit levels and supply quantities, satisficing or bounded rationality fails to provide both uniqueness and effective falsifiability. If one is to explain why a firm chose a specific level of supply, one must also explain why the firm did not choose any other possible level. Failing to do so begs the question and opens to door to unfalsifiability. Unless the model builder is specific about what the criterion is for a minimum level of profit (i.e., that which constitutes satisficing), there is always an available avenue to avoid refutation. If the firm chose a level outside of those allowed by bounded rationality, the model builder need only claim that the bounds moved or the minimum or satisficing level is less than thought. It might be countered that the neoclassical assumption of utility maximization is also unfalsifiable in the same way – that is, direct refutation is not possible (or allowed [Boland 1997, chaps. 5

and 6]). This counter argument would be true so long as any model built using bounded rationality yields some refutable implication. But remember, neoclassical economists do not expect direct refutability of utility maximization explanations but instead try to deduce refutable theorems [Samuelson 1947/65, p. 4]. In other words, for those theorists requiring falsifiable assumptions (perhaps to avoid tautologies), the assumption of bounded rationality is no better off than the maximization assumption – or perhaps worse.

New Institutional Economics as Super-Long-Run Neoclassical Economics

There is one view of transaction costs and New Institutional Economics that clearly does not reject neoclassical economics. According to this view, transaction costs are merely one element of production costs in the case of intra-firm exchanges or transportation costs in the case of inter-firm exchanges. As noted above, one can deal with such extra costs of production and trade by modifying Marshall multi-period analysis. To do so requires only some assumption concerning the variability of transaction costs relative to the variability of other factors of production or trade.

As I noted above, Marshall defined the long run as a length of time (several years) needed before technology could change and within which one could however change the quantity of capital as well as labor. And I noted that this type of change presumes a fixed institutional structure of the firm but one that might be changed if one could allow for an even longer length of time – my 'super long run' – such that the institutional structure of the firm might be changed. And whenever the firm has time to change something, that something becomes an object of choice. Of course, objects of choice are amenable to neoclassical analysis and its maximization hypothesis.

So, what needs to be accessed is whether, by recognizing transaction costs, the New Institutional Economists are merely introducing new factors to redefine the Marshallian period analysis and thus saying that they have not completed the explanation of the economy until they have finished considering the super-long-run results. Alternatively, perhaps, New Institutional Economists may only be redefining Marshall's short run. That is, they may introduce the limits of bounded rationality as a short-run limitation that might be overcome in the long run. But, in the terms of Chapter 2, until the opportunities of the long run are exhausted, the requirements of psychologistic individualism may be unfulfilled. And the best they can hope for is the satisfaction of the methodological requirements of methodological individualism or more specifically, of institutional individualism. In other words, so long as New Institutional Economists take psychologistic individualism as the ultimate goal of economic analysis, if neoclassical economics is to be rejected, it would only be the short-run version utilized by Marshall that is rejected.

Viable institutionalism: Infinite regress vs. methodological individualism

One of the main methodological problems facing New Institutionalists who do wish to recognize that 'institutions do matter' (when considering economic behavior) is one of a resulting problematic: posing an infinite regress in the long run or the classic 'chicken or egg' dilemma in the short run [Hodgson 1998, pp. 181–4]. That is, how does one fulfill the requirements of psychologistic individualism that is taken for granted in neoclassical economics (all exogenous constraints other than those naturally given must be explained) and still allow institutions to matter? If the institutions are explained as the outcomes of decisions made solely by individuals, then the only things that matter are the decisions made by individuals and the natural constraints they face. Critics of New Institutional Economics point out that the process of making any decision – including one that leads to the creation of an institution – depends on the existence of institutions. For example, market behavior depends on the existence of the market. Thus, if the creation of one institution depends on the prior existence of other institutions, then the explanation of one institution will lead to an infinite regress since those other institutions must also be explained in the long run.

Chicken or egg dilemma: An example

Going further, one could even question the notion that an individual, as an autonomous entity, exists separately from social institutions. To see this, consider Henrik Ibsen's play, *The Doll's House*, which provides a clear demonstration of the dependence of individuality on the social situation. In this play Nora, the main character, begins as a 'doll' in her husband's household but ends up discovering herself and thereby becoming an autonomous individual at the end of the play as a result of recognizing the lies and deceptions that constituted her marriage. As a doll, Nora depended completely on the social game she was playing with (and created by) her husband as well as some of the other characters. So, which comes first, the institutional situation that defines an individual or the individuals that create the institutional situation? In the short run, it is not clear hence the need to provide a super-long-run explanation of the institutional situation in which only individuals determine events. But, as already noted, such an explanation seems to lead to an infinite regress.

Institutionalism without transaction-cost analysis

New Institutional Economics seems to be muddled and so I will take this opportunity to provide an alternative explanation of institutions, one that does not *necessarily* involve the economics of transaction costs.

I think the problem for New Institutional Economics arises only when one insists on maintaining the narrow, psychologistic version of individualism. Popper's methodological individualism does not have this problem and nor does his explanation of the social situation. As noted in Chapter 3, Popper's approach to explaining the individual's decisions or choices involves his situational logic that in turn involves recognizing the problem that the individual seeks to solve. For example, according to neoclassical theory, the consumer faces a problem of maximizing satisfaction while facing the constraints consisting of his or her budget as well as the market-given prices. The neoclassical economist claims that the individual consumer solves this problem by applying simple calculus in a manner that involves identifying the marginal gains or losses obtained by varying the choice made along a 'continuum' of options (see again Chapter 3, especially, Figure 3.1). For Popper, the key notion is that of a problem and not whether the consumer can apply calculus.

Institutions as embodied social knowledge

In the late 1960s while teaching a first-year sociology class I applied Popper's approach to what was then a central issue in social theory: the explanation of social institutions. My approach was simple. To understand any institution one needs to identify a problem that is solved by the institution. Note that there was no presumption that all institutions maximize or minimize something. While minimizing transaction costs might be a problem solved by an institution, I made no such claim that this is the only problem to be solved. Instead, my concern was with institutional dynamics. The overall viewpoint was that institutions are the embodiment of social knowledge of how to solve specific social problems. The dynamics involved a two-stage process. The first stage was the creation of a *consensus* institution that might 'just happen' but only after a *sufficient number* of people agree that adhering to the institution does solve the relevant problem. Examples of consensus institutions include 'gentlemen's agreements', 'unwritten laws' as well as dictates of current fashions. Note, with this process there is no assumption that the social knowledge is true but only that a sufficient number of people think it is true and adequate to solve the problem. The second stage was the creation of *concrete* institutions to solve a dynamic social problem that would result from relying on potentially volatile consensus institutions – specifically, the questionable durability of the agreed upon solution. In other words, society's learning to solve social problems constitutes the creation of social knowledge thus society needs to have some means of giving this knowledge durability. In effect, a concrete institution's primary task is to durably represent a consensus institution. An organization's written constitution is an example of an attempted concrete institution – as are the *Robert's Rules* that are often referred to in the process of creating or altering the organization's written constitution.

Given my approach to explaining institutions [Boland 1979b; 1992a, chap. 8], considering all institutions to be of the consensus type would be a direct application of psychologistic individualism. It is important to recognize that the concreteness of concrete institutions is a consensus institution and this is what opens the door to the infinite regress I discussed above. As I noted in my original article [1979b, p. 965],

> The theory formed views institutions as social conventions which can be influenced by individual members of the society, but which also extend (in terms of time or space) beyond the individuals and thereby can influence the individuals either as constraints or as instruments of change.

How the institutions can be influenced depends on the institutions designed to deal with that problem. For example, election rules or a constitution's provisions for amendments are explicit institutional rules for change of a standing institution (e.g., a government or a constitution).

Institutional dynamics

Unlike the typical psychologistic-individualist neoclassical explanation of institutions, I made no claim that any concrete institution is forever a successful solution – only that it is thought that the consensus institution represented does solve the problem at the point of time. It is easy to see that many institutions are used as the bases for 'educating' youth by convincing them that the problem solved is an important problem. It is such an educational process that the 1960s' 'hippies' set out to challenge by showing that the problems the youth were being taught were not really problems. For example, would the world come to an end if some woman burned her bra?

To see institutions only as solving a problem of transaction-cost minimization presumes that a failure to minimize transaction costs is a social problem. To explain institutions this way seems to run the risk of opening up New Institutional Economics to the same criticism that faced neoclassical theorists in the 1940s who presumed that consumers were lightning-fast calculators of marginal utility. Instead, all that my approach presumes is that there is a widespread recognition or acceptance that the consensus institution is an effective solution to the perceived problem. Stated another way, from the viewpoint of society, an institution need only be effective at solving a perceived problem; it does not have to be efficient or otherwise optimal.

Towards evolutionary institutionalism

So, I think that it is easy to present a theory of institutions that does not assume all institutions are the result of *individuals* engaging in successful maximization but allows such a neoclassical explanation to be viable as a special case. Moreover, how I explained institutions in the multi-stage process allowed for an explanation of their evolution once one considered how institutions are educationally 'passed down' generation after generation. But, as we all know, education is not always completely successful. And to go down the path I outlined, one would have to give up psychologistic individualism. But my recommended process does raise some important questions of how a social group decides when a consensus institution represents an effective solution to a problem. An individualist perspective does not seem sufficient. Moreover, one could interpret every consensus institution as a transaction-cost reducing device, but doing so seems not to be very informative. And if such an interpretation is intended to be an exercise in psychologistic individualism, then the problems of an infinite regress and the 'chicken or egg' will rear their ugly heads again.

7 Equilibrium-based Explanation vs. Individualism

Wherever economics is used or thought about, equilibrium, is a central organising idea.

Frank Hahn [1973, p. 1]

it really is assumed ... that what you see when you look out the window is an economy in ordinary general equilibrium...

This view has obvious (and intended) affinities to nineteenth-century economic thought, Say's Law, and all that. Like that tradition, the new equilibrium school faces a basic problem: how can it account for the 'obvious' large-scale divergences from equilibrium that we think we see, especially in prolonged depressions?

Robert Solow [1979, p. 341]

The viability of a narrow, psychologistic-individualist neoclassical view of the world depends heavily on the specific possibility of all inputs to all production functions being variable – that is, on the possibility that Marshall's explanatory device of the long run applies (see the prior discussion on page 41). Only if this is possible can a neoclassical theorist explain all endogenous variables (including inputs) as being the consequences of only naturally constrained individual optimization, subject only to the psychologically given utility functions. If any input were not variable, then it would be a non-natural, non-individualist constraint on the ultimate equilibrium and thus on the equilibrium prices. Here I will argue, the primary endogenous variable (according to Marshall's approach to explanation) is the price of any good or service. And the main focus here will be any neoclassical model that claims that all prices are equilibrium prices.

Neoclassical explanation and equilibrium methodology

The centerpiece of neoclassical equilibrium economics has always been the empirical claim that the prices we see in the 'real world' are equilibrium prices. To understand the significance of such a claim it might be helpful to consider some alternative explanations of 'real world' prices. One could say that (i) prices are 'causally determined' by natural forces, or that (ii) prices are accidental (perhaps within certain 'reasonable' ranges) at least to the extent that they are never precisely determined. Both of these explanations of prices can be found in the economics literature. The former can be seen in the classical labor theory of value and the latter in more modern macroeconomic models where the everyday price is considered a stochastic (or random) variable.

Perhaps both explanations of prices are plausible and should not be dismissed without consideration. Nevertheless, both of these alternative explanations of prices would be considered undesirable from a methodological individualist perspective of neoclassical economics. Alternative (i) might easily be alleged to be a denial of 'free will', and alternative (ii) might be alleged to be a denial of the *possibility* of explaining prices. Stated another way, it may be easily admitted, rightly or wrongly, that the price is 'determined' when someone puts it on the price tag; we have no *reason* to expect any *particular* price to be placed on the tag. This raises an interesting methodological question. Is there a plausible way to reconcile these two alternatives to form a more acceptable option? One approach might be to modify alternative (ii) such that we can explain the limits on the range of possible (accidental) prices. We could combine (i) and (ii) by modifying alternative (i) such that the 'natural forces' are the 'causes' of the limits on any price decision. We could modify (i) by postulating that there are many possible 'causal determinants' of any price – which of the determinants are considered to be relevant for the person selecting the price may be accidental or at best arbitrary.

The acceptability of any of these alternative approaches depends on our theory of what constitutes an explanation. The theory of explanation that most economists take for granted is the one that can be traced back to a common belief that the famous seventeenth-century physicist Isaac Newton was undoubtedly successful in explaining the mechanics of the Solar System. Newton's explanation was that the Solar System is in a mechanical equilibrium, one that is completely and rationally determined. Accordingly, if we know all the facts, then given the laws of mechanics, we could determine all the particular aspects of the state of equilibrium (position, velocity, etc.) by means of ordinary rational argument. The philosophical impact of his alleged success was that it led economists to believe that all economic phenomena could be explained relative to an ultimate and unavoidable state of equilibrium (a balance of forces) by explaining each variable's role in the maintenance of that equilibrium.

Economics and Newton's mechanics

By the end of the nineteenth century, when economics was just being established as a serious academic discipline, the methodology of Newton's physics was being held out as the way to make economics into a comparable science. The ultimate failure of Newton's mechanics to explain all physical phenomena (including magnetic forces) was becoming apparent late in the nineteenth century [see Einstein and Infeld 1938/61, pp. 84–90] – but this was not apparent to the early neoclassical economists [Mirowski 1989, pp. 254–61]. For the late nineteenth century physicists, the failure of Newton's explanatory method presented a serious dilemma. In particular, how can we both recognize the apparent failure of Newton's method and still advocate the use of his rational method of explanation? One response to this dilemma was to attempt to rationalize the apparent failure of Newton's mechanics – that is, attempt to derive some sort of *ad hoc* mechanical explanation of the failure, thereby vindicating that method of explanation. Those who felt this was still possible continued to regard all explanations to be 'rational' to the extent that they could be represented by a mechanical equilibrium. Neoclassical economics was born in this atmosphere.

Not until the early twentieth century did physicists recognize that there is another 'rational' response which would allow for an alternative to Newton's mechanics. One version of the new alternative allows us to give explanations by accepting the concept of what might be called 'natural probability' in place of 'natural causes' or 'forces'. In this approach, to explain some event we need only to show that the event has a 'sufficiently high probability' of occurring under the circumstances. In light of this new approach – which is merely a sophisticated version of Conventionalism – Newton's theory could be reinterpreted to be a good approximation with a high probability of success. Clearly this is a defeatist position for those who require causal determination although it does retain an air of 'rationality' – a 'sufficiently high probability' is declared to be 'sufficient' reason.

Econometrics vs. causal explanation

In economics the probabilistic or stochastic view of rational explanation led in the 1930s and 40s to the development of econometrics, although the meaning of the term 'cause' has been restricted to how we distinguish exogenous from endogenous variables within a specified model (as I will discuss below). Moreover, the probability or approximation approach to explanation still allows for a 'win-win' methodology. Namely, it could still be said that either Newton's theory, or any theory, is true (because it can be rationally or inductively justified with observed facts) or its truth does not matter. If it does not matter it is because any explanation is alleged to be only a rational approximation of observed facts, or it does not matter since we can never know all the facts anyway. Clearly, another approach is still possible. We could admit that Newton's theory or any theory can be false and then set out to correct its flaws or replace it. But for those who believe in the 'mechanical' method of explanation, admitting that Newton's theory is false would be equivalent to admitting that there is no rational method which could guarantee the success of any of our theories.

For some of us, any theory can be either true or false since all theories are conjectures or guesses [Popper 1963/89]. Whether any theory is true or false does not depend on any extant human having a reliable method to prove the theory's truth status. Our theories may be guesses about the 'causes' of events or guesses about the 'probabilities' of events occurring, or merely guesses about the relationships between various objects in the 'real world'. But most important, any of these guesses may be false or they may be true. Of course, this view of theories applies equally well to our theories of explanation.

Equilibrium methodology and methodological individualism

With this brief commentary on the neoclassical economist's equilibrium-based mechanical theory of explanation in mind, let us consider the various approaches to explaining economic variables such as prices. To explain social phenomena such as prices, economists today build models – models are merely conjunctions of explicit *formal* statements used to represent relevant ideas. In the process of building their models, they explicitly distinguish between a model's endogenous and exogenous variables. This distinction was mentioned in Chapter 2, but let me now be more specific. By definition, endogenous variables are those determined *within the model* (i.e., they depend on the values of the model's other variables). Exogenous variables are those determined *outside of the model* (and thus do not change as a result of changes to endogenous variables). Thus, neoclassical theorists say that we would like to explain prices as endogenous variables – and more particularly, as consequences of individuals' choices. While recognizing that *any specific* price marked on a price tag must be decided by people, the question is begged as to why the particular price is put on the tag. Without a model to explain how the person putting it on the tag chooses the price, we have no reason to expect *any particular* price to be placed on the tag.

Despite the failure of the mechanical theory of the physical world, the concept of equilibrium has some attributes that make it even more interesting for economics where the question of 'free will' is a central concern. The concept of equilibrium seems to allow for any individual's 'free will' at the same time as giving a rational explanation of the economy as a whole. However, it remains to be seen whether an equilibrium explanation of prices can be constructed such that both 'free will' is preserved and a mechanical determination of prices made.

Being able to juggle the apparently conflicting philosophical demands for 'free will' with the methodological demands of 'rational' determination and explanation is an interesting challenge, which to a certain extent, has been accomplished within the textbook version of neoclassical economics. By carefully considering this juggling act we can understand such things as why traditional neoclassical theory separates the determination of demand from the determination of supply. Perhaps economists think that by separating demand from supply we can build in a minimum, but essential, element of 'free will' for autonomous decision-making. For any particular prices charged, the autonomous individual agent acts *freely* in deciding what, or how much, to demand or supply. Here we are viewing the separation of demand and supply as a decision made by the theorist – i.e. deliberate methodological individualism. Since this theoretical decision seems rather arbitrary, or at least overly convenient, textbooks attempt to rationalize why it is made. Much of traditional theory has been developed to justify this separation by showing that when demand and supply are separated in the 'real world', autonomous decision-making is preserved and the 'real world' will be the 'best of all possible worlds'. Moreover, it certainly would not be the 'best' whenever individuals encourage collusion or are dependent on each other's approval. As the common view of Adam Smith's world would have us believe, we should never depend on authorities such as the church or the state since the 'best of all possible worlds' will be achieved when everyone is independently pursuing self-interest and is not inhibited except by the givens provided by Nature.

Prices as social institutions

To understand clearly our modern economic concept of equilibrium let us consider it differently. Our equilibrium theory of prices says that *prices are social institutions*. To say this, however, brings up in a new form the dilemma concerning 'free will' versus explanation. At the beginning of Chapter 2, I discussed two extreme views of social institutions that are diametrically opposed. On the one hand there is the strict methodological-individualist view which says that all institutions are merely aggregate manifestations of individual behavior and hence institutions are explained *only* in terms of the behavior of each and every participating individual – this is the optimistic view of institutions that was promoted by the early advocates of New Institutional Economics that I discussed in Chapter 6. For example, if prices are social institutions, then prices will be the equilibrium prices only if everyone agrees that they should not be changed. On the other hand, there is the strict holist view which says that some institutions have an existence (and hence a determination) beyond the individuals that use or help create them. For example, the real price may reflect its 'natural value' or its 'just value' or its 'labor value', etc. From the standpoint of explaining social institutions, it is strict holism that is specifically rejected when traditionally we reject 'natural' causes (such as labor embodiment) as sole determinants of prices.

Since most neoclassical economists today would immediately reject the holist view of institutions, their primary philosophical task is to reconcile a methodological-individualist concept of social institutions with the concept of *equilibrium* prices. The concept of an equilibrium price must be shown to be a strict methodological-individualist institution – that is, one which can be shown to be the result of the interaction of *all* individuals yet determined by no single individual or by no natural cause [cf. Arrow 1951/63].

Prices as uncaused effects

Almost all modern analytical studies of neoclassical equilibrium models are concerned with this task. Everyone seems to agree that the analysis of a static equilibrium alone will never be sufficient to explain prices in a manner consistent with methodological individualism [see Arrow 1959 and 1994]. Instead, what is needed is a clear understanding of the process of reaching an equilibrium – but is the process 'evolutionary' or something else? Expanding our view of prices to include disequilibrium states as well as equilibrium states would allow for individualism (the price tag marker) and at the same time recognizes prices as holistic but endogenous givens which constrain individual actions (e.g. by determining opportunity costs). The individual sellers can pursue what they think is in their own interest but in the long run (a run long enough for equilibrium to be obtained), they will find it in their own best interest either to all charge the going equilibrium price or to demand or supply the quantities that are consistent with the equilibrium price.

More needs to be said about the methodological questions raised by the recognition that equilibrium prices are social institutions. But before doing so, I need to examine equilibrium explanations in general. Afterwards, I will discuss the possible conflict between the requirements of the psychologistic version of methodological individualism and the willingness to see the price system (i.e., all prices being determined simultaneously) as a social institution.

Psychologism and general equilibrium

Let us begin, then, by looking at the general methodological problem of determining what are acceptable 'givens' in our theories of the consumer and of the producer. In short-run models, not all givens are exogenous variables. Specifically, there are two types of givens although the difference means little in the usual neoclassical short run. These types are the endogenous variables that are social givens (e.g. going prices, income distributions, wage-rates, etc.) that might be explained in an expanded long-run version of the model, and the exogenous variables that are supposedly 'natural' givens (e.g. tastes, availability of resources, learning abilities, biological growth rates, etc.) and will never change as a result of how the endogenous givens are ultimately determined. The first step in the development of an economic model is to explicitly specify a list of relevant variables. The immediate next step is to partition that list into variables that are givens (which includes all of the exogenous variables) and the variables that are to be explained as matters of choice (which includes all endogenous variables even though they may be considered 'independent' givens in the short run). While social institutions were discussed in Chapter 6, for now, I will leave open the question as to which side of the partition social institutions fall.

In the neoclassical/Marshallian definition of the short run, individuals are unable to change any of the specified givens even though some of them may be endogenous variables in the long-run version of the model or theory. When the short run is employed to explain the choices made by a single individual firm or consumer, the explanation is called a 'partial equilibrium' (see Chapter 3) since some of the givens still need to be explained. Beyond the short run, individuals can influence the social givens. The solution to the 'holist vs. individualist' dilemma apparently lies here. In the short run, prices are holistic social givens; in the long run, they are the consequences of individual choices. The question addressed in Chapter 6 concerning New Institutional Economics was whether social institutions should be considered endogenous or exogenous. But, what about the 'natural givens'? Are they not the 'natural causes' or 'forces'?

For reference: A simple model of general equilibrium

Let us consider a model designed to represent a simple world in general equilibrium [cf. Samuelson 1950b]. By a simple world, I mean one where the list of relevant variables includes just two inputs, two outputs and two individuals. General equilibrium theorists usually refer to this as the '2×2×2' model. The *total* amounts available of the two inputs (so-called 'resources') will be considered exogenous. The two outputs correspond to two separate firms and are endogenous variables. The amount of each input used by each firm is endogenous – that is, the allocation of society's resources between the two firms is endogenous. And the amount of each output consumed by each individual is also endogenous. In the simplest model, the budget available to each individual would be exogenous and each would be price-takers; in more complicated models, the budgets would depend on how much of each of the inputs is owned by each individual and/or the individuals might be allowed to directly participate in the determination of the prices. Either way, the list must also include prices for the inputs and outputs. The remaining tasks would be to specify the input-output relationship (the production function) for each firm and the 'utility function' or preference relationship for each individual consumer. And this is followed with a specification of the behavioral assumptions to be used to determine the values of all of the endogenous variables.

Leon Walras is famous for attempting to specify the behavioral assumptions that would mathematically ensure the existence of a set of prices consistent with a general equilibrium of price-takers for any set of exogenous givens. He was interested in a state of equilibrium where each individual is maximizing subject to their personal constraints (e.g., their budgets) and facing the same set of prices as everyone else. For Walras, the model builder's main task would be to represent the preference and production relationships with formal calculus-based mathematical functions. In effect, the determination of any set of equilibrium prices amounts to solving a set of simultaneous equations where the equations correspond to the calculus-based maximizing conditions for each individual decision-maker. Initially Walras thought that it was enough to ensure that the number of equations equaled the number of endogenous variables. But, the question is much more complicated [see Wald 1936/51]. If for no other reason, any real economy usually has a very large number of individuals and so the system of equations would be difficult to solve except in very special cases. Nevertheless, theorists still refer to such a set of (general) equilibrium prices as Walrasian prices.

'Determination' as mechanical explanation

When general equilibrium theorists say 'determine' they usually mean 'explain' in the sense that for the given values or states of the exogenous variables and the specified behavioral assumptions relating all variables and givens, the values obtained for all of the endogenous variables are the only ones that would allow all of the equations to be true simultaneously. That is, on the basis of the specified behavioral theory and model that purports to represent the simple world, the explained set of values are said to be the only set which corresponds to the one particular set of values (or states) of the following 'givens': 'tastes' (which are what each individual consumer's preference map represents); 'technology' (which is what each firm's production function represents); available resources (viz., the total amount of available inputs that exists in the simple world) and, in complicated models, the wealth distribution (the portion of inputs owned by each individual consumer). Although I did not mention this above, sometimes there is an additional natural given in the form of an 'interest rate' which may represent the opportunity costs of consuming today rather than using one's capital to produce something for tomorrow (e.g. it may also represent the biological growth rate which follows planting of seeds).

This form of explanation can be easily interpreted as a mechanical explanation. But as such, it is very limited. It says that if the model is true, no matter what the firms or consumers think they are doing, ultimately they must make the decisions indicated by the determined values of the endogenous variables. Since these values have been determined to be the ones that allow all firms and individuals to be maximizing, if any firm or individual deviated from these values, they would not be maximizing. And most important, what this mechanical view of explanation allows is that the model builders never need to consider the *process* of maximizing. This would also mean that consideration of bounded rationality or any other issue about the decision process can be ignored. But, critics have charged that this is thus an unrealistic, static view of economics that might satisfy mathematicians, but anyone interested in the behavioral questions that need to be addressed to explain how the equilibrium is reached will not be satisfied.

Static vs. dynamic determination

So long as the (exogenous) 'givens' do not change and the long-run equilibrium has been reached, the long-run equilibrium values of the determined variables will *never* change! In other words, so long as the exogenous 'givens' do not change, our analysis is essentially static even though individuals may be thought of doing things continuously – such as changing inputs into outputs. Every week, each individual buys or sells the same quantity in the market because in this 2×2×2 world there is no change in the endogenous demands or supplies without a change in at least one exogenous variable. Clearly then, any interesting 'dynamic' analysis must somehow deal with changes in the exogenous 'givens'. I will return to examine the issue of static vs. dynamic in a different way in Chapter 10.

Mechanical explanation vs. methodological individualism

Even in simple 2×2×2 models of the economy like the one identified above, the possibility of a mechanical interpretation leads to problems for the methodological-individualist interpretation of the neoclassical explanation of prices. As suggested already, no matter what decisions individuals made in the process of reaching an equilibrium, there might be only one set of determined values for the endogenous variables given the specified set of exogenous variables. (If there is more than one set of equilibrium values, the explanation would be incomplete as there would be no explanation for why one equilibrium state is reached rather than another – and hence the recurring problem of multiple equilibria that was noted near the end of Chapter 3.) Does the existence of only one possible set of determined values for the specified exogenous givens mean that the set of givens is the 'cause' of the determined values and thus that our explanation of prices denies 'free will'? Unfortunately, it is difficult to see how the answer is not affirmative whenever the givens are considered unalterable by any individual involved – such as in the case with long-run models. Clearly this is a serious problem for methodological individualism. Can this obstacle be avoided or dismissed? Most economic theorists seem to think so. For example, some theorists [e.g. Samuelson 1947/65, p. 49; Kreps 1990, p. 100; Weirich 1998, p. 149] accept 'multiple equilibria', that is, more than one set of values which correspond to the one set of givens. This unfortunately is a defeatist position – no matter how liberal it may appear to be. Any hope of explaining the variables in question in terms of individual choices is conceded. But worse, if it is argued that there are many possible sets of equilibrium values then each individual's set of choices is to some extent *arbitrary*. For some of us, such arbitrariness is just as bad as a denial of 'free will'.

Another approach to this individualist dilemma is to admit that the 'givens' are not really given since each can be influenced by individuals in the economy. Unfortunately, if carried too far – that is, if all the givens are made endogenous *within* our model of the economy, then the explanation of all variables becomes circular. One way to avoid circularity is to explain the 'givens' *outside* of the model in question. The most commonly accepted approach to allowing certain givens to be explained outside the model is to confess that since 'we are all humans' everything reduces to psychology. This approach is just the narrow, reductive psychologism that I have been discussing and as such it would require us to explain even the impersonal givens such as technology, resource availability, interest rates, or wealth distributions, within any neoclassical model. However, some or all of the nature of individual tastes (or their variability) would have to be explained outside the model to preserve a minimum degree of exogeneity and avoid circularity. This psychologistic method of allowing economists to explain everything except the natural givens goes virtually unchallenged in neoclassical economics literature and textbooks since, as explained in Chapter 2, it still seems to many to be the only way to accommodate the demands of the psychologistic version of methodological individualism.

The price system and psychologistic individualism

Almost all elementary textbooks assure us that if we follow Adam Smith's eighteenth-century rationalist prescriptions and put all of our social interactions in markets, then so long as the markets are unencumbered, in the long run all of society's resources will be optimally allocated to the production of desired goods and services. This means, textbooks tell us, (1) every individual will be able to maximize utility and obtain the goods they want, (2) that every supplier will maximize profit, and moreover, (3) nobody will be 'ripped-off' since the market prices will not exceed the full cost of production. Together, these benefits of a market-based long-run equilibrium surely constitute a social optimum. However, the achievement of such an equilibrium depends on how prices are determined in the market. Who sets the price? How do they know what to set it at?

The problem of social institutions

In textbook neoclassical economics it is taken for granted that market-equilibrium determined prices are beyond the individual and thus constitute constraints on the choice situation facing the individual. As noted above, putting price determination beyond the individual means that an economy's system of prices (viz., the list of prices for all goods and services) is an exogenous social institution which is considered given for the choice situation of each individual decision-maker. The term 'social' usually means the establishment of the system involving the decisions of many individuals. But as I have continued to stress, by saying that neoclassical economics is based on psychologistic individualism, neoclassical theories or analyses must permit only two types of exogenous givens: natural constraints and psychological states. Of particular concern is the psychologistic-individualist requirement that no social institution that appears in our long-run explanations must be allowed to play the role of an exogenous given. That is, other givens may be allowed in short-run models, but they must eventually be explained as being the long-run consequences of decisions made by all individuals in concert. For reference and recalling the discussion of Chapter 6, let us call this particular requirement the 'problem of social institutions'. Specifically:

> The *problem of social institutions* is: how do we assure that every institution which is introduced as a given in the short-run (or partial equilibrium) version of a model can be explained in terms that include only the exogenous variables permitted in the long-run (or general equilibrium) version of the model?

It should be recognized, however, that New Institutional Economics does not try to solve this problem since it would extend this to allow for a super-long-run explanation of institutions. But let us leave this aspect for now and focus on the traditional neoclassical perspective, namely, psychologistic-individualist long-run equilibria.

The price system as a social institution

The idea that the price system might be considered to be a social institution is not new. Recall the quotation that appears at the top of Chapter 2 where Joseph Schumpeter noted: 'prices are obviously social phenomena' [1909]. What did he mean by this? Did he mean that the price system is an exogenous social institution? Or is it merely an epiphenomenon of the psychological states of the individuals in society? If, as required by psychologistic individualism, it is only an epiphenomenon, then two conditions must be met: (A) the actual price system can be influenced by each individual and (B) in our explanation of the price system, the value of all prices can be determined only by reference to all exogenous variables, namely, the natural givens and the psychological states of *all* individuals.

Condition (A) is the basis for some of the interesting theoretical questions raised by the 1972 Nobel prize-winner, Kenneth Arrow [1951/63, 1959 and 1994], that I discussed above. Specifically, in what circumstances is it *possible* for all individuals to be influencing the determination of the market price, yet at the same time for no one individual alone to determine the actual price and thereby deny the influence of all other individuals? Furthermore, just how can we be explaining demand and supply decisions as being those of price-takers?

Arrow argued that condition (A) is satisfied only when the market is in equilibrium. When the market is in equilibrium all individuals influence the price by their participation on the demand side or the supply side, since if they withdrew from either side, the price would change. Also, in equilibrium no individual can force the price to change to a specific price other than the value of the equilibrium price, since any effort to do so would cause a disequilibrium. We see then that according to the neoclassical (i.e., psychologistic) view of the market determination of actual prices, the individual's 'influence' on the price level is only indirect or 'unintended'. Given this, all that is required for the logical adequacy of this view is that the states of all the permitted exogenous variables do indeed entail a determinant price system (i.e., all markets are potentially stable). This is the requirement that, for any model of the price system, there must exist a solution for the values of all the prices – i.e., we must be able to provide a so-called 'existence proof' [see Boland 1992a, chap. 4].

Over the last seventy years the mathematical requirements for any existence proof have been explored and analyzed in excessive detail, to the boredom of most economists. Such proofs are no longer the basis of research programs in economic theory, although it could be argued that the existing proofs still are too demanding for observers of the real world. There nevertheless remains an unanswered part of Arrow's argument. What happens to the methodology of psychologistic individualism when the market is not in equilibrium? Arrow argues that in order to explain the determination of prices, we violate either the requirements of psychologistic individualism or condition (B), since in order to get the price to return to the equilibrium, at least one individual (i.e., the bidder) must set the price, and that means that at least one individual alone is determining the price! This observation of Arrow led to two schools of thought. One argued that we need a theory of 'disequilibrium trading' [e.g. Clower 1965]; the other argued that we need a neoclassical theory of the individual bidder [Gordon and Hynes 1970]. Neither school was completely successful, thus Arrow's challenge still stands. Today, one would think that game theory might offer a solution, but little seems to have been accomplished. I will return to the questionable success of various versions of game theory and evolutionary economics that address issues of dynamics in Chapters 9 and 10.

We have here another case of the repeating theme. Specifically, the theoretical puzzles based on condition (A) are the direct consequence of the acceptance of the methodological requirements of psychologistic individualism and, in par-ticular, of condition (B) – namely, the psychologistic requirement that all insti-tutions must be endogenous. And in particular, it is easy to see again that the problem of social institutions has immediate consequences for our concept of the price system as a social system that can *endogenously* coordinate all individuals and in which they are all presumed to be engaged in independent, 'rational' decision-making. This, of course, is an example of Hodgson's chicken-or-egg problem discussed in Chapter 6.

Until New Institutional Economics began to earn a following, the concept of a social institution was not often specified in economic models. Generally, in short-run neoclassical models it was accepted that institutions exist potentially to constrain all individual decision-makers. But what makes institutional constraints important in any model is that they are not naturally given but have themselves been created by other individuals acting *in concert*. That any institution may effectively constrain only one individual is not the issue here; rather, the issue is that its existence is dependent on the activities of many individuals, including any individuals who may be constrained by the institution.

In order to distinguish institutions from individual actions in the most general terms, let us say that any constraint, the establishment of which requires the implicit or explicit participation of many individuals, is in some sense a social institution. As a result, some economists consider a system of all market-determined prices to be a social institution whose function is to provide the decision-maker with a 'summary of information about the production possibilities, resource availabilities and preferences of all other decision-makers' [e.g., Koopmans 1957, p. 53]. In the neoclassical world of simultaneous market equilibria where everyone faces the same set of prices, the price system in this neoclassical way is an institution with which individuals' social behavior can be coordinated without the intervention of a government or a central planner.

Individualism vs. coordination

Methodologically speaking, as I continue to stress, the neoclassical theorist cannot rest until it is shown that the nature of any institution is what it is only because people have directly or indirectly chosen that it should be what it is. Recognizing the price system as an institution is interesting in this sense because the price system serves a dual purpose. On the one hand, it has to be *responsive* (no matter how small the degree) to every individual's psychological state and, on the other, it has to be a relatively *stable* signal indicating to every individual decision-maker the wishes of every other individual in society. How can a social institution serve such a dual purpose? How can something be both volatile (i.e., responsive) and stable?

To answer these questions, we need to understand the neoclassical conception of market-*equilibrium* prices (i.e., socially coordinated prices) beyond what was discussed in Chapter 3. Specifically, we need to understand how prices would have to be determined in a neoclassical model in a manner consistent with psychologistic individualism. As Arrow argued, in a consistent neoclassical model, prices are determinant only when the influences of *all* individuals are, in some non-accidental way, *in balance*. But, as suggested by Koopmans, if the price system is to fulfill the requirements of a social institution, we must assure the possibility of such a balance being a stable institution; and this is done by showing that the balance must *also* be an *equilibrium*. Specifically, it must be the case that any accidental disturbance of the balance will be corrected without the extraordinary influence of any one individual or institution. Any going price will be the one price at which the influences of participating individuals (through their willingness to demand or supply some of that good) are in balance. What the existence of an equilibrium implies is the following. The going (observable) price of a good is not an accidental price. It is not accidental because had it been higher or lower there would have been *reasons* for it to return to the balancing price.

Unfortunately, an existence proof does not usually provide behavioral reasons for the occurrence of an equilibrium. All of the mathematical studies concerning existence proofs only assured the existence of a possible *balance* (for example, as a solution of a system of simultaneous equations representing demand and supply functions). Nothing more was intended [Hahn 1973]. The question still may be open as to whether a potential balance is also an equilibrium. To many, the distinction between a balance and an equilibrium may not appear to be very significant because in economics textbooks, as noted in Chapter 3, the concept of equilibrium is often confused with that of a balance. But the distinction is essential to an understanding of many popular theoretical research programs.

Again, if there are reasons why a balance is not accidental (e.g., if it is the result of successful competition), then those reasons imply that the balance is stable, i.e., it is an equilibrium. In neoclassical theory this is of particular importance to the concept of equilibrium prices. The equilibrium price can be thought to be determined by the reasons which guarantee that demand and supply will be in balance, because these are the reasons which guarantee the existence of a stable balance. But to accommodate psychologistic individualism, the reasons must be related to individuals' psychological states.

Coordinating equilibrium and psychologism

The biggest challenge for those who accept psychologistic individualism concerns the neoclassical concept of a market equilibrium. Specifically, how can the psychologistic-individualist explanation of equilibrium overcome the conflicting demands of responsiveness and stability? On the basis of a posited relationship between the quantity demanded of a good and its going market price, and of a posited relationship between the quantity supplied of that good and the *same* going price, a stable equilibrium price will of necessity be the one price that brings into balance these two quantities as an unintended consequence of competition. What that price will be depends on the two posited relationships. Generally, if either relationship changes, the result will be a new equilibrium price. It is the sensitivity of the demanded (or supplied) quantity's relationship to the price which assures the responsiveness of the equilibrium price to changes in individual psychological states. In neoclassical theory the relationship is merely a consequence of maximization based on given utility functions. If psychologistic individualism is to be maintained, changes in the psychological state of any individual must have some effect on the equilibrium price (even though, when there are many individuals, the result may appear to be negligible). But, what motivates the responsiveness when there is a stable equilibrium?

As I have stressed earlier, the relationship between the quantity demanded (or supplied) by any individual is asserted to be the consequence of maximization (i.e., 'rational' decision-making). And, again, one aspect of maximization is that its consequences are usually determinate (and non-arbitrary); that is, it leads to a unique quantity for any given price (the budget being given). If one is given the going price, then theoretically one can calculate the correct quantity to be demanded of any good for utility to be maximized or to be supplied for profit to be maximized. If there is a discrepancy between the quantities demanded and supplied, then it must be the case that at least one individual is not maximizing! For example, consider Figure 7.1 where I have drawn the usual case in which the demand curve is negatively sloped and the supply curve is positively sloped. In this figure, I have shown the going price (P_1) being lower than the one which would clear the market (viz., at the intersection point), thus the transacted quantity must be less than the quantity that would be demanded if every individual were able to be maximizing his or her utility (at that price). In other words, whenever the market is not in equilibrium (below the clearing prince) not all individuals can be maximizing according to their psychologically given utility functions. A similar example would occur when the price is above the one that would clear the market. In this similar case, not all producers can be maximizing profit at the higher price. In either case, any individual who is not maximizing has an incentive to bid the price up or down. That is, in the situation depicted in Figure 7.1, by bidding the price up, the non-maximizing demander competes with other demanders for the available supply but also changes the constraints for every consumer such that all consumers reduce their demand. This process will continue until there is no excess of demand over supply. A similar dynamic takes place when the price is above the intersection; any supplier who is not able to maximize prices offers its supply for a lower price which affects the price constraint for all producers of that product.

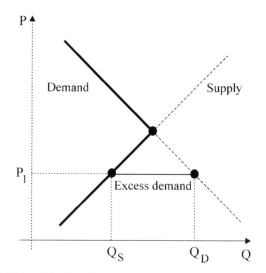

Figure 7.1. Suppliers maximizing but demanders not

Equilibria and incentives

This point needs to be stressed, since it is the center of the methodological problem that continues to face neoclassical theorists today. *The neoclassical theory that all individuals are successful maximizers can be true only if all markets are in equilibrium.* For an equilibrium to exist, there cannot be any incentive for any individuals to change their behavior, that is, change their choices. If an incentive does exist, then we would have to explain why it has not been pursued. If the individual chose not to pursue it, it could not have been an incentive. If the individual is in any way constrained from pursuing it, then additional constraints must be included among the exogenous variables of our explanation. This leads to the central theoretical problem of neoclassical economics that still is unsolved even today. How can there ever be any disequilibria? Would anyone choose a state of disequilibrium? As was discussed in Chapter 5, a disequilibrium can be accommodated with some sort of ideal-type methodology (as a deviation from an ideal equilibrium) but this still begs these questions. Some theorists today are eager to answer such questions by claiming that a disequilibrium is the result of errors made by decision-makers and that the errors occur because the decision-makers are in some way ignorant. More specifically, it is claimed that mistakes are the result of 'imperfect knowledge'. While this claim can be related to the discussion of Chapter 1, there is more to discuss whenever the matter of alleged imperfect knowledge arises but I will postpone such discussion until Chapter 8.

Before discussing the general methodological problems of disequilibria, let me be clear about the more elementary relationship between equilibria and incentives. Basically, a true equilibrium says that all possible gains from trade or from adjustments to behavior have been exhausted. If possible gains were available, then there would be reasons for change. In a state of market equilibrium there cannot exist any incentives for change. This does not mean that there are no constraints, but only that all operative constraints must be beyond choice.

Psychologism and the elementary world of Adam Smith

Surely, one would think, the problems created by allowing for both responsiveness and stability in a market system have been solved long ago. Unfortunately, they do not seem to have been. These problems (which were raised by Arrow in the late 1950s) continue to lurk in the shadows of neoclassical economics. And I argue that, of course, the reason for their persistence is the unexamined and uncriticized acceptance of the need to fulfill the requirements of psychologistic individualism. However, it could be that neoclassical economists put too much reliance on the matter of ultimately attaining a long-run equilibrium. To better understand the role of markets in Adam Smith's world, Schumpeter saw the long-run equilibrium as a starting point rather than an ending point. What does this alternative say for psychologistic individualism?

Self-interest vs. social optima

For the purposes of psychologistic individualism, it is essential that all incentives be available to individuals and not limited to society as a whole. Consider, for example, the profits of the individual firm in a competitive economy. For there to be an unambiguous long-run equilibrium, we say that in the long run excess profit of every firm (i.e., its total revenue minus total costs) must be zero. Perhaps from the social point of view this may be desirable, but to be consistent with psychologistic individualism we must not allow social objectives to be imposed on individual firms. Even from the social point of view, profit itself is not necessarily interesting. As Schumpeter pointed out, 'as the rise and decay of industrial fortunes is *the* essential fact about the social structure of capitalist society, both the emergence of what is, in any single instance, an essentially temporary gain, and the elimination of it by the working of the competitive mechanism, obviously are more than "frictional" phenomena, as is that process of underselling by which its achievements result in higher real incomes all round' [1928, pp. 380-1]. The point of Adam Smith's classical vision is that the pursuit of private interest *unintentionally* produces a social good. It does this only in a world of competition where profits are unintentionally eliminated. That is, zero profits are an 'unintended consequence' of the combination of competition and profit maximization.

Amazingly, maximization is the only behavioral assumption used in the neoclassical textbook's view of the firm – and, most important, maximization is a private, individualist matter. Specifically, the only individualist incentive used to explain the behavior of a textbook firm in the short run is the maximization of profits. When *total* revenue equals *total* costs, *average* revenue (viz., for units of output) must obviously equal *average* cost. For a profit-maximizing firm, however, average revenue and cost is irrelevant *with regard to maximization*. As is well known today, it is *marginal* revenue and *marginal* cost that matter.

The firm can respond to its incentives (viz., possible improvements in its profits) in two different ways. Primarily, it can internally and independently alter its output to adjust its costs and revenue. As a matter of elementary calculus, if it is maximizing its profits, then, of course, for any small adjustment marginal revenue must just equal marginal cost. But also, if it is maximizing profits, any increase in output must produce a situation in which marginal cost exceeds marginal revenue. So long as the firm is not incurring losses, there is no incentive for it to change its output. Secondarily, it can also deal with its situation by altering its external situation – but only if there exist other possibilities. If it is making losses (even though it may be minimizing them), it can do nothing to change its situation unless there exist better alternatives. But such contingencies are beyond its control in a competitive economy. Either a losing firm eventually quits or it switches to another industry. Its decision is a private matter. However, availability of an alternative industry is not a private matter.

Note that no reason is usually given for why the one firm is losing (i.e., its price is less than its average cost). Are all firms in that industry losing? If so, why is just one firm leaving the industry? How does the firm know which industry to switch to? Microeconomics could never answer these questions without reference to some sort of macroeconomic perspective. Let us leave this difficult consideration until Chapter 9 and instead just recognize that the sociology of the market place is usually ignored in the neoclassical textbook.

The textbook's assumption of profit maximization, then, only assures that marginal cost equals marginal revenue. Which of the individualist variables assure the attainment of zero profits? If some firms in one industry are making profits while firms in another are making losses, then there is an incentive for the losing firms to switch industries. In doing so the firms entering the profit-making industry only drive the market price down or reduce every other firm's share of the market and, either way, reduce everyone's profits. Even so, the existence of profit is an incentive for individual entrepreneurs to enter. The incentive to enter disappears only when the firms' profits are driven down to zero – however unintentionally.

So the individual's pursuit of self-interested profits internally and externally eventually leads to zero profits. But zero profit combined with profit maximization does not necessarily mean that the social goal of optimum resource allocation has been served. Or does it? It does whenever all maximizers are also price-takers, that is, when they are in effect 'small fish in a big pond' and thus unable to change the given market price.

Social optima as forced, unintended consequences

The allocation of society's resources is optimum only if there is no possibility of reducing their utilization without reducing outputs. Traditionally, this is illustrated by a U-shaped average cost curve such as the one labeled AC in Figure 7.2. Before I discuss this diagram, I should warn readers who have successfully negotiated their way through an economics course or two that I will try to limit the diagrams to very elementary and well-known standard drawings. The warning is that one should not be misled by the simplicity of the diagram to think that there are no methodological problems lurking between the lines, so to speak. So as to bring out these problems, I will try to be careful to explain the diagrams in a manner that even a novice will understand. My reason for this is that the way some textbooks explain such diagrams often obscures the interesting questions that a novice might like to raise. With this said, let us now turn to Figure 7.2.

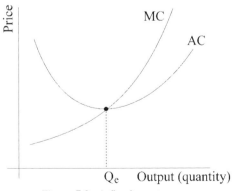

Figure 7.2. A firm's cost curves

The AC curve shown represents all the possible levels of the cost of the resources used *per unit of output*. If average cost (AC) can be decreased by producing a larger quantity of output, then the current output is not being efficiently produced. Maximum efficiency in this sense then occurs only at the level of output where average cost is minimum. This is the key to connecting the individual's concerns to the social objective. It is also the key to understanding the role of natural constraints.

Since the individual maximizer is only concerned with marginal values, we need to note an elementary point: the behavior of the average is not independent of its relationship to the margin. Specifically, to cause the average to fall, the margin must be below the average. Similarly, if the average is rising (as it is to the right of Q_e in Figure 7.2), it can only be because the margin is above the average. Thus, with this elementary point in mind, we see that whenever the average is at a true minimum and thus temporarily unchanging with respect to output, the margin equals the average. So, in order for model builders to have the firm using its resources efficiently, they need only have the firm producing where the marginal cost equals the average cost – namely, at output level Q_e in Figure 7.2.

But profit maximization, our individualist incentive, only assures the equality of marginal cost with marginal revenue – and this equality is a matter of simple calculus. Similarly, reducing profits to zero only assures that average cost equals average revenue – this equality is a matter of simple arithmetic. So far, there is nothing here to bring average and marginal cost into equality. Now here is where the idea that firms (and buyers) are price-takers becomes crucial. If a firm is a price-taker – that is, the price is given by the market (which is an exogenously given institution) and does not change in response to the single firm's behavior (which is the case when either there are very many very small firms or prices are externally fixed) – then marginal revenue will necessarily equal the average revenue (the latter of which is just the fixed or unchanged price). In this *special* case, if the individual firm's profit is maximized, the price (which equals both marginal and average revenue) will equal its marginal cost. If the individual firm (perhaps by its entry into the market) inadvertently causes profits to be reduced to zero, its average revenue (i.e., the price) will equal its average cost. Thus, indirectly we obtain the socially desired efficiency in the use of society's resources; the firm's marginal cost will equal its average cost *without the deliberate action by any individual* in that regard!

The elementary analysis of the last paragraph can also be illustrated with a simple diagram. The idea that the firm is a price taker is represented by a horizontal line. There is one drawn for P_1 and one for P_e – and in both cases, since the price is given and fixed (i.e., by assumption, the firm must take it as given), the price is both the average revenue (AR) and marginal revenue (MR). A profit-maximizing firm will choose the quantity of output that maximizes profit per unit of output (viz., where the price equals marginal cost). When it faces the given price P_1 it will then choose Q_1 and it will be making an average profit (AP), which in this case is calculated and represented by the distance between the marginal cost curve (MC) and the average cost curve (AC). When facing P_e it will choose Q_e; but in this case it makes zero profit and so marginal cost and average cost coincide.

Zero profit would never be the aim of a firm, of course, but should the given price be P_1 and thus mean that firms producing in this market are making profit, then whenever market competition in the form of a new firm entering the market causes the price to fall (so as to induce buyers to purchase its output), unintentionally the effect is a lower profit. And so long as there is profit to be made there is still an incentive for new firms to enter in this way. Once the price is caused to fall to the level of P_e and thus profits are eliminated, there is no longer an incentive for new firms to enter. So long as firms in this sense are price takers and there is free competition – that is, there are no barriers to the entry of new profit seeking firms – the social optimum is *inevitable*: there will not only be zero profits but maximum efficiency.

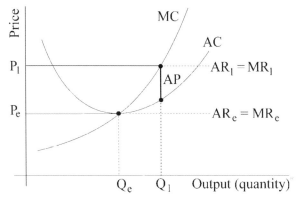

Figure 7.3. The firm as a price-taker

Do we need Adam Smith's world or is such a world even possible?

Admittedly Figure 7.3 is merely an elementary illustration of very elementary economics but it elegantly illustrates the virtues of Adam Smith's world. The social optimum of maximum efficiency in the use of society's resources is achieved solely as a result of the *individual* actions of self-interested profit-seeking firms. This is both the perversity and the beauty of Adam Smith's world. No individual has to have the *socially desirable* zero profits as his or her goal. Nor does there have to exist a central authority to set the optimum price. It is the free pursuit of private interest that, *unintentionally*, is claimed to be *sufficient* for the provision of this social good. But, behind this scene are a lot of social institutions that do not appear in the diagram. For example, it is presumed that there are institutions creating and protecting property rights. Without property rights, there would be no guarantee that one could keep any of the profits hence the incentives would be pointless. From the perspective of neoclassical economic model building, if a model did not include the social institution of property rights, there would be no point to methodological individualism.

Adam Smith's world of greed and virtue

There are more social considerations in Adam Smith's world. If one examined only the claimed sufficient conditions for an economy to be in a state of psychologistic-individualist equilibrium, the beauty of Adam Smith's world would be lost. Surely any entrepreneurs who took a broad perspective (or an elementary course in the principles of economics) would see that the outcome of any promotion of free competition must lead to the situation in which, without further changes in the natural constraints, everyone ends up making no profits beyond the costs of production. With this realization, it is easy to see why some critics of neoclassical theory might argue that the real incentive for any entrepreneurs is to restrict competition or eliminate their competitors so as to create so-called monopoly profits. Although they are correct when discussing a realistic world with governmental regulations and patents, this criticism completely misses the point of Adam Smith's unregulated world.

What Smith's world provides is an incentive for entrepreneurs to alter their technological constraints [see Schumpeter 1942/50]. For example, if we are all in a state of long-run equilibrium – in which, every supply price just covers the corresponding production costs – one way to get ahead is to improve one's technology of production in order to reduce the per-unit costs and thereby create short-run profits. The profits will be only short-run gains because in the usual view of Adam Smith's world, where there would be no patents, no marketing boards, etc., other producers will attempt to duplicate the cost-reducing technologies, and in this way everyone (i.e., each consumer) benefits from the original entrepreneur's 'greediness' – so long as free competition prevails. In this way 'virtue' is unintentionally the outcome of greed or 'selfishness' in Adam Smith's world.

Freedom vs. necessity

Adam Smith's world is concerned with the sufficiency of free competition when combined with rational decision-making for the achievement of a social optimum. It should be pointed out that some economic theorists have also been concerned with its necessity. Hayek [1937/48; 1945/48] – in a weak neoclassical but strong ideological moment – specifically wished to show that other world-views (e.g., 'collectivism') were not sufficient. His argument was that *exogenous* social institutions were informationally inefficient. Specifically, in Adam Smith's world the individual only needs to know his or her own situation (tastes, prices, income, and the location of the market). In the contrasting liberal-socialist world made up of individual decision-makers who are being constrained by an exogenously given bureau of social planners, the central authority would have to know the same information *but for all individuals*!

The primary message of Hayek's view is that if one realizes that all decisions require information and one assumes that the objective of every socialist economy is the achievement of a social optimum, then, if one adopts both psychologistic individualism and Hayek's view that only individuals know what is best for them, the determination of the social optimum must depend on the psychological states of all individuals. Hayek asserts that there is no way a 'socialist central planner' could ever be able to calculate the social optimum in order to implement policies to reach it. What he presumes is that in a psychologistic-individualist world there are private facts that affect each individual's view of what is best for him or her. Such private facts are by definition beyond the acquisition of any central planner, yet they are necessary for the calculation of the social optimum. Thus, with Hayek's view, we can see that, *given psychologism*, Adam Smith's world is a necessity, as all other world-views would give a role to an exogenous institution which would necessarily have insufficient knowledge to formulate adequate policies.

One has to admit that Adam Smith's view is magnificent, almost magical. But there is no magic here, only simple arithmetic (or simple analytical geometry in the case of Figure 7.3). What is magnificent is the apparent total reliance on just individual decision-making to motivate his world. No social institution (other than property rights) would seem to be necessary. The final outcome is the result only of the actions of individuals. But there may seem to be a paradox here. The key element to yielding the optimum (beyond maximization) is the *inability* of one individual firm or consumer to affect the going price; that is, competition must be perfect. Nevertheless, in the real world, individuals are not always powerless, since they are allowed to make their personal contribution to supply or demand. The end result is both a social optimum and an equilibrium. Apparently, all this can exist without any recourse to either non-natural or non-individualist variables or constraints. The only assumption in this neoclassical vision of Adam Smith's world is that every individual is an independent (i.e., self-interested) 'rational' decision-maker. If one could show that the currently existing world is possibly an instance of an Adam Smith world in long-run equilibrium, then one would have proven the logical feasibility of a psychologistic-individualist research program. But, what about the assumption that all decision-makers are price-takers? And how do we know when the world is in long-run equilibrium?

Long-run equilibria and psychologism

Theorists either explain why something exists or they explain it away [Agassi 1977; cf. Solow 1979]. For those theorists bound by psychologistic individualism, disequilibria must be explained away. In the absence of constraints, neoclassical theory would argue that an equilibrium must exist, since without constraints universal maximization is entailed. If there is a disequilibrium then it follows that there must be an operative constraint somewhere. Thus, for psychologistic individualism, it must be shown that what appears to be a disequilibrium is really a chosen event or the consequence of a natural constraint. This is because, of course, the only allowable exogenous (i.e., non-chosen) variables are natural constraints and psychological states.

Imperfect competition equilibrium vs. ideal-type methodology

The concept of equilibrium is a contingent proposition. There is a disequilibrium only if there are unexploited gains that *can* be obtained. Is it always a question of assessing the (transaction) cost of obtaining the gains? Maybe. But, possibly more important, how do we measure the potential gains? Too often the alleged gains are an illusion caused by comparing the existing state with an ideal state. As Ronald Coase put it,

> very little analysis is required to show that an ideal world is better than a state of laissez faire [viz., where there are no barriers to trade or competition] unless the definitions of a state of laissez faire and an ideal world happen to be the same. But the whole discussion is largely irrelevant for questions of economic policy since whatever we may have in mind as our ideal world, it is clear that we have not yet discovered how to get to it from where we are... [1960, p. 43]

The question here is whether the state of *laissez-faire* can be one in which there is imperfect competition. The approach offered by Coase allows us to argue that the ideal world is the one with perfect competition – that is, the one where the achievement of private goals indirectly assures the achievement of social goals. However, it may cost us too much to have that much competition. Imperfect competition may be the realistic *laissez-faire* optimum.

If this approach is taken in order to explain away the disequilibria (relative to the ideal world), then we would need to show that the resulting *laissez-faire* equilibrium (i.e., the imperfectly competitive equilibrium) is the result only of individuals' pursuits of their private interests. The question for us then is: how can an imperfectly competitive equilibrium be seen as a social optimum? To be an equilibrium, there should not be any possibility of an improvement, that is, there should not be any incentive. This is assured only if everyone is maximizing with respect to every variable of choice. This brings up the old problem of increasing returns [see Sraffa 1926]. Specifically, why would a firm facing increasing returns and thus facing the possibility of lowering its average cost be producing at a level of output less than the socially desirable efficient output?

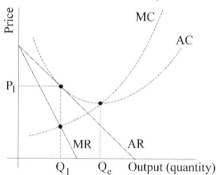

Figure 7.4. Imperfect competitor in long-run equilibrium

To *see* how the possibility of 'increasing returns' arises and thus why a firm might be maximizing profit even though it could lower its average cost, consider Figure 7.4. This figure is the elementary textbook's diagram of a firm in a state of imperfectly competitive (long-run) equilibrium. It is just a variant of Figure 7.3 as it retains the same cost curves. It differs simply because now we need to consider what it would look like if the firm is no longer a price taker. That is, here if the firm were to vary the quantity of its output (which it supplies to the market), it is now assumed to have an effect on the price it faces. For example, if it wishes to increase its output, it will have to lower its price in order to generate sufficient demand. This inverse relationship between the level of output and the price is represented by the downward-sloping average revenue curve (AR). Since the average revenue falls with increasing output, the marginal revenue must be less than the average and this is also illustrated with the marginal revenue curve (MR). (It is a straight line only because I drew a straight-line average revenue curve.)

Figure 7.4 clearly shows the firm's profit maximizing output (i.e., where marginal cost equals marginal revenue) to be at a level (Q_1). Note that at Q_1, the average cost curve is negatively sloped (i.e., to the left of the bottom of the U-shaped average cost curve). Reducing average cost means reducing the average use of resource inputs per unit of output – that is, reducing the ratio of inputs to outputs. If that ratio can be reduced, then its inverse – the returns for each unit of input – can be increased. This possibility is what was called a situation of increasing returns and this possibility presents a social problem. From a society's viewpoint, the possibility of reducing costs would surely benefit everyone in society. So, from the perspective of society, increasing returns imply a social disequilibrium, since the existing potential cost reduction is an unexploited incentive. Increasing returns, then, imply that we have not yet reached a social optimum. But here is the problem. Society may not have reached an optimum (in terms of the efficiency of the use of its resources), but the individual firm sees no incentive to change its use of its resources. That is, each firm can be in a state of equilibrium (profits are both zero and maximum), yet the imperfectly competitive *equilibrium* appears necessarily to entail increasing returns (since it is to the left of Q_e).

Although this is an elementary point of price theory, it must be treated with care. Let us then look again at imperfect competition from the perspective of the individual decision-maker who is supposed to pursue profit maximization. If a firm is an imperfect competitor, then by definition it cannot be assumed that the output chosen has no effect on its price. Whenever the price varies with the level of output, marginal revenue is not equal to the price. Furthermore, since it is always assumed that the demand curves are downward sloping, marginal revenue is always less than average revenue. Now, keeping this in mind, recognize again that profit maximization implies the equality of marginal revenue with marginal cost. If we also recognize that a competitive equilibrium painted in any color implies the absence of excess profits (over the cost of producing the chosen level of output) – and hence, the absence of incentives for new firms to enter the competition – then the price must equal average cost. Putting all these implications together means that profit maximization with competitively imposed long-run zero profits does not entail the lowest possible average cost – as we can clearly see in Figure 7.4. In particular, since marginal revenue is below the price and since profit maximization means that marginal revenue must equal marginal cost, then necessarily marginal cost is below average cost – which means that average cost must be falling (i.e., there are increasing returns) *whenever there is an imperfectly competitive equilibrium*. Thus, whenever there is an imperfectly competitive equilibrium, there appears to be a necessary conflict between the individual decision-maker's optimum (profit maximization) and what might be society's optimum (minimizing average cost).

How can the imperfectly competitive equilibrium ever represent a social optimum as Coase seems to suggest? If the individual firms' average cost could be reduced, society would benefit, since it seems that the available resources could be made to produce more output for the same input. Thus, the possibility of social benefits (reduced average cost) coexists with the absence of any incentive for the producer to change its behavior, since profits are both maximum and zero. But, on the other hand, if every producer is maximizing profits and profits are zero (and, remember, the demand curve reflects the simultaneous utility maximization by all individuals), how can there be any social disequilibrium? The common view of an imperfectly competitive equilibrium as a social disequilibrium may be only an illusion created by comparing it to an unrealistic ideal world that nobody really wants. If any imperfectly competitive equilibrium is a *laissez-faire* equilibrium (i.e., the consequence of everyone's free pursuit of profit or utility maximization), then there is no social or individual disequilibrium (unexploited gains) in the real world.

Imperfect competition vs. psychologistic individualism vs. New Institutional Economics

Let us consider the implications for possible theories of the imperfectly competitive firm – namely, of the firm which either is not a price-taker or has a sufficiently large share of the market such that its output decisions do affect the price. The general question is: in the long run, when ultimately the firm's profits are driven down to zero by competition but are still maximized for its nonnegligible share of the market, can the firm really be considered to be in equilibrium? Following the works of Joan Robinson [1933] and Edward Chamberlin [1934], most textbook theories say yes. But, unlike the perfectly competitive world where anything goes, the imperfectly competitive world seems to be based on an arbitrary institutional assumption that restricts competition. That is, the imperfect nature of the market situation has been exogenously given. Unless the degree of non-perfect competition is explained, it may be an unacceptable given in a neoclassical explanation. Does this mean that one cannot complete a psychologistic-individualist program if one attempts to develop a theory of an imperfect competitor in equilibrium? Or does this merely mean that an imperfectly competitive equilibrium is an illusion and thus that the imperfectly competitive firm is doomed to perpetual disequilibrium? Can an imperfectly competitive firm ever be in equilibrium and thus be explainable?

In order to explain how there can ever be an imperfectly competitive equilibrium, we only need to explain why the possibility of reducing average cost internally would be ignored. The explanation is that if average cost and average revenue are equal and if average revenue will fall faster (rise more slowly) than average cost (as in Figure 7.4), then there would be no incentive to reduce cost further. What does this explanation say about the 'apparent' increasing returns?

It says that they never really existed or, more generally, that the assessment of costs and benefits is misleading.

This raises an interesting methodological question. How do we know there are increasing returns? What is the source of the increasing returns? So as to avoid repeating all of the volumes of articles devoted to the puzzle presented by the concept of increasing returns, let me bluntly state the analytical case concerning the existence of increasing returns for a given production function, say f, where f is defined as

$$\text{Output} = f\,(\text{labor, capital}).$$

If we were to double both factors and the result is that the output more than doubles, then we would have a case of 'increasing returns'. But how is it possible for there to be increasing returns? If the doubling process has merely meant building an identical plant next door, what is the source of the increase in output beyond the doubled level of the original plant? Either the source is external or the production function has been misspecified, since there must be some third factor which has been more than doubled to account for the increased output. These two possibilities are really the same thing. Some constraint or input was not stated in the original production function. It should have been,

$$\text{Output} = f\,(\text{labor, capital, } X)$$

where X is the missing factor. As Harvey Leibenstein [1979] might have said, there could only have been the possibility of increasing returns because one of the factors (namely, X) was previously being used inefficiently; that is, the optimum quantity of X was not chosen. Stated another way, there could be the possibility of increasing returns only because the original plant was not maximizing profits with respect to *all* inputs.

Any attempt to explain the existence of increasing returns only brings into question the true nature of the production function [Samuelson 1947/65, p. 84]. If everything is variable, then exact duplication is possible; hence in this case no production functions can exhibit increasing returns. If increasing returns are possible, then there must be something constraining the variability of one or more of the factors so as to create the possibility of improving efficiency. But if there is something constraining the factors, then there is something which should have been included in the specification of the production function, that is, a missing factor. If it is not included, then we have the methodological problem prescribed by psychologistic individualism. Any such non-natural, non-individualist constraint must be explained away.

Explaining disequilibria away

Attempts to explain imperfectly competitive firms raise the key dilemma facing neoclassical theorists. On the one hand, if one is to fulfill the commitment to the psychologistic-individualist program, then, of course, there cannot be any unexplained non-natural, non-individualist constraints. Stated another way, there cannot be any disequilibria, since a disequilibrium is only possible because something is constraining the attainment of an equilibrium by constraining universal maximization. On the other hand, if imperfect competition exists, then there is something which is constraining or limiting competition, and thus something is left unexplained. Even worse, some may say that an imperfectly competitive equilibrium is still a disequilibrium in terms of the ideal world of perfect competition. Only in a perfectly competitive (long-run) equilibrium is it possible to fulfill all of the requirements of a psychologistic-individualist research program.

The key question here is the following. If we accept that a realistic concept of the existence of disequilibrium implies the existence of an endogenous constraint, do we also have to accept the reverse, namely, that the existence of an endogenous constraint implies the existence of a disequilibrium? If one considers the reverse, then the way is open to explaining away disequilibria. Of course, one can simply deny the existence of permanent (long-run) endogenous constraints. And if disequilibria can be explained away by any means then psychologistic individualism will be a feasible research program.

One obvious way disequilibria are explained away is to show that all non-natural constraints are matters of choice. Oliver Williamson's explanation of organizations such as prototypical corporations seems implicitly to advocate this [Williamson 1981]. Thus what appears to some to be a disequilibrium is really an equilibrium, as there are no real possibilities of improvement [Coase 1960]; if there were, they would have been pursued. This way may not appeal to everyone, since this is really an indirect argument that in some way assumes what it is supposedly proving. There is another way which, while more mysterious, is at least direct. It argues that the formal transaction prices are not reflected in the actual prices. The actual price is the sum of the formal price and the average cost borne by the *buyer*. For example, many people will wait in a queue to save money at a price-reduction sale – but the price would appear to be lower only if the buyer's time is relatively costless (i.e., there are little or no opportunity costs). Those who do not wish to wait may go elsewhere (perhaps because they have more profitable things to do with their time) and pay a higher price [see DeVany 1976].

This 'invisible-price' approach can go a long way toward explaining why some may see increasing returns when there really are none. The actual average cost curve *may* be minimum at the output level corresponding to the textbook's imperfectly competitive long-run equilibrium. The actual demand curve *may* be perfectly elastic (i.e., horizontal), since all reductions in prices are compensated by offsetting increases in transactions costs. If this is the case, then the formal imperfectly competitive long-run equilibrium is actually a perfectly competitive equilibrium! But, even more important is the consequence that the price any individual pays is no longer a social institution. Every individual's actual price is specific to that individual's psychological state concerning willingness to wait (but perhaps not if it is only a matter of there being opportunities to gain profit or utility by using one's time otherwise). In any case, this invisible-price approach gives new meaning to Hayek's view of the impossibility of a successful social planner.

Psychologism in the short run

Although in the long run *we* may all be dead, in any long-run equilibrium psychologism and Inductivism live. It is easy to see that psychologism is not jeopardized if we can adopt a view of the world where everything is in long-run equilibrium. Does this mean that if one wishes to build more realistic short-run models, one must abandon the psychologistic-individualist research program in favor of a more complicated disequilibrium approach?

The consensus among most neoclassical theorists until recently gave a negative answer to this last question. That is, there seemed to be agreement that a realistic short-run neoclassical theory must involve disequilibria that cannot be explained away, yet the requirement of psychologistic individualism must be retained. But, methodologically, this is self-contradictory – disequilibria imply the existence of non-natural and non-individualist givens, while psychologistic individualism implies only individualist or natural givens. The problem facing neoclassical theorists is to find a way either to explain the existence of disequilibria while allowing that individuals are seen to be free to follow only their self-interest or to explain disequilibria away. And so,

> theorists solve the problem by depending primarily on expectational errors as the prime source of divergences from full equilibrium. Economic agents optimize subject to what they perceive to be their circumstances... Agents have to form expectations about ... unknown or imperfectly known circumstances. One necessary part of the definition of equilibrium in this kind of world is that those expectations be confirmed, at least in some reasonable statistical sense. The way is now open to explain major departures from equilibrium as mainly the result of unusually large and/or unusually prolonged expectational errors. [Solow 1979, p. 341]

In the next chapter this 'expectational errors' approach to short-run disequilibria as well as the more general issue of imperfect knowledge assumptions will be examined. It will be argued that as a solution to the methodological problem of disequilibria it is an illusion, as it is based on the acceptance of Inductivism.

8 Imperfect Knowledge vs. Imperfect Behavior

> it is important to realize that the models with which we work are simplified representations of more complicated real-world problems... The world is rife with imperfections that we ignore when constructing models, and an equilibrium concept implicitly chooses among these imperfections to explain out-of-equilibrium behavior.
>
> Assumptions about closest worlds are typically built into equilibrium concepts in the form of trembles. The original game is replaced by a new game that matches the original with high probability, but that with some small probability is actually a different game.
>
> Larry Samuelson [1997, p. 14]

> Admitting that a rational player can make mistakes means drawing a distinction between deciding and acting, and a theory that wants to reconcile rationality and mistakes is committed to treating mistakes as entirely random and uncorrelated.
>
> Cristina Bicchieri [1993, p. 135]

While dealing with disequilibria remains a puzzle for most neoclassical economic theorists, fully dealing with the true nature of equilibria seems to be more a mystery. The main question that must be dealt with is how does each and every individual decision-maker acquire or learn the knowledge necessary for the achievement of a long-run (general) market equilibrium? The mystery arises because theorists have for many decades chosen to treat any insufficiency or inadequacy as a matter of 'uncertainty' which in turn is ill defined. Part of the mystery starts when theorists, following Inductivism, confuse information with knowledge. Another part follows from the acceptance of the popular notion that 'uncertainty' must always be a matter of probabilities.

The mystery is avoided when theorists limit their focus to the static nature of a long-run or general equilibrium – however, this begs too many questions. The attainment of a long-run equilibrium, for example, presumes that past investments were exactly correct. But, an investment must be based on a plan which in turn must be based on expectations as to the future state of the economy. How do the investors form such guaranteed successful plans? Specifically, how do they form expectations which allow for successful plans? When dealing with these questions, too often the theorists are inconsistent and when an inconsistency is recognized they beg even more questions.

The puzzles about how to deal with disequilibria are not new. Recall Solow's comment, quoted at the end of Chapter 7, that disequilibria have been explained away by referring to 'expectational errors'. Specifically, he noted that optimization requires the formation of expectations about 'prices that rule in the future, as well as other facts about the future that cannot now be known'. If an individual or firm is ever going to be successful in maximizing utility or profit – as is necessary for the establishment of an equilibrium – the expectations must be correct. Expectational errors may lead to a failure to maximize and thus to a disequilibrium rather than an equilibrium.

While disequilibria might be explained or explained away by noting the difficulties in forming correct expectations, Larry Samuelson in the above quotation recognizes that errors could be introduced in the implementation of the plan. In game theory these are identified as the results of a 'trembling hand'. In this case, your knowledge could be perfect, it just that your hand slipped. Obviously, any alleged disequilibrium could be the result of either type of error – maybe a combination of both.

The primary evidence of disequilibrium is the actual imperfect behavior and resulting errors that might be observed (leading possibly to changing behavior). If so, a fundamental methodological problem remains for neoclassical theorists. Specifically, neoclassical theorists wish to assume 'rational' decision-makers do not in equilibrium make errors and thus the ultimate explanation for the errors in this case will have to be imperfect knowledge. After all, even trembling hands could be the result of knowledge failure or incomplete learning in the sense that had implementation been fully contemplated, any trembling hand would have been foreseen and measures taken to avoid the errors. In this chapter I will be concerned more with the errors that result from alleged imperfect knowledge including 'expectational errors' – in particular, those errors resulting from false knowledge – rather than with imperfect behavior such as trembles.

In the following, I will not be saying that it is impossible to deal with the knowledge and learning necessary for neoclassical decision-making. Instead, I will be arguing in this and later chapters that many of the inconsistencies and inadequacies can be avoided by giving up Inductivism and Conventionalism and instead adopt a more realistic notion of knowledge and learning.

Does dealing with inadequate knowledge always require the use of probabilities?

> By 'uncertain' knowledge … I do not mean only probable. The game of roulette is not subject, in this sense, to uncertainty; nor is the prospect of a Victory bond being drawn. Or, again, the expectation of life is only slightly uncertain. Even the weather is only moderately uncertain. The sense in which I am using the term is that in which the prospect of a European war is uncertain, or the price of copper and the rate of interest twenty years hence, or the obsolescence of a new invention, or the position of private wealth-owners in the social system in 1970. About these matters there is no scientific basis on which to form any calculable probability whatever. We simply do not know. Nevertheless, the necessity for action and for decision compels us as practical men to do our best to overlook this awkward fact and to behave exactly as we should if we had behind us a good Benthamite calculation of a series of

prospective advantages and disadvantages, each multiplied by its appropriate probability, waiting to be summed.

John Maynard Keynes [1937, pp. 213–14]

The past ... has this virtue that we can have knowledge of it, knowledge of fact. The knowledge that we have, or can have, of the past is different in kind from what we can know of the future; for the latter, at best, is no more than a knowledge of probabilities.

John R. Hicks [1976, p. 135]

In Chapter 4, I briefly discussed the history that began with Frank Ramsey [1926/31] of employing probabilities to deal with situations where the individual is unable to assess the truth status of a statement or theory. The basic notion was that theorists chose first to substitute hypothetical or observed choices between gambles with known probabilities and then substitute those probabilities for measures of preferences between the options involved in the gambles. This, of course, was a very clever maneuver. But the problem with many clever tricks is that economic theorists too often use them in contexts beyond what is plausible or realistic – that is, by optimistically presuming their technical tricks are more general than is warranted. Much of this is involved when dealing with the question of uncertainty about the truth status of theories and expectations. The question I want to address here is whether probabilities are *always* relevant for questions of uncertainty.

Risk vs. uncertainty

Frank Knight [1921] is usually credited for promoting a distinction between 'risk' and 'uncertainty'. Risk is where probabilities are almost by definition relevant and uncertainty is where probabilities may have at best a limited relevance [see Runde 1998]. The distinction that Knight makes says that there are situations involving objective (i.e., observable) probabilities where in advance one does know the probabilities. There are two cases where probabilities may be known: The extreme case, for example, is one where we might randomly draw a playing card from a deck. In this case we do not know what the next draw will yield but, knowing what has been drawn so far, the probability of any particular card being drawn next can be calculated by means of combinatorial mathematics. The less extreme case depends on the prior observation of the frequency distribution. In this case, one knows the attributes of a statistical distribution such as the average age or height of a population, its range and standard deviations, etc. Thus, in both cases, one knows the *risk* of placing a particular bet on a particular outcome because one knows the nature of the probabilities (exactly in the former case and by inductive inference in the latter case if the whole population has not been observed). The term '*uncertainty*' is reserved for those situations where one does not know the nature of the probabilities and thus cannot calculate the risk.

John Maynard Keynes [1937] makes a similar observation but goes a step further to extend 'uncertainty' to situations where the notion of probability is irrelevant. Keynes' notion leads to questions that arise when we are talking about a singular or unique event.

The distinction I wish to make here along these lines is between a one-time event (such as whether or not some particular economist wins the Nobel prize this year) and one of many in a sequence (such as getting 'tails' when repeatedly flipping a coin). If one insists on assigning a probability to an event, unique events must have a probability of either one or zero – thus the notion of some sort of continuum over which there is a statistical distribution is irrelevant and perhaps misleading. Nevertheless, many economic theorists think probabilities other than zero or one are applicable to unique events. This is where Ramsey's trick comes into play and has led economic theorists to presume that individuals facing a decision that depends on a possible future singular event will necessarily choose to assign a probability to the singular event. It must be recognized that this presumption is a decision made by the theorist – and in particular, it is a presumption that might be false. That is, it is not necessarily true that everyone facing such a decision assigns a probability to a possible, unique event. And if they do not, the probability approach to uncertainty may be subjected to all of the recognized criticism of Instrumentalism.

Paul Davidson on the types of ignorance and uncertainty

Interestingly, critics of the overuse of probabilities in economics often quote Keynes as I have above but they often stop the quotation at 'We simply do not know'. But in what they leave out Keynes is not suggesting that probabilities must be employed. He is only saying that decisions still must be made. In the paragraphs that follow the quoted paragraph, Keynes indicates three alternative ways that decisions are made in the real world of uncertainties but none of them involve probabilities.

Paul Davidson [1991] offers a slightly different perspective by looking at the ways the decision-makers conceive of the uncertainties being faced. In one case, the decision-makers think uncertainties are a matter of objective probabilities in the same way traditional econometrics treats probabilities. The Rational Expectations literature of the 1970s was predicated on the assumption that all decision-makers in effect acquire needed knowledge using econometrics and thus knowledge is never certain but a matter of such objective probabilities – perhaps in the manner suggested by Ramsey. In a second case, the decision-makers think they need to subjectively assign probabilities to possible future events when making their decisions. Sometimes both objective and subjective probabilities are involved but there is no reason for the subjective probabilities assigned to be coinciding with any possible objective probabilities. In both of these cases of uncertainty, uncertainty is a matter of degrees and the probabilities are a measure of these degrees. Davidson says that, according to what Keynes was saying in 1937, 'true uncertainties' are not matter of degrees.

Keynes criticized econometrics in his review [1939] of the 1969 Nobel laureate Jan Tinbergen's demonstration of econometric methodology. Econometric methodology involves characterizing an economy with an explicit model – that is, with one or more equations with multiple coefficients – and then utilizes observable data to calculate what the model's coefficients would have to be for the model to be a sufficiently accurate representation of the observed data. In macroeconomic models, usually the data is historical and thus it is implicitly presumed that the coefficients represent statistical averages. To use such a model to represent one's knowledge of an economy in the process of forming an expectation of future observations requires a presumption that the past observations were, in effect, generated by what Davidson calls an 'ergodic' stochastic process. By this he means, 'averages calculated from past observations cannot be persistently different from the time average of future outcomes' [1991, p. 132]. Without such a presumption, one cannot possibly form a 'rational' expectation about future outcomes. But how could one ever know that the presumed stochastic data-producing process is ergodic independently from the model itself? It is just this type of knowledge that Keynes says that the decision-maker cannot have and thus must resort to other means of making decisions when the rationality of the decision depends on knowing (or on forming an expectation of) the future even as matter of degree.

Knowledge and equilibrium

Critics of neoclassical economics are fond of saying that neoclassical theory must be false simply because any long-run, general equilibrium model would have to require perfect knowledge. And given such a presumption of a necessarily perfect knowledge, most often this criticism itself is based on the presumption that all knowledge must be acquired by means of induction. That is, if perfect knowledge is required, the critics claim that it must be impossible since perfect knowledge would require a solution to the Problem of Induction.

It was noted in Chapter 3 that one of the necessary conditions for (general) market equilibrium is that all demanders and suppliers are maximizing, which implies also that all potential gains from trade are being exploited. It follows then that equilibrium of all markets entails the successful acquisition of adequate knowledge for the purposes of maximization (or that decision-makers acquired enough information to think they are maximizing – as I will briefly discuss later in this chapter and more in Chapter 17).

Conventionalism and the recognition of knowledge and learning in neoclassical theory

Now just what constitutes 'adequate knowledge for the purposes of maximization'? Decades ago Hayek argued that since the individual's acquisition of the (true) knowledge of his or her circumstances (viz., the givens) is essential for any (stable) equilibrium, in order to explain how the economy changes over time we must be able to explain how individuals acquire their knowledge [1937/48, p. 47]. Hayek's concern was that there was no (inductive) way to show how any individual could ever acquire true knowledge; and he pessimistically confessed his inability to offer an explanation for even one individual's knowledge acquisition process [pp. 47-8]. Explicitly, he admitted that he could not specify 'assertions about causal connections, about how experience creates knowledge' [p. 47]; implicitly, he was merely admitting the impossibility of an inductive proof.

Today, neoclassical theorists are more optimistic. Their optimism is based on the acceptance of Conventionalism (and an ignorance of such things as the paradox of confirmation which was discussed in Chapter 1). Mainstream theorists today do not require that any individual decision-maker have absolutely true knowledge because it would readily be admitted that inductive proofs have always been impossible. Instead, as we have seen, it would be argued that nobody's knowledge is ever absolutely true but only 'true' according to some degree of probability. Thus, a more moderate view of knowledge would be asserted. Today many theorists would argue that absolutely true knowledge has a probability of 1.00 and that a realistic view of knowledge would instead say the actual knowledge of any individual or group of individuals has a probability of less than 1.00. Of course, the closer the probability is to 1.00 the 'better' is the knowledge [Malinvaud 1966]. Given this Conventionalist view of knowledge, it could be argued that learning takes place whenever the probability of one's knowledge is increased – for example, whenever the degree of confirmation has increased.

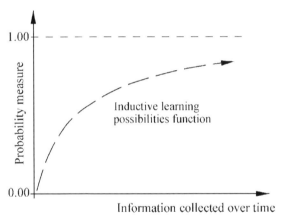

Figure 8.1   Sophisticated, inductivist learning

Learning and probabilities

Let us illustrate this view of learning and knowledge with a simple diagram, Figure 8.1, in which the curve indicates that the inferred probability of one's knowledge increases as information is collected. This curve will be called the 'inductive learning possibilities function'. It is a very short further step to argue that the probability of the truth of one's knowledge is like utility in a consumer's utility function and that learning is only a matter of increasing probability and knowledge is established when the probability is maximized. It is precisely this step that has been taken in the so-called Bayesian theory of learning [e.g., Harsanyi 1967-68; Hey 1981, chap. 6] as well as in the formation of the concept of rational expectations. As an explanatory theory, the Bayesian theory explicitly says that individuals facing uncertainty (or possessing 'imperfect' knowledge) assign subjective probabilities to a future event (or just to current imperfect knowledge) and then adjust or 'update' this subjective probability (i.e., the so-called 'prior') in accordance with Bayes's theorem in the process of collecting relevant information. Bayesian decision theory leads to the view that the individual makes a choice among options perceived to be available by maximizing his or her expected utility that has been calculated using probabilities in accordance with Bayes's theorem. In this manner, it is all too easy to explain away imperfect behavior as being the result of necessarily imperfect knowledge since all knowledge is about the probabilities of the truth of certain propositions or the likelihood of certain events.

The Bayesian 'solution' to the Problem of Induction?

Proponents of so-called Bayesian learning actually claim that using Bayes's theorem solves the Problem of Induction. Bayes's theorem is an equation that says the probability of a general event *B* given the particular event *A* equals the probability of event *A* given the event *B* multiplied by the probability of *B* and divided by the probability of event *A*. What proponents claim that Bayes's theorem says is merely that one can calculate the probability of a general event given the particular event from the probability of particular event given the general event in this manner. And going further, since this involves going from particulars to generals, this is claimed to be a solution to the Problem of Induction [e.g., Lindley 1987, p. 207]. But is it?

If it were necessarily true that all uncertainty must be expressed as a probability and if one denies the possibility of the probability of the truth status of one's knowledge being 1.00, then one could accept the conditional probability provided by Bayes's theorem as the best we can do. But to do so is at best merely to accept a sophisticated version of Conventionalism which substitutes probabilities for truth status. At worst, it is to accept a vacuous, uninformative theory of learning [see Albert 2001]. As I will explain in Chapter 12, one would have to be willing to give up the benefits of ordinary logic whenever one accepts the probability substitute for the proven truth status that induction was supposed to provide.

The Conventionalist theory of learning

The basis of virtually every neoclassical model that involves the recognition of limited or 'imperfect' knowledge is a Conventionalist theory of knowledge and learning – a theory which (as explained in Chapter 1) is merely a short-run version of the old Inductivist theory of knowledge and learning. Note also that when I say every neoclassical model I am including in this claim all models of rational expectations and efficient markets, as well as the game-theorist's use of the notion of imperfect information and uncertainty.

Let me quickly review the Inductivist theory of knowledge and learning. Briefly stated, this old theory said that individuals learn by collecting *particular* (objectively provable) facts and when they have enough of them they are able to induce (i.e., inductively prove) the true *general* theory which would explain the phenomena encompassed by those facts. Inductivism, as I have said, presumes that such an inductive process is indeed possible. For any specific case the only question at issue is whether enough facts have been collected, or possibly whether the quality of those facts is adequate, or both.

Now recall, the Conventionalist theory of learning recognizes that there really is no way to collect enough facts to prove absolutely the truth of any explanation. Instead, the best we can do is to maximize the quantity of facts collected or improve their quality (which sometimes turns out to be the same thing as collecting more facts). One learns either by improving the empirical support for one's theory or by finding a 'better' theory. Switching to another theory would be considered a case of long-run learning, and improving the support of one's present theory would be considered short-run learning.

The important point to be emphasized here is that the sophisticated Conventionalist theory of learning is merely a sophisticated version of the Inductivist theory. The difference is only that absolute proofs (i.e., which many Conventionalist believers will say requires that the probability equals 1.00) are no longer required. Learning, in a sense, has been quantified. Either one learns directly by collecting *more* information (i.e., information about additional variables deemed to be relevant), or one learns indirectly by collecting *more* secondary facts to improve the estimates contained in the present set of information.

The economics of information vs. the Rational Expectations Hypothesis

> One should hardly have to tell academicians that information is a valuable resource: knowledge *is* power. And yet it occupies a slum dwelling in the town of economics. Mostly it is ignored: the best technology is assumed to be known; the relationship of commodities to consumer preferences is a datum. And one of the information-producing industries, advertising, is treated with a hostility that economists normally reserve for tariffs or monopolists.
>
> There are a great many problems in economics for which this neglect of ignorance is no doubt permissible or even desirable. But there are some for which this is not true ...
>
> George Stigler [1961, p. 213]

> expectations, since they are informed predictions of future events, are essentially the same as the predictions of the relevant economic theory...
>
> The [rational expectations] hypothesis ... [is] that expectations of firms ... tend to be distributed, for the same information set, about the prediction of the theory.
>
> John Muth [1961, p. 316]

Once one adopts the notion that knowledge depends on the quantity of information available – such as is presumed in the case of naïve Inductivism or the sophisticated Conventionalist Bayesian theory of learning – the door is open for an economic analysis of knowledge and information. Such analysis can raise issues such as the efficiency of an information processing methodology [Hirshleifer and Riley 1979] or the optimality of one's choice of a theory or model given the consideration that collecting information (e.g., to improve one's probability estimates) is a costly process. How one proceeds through this door depends on one's purpose. Is it to explain away the need or the possibility of the 'perfect knowledge' that critics point to, or is it to just assert one's advocacy of Conventionalist methodology? The 1982 Nobel prize-winner George Stigler [1961] chose to explain away the plausibility of perfect knowledge by explaining why perfect knowledge would be too expensive and thus not economically optimal; promoters of the Rational Expectations Hypothesis chose instead to merely advocate a form of sophisticated Conventionalism.

Figure 8.2. Optimum search and dispersion

Stigler's 'The economics of information' revealed

In general, if one follows Stigler's methodology, one would begin with the identification of a quantitative aspect of the matter at hand, and in particular, an aspect that can thus be seen to be a matter of choice. Next one identifies a cost constraint such that the marginal cost of a unit increase in the object of choice can be compared with that unit's marginal benefit. For Stigler, the question at issue was whether or not to obtain an additional unit of costly information. To illustrate, if you are looking for the lowest price for a product, say a specific camera, think of having to put coins in a pay telephone to call stores to determine their price. At some point in a sequence of calls, you note a pattern such that the probability of finding a price that is lower than the lowest so far, and lower by more than the cost of the next phone call, is too low to warrant making the call. In Stigler's version of this methodology, one focuses on the acceptable dispersion of prices as viewed by demanders and suppliers. Figure 8.2 illustrates his view by adapting a standard market demand and supply diagram. On the vertical axis there is the degree of dispersion and on the horizontal axis, there is the quantity of search. Now think of the 'supply' curve (i.e., the positively sloped curve) as representing the buyer's minimum quantity of search chosen as a function of a given degree of dispersion (more dispersion leads to more search). And, the 'demand' curve (i.e., the negatively sloped curve) will represent the seller's maximum acceptable dispersion as a function of a given expected search by buyers (the more search expected, the less dispersion accepted). The intersection identifies the optimum amount of both search and dispersion. For Stigler this explains both why there would never be zero dispersion and thus why certainty will always be too expensive. Of course, anyone who advocates Popper's critical Socratic epistemology will find Stigler's effort to be a very clever example of Conventionalism yet one completely irrelevant for any philosophy of knowledge considerations. But other methodologists might find it a worthy example of applied economics. I will discuss Socratic epistemology later in Chapter 14.

Rational expectations as optimal knowledge

In the 1970s the proponents of the so-called Rational Expectations Hypothesis promoted a similar clever modeling trick. Of course, the term 'rational' is merely a reference to an assumption of expectations being formed in a manner that involves a constrained maximization based on something like the Inductive learning possibilities function illustrated in Figure 8.1. Their point is that expectations are rational if they are inductively based on the 'best' available information set. As Stigler already showed, the expectations will not usually be absolutely true for the simple reason that to make them so, even if it were logically possible, would cost far too much. Those models employing the Rational Expectations Hypothesis assumed merely that every decision-maker has acquired information as Stigler suggested, that is, only to the point that its acquisition is economical. In effect the Rational Expectations Hypothesis was a straightforward application of the maximization hypothesis to knowledge acquisition in a real-world setting where opportunity costs matter – along the lines of Figure 8.3. Some critics of the Rational Expectations Hypothesis characterize its use not as that of constrained maximization but as that of assuming every decision-maker is an expert at econometric analysis of available information (i.e., of observationally available data). But either way, the end result is merely to explain away imperfect knowledge not as a failure of induction but as a successful application of economics analysis to learning by showing that it is 'rational' to be satisfied with imperfect knowledge.

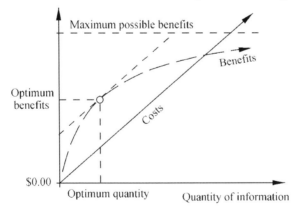

Figure 8.3. The economics of information

While it was once easy for neoclassical economic model builders to simply assume the truth of the Rational Expectations Hypothesis in order to make the mathematics of their models easier to deal with, today, few think it makes sense to assume every individual in an economy is making such calculations in order to decide how much information should be acquired. But, while most now reject this hypothesis, many still adopt the Conventionalist stance that knowledge must necessarily be imperfect. Their reason for rejecting any assumption that decision-makers would have to be expert econometricians may merely be that when confronting the real world with their models, neoclassical economists soon discover that real people do not behave as neatly as their models presume.

Tests of the probability-based explanation of how consumers deal with imperfect knowledge

Could it be that the behavioral theories are false? Or, perhaps people fail to make optimal decisions simply because – for good economic reasons – their knowledge is imperfect and thus their mistakes are understandable? Of course, if their knowledge is imperfect then the results of their decisions will be uncertain. And for all of the Conventionalist reasons I have been discussing, it is presumed that knowledge must be imperfect thus all decisions involve uncertainty. As I first noted at the end of Chapter 4, economic theorists have routinely assumed that whenever a decision-maker faces uncertainty he or she resorts to some sort of probability assessment. The standard approach has long been to assume that, for example, 'rational' consumers thus maximize their 'subjective expected utility' rather than maximize their direct utility.

The presumption of subjective expected utility maximization combined two separate ideas: expected utility based on probability assessment and subjective probability as an expression of the individual consumer's imperfect knowledge that has been arrived at in a Bayesian manner. The conditions that Savage [1954] laid out for subjective expected utility to be used in 'rational' decision-making were substituted for the usual conditions presumed about the form of the direct utility function used in the textbook treatment of the 'rational' consumer with perfect knowledge of his or her utility function as well as the prices faced and the consequences of the decisions made. But how do we know whether consumers facing necessarily imperfect knowledge do in fact make their decisions in a manner consistent with the conditions presumed by the assumption of subjective expected utility maximization? Better yet, is there any evidence that they do behave this way? According to some tests of this assumption, Daniel Kahneman (a 2002 Nobel laureate) and Amos Tversky [1979] concluded that decision-makers do not. More specifically, they claimed that the assumption of subjective expected utility maximization fails to explain observed behavior of real decision-makers in the test situations.

The question is open as to why the maximization assumption fails. Is it that the Savage conditions are not met for some sort of psychological reasons? Or is it simply because real decision-makers would rarely go to the trouble of employing the sophisticated mathematical calculations needed to engage in subjective expected utility maximization? Maybe they are just ignorant of the sophisticated mathematics needed? It may even be the case that, with the exception of habitual gamblers, few people feel the need to see uncertainty as a matter of probabilities and hence the assumptions of subjective expected utility and Bayesian learning are irrelevant mathematical toys.

Consequences of the failure to deal with learning and knowledge in neoclassical theory

> Economists are often reluctant to abandon the perfectly rational optimizing agents that frequent economic models. The trembles upon which an equilibrium refinement is built are often introduced with an appeal to the possibility that players might make mistakes.
>
> Larry Samuelson [1997, p. 14]

Mathematical toys may be appealing for their own sake, but I think they are invoked to deal with the Problem *with* Induction. Had economists long-ago dropped the presumption that all learning must be inductive, such toys might not have been needed. One obvious question that theorists have not faced is how does the consumer know *a priori* his or her entire preference map (or utility function)? When theorists talk about imperfect knowledge they are talking about the consumer's knowledge of the objective situation faced (prices, states of nature, etc.) rather than self-knowledge.

What is not always appreciated by demand theorists is that the consumer's preference map is an object invented by theorists to explain a choice already made by the consumer – and not just any map but one that satisfies certain mathematical conditions (continuity, convexity, non-satiation, etc.) that permit the use of calculus or some other mathematical technique that allows for the determination of a unique maximum. For example, refer back to Figure 3.2 where the choice being explained was point E. Theorists never provide evidence to show that the consumer agrees with the theorist's conjectured map. The only point guaranteed to be in common between the theorist's conjecture and the consumer's choice process is, by design, the chosen point E. How did the consumer decide that point E would maximize utility or satisfaction? There is no way a consumer could 'know' the whole map since the map represents an infinity of points (even along the budget line) and thus to know (based on experience) a whole map would require an impossible solution to the Problem of Induction. However, the consumer could conjecture that his or her map does look like the one invented by the theorist – and then, to make a choice, just assume that the map accurately represents what the consumer would experience should he or she choose to try consuming points other than E. But if so, then the map is a conjecture and thus conceivably false. So, with a conjecture as the basis for making a choice, how does the consumer know he or she is maximizing?

To illustrate the distinction between a consumer's conjectured map and what might be a map that truly represents what the consumer would experience beyond point E, consider Figure 8.4. Here I have both the same point E and the conjectured indifference curve through point E (and the one through point C) as in Figure 3.2 but have now added a second pair of indifference curves (the dotted curves) through points E (and C) and which represents what the consumer would truly experience if points other than E are consumed. The distinction between the conjectural (solid) and the true (dotted) maps allows for the separation of one's knowledge of an exogenous given and the true nature of that given. Here it allows for what may be a biological evolution of preferences (see Arthur Robson [2001]) about which the consumer may be completely ignorant and thus has no reason to know his or her true preferences.

I have drawn the dotted curves such that at point E it appears to satisfy the usual calculus conditions of a (local) maximum but violates the usual condition of (global) convexity. As such, the consumer is not truly maximizing satisfaction at E, but would be at point C. If the consumer were to test his or her assumption concerning the accuracy of the conjectured map, he or she might discover the error but this would depend on how the consumer decides whether he or she is maximizing. If we allow for testing in order to learn the true map, what choice is the consumer theorist explaining? Perhaps the observed choice was one entertained to test whether the conjectured optimum is the true optimum and thus, possibly, it is not the optimum choice as the theorist assumes. (A full discussion of the 'testing consumer' can be found in [Hammes 1985, chap. 8].)

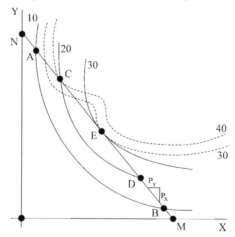

Figure 8.4. The 'ignorant consumer'

Surely what I am arguing here is at least plausible. The failure of theorists to deal with how consumers decide might explain the didactic success of critics such as Simon, Kahneman or Tversky. In the case of Simon, the task is easy since one could never inductively guarantee that their consumption choice is the optimum. And since few real world consumers are experts in statistical hypothesis testing, all sorts of strange choices might be made by consumers that critics might point to as being 'imperfect behavior' or consequences of a 'trembling hand', that is observable choices that are inconsistent with the explanations provided by consumer theorists.

Some theorists will likely want to explain away my characterization of an 'ignorant consumer' by simply invoking the accepted Problem *with* Induction. That is, they will say that, of course, the consumer could never inductively know their true indifference map. But, if so, they need to explain just how the consumer arrives at the conclusion that they are in fact maximizing their satisfaction or utility. Moreover, they need to explain why the observed choice is not really imperfect behavior given their theory of the consumer. Mark Machina [1987] does appear to address this concern but does so only by introducing even more exogenous variables and thus makes the explanation of the decision-maker's behavior less testable. On the one hand, perhaps he is right and this is the best we can do. On the other hand, maybe we should start addressing the question of how the consumer learns his or her preferences since the learning strategy may ultimately be the only possible empirical explanation of decision-making. By saying this, however, I am not saying that one must resort to the study of psychology [see Boland 1992a, chap. 10].

Since few will be satisfied with my just raising this critical issue and then dropping it, I will return to the matter of how one should go about including plausible (non-psychological) learning and knowledge assumptions in our theories of individual behavior in Chapter 16.

9 From Macroeconomics to Evolutionary Game Theory

The most interesting recent developments in macroeconomic theory seem to me describable as the reincorporation of aggregative problems such as inflation and the business cycle within the general framework of 'microeconomic' theory. If these developments succeed, the term 'macroeconomic' will simply disappear from use and the modifier 'micro' will become superfluous... We will be tempted, I am sure, to relieve the discomfort induced by discrepancies between theory and facts by saying that the ill-understood facts are the province of some other, different kind of economic theory. Keynesian 'macroeconomics' was, I think, a surrender (under great duress) to this temptation.

Robert Lucas [1987, pp. 107–8]

there is a persistent refrain in recent macroeconomics that the only acceptable macroeconomic models are those that have adequate *microfoundations*.

Kevin Hoover [2001, p. 59]

It is now 30 years since the [behavioral] revolution which began in growth theory and then swept through microeconomics. The new microeconomics is standard in all graduate programs... Adoption of the new macroeconomics has been slower, but the revolution is coming here as well. If there is any subject in economics which should be behavioral, it is macroeconomics. I have argued ... that reciprocity, fairness, identity, money illusion, loss aversion, herding, and procrastination help explain the significant departures of real-world economies from the competitive, general-equilibrium model. The implication, to my mind, is that macroeconomics *must* be based on such behavioral considerations.
    Keynes' *General Theory* was the greatest contribution to behavioral economics before the present era. Almost everywhere Keynes blamed market failures on psychological propensities (as in consumption) and irrationalities (as in stock market speculation). Immediately after its publication, the economics profession tamed Keynesian economics. They domesticated it as they translated it into the 'smooth' mathematics of classical economics.

George Akerlof [2002, pp. 427–8]

The point of departure for an evolutionary model is the belief that people are not always rational. Rather than springing into life as the result of a perfectly rational reasoning process in which each player, ... solves the game, strategies emerge from a trial-and-error learning process in which players find that some strategies perform better than others. ... In games that are played ... repeatedly, players will adjust their behavior, rejecting choices that appear to give low pay-offs in favor of choices that give high payoffs. The result is a process of experimenting and groping about for something that seems to work, a process in which strategies that bring high payoffs tend to crowd out strategies that do not.

... Evolutionary game theory ... assumes that the behavior driving the process by which agents adjust their strategies may not be perfectly rational, even though it may lead to 'rational' equilibrium behavior. In particular, the adjustment process driving evolutionary game theory sounds much like the process by which competitive markets are typically described as reaching equilibrium, with high-profit behavior being rewarded at the expense of low-profit behavior. The evolutionary approach thus marks not a new departure for economists but rather a return to their roots.

Like traditional game theory evolutionary models ... produce a tremble-based theory of equilibrium, but with a new notion of tremble. ... If we are involved in a game of chess and believe that play is proceeding according to some equilibrium, what should we believe when our opponent makes an unexpected move? Traditional game theory calls for us to believe that the opponent meant to make the equilibrium move... Evolutionary game theory would suggest that we consider the possibility that the player has reasoned differently about the game...

Larry Samuelson [1997, pp. 15–16]

There is virtually no discussion among economists of a need for macrofoundations for microeconomics, except, perhaps implicitly, in the writings of some old and new institutionalists. In contrast, many leading economists of their day [e.g., Phelps, *et al.* 1970; Okun 1980] often considered the demonstration of the existence of microfoundations for macrotheories essential. The reason was the same for both and is easy to find. Although rarely articulated, demonstrating the dependence of all macroeconomics on microeconomic principles was considered essential for the fulfillment of the psychologistic-individualist requirements of neoclassical economics. However – and this is not widely pointed out – this 'necessity' presumed that microeconomic theory, in the form of general equilibrium theory, is a completely successful individualist program. In some quarters, as I explained in the previous chapters, this is still an open question. And so, rather than worry about whether macroeconomics is compatible with psychologistic individualism, I wish to raise a new question. Given that evolutionary game theory does not presume the existence of a general equilibrium but does deal with a whole economy, and given that, as Larry Samuelson suggests, it considers simultaneously processes of experimenting and groping by individual players, can evolutionary game theory be a plausible alternative to macroeconomic theory and thus render macroeconomic theory irrelevant? Before going much further to answer this question, I need to make sure that my use of the widely used terms 'general equilibrium' and 'macroeconomics' are clearly defined and distinguished from the usual understanding of the term 'microeconomics'. Once this is done, I will try to determine whether evolutionary game theory is a worthy competitor or just an alternative microfoundation for macroeconomic theory.

General equilibrium vs. macroeconomic theory

As I noted in Chapters 3 and 7, the concept of a general equilibrium is usually distinguished from that of a partial equilibrium. Specifically, microeconomics is concerned with the individual maximizer or an individual market. The use of the Marshallian partial-equilibrium strategy of *ceteris paribus* implies a temporary methodological disregard for other individuals or other markets. Thus, followers of Marshall's partial-equilibrium methodology focus on one market so as to make clear that they have not yet assumed that all other markets are in equilibrium. However, as was noted before, any one market is in equilibrium only if all of its participants are maximizing [see Hicks 1939/46; Clower 1965] thus only a presumed general equilibrium could be a consistent and complete explanation of prices and equilibrium transactions (buyers meeting suppliers).

Macroeconomics: Keynes' 'departure'

In his 1937 *QJE* article, Keynes attempted to explain to his critics how his *General Theory* was a departure from 'previous theories' – presumably from those utilizing partial equilibrium analysis. He discussed two major points. First was the matter (that I discussed in Chapter 8) concerning uncertain expectations:

> recent writers like their predecessors were still dealing with a system in which the amount of the factors employed was given and the other relevant facts were known more or less for certain. This does not mean that they were dealing with a system in which change was ruled out, or even one in which the disappointment of expectations was ruled out. But at any given time facts and expectations were assumed to be given in a definite and calculable form; and risks, of which, tho admitted, not much notice was taken, were supposed to be capable of an exact actuarial computation. The calculus of probability, tho mention of it was kept in the background, was supposed to be capable of reducing uncertainty to the same calculable status as that of certainty itself...
>
> Actually, however, we have, as a rule, only the vaguest idea of any but the most direct consequences of our acts...
>
> I accuse the classical economic theory of being itself one of these pretty, polite techniques which tries to deal with the present by abstracting from the fact that we know very little about the future. [1937, pp. 212–13, 215]

His second major departure, according to Keynes, was concerned with the absence of an adequate macrotheory, specifically with

> the traditional theory['s] ... apparent conviction that there is no necessity to work out a theory of the demand and supply of output *as a whole*. Will a fluctuation in investment ... have any effect on the demand for output as a whole, and consequently on the scale of output and employment? What answer can the traditional theory [which he noted above 'takes the amount of factors as given'] make to this question? I believe that it makes no answer at all, never having given the matter a single thought; the theory of effective demand, that is the demand for output as a whole, having been entirely neglected for more than a hundred years.
>
> My own answer to this question involves fresh considerations. I say that effective demand is made up of two items – investment-expenditure ... and consumption-expenditure. Now what governs the amount of consumption-expenditure? It depends mainly on the level of income. People's propensity to spend ... is influenced by many factors such as the distribution of income, their normal attitude to the future and ... by the interest rate. But in the main the prevailing psychological law seems to be that when aggregate income increases, consumption-expenditure will also increase but to a somewhat lesser extent... This psychological law was of the utmost importance in the development of my own thought, and it is, I think, absolutely fundamental to the theory of effective demand as set forth in my book. [1937, pp. 219-20]

It is easy to conclude from these fragments of Keynes' own view of his departure that he was not arguing that macroeconomics lacked microfoundations. Rather, he was arguing that the traditional (micro) theory lacked necessary macrofoundations! It should also be noted, for future reference, that Keynes did not disagree with the hidden agenda of neoclassical microeconomics. First, when he referred to the lack of a 'scientific basis' for expectation formation he merely meant the lack of an *inductive proof* – that is, he still accepted the Problem of Induction. Second, to deal with the Problem of Induction in the 1937 article he specifically identified three different Conventionalist bases for the formation of expectations [1937, p. 214]. And third, his acceptance of psychologism is openly admitted in the above quotation.

In effect, by denying the adequacy of the macrofoundations of traditional theory, Keynes was simply arguing that microeconomic theory is *false*! Presumably, it is false because it is not logically consistent with all macrophenomena – such as persistent disequilibria – and thus, by *modus tollens*, at least one of the assumptions of microtheory is false and hence microtheory as a whole is false. If this is granted, why in the 1960s and 70s was there a concern for the microfoundations of macrotheory? I can think of at least two reasons. On the one hand, many believers in the truth of traditional microeconomic theory think that by showing Keynes' macrotheory to be logically consistent with microtheory (by providing the microfoundations), the strength of Keynes' critique of microtheory would be defused by the embarrassment of an inconsistency in Keynes' position. On the other hand, opponents of neoclassical economics could demand true microfoundations for macrotheory while knowing full well that what they demand is impossible. But I do not think these reasons are enough to support all of the concern for microfoundations. Rather, another reason may be the implicit recognition that Keynes appears to accept the neoclassical hidden agenda and this has thereby led many to think that he accepts neoclassical microtheory and, in particular, general equilibrium theory. For anyone who accepts microtheory, it would be easy to argue that Keynes' macrotheory – namely, that his theory of aggregate demand and supply – must have microfoundations.

Aggregative economics vs. macrofoundations

Walrasian general equilibrium models that I discussed in Chapters 3 and 7 are straightforward attempts to satisfy psychologistic individualism. In such models only individuals are represented – consumers by their nature-given utility functions and resource and talent endowments and producers by their nature-given production functions and technical know-how as well as their nature-given endowments of productive resources (e.g., land). In this regard, it should be noted that much of nineteenth-century economic theory focused on the producers in an agriculturally dominated economy so technology was embodied in the productivity of land and the farming skills of the individual farmers. For most of the twentieth century, production was dominated by industrial production which raises questions concerning the non-natural givens such as large corporations as well as social institutions like the market system. As we saw in Chapter 7, general equilibrium theory would now be seen to be lacking if it is still thought to be satisfying psychologistic individualism. I will leave it to the New Institutional Economics theorists to worry about this issue. Here I want instead just to distinguish between general equilibrium theory and aggregative or macroeconomic theory.

Aggregative economics is nothing more than what its name implies. To see it, one would simply choose variables that are common with all consumers or all producers and then add them up – for example, the total amount of personal incomes or expenditures for the whole economy, the total amount of capital used by all firms, etc. As such, aggregative economics does not violate psychologistic individualism any more than general equilibrium theory does. There is no claim that such totals obtained by aggregation are directly observable entities and thus nothing is raised that would require explanation beyond what has been identified in the general equilibrium model.

Before John Maynard Keynes produced his famous *General Theory* [1936], there was no micro vs. macroeconomics; there was just economics (e.g., typical textbooks might discuss 'value theory', 'monetary theory', 'cost theory', etc.). About the same time as Keynes was publishing his book, some old institutional economists began aggregating such things as the national income, gross national product, total savings, total investment, etc., in the hope that by understanding the relationships between such aggregates we would better understand economics. But for some strange reason (about which I will speculate later), by the 1950s, every elementary textbook was divided into two parts. There was a micro part that was based on Marshallian and Walrasian economics and the macro part that usually began with a chapter about national income accounting and then went on to discuss something that was claimed to be derived from Keynes' *General Theory*.

Aggregative economics and microfoundations

In one sense, the market, by textbook definition of the market functions, is an aggregation of the planned demands and supplies. That is, a minimum condition for a market equilibrium is that the *sum* of all planned quantities demanded must equal the *sum* of all planned quantities to be supplied. What if we extended the aggregation to an entire economy? This is just what was accomplished with the Hicksian grand synthesis in 'Mr. Keynes and the Classics' [1937]. We are led to believe that all we need are some big demand and supply curves in the macroeconomic sky which can be seen to imitate microanalysis of demand and supply. That is, what we need are curves representing a macro view of the economy. There are two ways to go in the direction leading to macroeconomics, although to be logically consistent they cannot be different. One is the direct aggregated demand and supply analysis which Keynes introduced. The other is the Hicksian IS-LM analysis. Either vision is difficult to keep in focus, since nobody can ever directly see the aggregated quantities.

Nevertheless, the basis of macroeconomics is the view that it is possible to keep the aggregated quantities in focus. But most important is the view that all of macroeconomic analysis is methodologically and perfectly analogous to micro-economic analysis. In this sense, one must be able to transfer all the microeconomic principles of market equilibria into a macro or aggregative context. Thus whenever aggregate demand exceeds aggregate supply, the price index of all goods aggregated must rise in the same way that the individual market price rises whenever the market's demand exceeds the market's supply. Of course, this analogy presumes that the microeconomic theory of individual prices is true.

The 1970s problem of microfoundations

The centerpiece of microeconomics is the purely competitive auction market in which buyers and sellers participate atomistically as price takers and where supply and demand are equated continuously by variations in price. These individual markets aggregate into a Walrasian general equilibrium model. ... In that aggregation of perfect markets, shifts in nominal aggregate demand affect only prices and never quantities.

Macroeconomics contrasts sharply with these implications of aggregated microeconomics. It begins with the observation that output and employment display significant deviations around their supply-determined trends... These fluctuations around the trend of real activity are the 'business cycle'... Clearly, the business cycle could not happen in aggregated classical microeconomics. Thus any macroeconomics that is connected to microeconomics by a solid bridge must explain how it departs from the classical micro model in its conception of the operation of markets.

Arthur Okun [1980, pp. 817-19]

Once microeconomics is seen as defining the very nature of economics, any macroeconomic phenomenon will be seen to need a reductive explanation. Of course, it is one thing to want such an explanation and quite another to have it. ... no one believes that economists can practicably trace the decision problems of millions of individuals and aggregate them to discover macroeconomic behavior. The intellectual triumph of microfoundations is grounded not in methodological individualism (that is, in a strategy of basing all empirical explanations on the behavior of individuals) but in *ontological individualism* (the conviction that the only real entities in the economy are individuals). Who could disagree with that?

Kevin Hoover [2001, pp. 70, 72–3]

In principle, *if* neoclassical microeconomic theory were successful in terms of psychologistic individualism, then any neoclassical macroeconomic theory must eventually be explicable in terms of the microtheory. Methodologically speaking, this means that neoclassical *macro*economic theory must not have any prohibited exogenous variables which do not exist in neoclassical *micro*economic theory. If it does, then the completeness of microtheory would be in doubt. This is the problem of microfoundations. In these terms, the problem of providing microfoundations for macroeconomics becomes a purely technical matter. The problem of microfoundations is to show that necessarily the logical validity of any macroeconomic theory depends only on the logical validity of the underlying microeconomic principles. A corollary of this problem is that if there are problems with macroeconomic theory, as some have claimed [e.g., Weintraub

1977], then there must be a problem with the (general) microeconomic theory underlying it.

If microeconomic theory is true, then the nature of the macroview or the aggregated view of the economy cannot be inconsistent with the microview. Some critics of neoclassical theory thus have an alternative route to undermining neoclassical economics. As I mentioned above, they can demand a demonstration of the foundations – which, of course, must exist if the individualistic microtheory is true. But the failure to solve the implied problem of microfoundations today does not mean that they are impossible to provide. The critics would be better off taking the bull by the horns and trying to prove that it is impossible to provide them in the future. Without such a proof, the only uncertainty might be about how long it might take to solve the alleged problem of microfoundations. But, two key questions remain.

One key question underlying the 1970s dispute over microfoundations was: Are there any limitations to the success of the neoclassical microtheory in terms of psychologistic individualism? For example, does the individual decision-maker require perfect knowledge? Similarly, do the knowledge requirements (whatever they are) presume induction? As we saw in Chapter 8, whenever induction is presumed, it is possible to postpone consideration of perfect knowledge. Nevertheless, if equilibrium requires the absence of possible gains from further recontracting, then equilibrium is reached only if there really are no possible gains *and* every individual decision-maker knows that there are no further gains to be had. How does he or she know this?

The other key question concerns the possibility of disequilibrium or what Larry Samuelson [1997] calls 'out-of-equilibrium behavior'. If there are possible gains, then it is possible for at least one individual to perceive them. But does the absence of possible gains assure an equilibrium? If there really are no possible gains but someone *thinks* there are, the equilibrium will be upset. On what basis will individuals actually hold the correct view that there are no gains? What forces anyone to form the correct expectations? If induction were to work, then individuals would be forced to hold the correct expectations – although that might require a long time. But even if everyone currently thinks, erroneously, that there are no possible gains, we have no reason to think that nobody will ever change his or her mind. At the very minimum, the existence of an equilibrium in prices and quantities would seem to also presume an equilibrium in knowledge acquisition perhaps along the lines of the 1970s Rational Expectations Hypothesis.

Macroeconomics as a Conventionalist construct

If, given a true neoclassical microtheory, all macroeconomics variables must be explainable as 'epiphenomena' – that is, by showing that they follow from the principles of microeconomics alone – why do we even have the sub-discipline we call macroeconomics? The answer is to be found in the combination of two factors. The first is that many, following Keynes, consider neoclassical *micro*economics to be false. Their reason may only be the claim that there are exogenous variables other than those allowed by the neoclassical psychologistic individualism. Or their reason may simply be that a neoclassical equilibrium world, although easy to define, is impossible to realize, hence could never be the basis of a true explanation of the state of a real economy. The second factor is more philosophical, as it is a consequence of the attempts to deal with the Problem of Conventions. Specifically, Conventionalism, today's primary item on the hidden agenda of neoclassical economics, does not allow theories to be considered true or false. If claims for truth or falsity were allowed and Keynes was correct in claiming that neoclassical theory is false, then at the very minimum his version of economics would have to supplant neoclassical microeconomics completely. But since Conventionalism does not allow theories to be considered true or false and since there are no universally accepted or absolutely true Conventionalist criteria, there is always a danger that economics could be destroyed by a life-or-death struggle because it is still presumed that one theory must be chosen as 'best'.

One of the complaints against Inductivism was that it fostered such life-or-death struggles and outright dogmatism over whose theory was the one and only true theory [Agassi 1963]. Conventionalism attempts to avoid such battles from breaking out in one, or a combination, of two ways. One way is to demonstrate that competing theories are merely two different ways of looking at the same thing – that is, the two competitors are logically equivalent. Successfully showing either that macrotheory is just a different way of looking at general equilibrium theory or that macrotheory does indeed have microfoundations would be such a demonstration. However, showing this may take a long time. The other way is to compartmentalize the discipline, giving each competitor its own department. For example, in response to Keynes' 'departure' two new categories were created – micro to accommodate those who wish to retain individualist neoclassical 'value theory', and macro for those of all sorts who wish to consider aggregate variables. However, this second way is only a temporary measure whenever competitors deal with the same phenomena. Unless they are shown to be logically equivalent, there remains the possibility that the economics profession could be destroyed by a life-or-death struggle caused by those economists who think that neoclassical microtheory is true or at least applicable to all economic phenomena and thus think that there is no need for a separate macrotheory [e.g., Lucas 1987]. For these economists macroeconomics can be accommodated *only* if it is shown that macrotheory is built upon a foundation of microeconomic principles.

Accommodating Keynes' theory of the economy 'as a whole'

The essential point here is that Conventionalism is a refuge for those who cannot tolerate disagreements over the truth or falsity of theories. The basic premise – recalling the discussion of rationality in Chapter 3 – is that whenever any two individuals accept all of the assumptions of a logically valid argument (i.e., microeconomics) they must agree with the conclusions validly reached. The Conventionalist position is that if any two individuals disagree, there must be some prior assumption which they do not both accept. Otherwise, at least one of them is crazy or 'irrational' [Pirsig 1974]. This then provides the avenue for avoiding disagreements – we should search for assumptions which form a foundation for agreement.

With this view of the fundamentals of Conventionalist agreement in mind, let us now examine the way in which Keynesian macroeconomics has been accommodated. The following is a speculative 'rational reconstruction' of the accommodation. The accommodation is founded on the following premises. It must be agreed, first, that (to be consistent with psychologistic individualism) neoclassical macroeconomics must not be more than an aggregation of micro-economics. Second, equilibrium is the primary basis of macro behavior, that is, of observable non-individualist behavior. Third, general equilibrium assures the existence of a set of fixed prices which facilitate aggregation. Fourth, the nature of any set of general equilibrium prices can be explained by neoclassical microeconomics using only natural and (psychologistic) individualist exogenous variables.

Let us see the ways in which these principles allow for an accommodation. Since so much of Keynesian economics is about aggregates, the primary obstacle in the way of an accommodation is what used to be called the 'Problem of Aggregation' [e.g., Klein 1946; Leontief 1947; see Blaug 1997, p. 451; Hoover 2001, pp. 74–82] – the problem of constructing Keynes' aggregate demand and supply quantities from the demand and supply curves of individuals or other sub-macro entities. We can always calculate unambiguous aggregates if we assume prices are fixed. The Problem of Aggregation is about whether the fixed-price aggregate quantities correspond to the quantities that would have to hold if one viewed the aggregate economy from a general equilibrium perspective.

Samuelson says there's no Santa Claus?

Today, few if any neoclassical theorists think the Problem of Aggregation is worthy of their time. There are two reasons for this. Before considering them, I need to briefly discuss again a technical issue that if not kept in mind seems to get in the way of dealing with the differences between general equilibrium theory and aggregative or macroeconomics. It concerns the two key necessary conditions for long-run and general equilibria that were discussed in Chapter 7: profit maximization which is a private matter of the firm and zero profit which is a social matter in the sense that its significance depends on whether other firms in other industries are making positive profits and this in turn depends on whether the firms are participating in a social environment of free competition. In the case of maximization, if there is a long-run, general equilibrium, there must not be any incentive for individual firms to change their decisions about how much to supply or, equivalently, how much of the inputs to purchase or employ. As noted in Chapter 7, the only reason to change behavior is that the decision-maker is *not* maximizing profit or utility. From the perspective of the firm's output decision, as we saw, if the firm is producing where marginal revenue equals marginal cost, it will not want to change its level of output. From the perspective of the firm's input decisions: if it is maximizing profit with respect to any input, it will not want to adjust the level of input. This is because maximization means that the firm is employing that input at the point where the value of its 'marginal product' equals the price of that input – meaning, for example, when the last additional unit of labor is used and it causes output to increase by one tomato, the labor is paid a wage equivalent to one tomato. As for the zero-profit condition, the issue for aggregative economics is a matter of simple arithmetic. If every firm in the economy is making zero profits, then the price of each supplied good is just enough to cover costs with nothing left over. This means that when we aggregate the values of the outputs of all firms, the aggregate total revenue of the suppliers must exactly equal the aggregate total income of the demanders – with nothing left over.

This brings us to the technical issue that was discussed in Chapter 7 but without reference there to macroeconomics. The issue involves the nature of Marshallian long-run production functions. Specifically, by definition of the Marshallian long run, all long-run production functions must be linear and homogeneous (and thus exhibit constant rather than increasing returns). For a production function to be linear and homogeneous, doubling inputs must always exactly double output (and thus average cost does not vary with the output). By definition of Marshall's long-run period of time, all inputs are variable (i.e. there are no fixed production factors). So, it was noted in Chapter 7 that whenever all inputs are variable, we can double output in two different ways. One would be to double the size of the firm (viz., double all inputs) and hence double its output. The other way would be to double the output by 'cloning' the firm next door. If either way does not exactly double the total output then either one of the inputs is fixed and thus cannot be doubled or cloned or we have not identified all of the inputs (and thus not doubled or cloned them) [Samuelson 1947/65, p. 284] – and in this case, there would be something left over in the form of excess revenue or excess cost of production. If it does not matter which way we double output, then the production function must be linear (doubling inputs doubles output) and homogeneous (no missing or fixed inputs). Thus, when it is not clear that all inputs are variable, one can be sure that each long-run production functions is *in effect* linear and homogeneous only if there is a 'Santa Claus' (to use Samuelson's term [1972, p. 485]) who could make up for missing inputs or revenue.

In Chapter 7, this technical issue was discussed because the concern was whether the production function could exhibit the increasing returns necessary for an imperfect competition equilibrium. Here the issue is the need for constant returns when dealing with the relationship between micro and aggregative economics. The primary 'benefit' for the theorists who assume that their model's production functions are linear-homogenous is that in the long run when the profit-maximizing firm pays each input the value of its marginal product, the firm, as a matter of simple mathematics, must be making zero (excess) profit [Boland 1992, pp. 68–9]. Let me stress this. This means that zero profits become a private, microeconomic matter of the mathematics of the production function and not dependent on whether the firm operates in a social, macroeconomic environment governed by free competition.

So, one reason for ignoring the old Problem of Aggregation is that if one is sure all production functions are linear-homogeneous, the problem cannot arise. More likely, in this regard, model builders will unthinkingly assume the production functions of their model are linear-homogenous and thus preclude a Problem of Aggregation. Thus, assuming production functions are linear-homogenous is one way to avoid having to solve the presumed Problem of Aggregation.

Now, the alleged Problem of Aggregation might be avoided in another way – specifically, by assuming all prices are fixed at their potential long-run equilibrium values (where all production functions would be locally linear and profit would be zero). This is where general equilibrium comes to the rescue. It can be shown that for any given set of resource endowments (which are fully employed) it is always possible to define a set of Walrasian prices which would clear all markets in a general equilibrium sense [Dorfman, Samuelson and Solow 1958]. The beauty of the general equilibrium sense is that the only exogenous givens are the individual utility or production functions and the naturally given resource endowments. All other variables can be calculated [cf. Boland 1989, chap. 6]. When using general equilibrium prices, it is always possible to perform an aggregation, if one assumes that the economy is in competitive equilibrium (zero excess profits). The economy is in equilibrium only if all individuals are maximizing, given these prices, and the absence of profits guarantees that the aggregate value of the resources must equal the aggregate value of the outputs. While I have said that this is another way, in the end, it does not seem so. And thus, one can see why long-run aggregate (macro) equilibria are difficult to distinguish from general equilibria.

The Walrasian prices correspond to the Marshallian long-run equilibrium prices where every producer is making zero excess profits. Thus, since in the short run non-zero profit is possible, the actual short-run prices cannot always be used for aggregation. But, from the macro perspective of Walrasian general equilibrium, the *total* profits in this case cannot be other than zero (otherwise, we would need a Santa Claus to provide the aggregated positive profit) but this does not preclude the possibility of short-run profits and losses of individual firms canceling each other out. So, in the short run the actual prices cannot be used for the aggregation except when one assumes that all production functions are linear-homogeneous. As was argued above, if all production functions are linear-homogeneous, whenever all firms are maximizing profit (by paying each of their inputs the value of its marginal product), then every firm will be making zero profits. If one assumes that the *aggregate* production function is linear-homogeneous (e.g., by assuming a Cobb-Douglas production function), then it might appear that, since the aggregate profits cannot be non-zero, the Keynesian aggregate supply function must reflect profit maximizing outputs, just as the individual supply curves of microtheory are determined by the profit maximization of the individual producers. But it must be realized that unless all individual production functions are linear-homogeneous, the so-called Problem of Aggregation has not been solved – and this is because the actual (i.e., short-run) prices do not necessarily correspond to the Walrasian prices that could be used to successfully perform the aggregation.

Technically accommodating Keynes' 'departure'

For many economists the air around the mathematics of general equilibrium theory is much too thin and the assumption that all production functions are linear-homogeneous begs too many questions. While a general equilibrium over the relevant period of time is a sufficient condition for the fixity of prices, it is not always necessary. It is much easier merely to assume that prices are fixed over the period of time needed to calculate any aggregate quantity such as the national income (or GDP). In this sense the aggregate quantities can be calculated and thus 'observed' even when there is no way to show that they correspond to the logically consistent but unobservable Walrasian general equilibrium prices. For many theorists this is the only viable and realistic way to accommodate Keynes' aggregative economics.

In order to be consistent with neoclassical theory, in the 1960s and 70s, the disagreement between micro and macro theorists could always be explained away as mere pedagogical differences over whether prices are actually fixed. If the economy were in general equilibrium then as long as exogenous givens did not change over the relevant period, prices would be fixed. So neoclassical economics could easily tolerate Keynesian aggregate economics if the only difference is that macroeconomics presumes fixed prices [Okun 1980]. That one or more markets may have 'sticky' (and non-equilibrium) prices can only help in the aggregation. Even when there exist one or more markets that are not cleared, as long as their prices are sticky, the fixity of prices is assured without recourse to an assumption of general equilibrium. This still begs the question as to whether the inflexibility of the prices is due to an implicit introduction of a non-individualist and non-natural exogenously constraining variable.

Some neoclassical economists interested in explaining non-fixed price situations, as with inflation or deflation, obviously cannot accept accommodation on these terms. Instead, to the extent that macroeconomics involves changing macrovariables and to the extent that equilibrium theory is essentially an explanation of why prices could be fixed at particular levels, it is argued that, for macroeconomics to be consistent with microeconomics, prices must change only because a temporary disequilibrium exists. And as the 1987 Nobel prize-winner Robert Solow notes [1979] (see again the quotation at the end of Chapter 7), disequilibria are attributed to 'expectational errors'. The Rational Expectations Hypothesis can then be used to explain the 'expectational errors' away. In this way macroeconomics is accommodated as epiphenomena of the microeconomic decision problems which are caused by uncertainty. Either way, the accommodation tolerates the Keynesian 'revolution' only if Keynesian macroeconomics is concerned with temporary short-run phenomena – Robert Clower [1965] called such an accommodation a 'Keynesian Counterrevolution'.

The Keynesian challenge to neoclassical theory

Critics of this accommodation argue that it is completely against the thrust of Keynes' *General Theory* [e.g., Clower 1965]. Keynes identifies 'classical theory' with the case of 'full employment'. What is wrong with the concept of full employment? First, full employment is a presumption of the orthodox Walrasian general equilibrium analysis which only attempts to identify the sufficient conditions for the existence of an equilibrium allocation of society's given (and fully employed) resources. Second, full employment is a necessary condition of any long-run equilibrium in a Marshallian world of price-takers. Again, if all production functions are linear-homogeneous, then profit maximization in the long run produces 'full employment' in the sense that further employment cannot yield higher utilities for anyone without lowering the utility of others.

Now Keynes claimed to be opposed to all of these aspects of full employment. But if full employment is a logical consequence of any perfectly competitive, maximizing economy in the long run, how can Keynes' opposition to theories based on full employment be reconciled with classical theory? Is it only a matter of whether Keynes was speaking about a short-run world, or is it something more? Specifically, is it only a question of Keynes' macrotheory being a special case of classical theory? Is it that the short run has some temporary exogenous variables which in time can be made endogenous and that these temporary exogenous variables are the only cause of the deviations from full employment?

Can the so-called counterrevolutionaries safely explain away Keynes' opposition to classical theory in this manner? Keynes' specific indictment, according to Clower, is that Keynes only denies that orthodox neoclassical economics provides an adequate account of disequilibrium phenomena [Clower 1965, p. 109]. But can this interpretation of Keynes' indictment be correct? All explanations are based on specifically recognized exogenous variables. If one can show that each of Keynes' disequilibrium conclusions follows only because of the intervening *temporary* exogenous variables, their existence *is* the basis of an explanation! It would appear that both Keynes and Clower were wrong.

This is the center of the whole sad matter. If the classical or the counter-revolutionary explanation is based on temporary exogenous variables that are neither natural nor individualist, then Keynes would be right all along. Keynes was right because the classical or counterrevolutionary position is nothing more than standard neoclassical theory and, as I have been arguing, neoclassical explanation allows only natural or (psychologistic) individualist exogenous variables. If the counterrevolutionaries must rely on the wrong type of exogenous variables to win their case against Keynes, they simultaneously violate their own requirements for a successful theory of economic phenomena. They can only win if the temporary exogenous variables are either naturally given or are aspects of individualism, such as psychological states.

Keynes' psychologism and Inductivism

Some of Keynes' defenders, notably Joan Robinson, argue that what Keynes was saying was that the results of past decisions are necessarily exogenous for current decisions and those results are neither natural nor individualistic [Robinson 1974]. That is, the individual decision-maker often makes mistakes which cannot be undone. Being mistakes, they cannot be explained as the outcomes of maximization; hence neoclassical explanations cannot be produced to explain away the temporal and temporary exogenous variables which supposedly yielded the short-run, disequilibrium situation.

On the surface Robinson's interpretation would appear to do the logical job that she intended. And it certainly appears to be consistent with the spirit of Keynes' 1937 argument. But if we accept this interpretation of Keynes' criticism of the classics, does his theory fare any better as an explanation of so-called disequilibria than the more recent invocation of 'trembling-hand' imperfection and the like that I discussed in Chapter 8? I will argue that it does not.

In his 1937 *QJE* article Keynes took the opportunity to restate his objections to classical theory in more direct terms. But, unfortunately, he exposed his hand too much. As was noted above, when referring to his theory of the consumption function he said, 'This *psychological law* was of the utmost importance in the development of my own thought...' (emphasis added). This is not an idle reference to psychological laws. Keynes was famous for his theories of *subjective* probability. And, as also noted above, one of his primary arguments against classical theory was that the individual decision-maker must form subjective expectations concerning the future and those expectations cannot be inductively proven, hence decision-makers *must* make mistakes. This view has been admirably developed by George Shackle [e.g., 1972].

Keynes' general theory as 'internal' criticism

While believers in the Keynesian revolution may think the *General Theory* provides a blueprint for a new economics and while it is possible to find a few passages there to support their optimistic view, a better understanding of his *General Theory* is obtained by recognizing that Keynes was primarily interested in criticizing Marshallian neoclassical theory (his so-called 'classical theory'). And it would appear that Keynes understood that if the purpose of criticism is to change the minds of the proponents of neoclassical economics, then the criticism must be 'internal' [cf. Salanti 1989]. An effective criticism must be in terms that the proponents of neoclassical economics will accept. Such an effective criticism is in the form of a rational (i.e., logically valid) argument along the lines I discussed in Chapter 3.

Neoclassical critics of Keynes usually dismiss his *General Theory* by pointing out that it presumes that the world we see out our windows is one of a disequilibrium rather than one of an equilibrium which we would be able to explain. Moreover, the neoclassical critics often claim that Keynes' viewpoint is merely a special case because without artificial constraints the long-run equilibrium is a necessary outcome of market competition. But the basic thrust of Keynes' criticism was to the contrary; that the long-run equilibrium that neoclassical theorists are so fond of is itself the special case. That is, the everyday world is a short-run world since at any point of time there are always factors of production that are fixed because either changing them would take time or they are beyond the direct control of anyone. Thus, while there are very many possible states of short-run equilibrium (i.e., where firms are maximizing profit with respect to the amount of labor used but not necessarily with respect to the fixed amount of capital being used), only one of them would fulfill the requirements of a long-run equilibrium (i.e., where also the amount of capital being used is the amount that the firm would choose to maximize it profit).

If the world of Keynes is at least an economy in a short-run equilibrium, then the question is begged as to what is constraining the economy from reaching the long-run equilibrium. The answer may simply be the existence of exogenous constraints that neoclassical economists will always try to explain away. Obvious examples are social institutions (as discussed in Chapter 6); yet these are elements of the real world that are necessary for the functioning of even a neoclassical market economy. At minimum, there are constraints that are the result of past decisions and as such cannot be undone (particularly when their creation uses irreplaceable resources). This is not saying that such past decisions were 'irrational'. Rather, in his 1937 *QJE* article, Keynes explicitly noted that, at any point in real time, decisions have to be made that require assumptions (or expectations) about an unknowable future. If these assumptions are (unknowingly) false, then mistakes can be made even when one's logical argument for the decision made is a perfectly valid argument. The bottom line then is that past decisions which result in possibly non-optimal constraints cannot be explained in a neoclassical manner – that is, in a manner that assumes all variables other than natural givens can be explained as being optimal (i.e., successful optimizing) outcomes of previous decisions.

Short-run equilibria and non-natural exogenous givens in macroeconomics

While stressing that any decision involves assumptions about the future might be problematic for neoclassical theorists, a more general issue is raised whenever the economy 'as a whole' is considered to be a matter of macroeconomics. The general issue I have in mind is not widely recognized. It follows from John Stuart Mill's position that economics may be about the mechanics of production but does not extend to social decisions about who gets what. But, if the income distribution is somehow changed, will it have an effect on the ultimate product mix of an economy? It will have an effect if people have different utility functions. If there is an effect on the product mix, there will also be an effect on the equilibrium prices and on the resulting income distribution. A similar question can be raised about the given wealth distribution.

Matters of distribution are macro matters. Microeconomics – particularly the Marshallian version – does not deal with given distributions but focuses only on single individuals in isolation facing market-given prices. Early twentieth century economists thought that the income distribution is explained by recognition that labor and capital are each paid their respective marginal products and thus explaining production indirectly explains the income distribution – at least between labor and capital. But once one recognizes that labor (or capital) is not homogenous with regard to talent or productivity, then the distribution of talent or productivity has an effect on the income distribution even when the marginal-productivity based explanation is considered. In response, it might simply be said that this is not a problem for neoclassical microeconomics since talent or productivity might merely be a nature-given attribute and thus exogenous. If the talent or productivity is acquired in a social context – that is, constrained by social institutions and social pressures of culture – then perhaps it or its distribution cannot be considered a nature-given exogenous variable. Again, if the social context is a matter of past decisions that may not have been optimal for today's conditions, neoclassical economists cannot easily expect to explain away the constraints that might prevent the achievement of a long-run equilibrium. That is, the best that can be achieved is a short-run equilibrium and only by chance will that short-run equilibrium also be a long-run equilibrium.

So, if the world we see out our window is at best a short-run equilibrium, then our explanation of that world must involve the recognition of constraining macro variables such as the given distribution of wealth, talent, etc. Such consideration can easily lead to the conclusion that rather than worry about the microfoundations of macroeconomics, we should be concerned with the macrofoundations of (short-run) microeconomics – if we wish to explain the real world we see out our window. (In Chapter 17, I will return to explore the epistemological aspects of macrofoundations.)

If economic theory needs both micro- and macrofoundations, perhaps the distinction was a false one from the beginning. Interestingly, at the same time that Keynes was introducing us to the economy 'as a whole', other theorists were trying to extend microeconomics by including 'representative firms' and later 'representative consumers'. Such devices are popular even today. But they have always invited criticism. While the invocation of such devices implies recognition that not all firms and not all consumers are alike, there is no recognition of the distribution of differences within a given population. How would we know whether the real macro distribution is represented? Actually, the device is incapable of dealing with the macro distribution and thus is nothing more than just another Instrumentalist false hope of hanging on to neoclassical microeconomics so as to avoid the challenge of Keynes.

Is evolutionary game theory a more fruitful alternative to macroeconomic theory?

> to explore the fine structure of technical advance with a neoclassical model requires an enormous amount of '*ad hoc*-ery' that is uncongenial to the basic neoclassical theoretical viewpoint. It is therefore virtually inevitable that, if a neoclassical perspective is preserved for the analysis of the macro phenomena of economic growth, a scholar working on micro phenomena and a scholar working on macro phenomena will be unable to talk to each other using a common language. And an individual scholar interested in both aspects of the problem will find his knowledge compartmentalized. A major advantage of an evolutionary theory is that it provides a way to avoid this difficulty.
>
> Richard Nelson and Sidney Winter [1982, p. 272]

The standard interpretation of noncooperative game theory is that the analyzed game is played exactly once by fully rational players who know all the details of the game, including each other's preferences over outcomes. Evolutionary game theory, instead, imagines that the game is played over and over again by biologically or socially conditioned players who are randomly drawn from large populations. More specifically, each player is 'pre-programmed' to some behavior – formally a strategy in the game – and one assumes that some evolutionary selection process operates over time on the population distribution of behaviors. What, if any, are the connections between the long-run aggregate behavior in such an evolutionary process and solution concepts in non-cooperative game theory?

Jörgen Weibull [1995, p. xiii]

An evolutionary model combines two processes: one *selection* process that favors some varieties over others, and one process that creates this variety, to be called the *mutation process*. In evolutionary game theory, the varieties in question are strategies in a game.

In nature, the basic selection mechanism is biological survival and reproduction, and the mutation process is basically genetic. *In the market place*, the basic selection mechanism is economic survival, and the mutation process is experimentation, innovation and mistakes. In both cases there is also an element of individual and social learning. *In other social and economic interactions*, the selection mechanism can in extreme cases be that of biological or social survival, but under more normal circumstances individuals and households adapt by way of individual and social learning.

A qualitative difference ... between evolutionary and rationalistic approaches is that while the second focuses on individuals and what goes on in their minds, the evolutionary approach usually instead analyzes the population distribution of behaviors (decision rules, strategies). One could say that the selection process replaces the mental process of choice made by rational players in classical non-cooperative game theory, while the mutation process replaces the mental process of exploring the strategy set and strategies' payoff consequences.

Jörgen Weibull [1998, p. 3]

The competitive environment within which firms operate is one of struggle and motion. It is a dynamic selection environment, not an equilibrium one. The essential forces of growth are innovation and selection, with augmentation of capital stocks more or less tied to these processes.

Richard Nelson and Sidney Winter [1974, p. 890]

So, the situation today (and for the last fifty or sixty years) is that macro-economics exists without clear microfoundations – if they are needed – and there is little chance that there ever could be microfoundations that would satisfy followers of Keynes. In the remainder of this chapter I wish to consider whether either evolutionary economics or evolutionary game theory might be a more acceptable and more likely method of reconciling microtheory and macrotheory. It will be argued that the evolutionary economics promoted by Nelson and Winter [1974; 1982], in effect, amounts to a different microfoundation for a different macroeconomics. And it will be argued that all too often evolutionary game theory is pushed to the point where success is to be measured by whether it duplicates neoclassical economics.

Evolution as a macroeconomic phenomenon: The key benchmark

The benchmark of neoclassical economics has always been what we now call a state of long-run equilibrium – the state of an economy where everyone is maximizing and all possible decisions that might improve the situation have been made. In Adam Smith's day the focus was on the benefits of a division of labor that can be achieved by a firm's expansion (in turn limited by the size of the market). A division of labor allows the growing firm to hire specialized workers that are doing what they do best rather than hiring workers who have to do many different jobs including ones that the worker is not the best at doing. A free market combined with sufficiently motivated producers was seen to be a sufficient means to achieve such an equilibrium state. One can easily interpret this scenario as being one of evolution where each expansion of a firm leads to improved production techniques. But, there is a limit to possible improvements, namely, when every worker is doing just one job and that job is the one he or she is best at doing. Once that limit is reached no more improvements can be made unless a new product or a new technology is introduced. And, as was explained above, once the long-run equilibrium is reached, all firms are charging prices that just cover their costs of production and thus there are no abnormal or 'excess' profits being made ('excess' being defined as a level above that necessary to stay in business). However, this limited evolution is not what is usually considered to be a useful evolutionary perspective. Joseph Schumpeter [1928; 1942/50] alters this perspective by focusing more on what happens after a long-run equilibrium has been reached. Specifically, such an equilibrium is the end of the line when there are no more innovations; that is, without innovators, there would be no movement beyond the equilibrium state.

When one adopts Schumpeter's post-equilibrium perspective, evolution is seen to be an ongoing and unending process (as long as there are innovators). And, as he pointed out [1928], the dynamics of this evolution involves winners and losers. The incentive for innovating is provided by equilibrium profits being limited to the normal profits for when prices just cover costs of production. So, if you want to make above-normal profits (without cheating), you will need to innovate either in terms of production techniques or in terms of introducing new products. Those that succeed by discovering innovative cost-saving techniques will thereby be able to make extra profits and this will give them a temporary advantage over those that do not innovate. Those that fail to innovate successfully will be the losers either because they continue to face relatively higher production costs or because they continue to offer products that are obsolete and thus less demanded. In short, as Armen Alchian [1950] subsequently argued (for different reasons), the losers cannot survive.

Recent proponents of evolutionary economics are quick to credit Alchian with moving economics further along the lines of evolutionary explanations of economic dynamics [e.g., Hodgson 1999], but this is misleading. As Alchian publicly stated at a conference session that honored his 80th birthday, he introduced the Darwinian 'survival of the fittest' only as a counter-argument against those critics of the realism of the neoclassical economics assumption of maximization – he was not advocating evolutionary economics as an alternative to neoclassical economics. As I discussed in Chapter 3, Alchian's view is that conscious maximization is not necessary since it is a natural consequence of equilibrium survival – that is, in the state of long-run equilibrium any survivor is just covering its costs and this is the best anyone can do. For there to be an equilibrium, there cannot exist any fair way to make positive (excess) profits since if there were, by now everyone would have imitated that profitable production process or introduced their version of the new product. Thus, anyone not making zero excess profit must be losing money and will not survive. Zero excess profit is the best that anyone can do and hence profit is being maximized; thus those making zero excess profit in long-run equilibrium are all maximizers whether intentionally or not. But, regardless of Alchian's intentions, it would appear that more can be made of his introduction of evolutionary considerations than he was willing to make of his defense of the maximization assumption.

Evolution as a macroeconomic phenomenon: Nelson and Winter

Now, Smith's division of labor dynamics by itself does not yield evolutionary explanations nor does a Schumpeterian emphasis on the role of the innovator in the growth of a firm. However, these two notions are put to use in an evolutionary theory of growth by Nelson and Winter [1974] when they consider what they call 'a "behavioural" approach to individual firms' [p. 891]. The basic idea is that firms could never know enough to have perfect production routines and instead opt for what is usually called 'rules of thumb'. About this they note, 'While neoclassical theory would attempt to deduce these decision rules from maximisation on the part of the firm, the behavioral theory simply takes them as given and observable' [*ibid.*]. This new consideration allows for imperfections in the rules and thereby allows for a diversity of firms – and given that firms may use different rules means that they can always consider changing their rules. About this Nelson and Winter say, 'Prominent among the processes of rule change in the individual firm are those that involve deliberate, goal-oriented "search" or "problem-solving" activity' [p. 892]. All this leads them to say that 'Evolutionary theory involves ... explicit analysis of the economic selection mechanism – the change in the weighting of different decision rules that comes about through the expansion of firms using profitable rules and the contraction of firms using unprofitable ones' [p. 893]. Thus, they claim that their

> conceptual scheme ... has distinct advantages over neoclassical theory as a basis for interpreting the phenomena of economic growth. First of all, it offers a natural definition of innovation – change of existing decision rules... Secondly, and relatedly, explicit introduction of the concepts of profit-motivated search and problem-solving behaviour provides a basis for the discussion of a distinctive entrepreneurial function. By contrast, the neoclassical over-emphasis on consistent maximising behaviour by one and all renders entrepreneurship otiose... Thus the proposal offers a systematic framework for a Schumpeterian analysis of the competitive process. [p. 894]

Moreover, using a simulation study, they demonstrated that such a view of the firm can be used to generate 'aggregate time series with characteristics corresponding to those of economic growth' for an entire national economy [p. 899].

Evolution as an economic phenomenon: The essential ingredients

Starting with Adam Smith and continuing through with the explicit evolutionary approach of Nelson and Winter, the necessary ingredient (even when unstated) is the recognition of a diversity that follows from singular innovations. Even without innovations, the mere recognition of imperfect knowledge on the part of the firm (i.e., the 'behavioural' approach) means that there is no reason for all firms to be alike (i.e., having the same decision rules or technology) and thus diversity still follows. Either way, the recognition of diversity necessitates a *population perspective* that raises a question of the distribution of the differing types of firms – that is, firms with differing decision rules to deal with the imperfections in their knowledge of production or of how to respond to market changes. Without diversity, macroeconomic aggregates are too easily obtained in neoclassical economics: No diversity means all firms producing the same product do so with the same technology and thus the aggregates are just multiples of any representative firm. But Nelson and Winter will have none of this. They conclude [p. 903]:

> It is obvious that a great deal of diversity and change is hidden by the neoclassical macro approach based on aggregation, maximisation and equilibrium. Indeed, the principal virtue of those tools is the gain in analytic tractability and logical coherence that has been obtained precisely by abstracting from all that diversity and change.

Before considering how evolutionary game theory might be a basis for reconciling macro- and microeconomics, I want to consider the necessary ingredients for any evolutionary analysis. One essential ingredient, as I have mentioned above, is the notion of a *diverse population* of individuals (i.e., of firms or people or types of individuals). If one wants to consider macroeconomics in these circumstances, the existence of diversity means that one would need to consider the *distribution* of the different types of individuals. For example, while microeconomics can be used to describe any particular individual type of firm, a different distribution of the individual types can yield a different macro aggregate of the outputs or inputs for all of the firms being considered.

If we follow Nelson and Winter and allow firms to innovate or to search and possibly imitate a competitor's innovations, this means that we are allowing for them to change how they use their inputs. But while changeability is always there to be considered, Nelson and Winter also want us to recognize that, in effect, the rules are the embodiment of what firms have learned about how to produce their product. Explicit decision rules are actually a way to provide a certain degree of *durability*. I would say that the firm's decision rules are like a society's institutions in that institutions are at any point in time the embodiment of social knowledge (see the discussion of my 1979 explanation of social institutions at the end of Chapter 6). In the case of a firm, its decision rules are embodied technical knowledge. One can think of such rules being published in a shop manual that both gives them some minimal durability but also gives them scope since everyone in the firm can possess the written rules – that is, one does not just depend on the memory of one worker to remember the rules. To the extent that a firm's rules are kept private (or protected by copyright and thus not distributed to competing firms) allows for a certain degree of concrete *separation* between firms.

If we also follow Adam Smith, imitation alone would eventually lead to a statically uniform distribution, that is, to an equilibrium state where all firms are alike. But as noted above, Schumpeter was interested in what happens next. An essential ingredient was the unstoppable innovation that accompanies competition and such innovation would disrupt any Smithian static equilibrium state. In other words, innovation provides a constant and *motivated source of change*. Innovation thus means that the distribution of the diverse population is constantly changing rather than converging to a static equilibrium.

In economics, it is important to recognize that all of these ingredients – population diversity and its distribution, knowledge embodied in durable rules or institutions, the availability of means of protecting and thus separating different firms or social systems (i.e., a collection of social institutions) and a motivated source of change – are seen to be what characterizes a competitive market system. Specifically, the market system's workings provide the remaining essential ingredient, a *selection process* that favors the survival of the winners over the losers. In the case of the market system, and as Alchian stressed, the selection process is based on the necessity of a firm making at least normal (viz., zero excess) profits – winners can, but losers cannot.

Evolutionary economics vs. neoclassical macroeconomics

With these ingredients in mind, does the Nelson and Winter approach to evolutionary economics amount to a program to provide a different microfoundations or a different macroeconomics? It certainly does not yield the Smithian static equilibrium state that is the focus of both the neoclassical microeconomics and neoclassical macroeconomics that can be analyzed with general equilibrium analysis. The usual way of presenting the necessary conditions for a general equilibrium is to say that it must be possible to select any two individuals out of the population and show that they are also in a state of exchange equilibrium. An example of an exchange equilibrium between two individuals was shown in Chapter 3, specifically, Figure 3.3. Whenever this is possible (and, it does not matter which two individuals are selected), microfoundations for macroeconomics have been achieved. But, in the case of Nelson and Winter, where there is a diversity of firms, it would matter which two firms have been selected. And thus, as I have suggested, the recognition of diversity requires a recognition and explanation of the entire population and how the differing types of firms are distributed in the whole economy. Such a recognition and explanation amounts to a different macroeconomics – one that could never have neoclassical microeconomics as its foundation!

Evolutionary game theory as an alternative to general equilibrium analysis

Evolutionary game theory has elements of the general equilibrium theory version of microeconomics yet recognizes the process of experimenting and groping that is characteristic of what might be going on in a market before the attainment of a long-run equilibrium. The evolutionary aspect also addresses the macro view by dealing with whole populations but in the same way that general equilibrium theory does. That is, like the exchange analysis of general equilibrium theory, evolutionary game theory analysis focuses on the interactions between pairs of individuals but where the interaction is to be characterized as a game being played by the two individuals. The game is usually one of non-cooperation (i.e., of competition) or one of common interest depending on what is being modeled.

The main difference between a general-equilibrium-theory exchange and an evolutionary-game-theory interaction is that the former, being based on the necessary conditions for equilibria, is essentially a case of static analysis and the necessary conditions do not directly depend on the (distribution of) other individuals in the population. Evolutionary game theory interactions can have an effect on the distribution of other individuals as well as on both the actual history of how the distribution changes and what the final distribution becomes. While ignoring the distribution of people in a population may not be essential to general equilibrium theory, it is the typical analysis. In the case of evolutionary game theory, recognizing the distribution is essential for any consideration of 'evolution'. I will have more to say about the importance of recognizing distributions later. For now, the point is simply that to do evolutionary analysis one must assume the existence of a population consisting of people with different characteristics (e.g., different competitive strategies) such that one can address the distribution of those characteristics and how the distribution changes over time. Whenever general equilibrium theory, or microeconomic theory in general, is based on 'representative' individuals (consumers or firms), it thereby eschews any need to address matters of distribution. This is particularly troubling for anyone who wishes to use microeconomics as a foundation for any macroeconomic theory that recognizes diversity as required by recognition of the dynamics of the view of either Smith or Schumpeter.

Biology as a source of metaphors for evolutionary economics

While Alfred Marshall murmured about biology in his famous *Principles of Economics* [1920/49], I think his only interest in biology (and possibly evolution) was that it involved a gradual, slow and progressive change along a continuum [see Boland 1992a, pp. 40–2] and moreover, it was seen as an alternative to mechanics [*ibid*. pp. 43–4]. In Schumpeter's day, biology analogies were not popular and so it can be argued that he avoided invoking Darwin to explain the dynamics of post-equilibrium described above [Hodgson 1997]. And as I have said, Alchian invoked his social-Darwinism only to counter the critics of deliberate maximization and thus he did not fully embrace biology analogies. And while there is much discussion of 'selection' and 'natural selection' in the early work of Sidney Winter [1964; 1971], not much is taken up by neoclassical economists that would involve biological analogies.

Today, however, there are many mathematically oriented economic theorists actively promoting biology as a source of powerful metaphors under the umbrella of evolutionary game theory. The metaphors that evolutionary game theory focuses on usually include 'selection', 'replication' and 'mutation'. When modeling evolution in game theory, a model of the biological selection process represents the elimination process that market competition invokes on the losers. A model of replication will sometimes be used to represent the imitation that is thought to take place when firms choose to copy their competitors' new techniques rather than innovate. Mutation is straightforwardly seen to represent innovation. In biology, genes and DNA are seen to be the way to retain any effective changes caused by mutations. In economics, there are no genes or DNA, *per se*. Obviously, Nelson and Winter thought that a firm's decisions rules were stable enough to provide some sort of gene-like behavior that might be used to distinguish between firms.

Evolution as social learning

While Nelson and Winter have been trying to provide a 'fundamental reconstruction of economic theories dealing with technological change and phenomena related, as to cause and effect, to technological change' [1973, p. 440], evolutionary game theory provides a different perspective. Evolutionary game theory tries to see evolution as a way to focus on a burning problem facing game theorists. Specifically, game theorists too often face multiple equilibria and if one is going to use an inevitable equilibrium state to explain or describe the behavior of a pair of individuals engaging in an economic exchange, then one needs to be able to explain how the players acquired the needed knowledge to play the game – or in other words, explain how the resulting equilibrium was *selected* from the multiple possibilities. If we could explain how the individuals learn to play the game and thus achieve the prescribed equilibrium, then the problem of equilibrium selection would be solved. Since game theories always involve more than one individual, learning is not considered to be just the possibly private matter of one individual but instead a matter of social learning. Evolutionary game theorists see this as a perfect place to apply the notions provided by biological evolutionary theory.

The reasons for their making a connection between evolution and social learning are not always obvious. One could easily conjecture that some game theorists became aware of the view of some biologists [e.g., Pringle 1951; Maynard Smith 1970] who argue that there is a connection since both involve an increasing complexity. But unfortunately, this basis for a theory of learning is open to question, as it does not involve a theory of knowledge. The connection may only be metaphorical or it could be just an obvious presumption of Inductivism. Either way, this approach does raise a few questions that are not answered in the literature of evolutionary game theory.

There is one branch of evolutionary game theory that goes far beyond Nelson and Winter and uses the idea of a gene to model social learning. The notion is to deal with a population's diversity by representing each individual element of the population as a gene which in turn is represented by a binary fixed-length string of 0s and 1s. Again, the focus is on the behavior of the whole population rather than the behavior of one of the maximizing individuals of neoclassical economics. Specifically, the biological notion is that the population evolves by 'replication', 'recombination' and mutation. Evolutionary game theorists are primarily motivated by the problems of mathematically modeling evolutionary economics. So, replication, which here is thought to be the metaphor for the market's entire selection process, is represented by a mathematical or computer-programmable device they call 'replicator dynamics' [see Taylor and Jonker 1978]. As a game-theory exercise, it is thought that the two individuals are randomly selected from the population to play a game and the one with the 'best' strategy (as defined by the game and its payoff table) wins. In this version of evolutionary game theory, the focus of the macro-distribution is not the individuals that make up the distribution but various strategies that they can employ. For example, we might be concerned with which pricing strategy would survive a competition, 'cost-plus' or 'marginal-cost' pricing. In other words, any population may consist of several sub-populations where within the sub-population all the individuals use the same strategy. Thus, as some strategies win and others lose, the distribution (of the relative sizes of the sub-populations) changes. Surprisingly, changes in the distribution are thought to represent social learning – and since learning in evolutionary game theory lacks a theory of knowledge, it is not clear whether the notion of learning discussed has anything to do with what most people would think learning is. However, there is one sense in which social learning does have a connection with knowledge and that is when the resulting distribution is seen to establish a social institution – or, in my [1979b] terms, when an institution is seen to be the successful embodiment of past social learning.

In economics, the notion of 'recombination' would seem to occur only when firms from different industries merge, but in biology it is more general and usually has to do with reproduction and the sharing of the genes of the parents. Nevertheless, much effort is devoted to building game theory models using genetic strings in a manner where part comes from one player and the remainder from the other and then seeing where the distribution of gene types evolve. This genetic approach to economic evolution relies on the effects of generational changes that result from the replicator dynamics. The selection process determines the subsequent generation's distribution. In this case, the win-loss situation is measured by how prolific one type of gene is relative to another.

A common complaint about using biological evolution as a metaphor for social or economic learning (even ignoring the absence of a theory of learning) is that evolution is a matter of mechanics but social and economic learning involve thinking beings that make choices. Contrarily, in the real world it could be pointed out that, as thinking beings rather than mere stimulus-response mechanisms, individual decision-makers make mistakes. And it is this point that Nelson and Winter stress in their promotion of evolutionary economics. But, evolutionary game theory is more concerned with the mathematics of model building and as such evolutionary game theory is just another exercise of Instrumentalism. Thus its proponents will never see a methodological reason to question the realism of the assumptions of evolutionary game theory.

On evolutionary game theory as a foundation of evolutionary macroeconomics

Of more concern in this chapter is whether, by focusing on games between individuals with imperfect knowledge, evolutionary game theory could ever provide the analogous macro perspective that general equilibrium theory provides with its pair-wise exchange analysis. It turns out that it does so long as we are limited to the micro-foundations for neoclassical macroeconomics. The reason is simple. The mathematical concern of the evolutionary game theorist is to see how to model the selection of one of the possibly many equilibria allowed by the definition of any particular game in question. Even when considering the exotic notion of mutations – that is supposed to metaphorically represent innovation – by adopting the idea that a mutation is an alteration of a binary string with a fixed-length there is still a limit to the evolution implied. This is because, as a matter of simple combinatorial mathematics, any binary fixed-length string allows only a finite, maximum number of possibilities even when all possible configurations of the string are considered. Evolutionary game theorists who attempt to borrow from mathematical biology (e.g., from Maynard Smith [1970; 1982]) will be using their mathematics to determine the existence of an 'Evolutionary Stable Strategy' which provides a population with a distribution that is impervious to mutations. But this is only a different type of equilibrium. Worse, it is a return to the neoclassical program that Nelson and Winter were trying to overcome. Certainly, without a theory of knowledge, learning – or even evolution – in evolutionary game theory is at best nothing more than another, possibly unrealistic, exercise in Instrumentalism.

Evolutionary economics and game theory vs. psychologistic individualism

One can also question whether evolutionary theory, by relying on biological mechanisms or just the collective competitiveness of the other individuals in an economy, can ever satisfy the requirements of psychologistic individualism which is at the foundation of all of neoclassical economics. The issue is not whether there are institutional constraints facing the decisions made by individuals (whether they are playing a game or just deciding whether to invest in research and development), but whether evolutionary theory presumes that 'things' make decisions. By modeling the growth or change of a society or of an economy as being like that of biology where no decisions are consciously made, seems to put evolutionary economics or game theory beyond the limits placed on explanation by psychologistic individualism – or perhaps even beyond that which the more general institutional individualism allows.

10 Time and Evolution in Economic Theory

When I was a boy, I had a clock with a pendulum which could be lifted off. I found that the clock went very much faster without the pendulum. If the main purpose of a clock is to go, the clock was the better for losing its pendulum. True, it could no longer tell the time, but that did not matter if one could teach oneself to be indifferent to the passage of time. The linguistic philosophy, which cares only about language, and not about the world, is like the boy who preferred the clock without the pendulum because, although it no longer told the time, it went more easily than before and at a more exhilarating pace.

Ernest Gellner [1959/68, p. 15]

Often in the writings of economists the words 'dynamic' and 'static' are used as nothing more than synonyms for good and bad, realistic and unrealistic, simple and complex. We damn another man's theory by terming it static, and advertise our own by calling it dynamic.

Paul Samuelson [1947/65, p. 311]

We ... learn that historical and institutional factors cannot be ignored. This is not a hard lesson for biologists, for whom the realities of genetic inheritance and the accidents of geography are brute facts that cannot be overlooked. But economists remain resistant to the idea that the same game might receive a different analysis if the players have a different history of experience, or live in different societies, or operate in different industries. One sometimes even reads that theories that ignore such considerations are 'superior' to those that do [not] because they are able to generate predictions with less data! However, if there is one fact that work on evolutionary games has established beyond doubt, it is that some details of the equilibrating process can have a major impact on the equilibrium selected. One of the major tasks awaiting us is to identify such significant details so that applied workers know what to look for in the environments within which the games they care about are played.

However, such a program is for the future. ... Evolutionary game theory is here to stay...

Ken Binmore [1995, pp. x–xi]

An evolutionary law is a proposition that describes an ordinal attribute E of a given system (or entity) and also states that if $E_1 < E_2$ then the observation of E_2 is later in Time than E_1, and conversely. That is, the attribute E is an *evolutionary index* of the system in point. Still more important is the fact that the ordinal measure of any such E can tell even an 'objective' mind – i.e., one deprived of the anthropomorphic faculty of sensing Time – the direction in which Time flows. Or, to use the eloquent term introduced by Eddington, we can say that E constitutes a 'time's arrow'. Clearly, E is not what we would normally call a cause, or the unique cause, of the evolutionary change.

Therefore, contrary to the opinion of some biologists, we do not need to discover a single cause for evolution in order to arrive at an evolutionary law. And in fact, almost every proposal of an evolutionary law for the biological or the social world has been concerned with a time's arrow, not with a single cause.

Of all the time's arrows suggested thus far for the biological world, 'complexity of organization' and 'degree of control over the environment' seem to enjoy the greatest popularity. One does not have to be a biologist, however, to see that neither proposal is satisfactory: the suggested attributes are not ordinally measurable.

Nicholas Georgescu-Roegen [1971, p. 128]

While in the 1970s the alleged lack of microfoundations for macroeconomics was once considered a telling criticism of neoclassical economics – and to a certain extent, even of Keynesian macroeconomics – a different line of criticism was subsequently promoted by post-Keynesian economists including George Shackle, Joan Robinson and Paul Davidson. Typical examples are: 'in its strict form, the theory of rational conduct ... must place itself in a timeless world, a world of a single moment which has neither past nor future' [Shackle 1973, p. 38]; 'The lack of a comprehensible treatment of historical time, and failure to specify the rules of the game in the type of economy under discussion, make the theoretical apparatus offered in neo-neoclassical textbooks useless for the analysis of contemporary problems, both in the micro and macro spheres' [Robinson 1974, p. 11] and 'The general equilibrium model ... abstracts from precisely those features that make the real world real – namely, the irreversibility of time and the uncertainty of the future' [Davidson 1981, p. 158].

What we should be asking is not whether neoclassical economics is timeless but whether its treatment of time is adequate. For any treatment of time to be adequate, it is necessary for the given model to be *in* time – that is, real time must matter in some fundamental way. The critics might thus argue that an adequate 'dynamic' model must include at least one dynamic process. But the question that I think we need to ask is: Can such a model ever be consistent with the hidden agenda? As discussed in the previous chapter, it is questionable whether any evolutionary model could ever satisfy the requirements of the psychologistic version of methodological individualism.

The elements of dynamic models

While Schumpeter-based evolutionary economics does seem to offer a recognition of a role for the dynamic process involving innovation and reactions to it, not much progress has been made within neoclassical theory towards an adequate approach which deals with *endogenous* dynamics. This is due partly to a failure to distinguish between dynamics and dynamic processes. To a great extent, Samuelson is to blame for this. He foisted a simplistic version of the physicist's distinction between 'statics' and 'dynamics' on us. This version of the distinction is not appropriate for economics problems. According to Samuelson, 'a dynamical system might be regarded as any set of functional equations which together with initial conditions ... determine as solutions certain unknowns in function of time', while 'timeless, statical systems are simply degenerate special cases in which the functional equations take on simple forms and determine as solutions functions of time which are identically constants' [1947/65, pp. 284–5].

The major difficulty with this simplistic distinction is that it confuses 'timeless' with 'static'. Whether or not a system is static is more properly a question of dynamics. Specifically, a system is static only if the given 'initial conditions' are constant over time. In this sense, the distinction between static and dynamic is no more informative than the Marshallian assumption that some givens are constant over a relevant time period. A more realistic distinction between static and dynamic is needed; one that more accurately reflects the sense in which the critics claim that a static model is limited by comparison with a dynamic model. For this purpose, I think we need a distinction that involves how we use a model's exogenous variables. Remember that a model's exogenous variables are the ones that we are not trying to explain because they are caused outside of the model and thus cannot be explained by the model. For an adequate dynamic model, the dynamics must be endogenous. So the question will always be whether true dynamics could ever be endogenous.

Dynamic explanation vs. explanations of dynamics

The basis of all explanations in economics is the behavior of exogenous givens. Once one has explained all the values of endogenous variables in any given model, their values cannot change without a change in at least one exogenous given. Whenever neoclassical models involve at least one dynamic exogenous given (i.e., its value changes with the passage of time), it can be argued that such models are dynamic explanations. There are two aspects to this observation about neoclassical models. One involves the necessity of exogenous variables; the other involves what constitutes an explanation of changes over time.

All explanations are essentially causal explanations – there is no other type of explanation [Hicks 1979]. No one model can explain everything; there must be some givens. Every model, which is not circular, has at least one variable that is exogenous. The values of endogenous variables are, in this sense, 'caused' by the values of the exogenous variables. When there is more than one exogenous variable, we cannot consider them to be causes in the ordinary sense. That is, we cannot say, for example, the price is determined by demand, since it also depends on the supply possibilities. This has long been a source of confusion in economics but it would be easily cleared up in the case of multiple 'causes' by referring to them as causal influences.

I point all this out only because the arguments raised below are not those raised by multiple 'causes' but rather those raised by the logic of explaining dynamic processes. Typically, changes in endogenous variables are explained by showing that they have been caused by changes in one or more exogenous variables – this is a simple matter in the case of one exogenous variable but a little confusing in the case of more than one. Since 'change' usually implies the passage of time, one could go further and explain the history of the endogenous variables as being caused by the history of the exogenous variables. In either case most economists would call these dynamic explanations. What I will consider here is whether one can have a dynamic explanation of the dynamics of any dynamical model. I shall argue that any model involving *only* exogenous dynamic processes that does not explain those processes is, at best, incomplete.

Change in neoclassical models

It is important to remember that in neoclassical economics there is only one behavioral assumption – the neoclassical maximization hypothesis. Only this assumption can be used to explain why anyone would change their behavior. And thus (as I said in Chapter 7) the only reason to change one's choice of a quantity to supply or to consume is that at the present time the quantity being supplied or demanded is not the one that would maximize profit or utility. A current failure to maximize could be the result of a previous change in the situation faced by the decision-maker. For example, the price may have changed or the technology of production may have been changed. While we may wish to explain the change in situation facing a consumer by saying tastes have changed, it should be recognized that some neoclassical economists (particularly George Stigler and Gary Becker [1977]) urge us to avoid this approach to explaining behavioral changes. One reason for avoiding the use of changes in taste to explain changes in a consumer's choices is that it would invite a retreat into behavioral psychology and thereby minimize the significance of economics. Minimization aside, while psychologists might like to explain changes in tastes, it is not clear that anyone could ever explain tastes as purely a matter of psychology any more than one can completely explain tastes as a matter of sociology [cf. Newman 1972]. But, perhaps Stigler and Becker may be over reacting or maybe they are just saying that the change must be endogenous and any change of taste would be exogenous and thus unexplained. For my purposes here, either way, refusing to recognize changes in tastes would seem itself to be a minimization of the significance of the neoclassical view of the role of a market system. After all, proponents (such as Stigler and Becker) of an exclusive reliance on the market to coordinate social activity strongly emphasize its effectiveness in responding to changes in tastes. All of this means that we can allow tastes to change as well as any other exogenous variables but if we want to explain the changes then we need to address how change can be made endogenous beyond just recognizing any failure to maximize.

The dynamic skeleton in the closet

Kenneth Arrow [1959] (following 1969 Nobel laureate Ragnar Frisch [1926/71, 1936]) long ago recognized that neoclassical economics still needs an explanation of how the price is adjusted to the equilibrium price. The usual textbook's hand-waving that just says the price is bid up or down whenever demand is not equal to supply begs the question. The question was discussed before with particular reference to Figure 7.1. What remains most important with this question is to recognize that to satisfy methodological individualism *things* cannot decide and thus neoclassical theorists need to explain why some individual would bid the price up or down. Of course, as was noted there, the reason for bidding the price up is that demand exceeds supply such that at least one demander is unable to maximize utility. That is, at least one demander cannot buy enough to be able to maximize his or her utility and thus offers a higher price to suppliers. If a supplier chooses to redirect its output to the higher-paying consumer, then some other consumer will be left out and thus can no longer maximize. The higher price also creates a situation for suppliers who, for this price, are no longer maximizing and thus change to a higher level of output. This dual response continues until the supply quantity is increased and the demand quantity is reduced (in response to the higher price) such that the excess of demand over supply is eliminated. What Arrow observes about this is that nowhere does neoclassical economics explain how much the price is bid up or down. And however we might try to explain the 'how much', to be consistent the reason has to be something to do with maximization. The on-going failure to provide such an explanation is a skeleton in the neoclassical closet [see further, Boland 1986a, chap. 9].

A critique of traditional models of dynamic processes

> The definition of economic dynamics (that much controverted term) which I have in mind here is this. I call Economic Statics those parts of economic theory where we do not trouble about dating; Economic Dynamics those parts where every quantity must be dated. For example, in economic statics we think of an entrepreneur employing such-and-such quantities of factors and producing by their aid such-and-such quantities of products; but we do not ask when the factors are employed and when the products come to be ready. In economic dynamics we do ask such questions; and we even pay special attention to the way changes in these dates affect the relations between factors and products.
>
> John Hicks [1939/46, p. 115]

So, the requirements of any neoclassical model that intends to address the questions of dynamics are that each explanation must not violate methodological individualism and it must not include any behavioral assumption other than one having to do with maximization. Note that maximization can be used either directly or indirectly. The indirect version is merely the recognition that the decision-makers change their behavior whenever their current choices are not maximizing profit or utility.

With all of this in mind, let me examine how neoclassical economists have so far tried to incorporate time and dynamics in their models. Specifically, one way time has been incorporated was by simply recognizing that a hamburger that one buys today is not the same hamburger one bought two months ago. Thus, to distinguish products in this way, model builders, as the 1972 Nobel prize-winner John Hicks suggested, simply distinguish non-durable products sold at different points in time by adding a time-subscript to each. A second way is to make time one of the endogenous variables such that we can talk about the economics of time. A third way is to recognize that the yesterday's value of a variable can have a 'lagged' effect on today's choice. And a fourth way is to see variables as 'flows' rather than 'stocks' and thereby moving the questions into the mathematical realm of differential equations. I will examine each of these as questionable means of addressing the needs of a truly dynamic economic model

– that is, one for which the dynamics is endogenous. But before doing this, I want to briefly revisit Marshall's possibly false dynamics.

Is the long run vs. short run the basis for explaining dynamics?

Marshall explicitly defined long and short runs only as a way of addressing the needs of explanatory methodology – specifically to distinguish between variables that are easy to change from those that are more difficult. As discussed in Chapter 6, he defined his short run as a period too short for a firm to change its physical capital (i.e., machinery) but long enough for the firm to change the amount of labor it wants to use. But, again, the distinction is only due to his notion that one cannot explain something as a matter of choice unless there is a sufficient time to vary that choice. Nowhere did Marshall explain the dynamics involved; he just takes the difference in changeability as an essential part of any 'scientific' explanation.

The time-as-a-subscript approach to dynamics

Now, it is Hicks who explicitly tries to deal with the explanatory problems of dynamics in his famous *Value and Capital* [1939/46] but, as the quotation above shows, he introduced dynamics only by putting a date on every quantity. In a similar manner, Tjalling Koopmans [1957] and Gerard Debreu [1959] tried to overcome the temporal limitations of static models by dating all variables with subscripts and then building models covering many points in time. In these models they simply put time subscripts on all goods, such as I suggested above with hamburgers. Hamburger (H_t), at time $t = t_1$ is not the same as a hamburger (H_t) at time $t = t_2$. Of course, in a model representing an entire general equilibrium, we have many more goods than one could observe at any one point in time. Nevertheless, the notion is that we would build an intertemporal model covering all points in time and thus all goods. The paradigm of this model is the one due to Arrow and Debreu [1954].

In this form, an equilibrium model requires the specification of intertemporal preferences or utility functions so that it can explain all prices and all goods. As such, this type of model is essentially static for the entire period of time over which the goods are defined. There are no dynamics to be explained here because nothing is changing. Specifically, the values of the endogenous variables at any point can be shown to follow from the values of the exogenous variables statically given at the unique initial point in time. The maximizing individual makes his or her only decision at that singular initial point in time. That is, without further changes in the exogenous variables, there are no dynamics.

The 'economics of time' approach

> What we must not abandon are Böhm-Bawerk's ... true insights – the things that are the strength of the 'Austrian' approach. Production is a process, a process in time. Though there are degenerate forms ... the characteristic form of production is a sequence, in which inputs are followed by outputs.
>
> John Hicks [1973, pp. 193–4]

There are two different ways to include time as a variable in a neoclassical model. One is to treat time as a simple resource to be allocated (in the manner that a firm allocates its fixed resources in the production of a good) such as with the 1992 Nobel prize-winner Gary Becker's theory of allocating time [1965]. But this way only amounts to a static allocation of a commodity and in no way represents an explanation of dynamics. Eugene Böhm-Bawerk's period of production model [1889] goes much further in this pursuit and is easy to illustrate with a simple diagram, see Figure 10.1. Böhm-Bawerk's model can be used to explain how long to wait before the product is considered finished. Given a fixed amount of working capital (needed to pay labor in advance), the optimum waiting time will maximize the profit rate (i) as can be seen in this diagram. Specifically, the model involves two exogenous givens: one is a given working capital (C–F), the other is a given production function (PF) that indicates the level of the output for any particular amount of waiting time (such as, when trees are growing or wine is aging). The optimum waiting time will be obtained where the marginal cost of waiting (measured by the slope of the line A–B drawn through point C) equals the marginal product of waiting for a small unit of time. In the figure this occurs for the optimum 'average production period' (G–F).

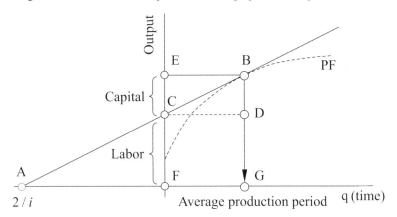

Figure 10.1 Böhm-Bawerk's optimum production period

Unfortunately, like Becker's model, while Böhm-Bawerk's model looks like it is dealing with time, it must be recognized that the only dynamics involved are provided by the exogenous production function (which relates output to the amount of 'waiting' time), that is, in the biology of growing trees or aging wine. And in such a model, the production function is thus exogenously given by Nature. No dynamics are being explained, that is, there is no *endogenous* dynamic variable involved – only a static allocation in the case of Becker or a statically given production function in the case of Böhm-Bawerk.

The 'variable givens' or 'lagged variables' approach

Rather than treat time or a time-based constraining function as a static, exogenous given, one could recognize that the exogenous variables change over time. That is, one might attempt to determine the *time-path trajectory* of the endogenous variables that would result from exogenously changing givens.

As with the time-as-a-subscript approach, one does not necessarily have to assume that the exogenous variables are from the same point in time as that of the endogenous variables. For example, one could assert that some of today's exogenous variables may be yesterday's endogenous variables [Nerlove 1972]. With such a 'lagged variable' approach one could derive a time-path trajectory for the endogenous variables. However, as an extension of Böhm-Bawerk's model, the position of the trajectory over a given time period will depend only on the initial set of exogenous values for the givens.

Superficially, the direct approach of using exogenous time-paths for the givens, or the indirect approach using lagged variables, appears to be a successful approach to dynamics. But on closer examination, this appearance is an illusion. With the exogenous trajectory approach, endogenous variables are changing *only* because the exogenous variables are exogenously changing. With the lagged variables approach, the position of an endogenous variable on its trajectory is uniquely determined merely by the length of time that has transpired since the initial givens were established. The position of the trajectory itself is uniquely determined by the initial values of the exogenous givens alone. In both cases the *trajectories* of the endogenous variables are exogenously and mechanically fixed. Again, the only 'dynamics' of the model are exogenous. Since exogeneity of any model results from an explicit choice to not explain the givens or their behavior, the dynamic changes have not been explained *within* the model. In other words such models are still relying on a statically given time-path trajectory which is fixed over the relevant time period. Unless we explain why it is that trajectory rather than some other, there can be no endogenous dynamics. One could assume the given path was such that the exogenous variable grew at a fixed rate. When asked why one did not assume an increasing rate, one cannot justify this assumption solely on the grounds that it yields the observed time-path of the endogenous variables. Surely, the truth of one's assumptions regarding exogenous givens must be independent of one's conclusions regarding endogenous variables.

The 'flow variables' approach

My criticisms of those types of explanations of dynamics that merely add time by defining certain variables can be extended to those approaches that add a time-differential equation to an otherwise static model. But, as I have already noted, the one effort to directly deal with dynamics [Arrow 1959] remains a failure – except, it did recognize the need for a consistent explanation. We still need an explanation for how much a disappointed demander or supplier would bid the price up or down. As Arrow characterized the problem (briefly discussed in Chapter 7), we need an explanation for the differential equation that explains the speed of price adjustment as a function of excess supply:

$$(dp_t/dt) = h(S_t - D_t),$$

where $dh/d(S_t - D_t)$ is negative and $h(0) = 0$ (these latter two conditions are needed to assure that the price converges to an equilibrium price). But unless this additional equation is explained as a consequence of a process to maximize utility or profit, the dynamics are purely improvised and arbitrary. A make-shift differential equation for the 'dynamics' of the market does not even say who changes the price or why it is being changed. Until we can say why the price has changed (rather than describing how much it should change), we have explained neither the process of disequilibrium change nor the dynamics of the market. In other words, the minimal requirements of methodological individualism and the specific needs of neoclassical explanations have not been satisfied with these approaches to the explanation of economic dynamics.

Real time vs. long run

Significant as some may consider such criticism to be [e.g., Gordon and Hynes 1970], matters are even worse for the determination of the equilibrium level of prices. Most models that attempt to explain price dynamics using time-differential equations only guarantee a solution in the long run. Such models are incapable of yielding a determinant and non-arbitrary solution for the prices at points of real (calendar or clock) time where equilibrium has been reached. If by 'in the long run' we mean that it takes anything approaching an infinite amount of time to yield a determinant solution, we are in effect conceding that we do not have a real-time explanation of the observed behavior of the endogenous variables. Specifically, I will now make explicit the following methodological principle:

> *To assert the existence of a long-run equilibrium when its attainment requires an infinite length of time is to imply either that time does not matter or that we have no explanation.*

Obviously, the usual Conventionalist argument that true knowledge is impossible, based on what I called the inductive learning possibilities function (in Chapter 8), is also based on this methodological principle.

Time, logic and true statements

Having argued that all of the usual ways of including time in neoclassical economic models fail does not mean that neoclassical economics is timeless. The claim that neoclassical models are 'timeless' (which I mentioned at the beginning of this chapter) should be rejected because this type of criticism is usually based on a confusion between conceivably false (dynamic) statements, which may happen to be true at all points in time, with tautological statements, which are true at all points in time simply because conceivably they cannot be false. Also the critics usually fail to distinguish between a model's solution statement that can be a timeless logical relation, and the logical consistency of the specific joint logical relationship between the values of all the endogenous variables and the time-based truth of the statements of the values of the exogenous variables. This latter failure has probably been the major source of misunderstanding about the alleged timelessness of neoclassical models. That a model or any explanation can be shown to be logically valid does not say that its truth status is timeless. This is simply because *a model is not timeless if any of its parts is not a tautology*. All models must have at least one such non-tautological statement, namely, the statement representing the values of the exogenous variables.

Time and knowledge

> economic problems arise always and only in consequence of change... [T]he economic problem of society is mainly one of rapid adaptation to changes in the particular circumstances of time and place.
>
> Friedrich Hayek [1945/48, pp. 82-3]

The discussion so far seems to suggest that any reliance on neoclassical general equilibrium theory alone precludes an explanation of historical change. All the causes, motivations, or reasons for change are beyond explanation because they are being considered exogenous to the models. In other words, we always face the problem of having to choose between dynamic explanations and explanations of dynamics (i.e., of the dynamic processes). The question might now be raised as to what do we want for an explanation of dynamics. At minimum, as the Georgescu-Roegen quotation at the top of this chapter suggests, whatever we do, we must be sure that once a variable is changed by a decision-maker, it cannot be perfectly reversed. That is, true dynamics in the real world are irreversible – time's arrow only goes in one direction. Said another way: real, irreversible 'historical' time is not what Robinson [1974] calls 'logical time'. By the latter she meant that when considering various possible values of a model's exogenous variables, should one of them change and thus yield a new set of values for the endogenous variables, restoring the original values of the exogenous variables will restore the original values of the model's endogenous variables. So, if we are to construct models that include endogenous dynamics, then the time-dependent variable must not involve such logical time.

The problem with all of the ways of including time that I discussed above is that nothing prevents reversibility. Georgescu-Roegen's solution for this problem is to introduce the Second Law of Thermodynamics, the so-called Entropy Law. It says, in simple terms, that it is impossible to construct a perpetual-motion machine. Every action uses energy – even the action that tries to reverse a previous action. 'Entropy' is a measure of used energy. But, from the perspective of economics, this solution seems to be nothing more than a restatement of the irreversibility of time without any behavioral implications. We need somehow to identify an essential ingredient in every neoclassical model that will provide the required temporal irreversibility.

If in our effort to deal with the irreversibility of time we also wish to maintain methodological individualism, eliminating the dilemma would appear to be simple. Specifically, when constructing a simple general equilibrium model, we might add the decision-maker's knowledge (or 'expectations') as an explicit variable. Surely, learning is irreversible. This approach seems to be what evolutionary game theorists appear to be doing – as I suggested in the previous chapter. But, if knowledge or its acquisition process is treated as another exogenous or statically given variable, then the problem of explaining dynamics remains. Similarly, no model solves the problem if it merely requires an individual decision-maker to have the benefits of a correct economic theory (e.g., one that presumes the individual has correctly assessed the costs and benefits of collecting more information). Such a model is thereby just suppressing the role of the individual decision-maker's knowledge. Furthermore, if the individual's knowledge is suppressed only 'in the long run' (by assuming that there has been enough time to acquire true knowledge – see Figure 8.3) we are then brought back to the irrelevance of real time. To solve the problem of explaining dynamics, the individual's *process* of acquiring his or her knowledge must be endogenous; it must be something to be explained. In rational decision models in a dynamic context, the individual's process of learning and adapting must take place in real (viz., irreversible) time.

Towards an essential role for time

If the 1974 Nobel laureate Friedrich Hayek [1945/48] is right, the obvious way to explain dynamics in a methodological individualist context is to identify a reason for why individuals would *choose to change* their behavior. One of the primary means of explaining the existence of disequilibria – and thus the need for change – involves the recognition of 'expectational errors', which are always possible when making decisions that depend on one's view of the future. Every investment decision runs this risk. And moreover, an investment error is not usually reversible – at least not completely.

Along these lines, some progress towards incorporating real time in economics models would seem to have been made by various post-Keynesian theorists some time ago. For example, Shackle [1972] and Davidson [1972] argued that the existence of money in an economy is a direct consequence of the importance of real time. Specifically, except in a barter economy where all transactions are direct and immediate, market transactions can often require placing an order at one point in time and acquiring the goods or sales revenue at a later point in time. In many cases this involves a sales contract. A sales contract can specify the consequences of failure to deliver the goods. The penalty for failure is almost always expressed in monetary terms – hence an additional role for money in models of economic dynamics that goes beyond the traditional static role (store of value, unit of account or medium of exchange).

From the perspective of this post-Keynesian view, money makes real-time contracts possible. More important, contracts would be unnecessary without essential processes that involve the passage of time (e.g., growing corn, aging wine, etc.). But does recognizing money and contracts overcome the shortcomings of neoclassical models? If the only reason for the contracts is the exogenously given time-using processes, then we have not moved beyond the 'economics of time' approach of Becker and Böhm-Bawerk, both of which make the dynamics exogenous.

It could still be argued that the post-Keynesian view does provide the essential endogeneity of dynamics with its recognition of the role of 'expectations'. Specifically, what is recognized in Shackle's view is 'uncertainty' that would give cause for the formation of expectations. The fact that we cannot know for certain that our expectations are true makes contracts (and money) an essential part of an explanation of 'rational' decision-making. But unfortunately, it is all too easy for a clever neoclassical theorist to argue that the recognition of uncertainty, expectations and contracts merely leads us to explain why certain contracts are better than others and thereby to bring the contracts and uncertainty into the neoclassical research program.

What is the basis for the post-Keynesian view that expectations necessitate contracts and the use of money? Unfortunately, it is our old friend the inductive learning possibilities function. On its basis one's view of the future could never be true, since proof of their truth would require an infinite amount of time or data. But, relying on an exogenous learning function is no different than relying on exogenous trajectories of the exogenous variables. By just focusing on expectations in this manner, there would be no endogenous dynamics in these post-Keynesian models. And worse, as we saw with the Rational Expectations Hypothesis, it is all too easy to argue that the formation of expectations can be seen to be a 'rational' process using all available evidence and thus any errors could be explained away (see Chapter 8).

Parenthetically, it might be thought that this post-Keynesian perspective does nothing more than what New Institutional Economists (such as Williamson) might be promoting. Both seem to be advocating the recognition of the time-use cost of transactions. But, fortunately, the post-Keynesian view of money provides more than just the facilitation of contracts to deal with unknown future circumstances. Actually the existence of money facilitates error which in turn gives the needed reasons for change. This is true even if one could form 'rational expectations'. A rational argument in favor of one's expectations could still be a false argument. And as Hayek [1933/39] noted seventy years ago, when the errors made are systematic and thus shared by many decision-makers – particularly investors (such as when they are misled by allegedly mistaken government policies that were common in the early 1930s) – the errors can lead to macroeconomic disequilibria. And the responses themselves could be based on systematic errors and thus lead to poor economic performance by an entire economy.

Learning and time's arrow

It could still be argued that Georgescu-Roegen's entropy perspective does nevertheless directly deal with time's arrow. But, an increasing entropy could never be responsible for errors. Moreover, trying to model entropy as a factor in decision-making seems to beg credibility, anyway. A more credible approach might be to recognize the individual decision-maker's learning in the sense that people learn but they cannot *un*learn.

It could alternatively be argued (along the lines of the 'bucket theory of knowledge' that I will discuss in Chapter 16) that collecting information might be considered a process of knowledge acquisition such that, as I have already said, once such knowledge is acquired it cannot be unlearned. Presumably, the process would be some form of induction. But it must be kept in mind that at any stage short of an inductive proof, the acquired knowledge can be false. And, of course, there is no logic that could ever provide an inductive proof. Without such a proof, induction does not mean much. Moreover, short of an inductive proof, any acquired knowledge might be overturned by just one refuting observation (e.g., the knowledge that 'all swans are white' would be refuted with the observation of just one non-white swan). In this case, such a refutation can easily be interpreted as a case of unlearning. So, a growing collection of information cannot be used to provide a way of assuring that we have provided for time's arrow.

One key difference between Georgescu-Roegen's entropy perspective and a presumption of an inductive learning is that while the former has no endpoint (except if one thinks in terms of the Universe with its finite amount of energy that might someday be exhausted), proponents of Inductivism do conceive of an endpoint where true knowledge is inductively proven. Another difference is that while the entropy perspective is irreversible, induction-acquired knowledge can be undone (as I just explained in the previous paragraph).

Thus, what we need is a view of learning that, like the entropy perspective, is unending. That is, we need the perspective of the early Socrates. At the end of Chapter 8, I provided such a perspective with the discussion of how the consumer is assumed to know his or her preferences. The main point is that the consumer in the real world could never have such knowledge if it is assumed that knowledge must be acquired inductively. The Socratic alternative is to think of the consumer always testing his or her assumption of the nature of the preferences. This testing behavior would necessarily lead to a dynamic trial-and-error groping and thus never can be characterized as a static choice even when facing statically given prices and budgets [see further, Hammes 1985, chap. 8].

Several years ago, I discussed the dynamic aspects of the Socratic alternative [Boland 1986b]. The specific proposal was to explain how, as a neoclassical decision-maker, a typical consumer interprets collected information and, in particular, information that might refute the inductive inferences based on information collected prior to observing the refuting information. In this regard, I offered six different ways that a consumer might deal with any evidence when facing a static situation involving given prices, budget and his or her preferences or utility function:

> *Inductivist consumers* who think that one should not jump to conclusions and thus that one never knows the correct utility function until one provides an inductive proof – all done without ever making any assumptions. Such a consumer will always be forced to keep trying new bundles. Although facing a static situation, an inductivist consumer would appear never to be satisfied.

> *Sophisticated Inductivist consumers* who think it would be wrong to simply collect facts without thinking ahead. Even if one arbitrarily adopts a theory of the nature of one's utility function, one can still never

be satisfied until that theory is proven true. This approach can also lead to the appearance of unstable buying patterns. Nevertheless, if the theory is true, over time we should expect to see the adaptive buying pattern converging to a stable point.

Apriorist consumers who begin by 'knowing' the true utility function (either by assumption, introspection or 'rational expectations'), and thus no market evidence could ever cause them to change their mind. Their buying patterns are not only stable but they are also invariant.

Conventionalist consumers who, given the many conceivable utility functions, ask 'how does one pick one to start with?' If one gives up the requirement of a complete proof, various criteria can be adopted to appraise one's theory of one's utility function. In effect, the Conventionalist consumer need only be a good econometrician – perhaps, a Bayesian econometrician [Leamer 1983; Poirier 1988]. No claim is made that the true utility function is found, but only the best available according to the evidence and the adopted criteria. The pattern of consumption behavior will depend on the method used to process data. For example, how many tests of current theory are required before concluding one knows or does not know the true utility function? Competent Conventionalist consumers might test their theory every third trip to the market and still be able to explain away numerous refuting observations before being forced to change their pattern of behavior.

Skepticist consumers are always skeptical about proving any theory true. These consumers will change their mind about their personal utility functions the first time some purchased bundle does not meet their expectations. While the Conventionalist consumers can tolerate occasional disappointments and thus seldom alter their consumption patterns, the skepticist consumers will be jumping all over the map.

Instrumentalist consumers for whom it is not always clear what they might do since the truth of their theories of their utility functions supposedly does not matter. They might act *as if* they liked their purchases when indeed they detested them. As long as their social role does not change, one could predict that the Instrumentalist consumers might continue to buy the bundle of goods that is most useful for their chosen careers. Any change in career will be accompanied by a change in the consumption pattern.

Note that only in the case of the Inductivist consumer is learning a mechanical process. No autonomous thinking is going on other than assuming that knowledge is based on Inductivism. The main point here is that consumers must decide on their methodology. And given the variety, there is no reason for them all to adopt the same methodology. Consideration of the possibility that consumers may differ in how they deal with such methodological questions, should lead economic theorists to also question their own views of methodology. Not only do economists hold views about their methodology, but they also attribute such views to the individual decision-maker who likewise must be assumed to have some methodology to deal with the available facts. Explaining how individuals deal with factual evidence should be within the purview of methodology, so I will return in Part VI to a consideration of the economists' views of methodology.

Does evolutionary economics solve the problem of explaining dynamics?

> Science values static patterns. Its business is to search for them. When non-conformity appears it is considered an interruption of the normal rather than the presence of the normal. A deviation from a normal static pattern is something to be explained and if possible controlled... Naturally there is no mechanism toward which life is heading. Mechanisms are the enemy of life. The more static and unyielding the mechanisms are, the more life works to evade them or overcome them.
>
> The law of gravity, for example, is perhaps the most ruthlessly static pattern of order in the universe... One could almost define life as the organized disobedience of the law of gravity. One could show that the degree to which an organism disobeys this law is a measure of its degree of evolution. Thus, while the simple protozoa just barely get around on their cilia, earthworms manage to control their distance and direction, birds fly into the sky, and man goes all the way to the moon.
>
> ... 'survival-of-the-fittest' is one of those catch-phrases like 'mutants' or 'misfits' that sounds best when you don't ask precisely what it means. Fittest for what? Fittest for survival? That reduces to 'survival of the survivors', which doesn't say anything. 'Survival of the fittest' is meaningful only when 'fittest' is equated with 'best'... And the Darwinians ... are absolutely certain there is no way to define what that 'fittest' is...
>
> Biological evolution can be seen as a process by which weak Dynamic forces at a subatomic level discover stratagems for overcoming huge static inorganic forces at a superatomic level. They do this by selecting superatomic mechanisms in which a number of options are so evenly balanced that a weak Dynamic force can tip the balance one way or another.
>
> Robert Pirsig [1991, p. 142–5]

The idea that learning could be a source of dynamics is clearly understood by Nelson and Winter but other than a Schumpeter-type or Smith-type conjecture about what is allowed by market competition, the actual process of learning is never explained. Clearly, in the case of evolutionary game theorists and some macroeconomists, the only learning at issue is that directed toward how players arrive at a Nash or a Rational-Expectations equilibrium. And ordinary game theorists have merely assumed the necessary knowledge has somehow been acquired. As I have already noted, in the case of game theory neither type sees a need to address the theory of knowledge that the players would need to have in order to move toward the needed knowledge. Learning, as methodologists and philosophers of science understand it, is never a consideration for game theorists. At best, they presume a 1950s-type behaviorist (i.e., 'stimulus-response' or 'reinforcement') theory of learning – the one characterized with Pavlov's dog that was trained mechanically to salivate whenever a bell rang.

Now, an evolutionary economist might simply see my six conjectured ways that consumers could try to learn when dealing with their lack of full knowledge of their situation as merely six different decision rules that are subject to evolutionary selection. But, contrarily, my point for raising these particular learning methodologies is that each is based on a false theory of knowledge. If they are subjected to some sort of evolutionary selection process, whichever one is selected will still be an inadequate view of knowledge and learning. And if it also is presumed that the only successful outcome possible is the achievement of an eventual equilibrium in the absence of an exogenous changing in the static situation, there is no guarantee that the eventual equilibrium is the individual's desired optimum.

Without a theory of the individual's learning process, replete with assumptions about the individual's own theory of knowledge and its implications for how to go about learning, there is no endogenous dynamics in evolutionary economics. Instead, learning is unexplained; it is a mysterious, exogenous event analogous to biological mutations. As always, part of the reason for the lack of a theory of endogenous learning is that economic theorists take for granted either Inductivism as a long-run view or Conventionalism as a short-run compromise in lieu of an explanation. When it is Inductivism, learning is purely a matter of mechanically connecting one's knowledge to the available 'facts'. When it is Conventionalism, learning is a matter of connecting with the social conventions of the day and as such there is no dynamics; it is only a question of whether one's decisions are consistent with the statically given knowledge standards.

Evolutionary economics without an element of endogenous dynamics fails to provide an alternative to neoclassical economics. To the extent that evolutionary economics might try to explain how and when an individual firm chooses to innovate or imitate then, a Schumpeterian theory of economic dynamics would seem to be possible – and it would also address the needs of methodological individualism. But, should such a theory be constructed, it ceases to be evolutionary in the popular sense that equates learning with social evolution. And if all of the dynamics of the theory is invested in the act of innovating or imitating, then the evolutionary perspective that stresses the selection process would seem irrelevant. If it is relevant, then the act of innovating or imitating does not play an explanatory role – and it would fail to satisfy the requirements of methodological individualism. The dilemma of evolutionary explanations remains. If one explains the dynamics endogenously, it ceases to be evolution-based. If one tries to make the social aspects of learning play a role, the essential dynamics are exogenous. Adherence to methodological individualism suggests that we should try to explain how the individual learns what is needed to make explainable decisions in a manner to explain the dynamics of learning. I will give some suggestions along this line in the Part VI.

Part IV
A CRITIQUE OF TRADITIONAL ECONOMIC METHODOLOGY

11 Instrumentalism vs. Conventionalism: Against Rule-based Methodology

> It may be said without qualification that political economy, whether having recourse to the deductive method or not, must begin with observation and end with observation. ... there is a tendency to forget that the deductive method in its complete form consists of three stages, only one of which is actually deductive, the two others being the inductive determination of the premises, and the inductive verification of conclusions.
>
> John Neville Keynes [1917, p. 105]

> The subject matter of economics is regarded by almost everyone as vitally important to himself and within the range of his own experience and competence; it is the source of continuous and extensive controversy and the occasion for frequent legislation. Self-proclaimed 'experts' speak with many voices and can hardly all be regarded as disinterested; in any event, on questions that matter so much, 'expert' opinion could hardly be accepted solely on faith even if the 'experts' were nearly unanimous and clearly disinterested.
>
> Milton Friedman [1953, pp. 3-4]

In this and the next chapter I will examine the revealed methodologies of the leading currents in mainstream neoclassical economics. This chapter is about Instrumentalism beyond what was discussed at the end of Chapter 1. The next chapter will examine Conventionalism distinguishing between the various major versions practiced in neoclassical economics. Instrumentalism – unlike all versions of Conventionalism – is based on a rejection of any need to solve the Problem of Induction. I will try to clarify how Instrumentalism differs from a similar methodological viewpoint called Pragmatism. The extent to which Instrumentalism and Pragmatism can differ from Conventionalist methodology will also be addressed in this chapter.

Popular methodology alternatives

There is little new under the methodological sun. As explained in Chapter 1, most methodological rules and prescriptions can be traced to nineteenth-century reactions to Hume's recognition of the impossibility of providing a foolproof empirical basis for (scientific) knowledge. The most widely accepted prescription is the one usually attributed to John Neville Keynes: Thou shall not base positive economics on normative judgments. As the above quotation demonstrates, J. N. Keynes seemed to presume that if there were methodological rules (viz., 'stages') governing economics they would have to be the dictates of an Inductivist philosophy of science. His only problem was that he was a hundred years too late. Inductivism was on the way out as a result of Hume's arguments, and Duhem, Poincaré, Eddington and others were already developing an alternative viewpoint with respect to the philosophy of physics. Their view in some interpretations is what I have been calling Conventionalism. At about the same time Dewey, Mach and others were developing yet another alternative. This latter alternative is sometimes called Pragmatism and at other times called Instrumentalism, even though these two views are not always equivalent. Where Conventionalism and Pragmatism are direct competitors, Conventionalism and Instrumentalism are not. This may seem confusing but it is the reason why there is much confusion about the differences between Conventionalism and the methodology Friedman promotes in his famous essay [1953] (which it can be argued is merely a straightforward version of the methodology which Popper calls 'Instrumentalism' [Boland 1979a]). In their pure form, both reject Pragmatism but some proponents of Instrumentalism want to have it both ways [cf. Hammond 1993]. Furthermore, if one gives up interest in the Problem of Induction, none of these popular alternatives seems worthwhile.

Conventionalism and Pragmatism

What I am calling Pragmatism here has, like Conventionalism, its roots in our inability to solve the classic Problem of Induction. Hardly anyone today thinks the old 'scientific method' – namely, step-by-step, systematic proof by induction – is effective. Very many philosophers (but not all) think that the Problem of Induction still needs to be solved or dealt with in some other way; they think an alternative *must* be found.

Conventionalism and Pragmatism are still the most common competing ways of dealing with the Problem of Induction. Both are concerned with proofs of the truth of our scientific (or other) knowledge. However, it is possible to distinguish between two forms of Pragmatism: either one accepts practical success as a sufficient criterion of the truth of any theory or one retreats to a position whereby practical concerns demand the acceptance of workable premises as a matter of faith. This latter position is called 'fideism' [see Agassi 1985; cf. Bartley 1982]. Either way, if the theory works, it must be true, since that is all we ever want of a theory. Conventionalism takes a very different tack. It says that it is a mistake to think that scientific theories are true. Instead, any given theory is by some measure only 'better' or 'worse' than some other competing theory. In short, no theory is to be considered absolutely true, or provable by reference to facts. As we have seen for adherents of Conventionalism, a theory is a convenient description of, or filing system for, the existing facts. Apparently, some filing systems are better than others. Along these lines, according to Samuelson's [1965] version of Conventionalism, 'explanation' is merely the name we give to a 'better description'.

In order to distinguish Pragmatism from Conventionalism let me recast the nature of Conventionalism. Conventionalism is designed to deal with the classic Problem of Induction but it does so by redefining the problem by changing it into a problem that can be solved. Conventionalism is designed to solve the revised problem of choosing the 'best' theory among several competitors. The 'best' is always *relative* (i.e., subject to conditions). Obviously, there is no claim that the 'best' theory is necessarily the one 'true' theory; this is the quintessence of Conventionalism. There are many different versions of Conventionalism which differ only to the extent that there are different criteria to be used to choose the 'best' theory.

Non-fideistic Pragmatism takes a slightly stronger stand in that when a theory is judged to be working, its premises must be true, not just the 'best'. The fideistic version is more like Conventionalism in that there is a recognition of a theory not necessarily being absolutely true but given the pressure of everyday life to take a stand, fideistic Pragmatism will consider a theory that works to be true. For my purposes here, I will leave these fine distinctions aside and just refer to Pragmatism as the doctrine that goes beyond Instrumentalism by claiming that theories that work have the status of being true. Instrumentalism would simply say that a theory's truth status does not matter.

All versions of Conventionalism require generous amounts of hand-waving and clever philosophical analyses to be convincing. Pragmatism is much more straightforward. Whatever 'works' is true or must be considered true. If a theory does not work, it cannot be true. If it is true, it will work. If it is false, then eventually we will find that there is something for which it does not work.

The important point I wish to stress here is that both Conventionalism and Pragmatism are based on the acceptance of the necessity of dealing with the Problem of Induction. The former deals with the problem by 'moving the goal posts' – that is, by denying its original objective which was to establish the truth of scientific theories. The latter deals with the problem by accepting a weak criterion of truth – namely, 'usefulness'. Since Friedman's 1953 essay often invokes usefulness as its primary objective, its application to policy is often considered a version of Pragmatism. And for this reason, some followers of Pragmatism exhibit a vague ambivalence towards the methodology presented in Friedman's essay [e.g., Hirsch and de Marchi 1990, pp. 291–2]. They miss the point, however. The methodology of Friedman's *essay* also rejects Pragmatism!

Instrumentalism and 'usefulness'

It is nevertheless true that once one recognizes 'usefulness' as a criterion of truth one is immediately reminded of the many methodological prescriptions emanating from the so-called Chicago School. The source is allegedly the Instrumentalist methodology of Friedman's 1953 essay. Many of the followers of Friedman's essay claim that the only criterion to use when it comes to assessing a given theory is the theory's usefulness. The question which should be asked is whether by 'usefulness' they actually mean the same thing as do orthodox Pragmatists. To answer this we must look at what Friedman's essay contributes to the discussion – so let us now turn to a brief discussion of the philosophical basis of Friedman's methodology [I will be drawing on the more detailed discussions of Boland 1979a, 1980, 1981a and 1997, chaps. 1 to 4].

Any theory (or explanation) is just an argument in favor of certain given propositions or specific predictions. As such, a theory is a conjunction of assumption statements, each of which is *assumed* (or asserted) to be true. A theory is also claimed to be a sufficient explanation and as such at least one of its assumptions must be in the form of a *strictly universal* statement [Popper 1972, p. 350]. (For example, if one has an explanation with a less than strictly universal assumption that says '*some* people are maximizers...' to explain the actions of an individual, the question would be immediately begged as to how one knows that the individual is not a non-maximizer – the strictly universal assumption that says 'all people are maximizers' will apply without begging the question.) Without an inductive logic, the requirement of a strictly universal assumption seems to raise all the methodological problems discussed in Chapters 1 and 3. When can one assume universal maximization is a realistic (i.e., true) assumption? It is such difficulties that Friedman's essay attempts to overcome.

Friedman's essay argues that so long as a theory does its intended job, there is no apparent need to argue in its favor, or in favor of any of the realism of its constituent parts. For some policy-oriented economists, the intended job is the generation of successful *predictions* – a theory's predictive success is always a sufficient argument in its favor. In effect, the methodology of Instrumentalism is an answer to the question, 'what is the *role* of theories in economics?'. It says that theories are convenient and useful ways of (logically) generating what have turned out to be successful predictions or conclusions. So, when economists use Friedman's essay to deflect criticism of the realism of their assumptions, they are merely proclaiming their advocacy of the Instrumentalism as expressed in Friedman's famous essay. That is, they are avoiding the question of the *status* of theories in economics. Again, Conventionalism is an answer to this latter question since it claims that the status of theories is not 'true or false', but 'better or worse'.

Anyone who sees the object of science as finding the *one* true theory of the economy faces a task that cannot be simple. However, if the object of building or choosing theories (or models of theories) is only to have a theory or model that provides true predictions or conclusions, *a priori* realism of the assumptions is not required *if* it is already known that the conclusions – such as publicly available statistical data about the state of the economy – are true or acceptable by some Conventionalist criterion. Thus, from the viewpoint of Instrumentalism, theories do not have to be considered true statements about the nature of the world, but only convenient ways of systematically generating the already known 'true' conclusions.

As discussed in earlier chapters, Instrumentalism in this manner offers an alternative to the Conventionalist response to the Problem of Induction. Instrumentalism considers the truth *status* of theories, hypotheses, or assumptions to be *irrelevant* to any practical purposes, so long as the conclusions logically derived from them are successful. Although Conventionalism may be wary of the possibility of determining the truth status of theories or models, Instrumentalism simply ignores the issue. Of course, as Friedman's subsequent testimony [Friedman 1978] indicates, some followers of Instrumentalism may personally care about truth or falsity. Some may even believe in the powers of induction. Nevertheless, such concerns or beliefs are separate from the Instrumentalist view of the role of theories in science.

The usefulness of logic

In Chapter 3, it was pointed out that there are only two useful ways of employing formal logic. There is *modus ponens*, which again says that a valid logical argument is one where whenever all of the assumptions are true, all of its conclusions must be true and thus an argument can be used to argue in favor of the truth status of its conclusions. And there is *modus tollens*, which says that if any of the conclusions which follow from a valid logical argument is false then at least one of the assumptions must be false – this follows from *modus ponens* since were all of the assumptions true and the argument valid, then none of the conclusions that validly follow could be false.

For adherents of Instrumentalism, who think they have solved the Problem of Induction by ignoring truth, *modus ponens* will necessarily be seen to be irrelevant. This is because they begin their analysis with a search, not for the true assumptions but rather, for true or useful (i.e., successful) conclusions. *Modus tollens* is likewise irrelevant because its use can only begin with a search for false conclusions.

Note that neither Instrumentalism nor Pragmatism can validly use logic to infer the truth of an explanation's premises from the observed truth of its conclusions. The reason is simply that, as any elementary logic textbook will demonstrate, a logically valid argument that begins with false premises can still yield true conclusions. To think that one could argue from the truth of logically valid conclusions to the truth of the premises is called the 'Fallacy of affirming the consequent'. For Instrumentalism this is not a problem but for Pragmatism it is a serious problem (perhaps this is the reason why the fideistic version of Pragmatism needs to rely on faith).

Pragmatism vs. Instrumentalism

The point I wish to stress is that when we compare Instrumentalism and Pragmatism the criterion of 'usefulness' is not being applied to the same problem in each case. What Pragmatism desires is a truth substitute in order to provide what the old 'scientific method' was supposed to provide, a solution to the Problem of Induction. Instrumentalism, such as the view presented in Friedman's essay, does not seek a truth substitute. Instead, the Problem of Induction is dismissed. In fact, all such philosophical problems (and solutions such as Pragmatism) are dismissed. The only question at issue concerns which method is appropriate for success in choosing theories as guides for practical policies.

If followers of Instrumentalism reject Pragmatism, how do they assure the truth of the theories they wish to use? Of course, such an assurance is not required. True assumptions are not essential for practical success. As was noted in Chapter 5, our television repairman does not need to understand electromagnetics or quantum physics – so long as he fixes our ailing television, we do not care whether his theory of how televisions work is true. This is the key to understanding Instrumentalism. If emphasis is being placed on success and there are no doubts about one's success – for example, the television set does, in fact, now function properly – there is no immediate need for a philosophical substitute for inductive science. However, it is also clear that since truth is not necessary, there is no need to confuse success with truth. Thus we see, while success-in-use is a criterion of truth for Pragmatism, for Instrumentalism it is not. Unlike Pragmatism or Conventionalism, which both offer a way to resolve the Problem *with* Induction, Instrumentalism does not attempt to deal with that philosophical problem. That is, Instrumentalism does not attempt to establish the truth of scientific theories, since truth is simply not necessary for practical success.

The methodological differences

Convexity in the commodity space obtained by aggregation over a collection of insignificant agents is an insight that economic theory owes in its revealing clarity to integration theory.

An economist who experiences such an insight belongs to the group of applied mathematicians, whose values he espouses. Mathematics provides him with a language and a method that permit an effective study of economic systems of forbidding complexity; but it is a demanding master. It ceaselessly asks for weaker assumptions, for stronger conclusions, for greater generality. In taking a mathematical form, economic theory is driven to submit to those demands. The gains in generality that it has achieved as a result, in little more than a century, stand out when the first formulations of the theories of general equilibrium (... Walras ...) and of the core of an economy (... Edgeworth ...) are placed side by side with the recent treatments of those subjects. ... Walras's consumers and producers have been freed from many of their constraining characteristics; Edgeworth's universe of two consumers and two commodities has been vastly expanded.

Gerard Debreu [1991, p. 4]

This brings us to the alleged differences between Conventionalism and the Instrumentalism of Friedman's essay. So far, my argument here is that, contrary to popular opinion, the followers of Instrumentalism and Conventionalism do not necessarily disagree. Their differences are at cross-purposes. Conventionalism and Instrumentalism agree that there is no direct solution to the Problem of Induction; and that the Pragmatist, 'success-in-use' solution may be rejected. They disagree only about what we should do about the Problem. While Conventionalism looks for some criterion to provide a truth substitute, Instrumentalism looks for short-run criteria that can promise immediate success. There is no claim that Instrumentalist criteria are adequate truth substitutes. Where Conventionalism and Instrumentalism can be seen to differ is in their classic dispute is between 'generality' and 'simplicity'. The former criterion is typical of Conventionalist objectives; the latter is typical of Instrumentalist objectives.

Conventionalist 'simplicity'

If one were to consider the methodology in Friedman's essay as a solution to the Problem of Induction (which would be a mistake), then one might see his methodological prescriptions as direct competitors with orthodox Conventionalist prescriptions, since all versions of Conventionalism seek criteria to use in the allegedly necessary task of choosing between competing theories. In this sense, some economists see Friedman's advocacy of simplicity as a rejection of generality. But Conventionalism does not necessarily reject simplicity.

Let us consider how simplicity might be desirable from a Conventionalist's standpoint. Simplicity is advocated by those Conventionalists who believe that Nature is essentially simple. Historically, simplicity was invoked because many philosophers would invent complexities in order to overcome the failure of their explanations. The historical details do not matter here; so let me illustrate this with a modern example. Let us say that someone might see the demand curve as a mathematical function relating the price to the quantity demanded. Supposedly, if one knows the price, then one can calculate the quantity demanded. The demand function says that any time the price changes, the quantity changes in a predictable way. In some sense, then, the price is used to predict the quantity demanded. This would be the simplest possible explanation of the quantity demanded, as there is a minimum number of variables involved – two: the price and the quantity demanded. Now if it were observed that the price changed but the quantity demanded did not, how would one explain this? The only way is to introduce a third variable, say, income. Thus, it might be argued that although the price changed, so did the consumer's income, so that the effects of the price change alone were cancelled out by the income change. The obvious instance would be that whenever all prices double and incomes double, the demand will not usually change.

This illustration is not intended as a criticism of demand theory. Rather, I am suggesting that no matter how many variables are involved or introduced, we can always explain away any insufficiency in our original theory by introducing a new explanatory variable. But is the introduction of additional variables an acceptable way of dealing with failures to explain? Surely such a method of dealing with explanatory failures could get out of hand. We could have so many variables that there would be one variable for every possible change. With so many variables things could get very complex.

Sometimes we have to admit that our explanations are false. But if we are allowed to invent new variables to explain away our failures, such admissions can be postponed forever. This, historically, is the type of situation that fostered the desire for simplicity. The methodological rule used to be that whenever facing the choice of two competing theories, always choose the one with fewer variables or conditions. This rule would reduce the chance of opting for a complex theory which merely covers up an inherently false theory. Note that this rule of simplicity can be misleading, since the true theory may actually be very complex!

Not all followers of Conventionalism advocate simplicity; some like Debreu and Samuelson advocate generality. Generality is the criterion invoked by those followers of Conventionalism who wish to explain much by little. The Conventionalist view – that a theory is but a filing cabinet for systematically storing and describing available facts – leads to the view that the more that can be systematically stored, the better. This is the essence of the criterion of generality. The more situations that can be described, the more general is the theory. In terms of the theory of demand, the ability to deal with various types of goods (e.g. normal, inferior, and Giffen, as well as complements and substitutes) is a definite plus for the generalized form of demand theory which Samuelson presented in his *Foundations* [1947/65].

This, then, would appear to be the difference between generality and simplicity. But is the difference so (sorry...) simple? Even when the number of variables is low, the relationship between them could be very complex. What one is looking for, given the Conventionalist penchant for choice-criteria, is a theory which is both simple and general (as Debreu [1959, p. viii] advocates). Thus, on purely Conventionalist grounds, there is no necessary choice between simplicity and generality, as it may only be a question of personal tastes.

Instrumentalist simplicity

Adherents of Instrumentalism do not usually advocate generality and they desire simplicity for entirely different reasons. For Instrumentalism the only criterion to be considered is the practical success of a theory; otherwise anything goes. General theories are all right if they work. The reason why Instrumentalism values simplicity is that simple theories are easier to employ to provide practical predictions. They require less information. If there are few relevant variables, then there are few calculations to be made in the predictions. There is not much more to say than that. The only caution is to note that a small number of variables does not always imply simplicity. Two variables could be related in a linear fashion, as with a straight-line demand function. On the other hand, two variables could be related by means of a very complex polynomial of a very high degree. Thus it is possible for the relationship between three variables to be less complex than the relationship between two variables.

From the perspective of Instrumentalism, there is no need to impose arbitrary criteria such as simplicity or generality. The only relevant criterion is whatever works. Simplicity arises only because it is related to the practical question of the amount of information needed to implement any given theory. But the difficulty of collecting information may not always be a problem. In such cases, it is possible for the more general theory to be more useful than the less complex. So be it. From the stand point of followers of Friedman's Instrumentalism, the only prescription is to choose the theory which is most useful.

Critiques of Friedman's essay

Friedman's essay elicited a long series of critiques. The most popular of these were by Koopmans [1957], Eugene Rotwein [1959], Samuelson [1963] and, to some extent, Herbert Simon [1963]. All of these critiques fail because they fail to understand that Friedman is merely stating his version of Instrumentalism.

The 'Introduction' of Friedman's essay seems to have misled many readers. There he seems to be saying that he is about to make another contribution to the traditional discussion about the methodology of Inductivism and Conventionalism. Such discussion is usually about issues such as the verifiability or refutability of truly scientific theories. What he actually gives is an alternative to that type of discussion. Unfortunately, most critics miss this point. Consequently, the critiques are quite predictable.

Koopmans takes Friedman to task for dismissing the problem of clarifying the truth of the premises – the problem that Koopmans wishes to solve. The source of the disagreement is Koopmans' confusion of 'explanatory' with 'positive' [see 1957, p. 134]. Koopmans, adhering to Inductivism, would define *successful* explanation as being logically based on observably true premises, that is, ones that are in turn (inductively) based on observation. As noted above, in his essay Friedman does not consider assumptions or theories to be the embodiment of truth but only instruments for the generation of useful predictions. Thus, for Friedman 'positive' is not equivalent to 'explanatory' because he does not use *modus ponens*. Explanation in Koopmans' sense is irrelevant to Friedman's Instrumentalism. Followers of the methodology in Friedman's essay can easily escape from Koopmans' critique.

Rotwein merely asserts that everyone should adhere to an optimistic form of Conventionalism, which he calls 'empiricism'. Specifically, empiricism ascribes to Justificationism, the methodological rule that everyone must justify every claim they make for the truth of their conclusions or predictions. Amazingly, Rotwein as a follower of empiricism recognizes that Hume showed that 'there was no reasoning that could justify (inductive) expectations that past regularities would be repeated in the future' [1980, p. 1554]. But rather than drop the presumed need to justify one's empirical claims, Rotwein says: 'Hume, however, held that such expectations were to be accepted because, given the kinds of creatures we are, or the manner in which we form our beliefs, we had no alternative to their acceptance; and this view has been central to the empirical tradition ever since his time' [1980, p. 1555]. Somehow, in everyone's head there is supposedly a perfectly functioning inductive logic which does what we cannot do outside our heads. How do the empiricists who follow Hume 'know' that there is such a functioning induction? This form of empiricism is silly and Friedman's followers are quite free to dismiss it as such.

Simon's critique of Friedman's essay is based on the acceptance of a surrogate inductive learning function which Simon calls 'the principle of continuity of approximation'. Simon says that 'it asserts [that] if the conditions of the real world approximate sufficiently well the assumptions of an ideal type, the derivations from these assumptions will be approximately correct' [1963, p. 230]. This principle is nothing more than a sophisticated version of the inductive principle often used by mathematicians to avoid the intractable complications caused by the absence of an inductive logic. Formally, Simon's principle would appear to be a restatement of *modus ponens*, but, as will be explained in the next chapter, there is no valid *approximate modus ponens* [see also Haavelmo 1944, p. 56]. It is to Friedman's credit that he did not opt for this sophisticated subterfuge which smuggles successful induction in through the approximate back door.

Samuelson's critique [1963] is easily the most popular of all. Many critics of Friedman's economics are eager to believe that here is a critique which works. And since Samuelson's is so obscure, it is easy to accept it as an adequate critique because it is not well understood but does appear to work. Samuelson tries to criticize the methodology in Friedman's essay by attempting to argue that it is self-contradictory. Specifically, Samuelson offers a false theory of the motivation for Friedman's methodology and applies the false theory to explain the behavior of Friedman's followers. By implication we are supposed to conclude from the alleged successful explanation that there is some merit in his deliberately false assumptions. This implication is supposed to be a criticism of Friedman's use of the 'as if' principle, but it is a misuse of that principle.

Perhaps Samuelson is correct in attributing a pattern of behavior to the followers of Friedman and in positing that such a pattern can be shown to follow logically from his assumption concerning their motivations, but the 'as if' principle still does not warrant the empirical claim that his assumption about Friedman's (or Friedman's followers') motivation is true. More important, the 'as if' principle is validly used only when explaining true conclusions. That is, one cannot validly use such an 'as if' argument as a *critical* device similar to *modus tollens*. If the *implications* of using Samuelson's false assumption are undesirable, then one cannot pass the undesirableness back to the assumption. Furthermore, there are infinitely many false arguments that can imply any given (true) conclusion. The question is whether Samuelson's assumption is *necessary* for his conclusion. Of course, it is not, and that is because Samuelson is imitating Friedman's mode of argument, which relies on sufficient conditions for success.

The irony of Samuelson's critique is that *his* followers accept it *as if* it were successful. Logically, there is no way Samuelson's criticism can be considered successful, since such a line of argument requires logically necessary assumptions. But worse than this, most critics of Friedman's essay object to its dismissal of the necessity of 'realistic' assumptions, yet Samuelson's criticism is based on deliberately 'unrealistic' assumptions! These critics are caught violating their own requirement in order to criticize Friedman's essay. In effect they employ 'as if' arguments while criticizing their use. By their own rules they should reject their own critiques.

Conventionalist critiques of Instrumentalism

There have been many Conventionalist critiques of Instrumentalism [cf. Caldwell 1982/94 and Hands 2001]. All of them have viewed Instrumentalism as just another alleged solution to the Problem of Induction. What is surprising about this is that Instrumentalism is a rejection of the philosophical questions addressed by Conventionalism.

In my published defense of Friedman's essay against what I considered to be unfair critiques [Boland 1979a], I stressed the importance of distinguishing the Instrumentalism in Friedman's essay from the Conventionalist philosophers' alternatives that are more concerned with methodogical rules for establishing the universal acceptance (or probable truth) of scientific theories. The key issue is the separation of purposes, that is, the separation of immediate practical problems from long-term philosophical questions. Although Instrumentalism may be appropriate only for the former, the view that Conventionalism is the superior alternative is at least open to question. It is time to examine critically the logic of Conventionalism and its relationship to Instrumentalism.

Instrumentalism through Conventionalist eyes

The common error of seeing the necessary superiority of Conventionalism over Instrumentalism is the result of falsely assuming that one's own objectives are shared by everyone. If Friedman's Instrumentalism were intended to be an all-encompassing philosophy of science, any modern philosopher could easily be dissatisfied. But although Friedman in his 'Introduction' gives an appropriate nod to J. N. Keynes, Friedman's approach is to drop the traditional problem posed by Keynes because its solution would require an inductive logic. Friedman's method of dealing with the question of a 'positive science' is to limit the domain of the question in the case of economics to only that which is appropriate for a practical policy science. Limiting the domain of applicability for any method or technique is a rather obvious Instrumentalist ploy – one which can easily be justified in Instrumentalist terms.

Philosophical comparisons of Instrumentalism with Conventionalism are not uncommon; but I think they can be misleading if presented only in Conventionalist terms. The late Imre Lakatos was noted for considering Instrumentalism to be 'a degenerate version of [Conventionalism], based on a mere philosophical muddle caused by a lack of elementary logical competence' [1971, p. 95]. But his judgment is based on whether Instrumentalism is a means of achieving the objectives of most Conventionalist philosophers of science, and not on whether it is a useful guide for dealing with practical problems. In terms of Instrumentalist objectives, any advocate of Instrumentalism could argue that Conventionalist philosophy of science is obviously useless. Moreover, Lakatos is wrong; Instrumentalism on its own terms is devoid of the alleged elementary logical errors.

Some words of caution

Now before one jumps to the conclusion that the real choice is between Instrumentalism (i.e., the methodology promoted in Friedman's essay) and Conventionalism (i.e., the methodology of Samuelson or Debreu) and, worse, that if one rejects Conventionalism, one must then embrace Instrumentalism for all of economics, let me add some further advice. Instrumentalism is always limited to short-run practical problems. If one is looking for a more universal, lasting understanding of the workings of the economy – that is, a true theory of economics – then Instrumentalism will never do, since it ignores the truth of theories. Of course, Conventionalism fails here too, since it denies any truth status to theories. If a true theory of the economy is our objective, then we will just have to look beyond the dispute over methodology between Friedman's Instrumentalism and the Conventionalism of Samuelson or Debreu.

Rule-based methodology as an attempt to solve the Problem of Induction

> Our view ... is that there is only one generally applicable methodological rule, and that is the exhortation to be critical and always ready to subject one's hypotheses to critical scrutiny. Any attempt to reinforce this general maxim by a set of additional rules is likely to be futile and possibly harmful.
>
> Kurt Klappholz and Joseph Agassi [1959, p. 60]

At root, Friedman's essay was a response to the presumption of 'expert' philosophers who think there are rules for doing 'scientific' economics. The 'experts' that Friedman refers to in the quotation at the beginning of this chapter seem to think that economic science can be distinguished from other competing academic pursuits such as economic history, Marxist economics and old institutionalism [cf. Hands 2001, p. 37]. The basic notion is that true science can be seen to be the result of following the step-by-step rules of scientific method that I discussed in Chapter 1. School science textbooks usually begin by outlining these rules: Do not jump to conclusions but first, collect data; second, inductively form a hypothesis to explain the collected data; third, invent a means to test the hypothesis; fourth, if it passes the test, publish the hypothesis and the results of your test so that others can try to test it; and so on. Few economists ever thought economics could be characterized by such a scientific method.

Of course, one notion of an appropriate methodological rule that has been around for a long time is that scientific economics would never be based on 'normative' statements but instead 'positive' statements. More recent methodological rules involve explicit model building and the requirement that, of course, one's model must be 'testable' [Hutchison 1938; Winter 1964] or at least 'refutable in principle' [Samuelson 1947/65]. Some would-be followers of Popper think we should resist 'ad hoc' assumptions designed to overcome refutations of our models. One needs to ask in all of these cases, what does this have to do with true theories? Who is to say that the true theory of some phenomena might not actually be difficult to test or refute or that the added 'ad hoc' assumption might not actually be true?

Commenting on common 1950s views of economic methodology and the alleged 'slow progress in economics', Klappholz and Agassi observed that many defenders of mainstream neoclassical economics think that 'if only economists adopted this or that methodological rule, the road ahead would at least be cleared (and possibly the traffic would move briskly along it)' [1959, p. 60]. As noted above, they reject all rules except the non-specific rule that we should be critical. Beyond this anything goes so long as it is still subject to criticism.

In Chapter 13 I will return to examine the many misunderstandings of Popper's theory of science. But there is one misunderstanding that is relevant here, namely, the notion that Popper's 'Critical Rationalism', which Klappholz and Agassi were advocating in 1959, is a set of rules or procedures for the progress of economic science. Specifically, Bruce Caldwell [1982/94, p. 38] says that Popper's Critical Rationalism can be defined as:

> The way in which knowledge progresses is a twofold process: bold conjectures are advanced, and they are met by attempted refutations in which critical and severe tests are proposed and carried out. This is a trial and error process, and the hope is that we can learn from our mistakes. The penultimate rule of rational (and thus scientific) discourse is to subject every belief to critical scrutiny.

Except for his last sentence, it is not easy to see how this is not just a different way of saying what school science textbooks have promulgated. It is certainly not the view of Critical Rationalism advocated by Klappholz and Agassi.

Before returning to an examination of Popper's theory of science and in particular how the view advocated by Klappholz and Agassi might help economists avoid 'expert' rules without retreating to the questionable and potentially anti-intellectual position of Instrumentalism, we need to see how Conventionalism is practiced in economics. Of particular concern will be the Conventionalist rules of the game.

12 Optimistic vs. Defeatist Conventionalism

> The great virtue of mathematical reasoning in economics is that by its precise account of assumptions it becomes crystal clear that application to the 'real' world could at best be provisional...
>
> This view which I have always held has however been severely strained by relatively recent developments... For instance a recent macro-text starts with the mathematics ... for a single agent which seems distinctly peculiar for the macro-enterprise which is to distill something useful out of economic analysis. Of course these macro-economists are not mathematical economists. They use mathematics to be found in texts but are quite unrigorous in their analysis of what would have to be the case for their exercises to be applicable. Nonetheless it looks as if the scientific air of mathematical reasoning has misled them into believing that they are saying something scientific.
>
> Reflecting on this ... I have come to the conclusion that [mathematical reasoning] is not to blame. The blame lies in the first instance with Milton Friedman and in the second with the romantic desire to pass as a 'scientist'. It was Friedman's doctrine of 'as if' and the general babble about the virtues of 'simplicity', 'beauty' and 'elegance' which is largely responsible. If economics were a science with a body of doctrine confirmed by controlled experiments there might be something to be said for the Friedman line. But it is not and, as far as I know, no economic theory has ever been conclusively falsified by experiment, leave alone by statistical inference. To hang on the coattails of a theory of such seeming paradox as quantum mechanics, say, because 'it works' will be justified when economists' theories predict correctly to eight decimal places as quantum theory does. Until then, the direct plausibility of our assumptions remains a test a theory applied to the 'real' world must pass.
>
> Frank Hahn [1994, p. 246–7]

The discussions in most of the previous eleven chapters have centered on the hidden agenda of neoclassical economic theory and how it is expressed in various mainstream research programs. Chapter 11 examined how the methodology of Instrumentalism is used to *dismiss* questions of realism (viz., truth status) in economic model building. This chapter will examine how the methodology of Conventionalism is implemented in mainstream neoclassical economics to *avoid* questions of realism in economic model building.

Once one drops truth status as the primary regulative principle for conduct of one's theoretical pursuits, the fear may arise as to whether just anything goes without limit. Are there any limits? Are there methodological rules for doing economics beyond the hidden and visible agendas? If one examines the actual practice of economics as is evident in its leading journals, there would seem to be sufficient uniformity to suggest that maybe there are rules for doing economics even though no economists would ever want to make the rules explicit. Actually, there appears to be two sets of rules – there are even some articles that try to satisfy both sets of rules. Rules characterize mainstream Conventionalism which can be divided into two separate currents. One moves under the overt banner of 'positive economics', although not too many years ago it was merely called 'applied economics'. The other moves under the pretentious title of 'economic theory', although it is merely what was called 'mathematical economics' forty years ago. Their differences are essentially analogous to the differences between what I will call optimistic Conventionalism and defeatist Conventionalism. Optimism in matters of neoclassical economics tends in some circles to lead to anti-intellectualism. Pessimism too often leads to silliness. But I am getting ahead of myself. Let me begin this chapter with an examination of the optimistic version.

Approximationism as optimistic Conventionalism

In the absence of truth as the regulative principle, most positive economics must include rules to deal with some form of approximation. As I suggested earlier, analytical model builders run the risk of hiding behind Instrumentalism whenever challenged to say what their analytical tools represent in the real world, but this will not be the focus here. Instead, I wish to examine the rules of the analytical game when there is no need to resort to Instrumentalism. I will begin by examining the implicit rules of applied or positive economics in the first half of this chapter and then turn to the rules for mathematical or analytical economics in the other half.

Positive evidence about positive economics

The salient feature of all the applied or 'positive' economic analyses is their usual conformity to just one format. Specifically, after the introductory section of a typical positive economics article there is a section titled 'The Model' or some variation of this. This is followed by a section titled 'Empirical Results' or something similar, and a final section summarizing the 'Conclusions'. The question I want to consider is why do virtually all applied papers conform to this one format? As I shall explain, the reason is that this format satisfies the rules of optimistic Conventionalism.

A 'model' of neoclassical empirical analysis

A trivial explanation for why a specific format is universally used is that all journal editors require that format, but they are only responding to what they think the market demands. My concern here is not just why any particular individual might decide to organize a research paper according to the accepted format; I wish to examine why this particular format is so widely demanded.

One way to understand a methodological format is to emulate it – so let me attempt to build a 'model' of the format of a typical article in the literature of positive economics. Judging by what is often identified as a 'model' in positive economics, virtually every formal statement is considered a model. Nevertheless, there are some basic rules.

In order to build my model of neoclassical empirical analysis, as with any model, the assumptions need to be explicitly stated. Let me begin by stating the obvious assumptions which form the 'visible agenda' of neoclassical economics. My first assumption is that every neoclassical model must have behavioral assumptions regarding maximization or equilibrium. Furthermore, the results of the model must depend crucially on these assumptions. My second assumption is that every empirical model must yield at least one equation which can be 'tested' by statistically estimating its parametric coefficients.

Beyond these two explicit requirements almost anything goes when it comes to building the model. But there are two more rules that are part of the first item on the hidden agenda of neoclassical research programs. My third assumption is that every empirical paper must presume specific criteria of 'truthlikeness' – so-called testing conventions. For example, one must consider such statistical parameters as means and standard deviations, R^2s, t-statistics, etc. That is, every equation is a statement which is either true or false; however, when applying an equation to empirical data we know that the fit will not usually be perfect even if the statement (i.e., the equation) is true. So the question is: in what circumstances will the fitted equation be considered *acceptably* 'true'? The use of the testing conventions implies that the investigator is not attempting to determine the absolute truth of his or her model. Rather, the objective is to establish its acceptability or unacceptability according to standard testing conventions.

My last assumption is that in order to be published, every empirical paper must have contributed something to the advancement of 'scientific' knowledge. That is, it must establish some new 'facts' – namely, ones which were previously unknown – by providing either new data or new analysis of old data.

An 'empirical analysis' of some neoclassical literature

In order to test my model of the methodology of neoclassical positive economics, we must consider the available data. First we must decide on where to look for mainstream 'positive economics'. Obviously, we should expect to find it in the pages of the leading economics journals. So, let us sample one arbitrary year. In the first edition of this book I used the year 1980. This time I am using the year 2000 and again examining the contents of a few issues for that year of a leading journal. Further, I am again restricting my examination of the data to those articles intended to be positive analysis – explanations of observable data. That is, I am skipping those articles that are presidential-type addresses or those concerned with the more technical (mathematical) aspects of 'economic theory'. Also, I am ignoring topics such as 'history of thought' or 'methodology'. So, let us now examine the topics that remain (within these articles are variants indicated by * that appear to follow the format but without reference to actual data and variants indicated by ** that appear to try to conform to the old inductivist textbook version of the format where the data appear before the model):

- Optimal Adoption of Complementary Technologies
- Collateral Damage: Effects of the Japanese Bank Crisis on Real Activity in the United States *
- Endogenous Inequality in Integrated Labor Markets with Two-Sided Search *
- Mobility, Targeting, and Private-School Vouchers
- Saving and Growth with Habit Formation *
- Tax Policy and Aggregate Demand Management Under Catching Up with the Joneses *
- Habit Formation in Consumption and Its Implications for Monetary-Policy Models
- Habit Formation in Consumer Preferences: Evidence from Panel Data
- What Do a Million Observations on Banks Say About the Transmission of Monetary Policy? **
- Federal Reserve Information and the Behavior of Interest Rates **
- What Inventory Behavior Tells Us About Business Cycles
- Job Destruction and Propagation of Shocks
- Ownership Risk, Investment, and the Use of Natural Resources
- Orchestrating Impartiality: The Impact of 'Blind' Auditions on Female Musicians **
- Wage Shocks and North American Labor-Market Integration
- Mentoring and Diversity *
- Asset Pricing with Distorted Beliefs: Are Equity Returns Too Good to Be True? *
- Population, Technology, and Growth: From Malthusian Stagnation to the Demographic Transition and Beyond *
- Aid, Policies, and Growth
- A Reassessment of the Relationship Between Inequality and Growth
- Intelligence, Social Mobility, and Growth *
- Meetings with Costly Participation *

My examination of the articles on these topics seems to indicate that all of them conform to the format specified by my model (allowing for the two variations which either follow the format without data or parade as inductivist science). The only empirical question implied by my positive model is whether there are any exceptions to what I have claimed will be found in the mainstream journals. I can report that there are none in the data considered. My model of positive analysis does fit the data.

Some questions raised by my positive analysis

Now I do not wish to push this mockery of positive analysis any further, as it is not clear what positive contribution it would make. Nevertheless, it does emphasize the point raised that there is an amazing empirical uniformity among positive neoclassical articles. Empirical uniformities beg to be explained.

There is apparently no discussion of why papers should be written according to the observed format. Of course, there is no need to discuss the standard format if everyone agrees that it presents no problem and it is doing its required job. But what is the purpose of the standard format? My general theory is that the reason why the format is not discussed is that its purpose is simply taken for granted.

Taking things for granted is a major source of methodological problems and inconsistencies in economics, although the problems are not always appreciated. This is the case with the format of neoclassical empirical research papers. I will argue here that the purpose of the standard format is the facilitation of an inductive verification of neoclassical theory even though the format itself serves a more modest Conventionalist view of knowledge and method, a view which supposedly denies induction.

To understand the relationship between the standard format and the research program to verify neoclassical theory, consider the following questions. What constitutes a successful empirical analysis? What would be a failure? What is presumed in the use of 'testing conventions'?

The logic of model-building in positive economics

Every applied model in neoclassical economics is a specific attempt to model the essential idea of neoclassical theory – independent individual maximization with dependent market equilibria. In a fundamental way each model is a test of neoclassical theory's relevance or applicability to the phenomena of the real world. At the very minimum, each model is an attempt to make neoclassical *theory* testable.

Since my view of applied models is still not universally accepted, perhaps I should be more specific about the nature and purpose of model-building. While some economists use the term 'model' to specify the idea of a formal model as conceived by mathematical logicians, my use of the term reflects the more common usage in positive economics [e.g., Lucas 1980]. Although I have discussed the nature of models elsewhere [Boland 1977a, 1977c, 1989], it will be useful to review the essentials here.

The role of models in testing theories

One way to determine if a theory will work in a given practical situation would be to build a 'model' of the theory much in the spirit of design engineering. Design engineers might build a small model of a new airplane wing design to test its aerodynamics in a wind tunnel. In other words, engineers commit themselves to specific models. Of course, many different models may be constructed (all based on the same new wing idea) by varying certain proportions, materials, etc. Unfortunately, such opportunities for testing in this manner (i.e., with scaled-down models in wind tunnels) seldom arise in economics – although the growing interest in experimental and behavioral economics would seem to be a viable alternative [cf. Smith 1989].

Schematically, in model-building we traditionally start with a set of autonomous conjectures as to basic behavioral relationships which must include an indication of the relevant variables and which of them are exogenous and which are not. To these we add specifying or simplifying assumptions, the nature of which depends on what is being simplified or specified (i.e., on the behavioral assumptions). One reason why we must add these extra assumptions is that no one would want to make the behavioral assumptions of our neoclassical theory of the consumer (or producer) as specific as would be required in order to make it (or predictions deduced from it) *directly* observable. Applied models add another set of assumptions designed to deal with the values of the parameters either directly specifying them or indirectly providing criteria to measure them. This gives us the following schemata for any model (in the engineering sense):

(1) *A set of behavioral assumptions* about people and/or institutions. This set might include, for example, the behavioral proposition $Q = f(P)$, where $\partial Q / \partial P$ is negative. The *conjunction* of all the behavioral assumptions is what normally constitutes a 'theory'.

(2) *A set of simplifying assumptions* about the relationships contained in the above set. For example, the demand function stated in the theory might be specified as a linear function, $Q = a + bP$, where 'a' is positive and 'b' is negative.

(3) *A set of assumed parametric specifications* about the values of those parameters created in the second set above. For example, the parameter 'b' above might be assumed to have the value $b = -4.2$ or the specification that the above model fit the available data according to certain statistical criteria or perhaps one could 'calibrate' the model as discussed in Chapter 5.

Observing that any empirical model is a conjunction of these three sets of assumptions leads to the consideration of some problems concerning what constitutes a success or failure. Whenever it is shown that one of the predictions is false, then, by *modus tollens*, we can conclude that at least one of the assumptions (the constituent parts) must be false. Note, however, there is a certain ambiguity about which type of assumption is responsible for the false prediction. If any one of the assumptions is false, then some of the predictions will be false. But since any of them could be the false offending assumption, just noting that one of the predictions is false does not necessarily tell us anything about *which* assumption has 'caused' the false prediction. I call this the problem of the ambiguity of logical refutations (philosophers refer to this with the uninformative label: 'the Duhem-Quine thesis'). As will be seen, this is particularly a problem for model-builders who are using models to refute neoclassical theory.

The logical problem of testing theories using models

To expect to refute a *theory* by showing that it is false by means of empirical testing means that one must expect to show that *all possible models of the theory are false!* In other words, to get at the basic behavioral assumptions themselves one must consider all possible ways of specifying them (however simple or complex). But there will always be an infinite number of ways. Assuming that there are no logical errors, if *every* one of them, when conjoined with the behavioral assumptions, can be shown to lead to *at least one* false prediction, then one *knows* that at least one behavioral assumption is necessarily false. And if that were not the case – that is, if all the assumptions are (non-tautologically) true – then it is *possible* to specify the behavioral assumptions such that no false predictions could or would ever happen. Obviously, the requirement that one must show that *all* possible models are false is impossible for the same reason that it is impossible to verify a strictly universal statement. It must therefore be concluded that on this basis the empirical falsification of neoclassical theory *using models of the theory* is impossible. I will return to this issue below.

Now, what about building *specific* models of a theory intending to show that the theory is true? Well, this is again the old logic-textbook problem of the 'Fallacy of affirming the consequent'. In effect, every model of a theory is a special case and a confirmation of one model is good only for one given set of phenomena. Even though you may confirm a neoclassical model's application to one market during one period of time, you still have not proven that the same model can be applied to any other market or any other period of time. To say that a behavioral theory is true is to say that it applies to every situation to which it purports to be an explanation. That is, *if* a theory is true, then it is *possible* to build at least one model that will fit the data in *any* given situation. If an explanatory theory is not a tautology (i.e., not an argument which for logical reasons cannot be false), then to prove it true we would have to provide a potentially infinite series of models. That is, no finite set of confirmed models will do, since there will always be the logical possibility of a situation which cannot be modeled or fitted. It is easy to see that this is merely the Problem of Induction restated at a slightly different level of discussion.

The point of formalizing my view of models is to show that building models of a theory in effect insulates the theory from empirical testing if our purpose in testing is either refutation or verification. It can also be concluded that neoclassical economists who are not prone to making logical errors, but are nevertheless building models to apply or to test neoclassical economics, must have some other objective in mind – otherwise there would be more concern for these logical problems.

The empirical problem of testing theories using models

So long as one is willing to promote Conventionalist criteria for the acceptance of observation reports, one should be able to specify what it would take to construct a counter-example to any explicit explanatory model. But there are problems. As I demonstrated in Chapters 2 and 3 of my 1989 book, to construct a refuting counter-example for a relatively simple model – for example with four endogenous variables and the standard Cobb-Douglas production function – the number of needed observations may exceed 400,000! Nevertheless, in the same book (Chapter 8) I show how to overcome the problem of the ambiguity of logical refutations: by constructing a refuting test involving a test of both the theory in question and a relevant counter-example using the same observations and the same Conventionalist criteria. If one tests only by seeing if the model fits the observational data but does not consider whether the same data also fit the counter-example, no refutation (or confirmation for that matter) could be logically sufficient – even if the Conventionalist criteria are not in question. I will return to this view of testing below.

The problem with stochastic models

Some may argue that the logical problems discussed here are irrelevant for the neoclassical economist who is wedded to Conventionalism, since these problems concern only those cases in which someone is attempting to provide a proof of the absolute truth or falsity of any given theory. Instead, it would be claimed, we should be concerned only with the problems of building models which fit the data with acceptable degrees of approximation [Simon 1979]. But in response I would argue, if models are never refutations or verifications, what constitutes a successful model? When would a model-builder ever be forced to admit failure?

Virtually every applied neoclassical model today is a stochastic model. The reason for this is simple. Stochastic models are the primary means of accommodating the dictates of Conventionalism and at the same time externally solving the Problem of Conventions by appealing to universally accepted statistical testing conventions. One does not have to build stochastic models to satisfy Conventionalism, but it certainly helps.

The problem with the concept 'stochastic' (or more generally, with the doc-trine of 'stochasticism' – the view that realistic models must be stochastic models), is that it takes too much for granted. Some economists are fond of claiming that the world is 'a stochastic environment' [e.g., Smith 1969]; thus technically no model is ever refuted or verified, and hence there could not be any chance of our construing one as a refutation or a verification of a theory. This concept of the world can be very misleading and thus requires a critical examination.

My purpose here is to show that stochasticism involves model-building – since it requires an explicit assumption which is possibly false – and thus stochasticism should not be taken for granted. And, further, to argue that the retreat to stochasticism does not succeed in avoiding all of the logical problems of using models to test neoclassical economics.

The nature of stochasticism: Conventionalist or Instrumentalist?

The word 'stochastic' is based on the idea of a target and in particular on the pattern of hits around a target. The greater the distance a given unit of target area is from the center of the target, the less frequent or dense will be the hits on that area. Consistent with the discussion in Chapter 5, it can also be said that there are two 'worlds': The 'real world' of observation and the 'ideal world' of the theory or mathematical model. Thus, we might look at a model as a shot at the 'real world' target. When we say the theory (or model) is 'true' we mean that there is an *exact* correspondence between the real and the ideal worlds. There are many reasons why we might miss the target, but they fall into two rough categories: (1) ours was a 'bad' shot, i.e., our model was false or logically invalid, or (2) the target moved unexpectedly, i.e., there are random, *unexplained* variations in the objects we are attempting to explain or use in our explanation.

Proponents of ideal-type methodology may thus say that a stochastic model is one which allows for movements of the target – the movements are deemed to be like the notion of friction used to explain why the block does not instantly slide down the slope as it would in an ideal frictionless world. However, proponents of optimistic Conventionalism could say that stochastic models follow from a methodological decision *not* to attempt to explain anything *completely*; that is, even with true theories the *correspondence* between these two worlds (ideal vs. real) will always be approximate or inexact for many obvious reasons (e.g., errors of measurement, irrational mistakes, etc.). For optimistic Conventionalism, neoclassical models are usually stochastic models so as to explicitly accommodate the stochastic nature *of the correspondence*. For example, we can assume that the measurement errors, etc., leave the observations in a normal, random distribution about the values of the ideal world. This means that it is the correspondence which is the stochastic element of the model. Note, however, here I am saying that it is the model (or theory) which is stochastic rather than the world or the 'environment'. Any test of a stochastic model is a test as much of the assumed correspondence as of the theory itself.

One can see the world as being *necessarily* stochastic *only* if one assumes beyond question that it is one's model (the ideal shot at the real world target) which is true (and fixed) and that the variability of the correspondence is due entirely to the deviant movements of the target (the real world). Thus stochasticism can also be seen to be an Instrumentalist exercise that puts the truth of our theories beyond question. There is a serious element of potential intellectual dishonesty in asserting that the environment is stochastic. We *assume* that the assumptions of our theory or model are true because we cannot prove them true. Thus there is no reason for any assumption to be beyond question, as stochasticism seems to presume.

The logical problems of stochastic models

Let us leave aside any Instrumentalist reasons for stochasticism and for now grant that it is the models or theories which are stochastic and not necessarily the real world, then stochastic models are still subject to the logical problems discussed above. Does this mean that we must give up any hope of testing neoclassical theories? I have already argued above that it does not; it just makes things a bit more complicated and more involved. The logical problems involved in any test of neoclassical economics are not insurmountable if it is recognized that it is the model rather than the environment which is stochastic. That is, we can overcome the logical problems outlined above if we explicitly recognize the specific assumptions which make the model stochastic.

Unfortunately, when we build stochastic models, the logical problems are not always apparent. So let us review the discussion with respect to non-stochastic models. We cannot refute a theory by first building a model of that theory and then refuting the model because of the problem of the ambiguity of logical refutation. Specifically, we cannot logically identify the source of the refutation – is it the behavioral assumptions of the theory or is it only the 'simplifying' assumptions that we have added? This problem is solely the result of our having to add *extra* assumptions in order to build the model. Although stochasticism requires additional assumptions and thus suffers from this problem, it also adds an entirely different logical problem, one that is not widely recognized.

For now let us forget the problem caused by adding extra assumptions. Let us restrict our concerns to testing a model, not bothering about whether one can logically infer anything about the underlying theory. The logic of refutation is based on three propositions as follows. We go about refuting a logically valid model by using the model to argue *modus ponens*: (1) 'whenever all of our assumptions are *true* then every prediction which logically follows from their conjunction *must be true*'; which in turn allows us to argue *modus tollens*: (2) 'should any prediction turn out to be *false* then we know that the conjunction of all of the assumptions *cannot be true*'. If we actually observe a false prediction, does that guarantee that at least one of the assumptions is *false*? It is possible to argue in favor of such a guarantee *only* when we accept the *axiom of the excluded middle*: (3) 'A statement which is *not true* must be *false*'.

This is not a trivial word game about 'true' and 'false'. For example, if we adopt the sophisticated, stochastic-Conventionalist view that identifies absolute truth with a probability of 1.00 and absolute falsity with 0.00, then to say some given statement is not absolutely true would *not* imply that it is absolutely false. A stochastic statement with a probability of 0.60 is not absolutely true, nor is it absolutely false! This same ambiguity occurs when positive economists substitute 'confirmed' for the term 'true', and 'disconfirmed' for the term 'false' in the above logical propositions. Generally, 'not confirmed' does not mean 'disconfirmed'. In other words, when 'confirmed' and 'disconfirmed' are used in place of 'true' and 'false', proposition (3) is discarded. But when *the excluded middle* is discarded we sacrifice the logical force of any test. That is, we cannot construct an 'approximate *modus ponens*' such as (1′) 'Whenever all of our assumptions are "confirmed" then every prediction which logically follows from their conjunction will be "confirmed"' because it does not imply (2′) 'Whenever there is a "disconfirmed" prediction then all of the assumptions cannot be "confirmed"'. It is quite possible for all of the assumptions to be confirmed and, with the same data, for one or more of the predictions to be disconfirmed, too.

This is probably not the place to argue this, so I will leave the analytical proof or disproof up to the reader. But in simple terms, what I am saying is that the conjunction of several assumptions, each with a probability of 0.60, does *not* imply that all predictions will have a probability of 0.60. One example should be sufficient. Consider the following four statements.

(a) Urn A has 100 red balls and no green balls.
(b) Urn B has 100 green balls and no red balls.
(c) I have withdrawn one ball from A or B.
(d) The ball is red.

Together these statements, if absolutely true, imply that the following statement is absolutely true:

(e) I have drawn a ball from urn A.

Now, if statements (a) through (d) are true 60 per cent of the time (that is, they have a probability of 0.60 of being true), then what is the probability of statement (e) being true? Surely its probability need not be 0.60, since it compounds the probabilities of the other statements and it must be false whenever (c) is false regardless of the probabilities of the other statements. In other words, given a logically valid argument which works for absolute truth, the same argument need not work for any given degree of approximate truth. If my argument here is correct (and I think it agrees with Haavelmo [1944] when he recognizes the limitations of his advocated probability approach to econometrics), it has serious implications for the generally accepted view of the methods of testing stochastic models.

Testing with stochastic models

Above I have argued that, in accordance with optimistic Conventionalism, stochastic models are models which contain assumptions that detail the stochastic correspondence between the exact model and the observable real world. For example, a stochastic model might contain an assumption that observational errors will be normally distributed about the statistical mean corresponding to zero error. But, for the purposes of *logical* inferences, we must specify in what circumstances such an assumption would be considered 'false' and in what circumstances it would be considered 'true' (in order to use *modus ponens* or *modus tollens*). Usually this assumption will be some sort of parametric limit applied to the observed distribution of the actual errors. There will be a range of possible statistically estimated means and standard deviations. The criteria are designed either to avoid Type I errors (rejecting the model as false when it is actually true) or Type II errors (the reverse acceptance) but not both. Remember that, unless we are discussing absolute truth or falsity (i.e., statements with a probability of either 1.00 or 0.00), we need two different criteria because we can no longer rely on the proposition of the 'excluded middle'.

That statistical testing must choose between avoiding one or the other type of decision error is the key to the problem I wish to discuss now. If we build a model to test a theory by adding statistical decision criteria to the model (to specify when it applies to the available data) and then we deduce a test prediction (e.g., an equation to be estimated by linear regression), the results must be assessed by the same criteria. If the criteria specified minimum conditions for the assumptions of the models to be accepted as 'true' for the purposes of the logical deduction of the prediction, then it is logically consistent for us to apply the same criteria to assess the 'truth' of the prediction. For example, as above we could say if we accept the assumptions as 'true' when the fitted equation has a probability of at least 0.95, then we can accept the predictions as 'true' when they have a probability of at least 0.95. We still have not avoided the problems discussed above, but at least we can be logically consistent in our decision process. However, remember that this consistency is only for the purposes of deducing the confirming predictions. If all of the predictions pass the test, we can say without inconsistency that the theory is so far 'confirmed'.

What can one say if a prediction fails according to the decision criteria? When I said that we would accept a statement (an assumption or a prediction) which has a probability of 0.95, I did not say that failure to have at least a 0.95 probability implied that the statement was false or 'disconfirmed'. On the contrary, a criterion of acceptance of a statement's falsity might be a probability of less than 0.05. Should our prediction fail the confirmation criterion by having a probability of say 0.80, it would still be a long way from being logically considered false. There is then a fundamental asymmetry between the criterion of confirmation and the criterion of disconfirmation.

Since most stochastic model building in positive economics is concerned with deducing stochastic but 'testable' predictions, the usual choice made is to use 'confirmation' criteria rather than 'disconfirmation' criteria for the purposes of defining a valid deduction. Such models cannot automatically be useful when we wish to test a theory except for the purpose of finding confirmations. In order to test a theory by building stochastic models we must do much more.

I am arguing not just that whenever both criteria are employed there is a very large range of undecidable cases (e.g., where the probabilities are between 0.05 and 0.95 along the lines I have just illustrated) but also that even if one criterion is used, the results are often contradictory, leading to the conclusion that most statistical testing done in the neoclassical literature is more inconclusive than the reporting might indicate. Before one can show this, one must consider what it would take statistically to refute a theory using a stochastic model. Remember that with exact models we can refute a model by showing that one of its predictions is false (*modus tollens*). In effect, a false prediction is an instance of what I above called a counter-example; that is, it is a statement which would be denied by the truth of the exact model. This is a clue for the design of a logically adequate test of any theory. Let me illustrate this with the *exact* model concerning the selection of red or green balls from two urns. Whenever we can show that statement (e) is false and that the statement

(f) The ball was drawn from Urn B.

is true, at least one of the statements (a) to (d) must be false. In other words, (f) is a counter-example to the conjunction of (a) to (d). If we really wished to test the conjunction, then the statistical question would have to be concerned with the question of how to decide when the counter-example is *confirmed*.

There still is only one case in which this form of statistical testing has been successfully applied [Bennett 1981]. In that one pioneering case the results were dramatic. It was shown that if one were to take some of the well-known reports of tests of models of post-Keynesian theories and extend them by performing a similar test of models of corresponding counter-examples, the results would show that *both* the theories and their counter-examples were confirmed *using the same statistical test criteria*! What this demonstrates is that testing models using confirmation criteria (e.g., a statement is considered true if its probability is at least 0.95) can lead to contradictory results and that thus the usual published tests are often very misleading. But it should also be noted that Bennett's demonstration shows what I claimed earlier in the chapter, namely that it is possible to have decisive tests subject to the Conventionalist acceptance of specific stochastic decision criteria. For example, a refutation is successful, relative to given confirmation criteria, only if the predictions fail the confirmation test *and* the counter-example passes the same test. Few, if any, reported 'disconfirmations' would satisfy these requirements.

Positive success or positive failure?

This now brings us back to the question I keep asking: what constitutes a successful model in positive neoclassical economics? And, more generally, to decide what constitutes success we need to ask: what is the objective of neoclassical model building?

Consider now the available facts before considering answers to these questions. First, there are all the logical problems I have been discussing. Second, all the standard statistical parametric criteria have been designed or used to identify confirming predictions, even though some investigators have mistakenly attempted to use them to establish 'disconfirmations'. Since there has been very little recognition of the logical problems – a possible exception is Hendry [1997] – I can only assume that most positive economic model-builders are not attempting to deal with them. So it is the secondary evidence of the prevailing confirmation criteria and the recognition of the necessity to choose between Type I and Type II error avoidance that we must take into consideration.

It can now be argued that if the usual published positive neoclassical articles such as those noted at the beginning of this chapter are actually considered contributions to 'scientific knowledge', then it can only be the case that the hidden objective of such positive economics is a long-term *verification* of neoclassical economics. Specifically, each paper which offers a confirmation of the applicability of neoclassical economics to 'real world' problems must be viewed as one more positive contribution towards an ultimate inductive proof of the truth of neoclassical theory. My reasons for concluding this is merely that logically all that can be accomplished by the typical application of neoclassical theory to 'real world' phenomena is a proof that it is *possible* to fit at least one neoclassical model to the available data. Critics can always say that a model's fit may be successful in the reported case but it does not prove that it will be successful in every case. I am arguing that the agenda of positive neoclassical research programs presumes that if one can continue to contribute more confirming examples of the applicability of neoclassical economics, then eventually one will prove that it is the only true theory of the economy.

Analytical theory as defeatist Conventionalism: Propositions and proofs

> In recent years, mathematical tools of a more basic character have been introduced into economics, which permit us to perceive with greater clarity and

express in simpler terms the logical structure of important parts of economic theory...

It may facilitate reference if we set out the basic assumptions of the model to be discussed in a number of postulates. This may be looked upon as a device for separating the reasoning within the model from the discussion of its relation to reality. The postulates set up a universe of logical discourse in which the only criterion of validity is that of implication by the postulates. ... Only the logical contents of the postulates matter.

Tjalling Koopmans [1957, pp. 5, 43 and 133]

In all formal procedures involving statistical testing or estimation, there are explicitly stated but untested hypotheses... In ... econometric studies ... the 'premises' [e.g., profit maximization, maximization of satisfaction] ... play that role. More in general, any statement resulting from such studies retains the form of an 'if...then...' statement...

The 'if ... then ...' statements are similar to those in the formal sciences. They read like logical or mathematical reasoning in the case of economic theory, and like applications of statistical methods in the case of econometric estimations or testing. The heart of substantive economics is what can be learned about the validity of the 'ifs' themselves, including the 'premises' discussed above. 'Thens' contradicted by observation call, as time goes on, for modification of the list of 'ifs' used. Absence of the contradiction gradually conveys survivor status to the 'ifs' in question. So, I do think a certain record of noncontradiction gradually becomes one of tentative confirmation. But the process of confirmation is slow and diffuse.

Tjalling Koopmans [1979, p. 11]

In the remainder of this chapter I shall examine the nature of the other mainstream research program in Conventionalist neoclassical economics which also conforms to a specific format but one unlike that of 'positive economics'. Again I shall describe the nature of the format and the problems involved in its application and then explain the hidden agenda implied by its widespread use. But first we must see why anyone might think there is a need for an alternative research program in neoclassical economics.

The problem of 'positive economics'

Those neoclassical economists who are pessimistic about the possibility of ever constructing an inductive proof for neoclassical theory based on observed 'facts' have slowly developed a research program which on the surface appears to depart significantly from that employed in 'positive economics'. They might argue either that induction is impossible or that inductive proofs are never final, as 'all facts are theory-laden' [Hanson 1965; Samuelson, Nordhaus and McCallum 1988]. But if one doubts 'facts', what is left? Is economic theory an arbitrary game? If there are no final inductive proofs, does this mean that all theories are circular or infinite regressions? Is there no solid foundation for a scientific economics? Such questions are seldom asked any more simply because economic theorists avoid making broad claims for economic theories. It might be interesting to consider why such questions are avoided. I think their avoidance is likely for the same reasons as those identified in earlier chapters for similar omissions – such questions do not need to be asked, since the answers are considered obvious.

Here I shall argue that the reason why these questions need not be asked is that economic 'theorists' have found what may be considered a superior alternative to solid empirical 'facts'. The problem with empirical 'facts' or, more properly, with *reports* of observations is that they can easily be questioned. That is, theorists think empirical claims cannot be considered absolutely true since they are unprovable by induction. For many mathematical logicians [see Hughes 1981] *that* is the Problem *with* Induction. To begin any successful inductive argument what is needed are unquestionably true statements. It turns out that the only unquestionably true statements are those that are logically true.

Arguments as statements

For subsequent reference, I need to revisit two key distinctions. One is that between statements and arguments; the other is that between two types of statements: logical and contingent. The first is easy. When we form an argument or an explanation, we are conjoining two or more simple statements with the intention to convey the notion that whenever the constituent simple statements are all true, the statement of the phenomena we are claiming to explain must also be true. So, every argument is a compound statement whose constituent parts are simple statements. To be used in an argument, simple statements are either true or false and, most important, a compound statement is true only if all of its constituent parts are true.

There are two ways a statement (simple or compound) can be true: as a matter of its logical form and as a matter of its empirical content. The former type is the tautology, which I discussed in Chapter 3. Specifically, it is a statement which is true regardless of what the non-logical words in the sentence mean – any statement such as 'X is Y or X is not Y' is true regardless of what we might mean by X or Y. The other type is a contingent statement; namely a statement which is true only by virtue of the meaning of the non-logical words.

These two distinctions are important whenever we construct an argument to form an explanation; we are of course relying on the logical validity of the argument. As noted in Chapter 3, logical validity provides both universality and uniqueness. Specifically, anyone who accepts as true the constituent parts (the premises or assumptions) of our argument will have to accept the logically valid conclusions we can reach. The only issue is whether the meaning of the non-logical words matter. Everyone has to accept the truth of a 'logically true statement' (a tautology) regardless of whether they accept our meanings of the non-logical words. But this is not the case with an 'analytically true statement'. No one is required to accept an explanation that contains a constituent part of the form 'suppose X is a Y ...' unless one defines X as a Y. But whether this is an empirical claim or just an accepted definition, this part is a contingent statement as in both cases it is a matter of acceptance. And, of course, every claimed empirical argument would seem to be offered as a contingent statement as it would depend on its parts being empirically true.

Now the importance of all this is not to argue that empirical theory cannot be true or that theories are empty tautologies. Such is simply not the case. The point is that all explanatory theories are intended to be *contingently true statements*. But, unlike analytical statements, empirical statements are not a matter of acceptance – their claimed truth status depends on the truth of other statements whose truth status in turn may be unproven – i.e., theory-laden.

My argument is that today the research program of neoclassical economic '*theory*' is one of seeking analytically true statements – instead of simple (but unproven) empirical 'facts' – so as to push on with an *ersatz* inductive science. That is, everything must be directed to establishing *logical* facts – just as everyone once thought science established *empirical* facts. However, there is a limit to all this, since we do not wish to end up with only logically true statements (i.e., tautologies). The logical facts of interest are logically proven contingent statements – so-called proven 'theorems'.

The format of 'economic theory'

The paraphernalia of the pursuit of logical facts include the following 'buzz-words': 'proposition', 'lemma', 'proof', 'corollary', 'hypothesis', 'condition', 'definition' as well as 'theorem'. Over the last forty years, at least, these words have played a prominent role in the format of theory articles. Usually they are printed in capital letters to highlight the format. This was abundantly evident in the 'theory' articles that I excluded from my list of 'positive' economic articles at the beginning of this chapter.

The topics of typical theory articles cover a wide range but most are concerned with the theoretical problems I discussed in Chapters 5 through 10 above. The standard (analytical) theory format seems to yield an article with several numbered propositions or theorems, each followed by a proof. The standard format follows quite closely the format of Koopmans' first essay [1957], which in turn merely copied the format of many mathematics textbooks of its day. Procedurally, the standard theory article begins by defining a 'universe of logical discourse' or a 'model', as it is sometimes called. The rules of the game do not permit any new terms to be introduced after this step, as the object of the game is to show that some particular given theorem or situation of concern can be handled using only the stated universe of logical discourse.

Analytical model-building

Unlike 'positive' analysis, which attempts to show that a particular theoretical proposition is logically supported by available data, the 'theory' article attempts to show that a particular theoretical proposition is logically supported by available mathematical theorems. Where 'positive' economics seeks objectivity in repeatable or observable data, 'theoretical' or, more properly, 'analytical' economics seeks objectivity in the autonomy of the discipline of mathematics. And this, I will argue, is the problem with this neoclassical research program. While it may be easy to dispute empirical 'facts', surely it is not supposed to be easy to dispute the veracity of the mathematics profession. But there is a more fundamental question: what is the cost of our reliance on these given mathematical theorems?

Acceptable givens

In order to assess the methodology of economic 'theory' we need only begin with an examination of what are considered acceptable givens. That is, if one is going to prove some particular proposition, one still needs some assumptions, some premises, which are beyond question. One is successful at proving one's chosen proposition when one shows that the proposition logically follows from the conjunction of one or more acceptable premises. Years ago, there was a small set of mathematical theorems which would be invoked in almost every book devoted to the mathematical structure of neoclassical economics. The most frequently used theorems had names such as Kakutani, Lyapunov, Brouwer, and Frobenius. For a while, until perhaps the late 1970s, this game had been transformed into one of referring to theorems named after economists, such as Arrow's possibility theorem, Sheppard's Lemma, Stolper-Samuelson theorem, etc. Today, it is somewhat curious that theorists refer to very few named theorems. In any case, what is the set of acceptable givens now?

It would appear that one item on the portion of the hidden agenda devoted to the objectives of economic 'theory' is that we must appear to be self-reliant – that is, we must no longer appear to be dependent on the mathematics profession for our fundamental theorems. Nevertheless, the proofs do depend on established principles of algebra or set theory. But since students of algebra or set theory are required to duplicate the proofs of established principles, all major principles are in the 'public domain' by demonstration. Thus the current fashion in economic 'theory' methodology is to incorporate all givens in the 'universe of logical discourse' and provide a proof for anything else that is introduced. This means that apart from the terms introduced in the 'universe of logical discourse' the only things we are allowed to take for granted are the rules of logic, since everything else will be proven by the economic 'theorist' within the 'universe of logical discourse'.

One of the consequences of this admirable show of self-reliance is that many of the stated economic theorems and propositions for which proofs are published yield trivial results. Usually they are nothing but some familiar theorem from standard neoclassical theory. The contribution provided by the given article is a 'new' proof or an 'alternative' proof demonstrating that the theorem or proposition can be proved using only the specified 'universe of logical discourse'. Anything novel or informative will have to be provided in the 'universe of logical discourse'. What I am saying here is simply that economic 'theory' today continues to be nothing but exercises in mathematical puzzle-solving – along the lines described by the historian of science, Thomas Kuhn [1962/70].

Avoiding tautologies

If the only givens allowed, beyond the definition of the terms to be included in the model, are the rules of logic, what constitutes successful model-building? As noted above, unless a reference is made to some contingent proposition, the only outcome can be a tautology. This is because, for the purposes of logic, to prove a statement true means to prove that it is always true in the given circumstances (i.e., the given 'universe of logical discourse'). If no contingent propositions are introduced, then the only possible true statement is a tautology. (To reiterate, a tautology is any statement which is true by virtue of its logical form alone.) Since a tautology is true regardless of our 'interpretations' of its terms, then the 'interpretations' are irrelevant for the truth of the proven proposition. Critics of neoclassical 'theory' are free to argue in this case that there is nothing empirical or 'scientific' about formal neoclassical model-building.

Unfortunately, the critics are often a bit confused about the nature of tautologies. They tend to think that any argument involving definitions and logic must result only in tautologies. As explained in Chapter 3, although by their nature tautologies make the meaning of non-logical terms irrelevant, tautologies are not just a matter of definitions. To illustrate let us take an example of an analytically true statement from elementary neoclassical theory. We might say that every genuine demand curve is downward sloping, and if it is not downward sloping, it cannot be a genuine demand curve. Most economists would consider such a statement to be a tautology, since all possibilities are covered – but this depends on the definition of a 'genuine' demand curve. For all practical purposes, pure tautologies seldom arise in economics; it is almost always the case that when economists call an argument or theory a tautology, they mean that it is true by definition of its non-logical words. The difficulty is that, except for pure tautologies, the truth of any statement or argument always depends on the definitions of its non-logical words. Nevertheless, considering how complex a theory can be, it is quite easy inadvertently to construct what would be called a tautology by defining the terms in a manner which indirectly covers all cases and thereby leaves no conceivable counter-example.

This is not facing up to a fundamental question: why not seek pure tautologies, since they are always true statements? In other words, why are pure tautologies unacceptable as explanations? This is a delicate question and it is more difficult to discuss than might be expected. Consider, for example, a common explanation offered by neoclassical demand theory. When we offer any explanation, we put the truth of our assumptions at stake. In this case, when we explain someone's consumption choice as a consequence of the maximization of his or her utility, we put our assumption of utility maximization at stake. If it matters whether our explanations are true, it is because we want our theories to be true while at the same time allowing the possibility that our theories might be false. If they cannot be false (for purely logical reasons), not much will ever be at stake and thus nothing much can be gained.

All this may seem perverse, but it is really rather simple. An explanation is interesting because, while it is claimed to be true, it could just as easily be false (hence, it is not a tautology). If someone offers us an explanation which is true purely as a matter of logical form alone (i.e., all cases have been covered and thus all possible counter-examples are rendered inconceivable), we are not going to be very impressed, except perhaps with his or her cleverness. What makes the theory that all consumers are utility maximizers interesting is merely that someone might think there is a possibility for consumers being otherwise motivated.

We thus have to be careful to distinguish between the logical impossibility of counter-examples to our theory (due to the logical form of our theory) and the empirical impossibility of the existence of empirically true counter-examples (because our theory happens to be true). This distinction is difficult to see when we use only elementary examples. So let us consider a different example, one which is a bit more complex.

Many years ago, economic theorists accepted as true what they called the Law of Demand. This allegedly true statement considers the question of whether demand curves are always downward sloping. Immediately, given the above considerations, we might suspect that such an allegedly true statement may only be a so-called tautology, but let us suspend our judgment for a while.

Empirically it may be true that all demand curves are downward sloping, but it may also be true that a good with an upward sloping demand curve is still a possibility. For instance, consider the allegation that a good with an upward sloping demand curve was observed many years ago by the statistician named Giffen. Such an observation is not logically ruled out by maximizing behavior [Samuelson 1953]. The good demanded may have been an inferior good (a good for which the demand falls whenever income rises). And, almost everyone agrees, for a good to have an upward-sloping demand curve the good must be an inferior good. Even inferior goods may still have downward-sloping demand curves as long as they are not too inferior (that is, their positive 'income effect' does not overwhelm the negative 'substitution effect' of increasing their price). However, if one restricts consumer theory to the question of the demand for non-inferior (i.e., 'normal') goods, then as a matter of logic it is possible to show that all such goods will have downward-sloping demand curves whenever the only reason for demanding them is to maximize utility.

In a world consisting only of non-inferior (i.e., 'normal') goods and utility-maximizing consumers, upwardly sloping demand curves are logically impossible. In such a hypothetical world, Giffen's observations would be empirically impossible, since they are logically impossible. But this question of possibility depends on the special characteristics of our invented hypothetical world. There is no reason why the real world has to correspond to this restricted hypothetical world. In other conceivable worlds (or perhaps, in a different 'universe of logical discourse') it is quite possible for there to be upward-sloping demand curves (i.e., Giffen goods) (for a more detailed discussion, see Boland [1992a, chaps. 13 and 14]).

The point of all this complexity and perversity is that a statement which some might consider to be a tautology may only be a statement for which the hypothetical world has been designed logically to rule out all counter-examples. In fact, as I suggested above, in economics there are very few pure tautologies (statements which are true regardless of definitions). But, there are many theories and models which invent hypothetical worlds that provide what we might call 'pseudo-tautologies'. What is important at this stage is the recognition that when we want to provide a true explanation or theory for something, we do not want our explanation or theory to be true merely because it is a tautology. A tautology is a true statement but its truth is, in a sense, too easy.

A critique of 'pure' theory

Although it is not widely recognized, it is interesting to note that Paul Samuelson's monumental Ph.D. thesis [1947/65] was, among other things, concerned specifically with methodology. Its subtitle was 'The Operational Significance of Economic Theory'. One of his stated purposes for writing the book was to derive 'operationally meaningful theorems' from economic theory. By 'operationally meaningful theorems' he meant hypotheses 'about empirical data which could conceivably be refuted, if only under ideal conditions' [p. 4]. As far as I am aware, Samuelson nowhere tells us why one would ever want to derive 'operationally meaningful theorems' or why anyone would ever think economics hypotheses should be falsifiable. But everyone knows why. If a statement or theory is falsifiable, it cannot be a tautology.

The methodology of tautology avoidance

To a certain extent requiring falsifiability is *ad hoc*, since falsifiability is not necessary for the avoidance of tautologies. All that is necessary for the avoidance of a tautology is that the statement in question be conceivably false. Some statements which are conceivably false are not falsifiable. For example, a 'strictly existential' statement such as 'There will be a revolution *after* 2020' can be false but we could never refute it.

Now the reason why Samuelson found it necessary to invoke the *ad hoc* requirement of falsifiability is that he wished to promote analytical models of neoclassical economics. Specifically, he 'wanted to find the common, core properties of diverse parts of economic theory' [1947/65, p. ix]. In short, he attempted to show that the foundations of economic analysis are nothing more than the analytics of maximization (or minimization). Not only did he show the logical equivalence of the theories of consumer behavior and of costs and production but he also demonstrated that they are equivalent to the theory of equilibrium stability. That is, they can all be reduced to the analytical properties of a maximizing system in which 'analytical properties' are merely provable theorems.

Samuelson's methodological contribution was to recognize that if we wish to avoid tautologies then we must be concerned with the correspondence of the analytical model of an equilibrium to a dynamic process. That is, not only must our equilibrium explanation imply the existence of a potential balancing of demand and supply but we must also provide an explanation for *why* the market price or quantity converges to that balance point. He sometimes called this the *correspondence principle*. Unfortunately, it is all too easy to transform his correspondence principle into another analytical issue and thus to defeat the effort to make economics refutable. Specifically, this is the problem of explaining away disequilibrium which was discussed in Chapter 7.

Whenever someone attempts to satisfy the correspondence principle by adding a mathematically appropriate difference or differential equation for the rate of change of the price relative to the extent of disequilibrium (as discussed in Chapter 10), the question concerning the testability of the original model of the nature of market clearing prices goes begging. That is to say, if one refuted the augmented model (which added a rate of change equation), one would not know whether the source of the failure was the added equation or the original model. This is merely the same problem of the ambiguity of logical refutations which I discussed concerning model building in positive economics earlier in this chapter! This means that Samuelson's method for avoiding tautologies – requiring testability through a correspondence principle – can, in effect, make the original model untestable and thus is a self-defeating methodology.

Is falsifiability really necessary?

As my example above showed, if all we wish to accomplish is an avoidance of tautologies, then falsifiability is sufficient, but not necessary – since strictly existential statements can be false (hence not tautological), even though they are not falsifiable. An alternative way of avoiding tautologies is to consider the terms of the 'universe of logical discourse' to be contingent statements about the nature of the real world. That is, instead of the analytical model being defined by statements such as 'Suppose there are N goods, M people, constant returns, a competitive equilibrium....', some of those statements could be considered empirical statements about the nature of the real world. If this is allowed, then there is no necessary problem about the possibility of the model being conceivably false. Can the problem of tautologies be so easily solved?

The logical problem of analytical models

The question of the falsifiability or testability of economics is rather stale today among economists – but it still lives among some methodologists [e.g., Blaug 1980/92]. And, as I have just indicated, falsifiability is not really essential. Does this mean that analytical economics or 'pure' theory need not worry about the potential shortcomings of relying only on analytical proofs of (desirable) propositions? I hope to show that there may yet be a more fundamental problem.

In order to discuss this new problem I will need to review some technical issues of formal logic. My major concern will be the logical concept called the 'material conditional' – a concept which remains a skeleton in the closet of analytical philosophers who have fostered the format and methodology of 'pure' theory [cf. Hollis and Nell 1975]. What I have to say here may not satisfy the tastes of fastidious analytical and linguistic philosophers but they will have to clean out their own closets.

Let me state my 'universe of logical discourse'. First, suppose that only statements can be true or false – a theory is true or false only by virtue of its being a compound statement such as a conjunction of all its premises (or assumptions). Second, suppose, as I said above, that logical arguments (e.g., proofs) consist of one or more statements. An argument is sufficient only if it is logically valid – which only means that whenever all of its premises are true its conclusions (or predictions, as economists say) are also true without exception. Third, suppose that there is no universal or general means of proving sufficiency. We have only minimum conditions for sufficiency. And fourth (as I discussed in Chapter 3), suppose that an argument in favor of the truth of any particular proposition or statement has two essential parts. One asserts the *validity* of the argument connecting the truth of the assumptions to the truth of the proposition in question, and the other asserts the *truth* of all of the assumptions which form the conjunction representing the argument.

Since 'pure' economic theory takes formal logic as a given for the purpose of providing proofs of propositions, the only question of concern here will be what constitutes a minimally acceptable statement to be included in the logical argument. This is a question which, according to the traditional view of Aristotle's logic, briefly discussed in Chapter 3, requires the three minimum conditions. First, we must not change the meanings of the basic words (i.e., one cannot simply cross out the word frog and write in horse in order to use a statement concerning frogs in an argument about horses – this is called the *axiom of identity*). Second, statements in a logically valid argument cannot be simultaneously true and false (this is called the *axiom of non-contradiction*). And third, there are only two possible values of truth status of an admissible assumption, true or false (this is called the *axiom of the excluded middle*).

Most existential or universal statements would be admissible. For example, 'All consumers are utility maximizers', 'There is one equilibrium price', etc. are unambiguous candidates because we know what it means for them to be true or false, although we may not know how to prove their truth status. Now consider the key critical question. Are conditionals, that is, statements of the form 'if ... then ...', always admissible? I offer the following argument for why they may not always be admissible and thus why the basis of analytical economic theory is not as secure as we are led to believe.

Consider the standard form of a conditional or 'if ... then' statement: 'If P then Q', where P and Q represent admissible statements. (Note that I am discussing 'conditionals' and not necessarily 'implications' [see Quine 1965, pp. 18–22 and 65–68].) Some logic textbooks would have us believe in the material conditional, namely, that such a statement is false only when P is true at exactly the same time Q is false. In all other cases, we are supposed to accept the 'if ... then' statement as true because of the excluded middle. Now, I ask, why must we accept the material conditional?

There are two alternative answers to this question. Some logicians might say that the given 'if ... then' statement is logically equivalent to the statement 'It is not true that "P is true" and "Q is false"'. In these terms the 'if ... then' statement appears equivalent to a conjunction and is thus admissible. As a conjunction, it is false whenever one or more of its constituent parts is false. But this argument might lead to circularity if we question what is meant by 'logically equivalent'.

My preference is for a different explanation. I argue that the only reason for accepting the material conditional is that analytical philosophers want *all* compound statements which are not self-contradictory to be admissible into logical arguments. Specifically, let us consider the given statement 'If P, then Q' and grant that whenever P is false the statement 'If P, then Q' is *not false*.

Now I think it could be argued that whenever P is false the statement 'If P, then Q' can also be considered *not true*. Thus it could be argued that in these circumstances the statement 'If P, then Q' does not always satisfy the axiom of the excluded middle (since it is neither true nor false), hence it is not always admissible into a logically valid argument! The textbook argument accepts the material conditional, I conjecture, on the following basis. Textbooks claim that to say the statement 'If P, then Q' is not false means, on the basis of the excluded middle, that the statement is true. But it could be claimed that the invocation of the excluded middle presupposes that the statement is admissible – which is the moot point. That is, only if one presumes that the given statement is admissible can one infer that it satisfies the axiom of the excluded middle. If the question of its admissibility is still open, then we cannot infer that when it is not false it must be true.

If this argument here against the presumptions of the material conditional is accepted, then it would deal a serious blow to the presumed universality of analytical proofs and propositions. It means that the 'if ... then' propositions that abound in analytical economics are actually much more limited in their logical force than is presumed. Specifically, the truth status of the compound statement 'If P, then Q' is decisive only in one of the four possible combinations of the states of P and Q. Whenever P is false we cannot determine what the truth status of 'If P, then Q' is. In particular, the statement is logically decisive only when the statement is false. Saying that the compound statement is not always logically decisive in no way questions the truth status of its parts.

Analytical success or analytical failure?

So, I claim either one or the other of the following propositions is true:

PROPOSITION 1: I am wrong about the problems of the universal applicability of 'if ... then' statements; thus analytical economics is a successful program to establish logical facts. Furthermore, the ultimate objective of this program is the 'generalization' of neoclassical economics – that is, an inductive proof of its universal truth.

PROPOSITION 2: I am correct and thus analytical economics cannot provide proofs of universal propositions. It can only provide analytical refutations of contingent propositions. A successful generalization of neoclassical economics is thus an impossibility for the same reason that inductive proofs of universal statements are an impossibility.

I will not try to prove either proposition, as that would be contrary to my stated argument. But analytically these propositions cannot both be true. With regard to the first proposition, the second part follows from the conjunction of my previous argument that (dealing with) the Problem of Induction is a primary item on the neoclassical hidden agenda and my argument earlier in this chapter that analytical economics rejects 'positive economics' as an impossible means of establishing indisputable 'facts'. Instead only a logically valid argument could ever provide proof of a generalization, that is, could ever demonstrate the impossibility of counter-examples – and doing so would establish a logical fact.

The basis of the second proposition was argued in the previous subsection. Without the material conditional, analytical economics cannot establish any non-contingent or logical facts (i.e., proven propositions). Without universal propositions each proposition must be proven in each real-world case by proving that the givens are true. Without a logical proof, any claimed generalization is always open to dispute since exceptions (counter-examples) cannot be logically precluded.

13 Falsifiability without Popper on the Agenda

I argue in favor of *falsificationism,* defined as a methodological standpoint that regards theories and hypotheses as scientific if and only if their predictions are at least in principle falsifiable, that is, if they forbid certain acts/states/events from occurring.

Mark Blaug [1980/92, p. xiii]

Popper does not like to use the word 'falsification*ism*' in referring to his views on the methodology of science (1983, p. xxxi). The term is frequently encountered in the critical literature, however, and its usage is standard among economic methodologists.

Bruce Caldwell [1991a, p. 2, fn. 1]

falsificationism represents Popper's approach to the growth of knowledge as well as his solution to (or dissolution of) the traditional problem of induction...

Actually, Popperian falsificationism is composed of two separate theses: one demarcational (concerned with demarcating science from nonscience) and one methodological (concerned with how science should be practiced). The demarcation thesis is that for a theory to be 'scientific' it must be at least potentially falsifiable, that is, there must exist at least one empirical basic statement that is in conflict with the theory...

Briefly, ... Popper's falsificationist methodology requires the search for scientific knowledge to proceed in the following way. Start with a scientific problem situation: something requiring a scientific explanation. Second, propose a bold conjecture that might offer a solution to the problem. Third, severely test the conjecture by comparing its least likely consequences with the relevant empirical data... Finally, the last move in the game depends on how the theory performed during the third testing stage. If the implications of the theory were not supported by the evidence, the conjecture is falsified and it should be replaced by a new theory that is *not ad hoc* relative to the original. If the theory was not falsified then it is considered corroborated by the test and it is accepted provisionally...

It appears that in the final evaluation 'Popperian' economic methodology must be given low marks. Falsificationism ... seems extremely ill-suited to economics.

Wade Hands [1992a, pp. 20–1 and 36]

Those of us, like myself, who have advocated falsificationism as a normative methodology for economics have done so in order to improve economics, to weed out ideological doctrines dressed up as scientific truths, and to provide the discipline of striving for law-like explanations of economic behavior. That economists rarely practice falsificationism only demonstrates the need to preach falsificationism day in and day out, always assuming that falsificationism is in fact practicable in economics that the history of our subject displays some instances of it.

Mark Blaug [1992, p. 57]

I share Blaug's concerns. I too want a methodology that can reject some theories, but I also want one that will leave much (most) of current economic theory intact and allow for new theories to develop... Falsificationism ... is not a good methodology for letting theories grow, weeding out yes – but letting grow – no... [F]alsificationism is a great methodology for avoiding type II errors – it makes it impossible to ever accept a bad theory. On the other hand, since nothing seems to be able to pass the falsificationist test, it makes the chances of a type I error (rejecting a good theory) quite high. Blaug's main concern is avoiding type II errors, making certain the ideologues stay out; I am equally concerned with type I errors. I do not want a methodology that would force us to abandon most of modern economic theory, or one that would become a prohibitive barrier to the development of any new ideas.

Wade Hands [1992b, p. 62]

In this Part, I have so far offered a critical examination of the three obvious ways economists deal with methodology. That is, they might follow Milton Friedman's essay down a self-serving road of Instrumentalism thereby avoiding obvious questions of the realism of their theories and models. Or they may see themselves as followers of Conventionalism and thereby cleverly sidestep questions of realism by simply claiming that theories and models are not to be considered true or false. This cleverness is expressed in two ways. The optimistic version presumes one can substitute a measure of approximate realism and then push on as if the usual modes of logical analysis apply. The other version completely abandons any claim to realism and instead adopts a more risky attitude where logical truths (in the form of analytical proofs) are substituted for empirical realism. The latter attitude is risky because the most obvious logical truths are tautologies and thus empirically empty. To minimize this risk, all mathematical model builders think they are safe from methodological criticism on the sole basis that they make sure their models and theories are falsifiable.

Almost all economic methodologists have been misled by the prevalence of invocations of falsifiability by model builders. They have been misled in two ways: they see the invocation of methodology as a matter of 'big-M' methodology rather than the less pretentious 'small-m' methodology of model building; and they think the invocation of falsifiability implies an application of a so-called Popperian methodology. This latter mistake will be the central issue of this and the next chapter. It will be argued that there is no such 'falsificationist methodology' inherent in Popper's theory of science and that the notion of so-called 'falsificationism' results from the mistakes made by some prominent historians of economic thought. My hope here is that I can convince the reader that 'falsificationism' has little to do with Popper's theory of science but instead is just the latest version of Conventionalism being foisted upon economic methodologists.

Before going into the true nature of Popper's theory of science, I will provide an overview of the state of economic methodology today and explain how the legitimate interests of historians of thought can mislead methodologists.

Methodology and the hidden agenda

> A 'good' model ... will not be exactly more 'real' than a poor one, but will provide better imitations. Of course, what one means by a 'better imitation' will depend on the particular questions to which one wishes answers.
>
> Robert Lucas [1980, p. 697]

Methodology is not considered an urgent topic for neoclassical research programs simply because methodology has historically been concerned only with big-M philosophical questions, including those questions about the nature of the items on the hidden agenda. Being concerned with the items on the hidden agenda means that, to the extent that methodologists tend to question the adequacy of various views of the agenda items, the subject of methodology is paradoxically considered either a waste of time or too dangerous to handle. Consequently, novice economists are often advised to steer clear of methodology, as there is no way to establish a career based on methodology. It is claimed that no significant contributions can be made in that area. So, it can be asked, does this orthodox attitude towards methodology merely reflect a deep-seated insecurity about the hidden agenda? If it does, then there can be no doubt that the advisors are correct!

In the twenty years since the first edition of this book, methodology appears now to be a viable sub-discipline within the economics profession with regular conferences and at least two journals specializing in economic methodology. Nevertheless, in the mainstream of the economics profession, economic methodology is a sideshow that leading economics departments in North America would never accommodate by including methodology courses in their curricula. Presumably, research in methodology could never make a significant contribution to neoclassical economics. They may be right, but how could they ever know this if research on methodology is always prohibited?

Apparently, a 'significant contribution' to neoclassical economics can be made in only two ways. One can either (1) provide a new application of neoclassical theory, or (2) provide a proof of a theoretical proposition which is relevant for applications of neoclassical theory. It is easy to see that with such a limited range of possibilities there is little room for the study of methodology as part of a neoclassical research program.

So long as the domain of methodology is limited to the study of big-M questions about the hidden agenda, the logic of the situation facing an aspiring methodologist is limited. Primarily, given the presumed need to deal with the Problem of Induction and the logical impossibility of providing inductive proofs, the only methodological questions of concern to big-M methodologists are those relating to acceptable ways of solving the Problem of Conventions. If one could provide a new theory-choice criterion which is in some way superior to previous criteria, then such a criterion would be considered a significant contribution to methodology. But since the purpose of any methodological criterion is to provide a basis for justifying a given theory-choice, the givenness of the theory-choice precludes any methodological contribution. For example, in the methodological debates in the 1960s between the followers of Samuelson and the followers of

Friedman's so-called Chicago School, in the 1970s between the 'Keynesians' and the 'Monetarists' or in the 1980s and 90s between proponents of 'critical realism' [e.g., Lawson 1997] and mainstream neoclassical theorists, the appropriate theory-choice criterion is dictated by the nature of the competing theories. One still finds lukewarm remnants of old methodological debates with Samuelson and the other analytical theorists (who urge the dominance of a criterion of 'generality') on one side and followers of Friedman and other 'policy wonks' (who argue for 'simplicity' or for 'usefulness') on the other – but these remnants continue to exist only for lunch-room entertainment.

Many economists consider such debates to be sterile – although they do not hesitate engaging in methodological pronouncements whenever they want to say something important (e.g., Lucas [1980; 1987], Aumann [1985], Binmore [1997]). It might thereby appear that questions of methodology matter, but they really are not decisive, since each side is already committed to its respective theory. Methodology is only an afterthought. Those liberal methodologists who wish to defuse such extremist methodological debates try to confuse the methodological issues. Usually they recommend some *ad hoc* middle ground where both methodological views are represented and thereby make any methodological question irrelevant.

A major factor determining the irrelevancy of contemporary methodology is the lack of a logical consistency of purpose. As can be seen in the various quoted comments of Robert Lucas or Robert Aumann, there is a little bit from Instrumentalism (e.g., 'usefulness') and another bit from Conventionalism (e.g., 'better imitation' or 'better filling system'). Of course, such a mixture is consistent with Instrumentalism. Perhaps that is all that is revealed by the liberal compromise methodologies.

No matter how much methodological discussion is smuggled into neoclassical articles, as long as the theories presented are put beyond question, the methodology provided is irrelevant. But many neoclassical economists who do provide some mention of methodology seem to suggest that methodology potentially does matter in their choice of their theories; and this implies that their theories are not beyond question. Nevertheless, there is little a methodologist can contribute, given the second item on the hidden agenda – the explanatory problem of methodological individualism. As long as psychologistic individualism is considered to be the only acceptable form of individualism for neoclassical economics, the Problem of Induction will not be considered questionable. Thus, I think a key to the apparent irrelevance of methodology is the implicit acceptance of psychologistic individualism.

Methodology and the history of economic thought

> No assumptions about economic behavior are absolutely true and no theoretical conclusions are valid for all times and places, but would anyone seriously deny that in the matter of techniques and analytical construct there has been progress in economics?
>
> Mark Blaug [1997, p. 3]

progress in a discipline is better described by a sequence of theories, or models, not by a study of individual theories. A 'research program' is the organizing conception; to describe it is to characterize the various sequences of models that have family resemblance.

E. Roy Weintraub [1979, p. 15]

Methodology as a viable sub-discipline of economics has been able to grow primarily because it has been taken under the wings of historians of economic thought. This is probably influenced by that fact that the area where methodology is supposed to matter most is the study of the history of economic thought. But if methodology (as we are led to believe) is not decisive in the choice of any particular theory, how can methodology matter in the historical development of our theories? This contradiction is easily handled today, particularly by the leading economics departments. The common view is that the study of the history of thought does not matter either! Nevertheless, let us leave this controversial subject for a while and instead focus on the questions of methodology from the respectful host of the history of thought.

The study of methodology and the study of the history of economic thought go hand in hand. As the views of Koopmans [1957, p. 142] and Weintraub [1979, p. 15] indicate, a common methodological view says that we must see a research program as a 'sequence of models'. This immediately puts methodology into an historical context. What is probably not often appreciated is that putting methodology into an historical context is just a straightforward application of either Inductivism or Conventionalism.

Two views of the history of economic thought

Many historians of economic thought study methodology under the title of the 'Growth of Knowledge' [e.g., Latsis 1976; Loasby 1993; cf. Caldwell 1982/94 and Hands 1993]. What all such perspectives presume is that there is some sort of continuity. The continuity is established either by a logical relationship to some original theory or theorists or by a family and/or social relationship provided by the continuity of a specific community of scholars. The former view is usually in the old tradition of Inductivist histories of science [e.g., von Laue 1950] and the latter in the more recent tradition of Conventionalist histories of physics [e.g., Kuhn 1962/70].

In the older, the orthodox Inductivist tradition, the history of any science is the history of the development of an inductive proof of some 'scientific law'. According to Inductivism, a 'scientific law' is established by the presentation of logically sufficient facts – facts which have been gathered by true scientists. A 'true scientist', so the tradition goes, avoids making mistakes by striving to be unbiased and open-minded, that is, by not jumping to conclusions until all the facts have been collected. This takes a great deal of patience and hard work (the similarity to the 'labor theory of value' is not accidental). One's patience and hard work will be rewarded in the end, perhaps by having one's work included in someone's history of science! Since the speed and veracity of one's inductive proof depends so much on the quality of one's collected facts, the real test of any science is the personal character of the scientists involved. For this reason, inductivist histories of science tended to dwell on the personal qualities of leading scientists.

Agassi [1963] argues that the older historians of particular sciences tended to see what they thought they should see. As he says, they were often unable to 'avoid being wise after the event'. That is, by taking Inductivism for granted, many historians of science would selectively portray a given scientist as if he were pure in heart and mind and unable to make mistakes. This is because whenever a 'scientific law' had been established (i.e., inductively proven), the facts must have been scientifically clean, and that is possible *only* when the scientist is unbiased, open-minded, etc. To those of us in economics these histories of science seem a bit silly, but that is because very few orthodox inductivist histories of economic thought have been written in recent times.

The other approach to writing histories of science is much more common in economics. More and more, the history of economic thought is considered to be the history of an impersonal enterprise. Today one can discuss the 'marginalist revolution in economic theory' without going into any detail about the lives of Jevons, Marshall, Walras, or Menger. What is recognized today is that although each of these men contributed to the body of economic thought, their contributions depended on *acceptance* by other economists. Of course, the idea that anyone's contribution depends on acceptance by others is the keystone of modern Conventionalism. Where Inductivist scientists strived to provide empirical, objective proofs, Conventionalist scientists provided acceptable arguments and propositions. Whether one's intended contribution is accepted depends on whether one has satisfied the currently approved criteria of acceptance for one's evidence and for one's mode of argument.

There are two essential elements in the Conventionalist view of the history of economic thought. First is the continuity of the enterprise; second is the tentativeness of the certification of one's contribution. In some sense there was a continuity involved in the Inductivist view of the history of science but it was due to the presumed durability of any alleged inductive proof. The Conventionalist view, which denies the existence of both inductive proofs and absolute truth, takes a broader historical view. Any body of knowledge is treated like a river flowing through time. We can all attempt to pour our contributions into the stream but their significance will be judged downstream.

Implicitly, the continuity of the growth of knowledge would seem to presume that whenever somebody is to have made a contribution, it remains a contribution forever. But this implication of continuity has not always fitted the facts. That is, 'contributiveness' itself must be judged downstream. What may be considered a contribution today might tomorrow be considered an illusion. The resulting tentativeness of the judgment concerning whether one has actually made a contribution leads to a breakdown in the continuity aspect of the history of the enterprise.

In Chapter 4, I discussed the best illustration [Wong 1978] of the tentativeness of contributions in the history of Paul Samuelson's contribution to demand theory. Recall that in 1938 Samuelson said that he had solved the problem plaguing all psychologistic theories of behavior – namely, that the basis of such explanations of individuals' behavior is not 'operational', that is, is not observable. He offered a new way to explain an individual's demand. Instead of assuming the existence of a psychologically given utility function or preference ordering, we were to assume only that the individual was consistent in his or her choices. Consistent choices meant only that whenever one faced the same price-income situation one would make the same choices. In effect, one was supposed to be a slave to one's past history. On the basis of this postulate of consistency (and a few minor postulates that provide that the consumer does make choices), Samuelson was able to prove what he thought was the essential purpose of the orthodox theory of the consumer (as presented by Hicks and Allen [1934]) – a theory that seemed to require the existence of psychologically given preferences.

Now, the success of Samuelson's research program is widely accepted and even hailed by many as a major contribution to economic knowledge. What is interesting about the history of Samuelson's contribution is that by 1950 *he* readily admitted that a complete version of his demand theory was logically equivalent to the 'ordinal demand theory' which Hicks and Allen had developed [see Samuelson 1998]. Now, there is an inconsistency here. How can Samuelson's 'operational' theory of demand be both different from and logically equivalent to the Hicks-Allen theory? What appeared as a major contribution in 1938 disappears as a mirage in 1950. Probably more significant, what was hailed as a major breakthrough in economics methodology has disappeared in a puff of philosophical smoke. Such are the ways of Conventionalist histories of economic thought!

Methodology and continuity-based histories

The paradigm of continuity theories of the history of science is, of course, Thomas Kuhn's view, which he presented in his *Structure of Scientific Revolutions* [1962/70]. According to his view, we are to see a steady progress in everyday 'normal science', with the steady accumulation of solutions to theoretical puzzles. What distinguishes a puzzle from a problem is that a puzzle is approached on the basis that definitely there is a way to solve it – if only we can find it. On the other hand, a problem may not always have a solution, no matter how long we look for one (e.g., the Problem of Induction). No one claims that the solution to the puzzle constitutes absolute proof. Nevertheless, each piece added to the puzzle warrants much the same reward as the discovery of each additional fact leading to an inductive proof.

It might be asked, if Kuhn's book is so concerned with puzzle-solving (viz., normal science), why is the title concerned with 'revolutions'? The answer is that puzzle-solving is not very progressive and historians are more concerned with significant progress. Historians record the abandonment of one puzzle deemed to be a bit stale and its replacement by a new and more promising puzzle. He calls these puzzle-replacements 'revolutions', since each old puzzle is abandoned only after internal sociological developments within the scientific community. In particular, there are no devastating refutations, as might be suggested by Karl Popper's view, but instead a steady evolution along social-Darwinian lines. A given puzzle is not abandoned until a 'better' puzzle comes along *and* is accepted.

The question of acceptance brings us right back to the Conventionalist basis of Kuhn's view. Although would-be revolutionaries have been stimulated by Kuhn's book, it was really just an effort to explain so-called 'revolutions' away rather than to promote them. A 'revolution' is never a complete break but depends on the acceptance of an on-going community of scientists. The acceptance of a 'revolution' depends on the acceptance of any criteria used to assess the intended 'revolution'.

Methodologists could easily argue that a real revolution would require a revolution in criteria – but on what basis would the new criteria be assessed? Some may argue that such considerations show that Conventionalism is circular, but this is not the point I am making. What I wish to point out is that changes in any social enterprise require the stability of some frame of reference. In order to assess any change in methodological criteria we would still need some fixed basis from which to assess the changes. We could appeal to some outside authority (such as philosophers of science) but this would only bring into question the basis of their authority. To assess methodology within an enterprise such as neoclassical economics requires the acceptance of neoclassical theory. Given this theory of social change, there could hardly ever be a genuine revolution.

Conventionalism and the 'growth of knowledge'

If it is difficult to specify a revolution within the context of a Conventionalist concept of the history of economic thought, can one at least identify unambiguous signs of 'progress'? If one can no longer identify progress with establishing new 'scientific laws', then what is now regarded as progress? Consider Axel Leijonhufvud's [1976, p. 67] comments:

> Traditionally, the history of economic doctrines has for the most part been written as a 'straight' historical narrative – as a chronological story of 'progress' by accumulating analytical improvements in a field of inquiry of more or less stable demarcation and with a largely fixed set of questions.

The term 'stable demarcation' refers to what I am calling acceptance criteria. In this sense, given a criterion which specifies when a model or theory is 'better', one could simply say that progress is identified with finding a 'better' theory. But this reveals that there still is an element of the Problem of Conventions here, as long as there are judgments to be made about whether progress has been made.

So when Blaug asked, 'Has there been progress in economic theory?' his answer was a clear 'Yes' and his initial specification [1997, p. 7] was a long list of Conventionalist criteria:

> analytical tools have been continuously improved and augmented; empirical data have been increasingly marshalled to verify economic hypotheses, metaeconomic biases have been repeatedly exposed and separated from the

core of testable propositions which they enmesh; and the workings of the economic system are better understood than ever before.

In more general terms he says [p. 7]:

The development of economic thought has not taken the form of a linear progression toward present truths. While it has progressed, many have been the detours imposed by exigencies of time and place.

Although Conventionalism and its presumption that there are standards of acceptance seems to dominate the historian's view of the methodology of economics, there does not seem to be as much agreement over what constitutes acceptable progress in economics as some historians might like us to think.

Conventionalism and the sequence of models

The view of Koopmans [1957] and Weintraub [1979] that a research program in economics should be seen as a sequence of models is an example of the Conventionalist continuity theory of the history of economic thought. Is there anything more that one can infer from such a view? Probably not, since the recognition of a sequence does not imply that each step represents unambiguous progress, although that may be what Koopmans and Weintraub have in mind. Today, few economics writers find it worthwhile to add some romantic comments about how far we have progressed beyond our primitive forefathers. This is simply because real progress was always the promise of those who believed in inductive sciences or, as I would now say, in an inductive learning possibilities curve which reaches the probability of 1.00 in real time. Now, today, we are apparently more modest, as it is agreed that there is always room for improvement. Each subsequent model in the sequence may be *more* realistic but nobody will claim that it *is realistic* – that is, that it is true. Each model may be more useful but, as Lucas said, that depends on what you want to do. Given all this modesty, one might wonder why anyone bothers with neoclassical research programs.

Revealed methodologies

The picture of contemporary methodology in neoclassical economics I have now painted is rather bland. Perhaps I should say that I have constructed a collage. The unifying element is the predominance of Conventionalism which is only lightly colored by its Inductivist origins. Model-building is the primary focus of all recent studies of methodology – supposedly, we are to think that 'progress' is any movement along some continuum formed by the growing sequence of accepted models. No single model is ever claimed to be true, of course. Successful model-building is only tentative; our final judgment is to be postponed.

So I ask again, why do so many economists strive to contribute to the body of knowledge if their success is to be considered so tentative? The answer, which I have been developing throughout this book, is that although there is much talk that might indicate a belief in the postulates of Conventionalism (namely, since we do not have an *operational* inductive logic, theories are not true or false but only 'better' or 'worse'), the acceptance of Conventionalism is only a short-run measure. When philosophers tell us that we cannot conduct an inductive proof, neoclassical methodologists have interpreted this to mean that we cannot give an inductive proof in our lifetime, and perhaps this does not logically preclude an inductive proof in the *very* long run. What contemporary methodologists and historians of economic thought may presume is that our short-run tolerance of acceptably false models will be rewarded with the one true model in the long run. Eventually the sequence of models has to lead somewhere. Again, each model added to the sequence is like one more fact in the process of providing an inductive proof. And again, neoclassical methodologists accept Conventionalism in the short run but hold out for Inductivism in the long run – perhaps Blaug's methodological view of the history of economics [1978; 1997] can be considered the paradigm of this perspective.

Misappropriation of Popper's theory of science

Contrary to my view that contemporary methodology is dominated by Conventionalism, given all the popular references to falsifiability of economic theories some might think that most methodologists have adopted Popper's theory of science today. For example, consider the following views:

> The hallmark of a metaphysical proposition is that it is not capable of being tested... Adopting Professor Popper's' criterion for propositions that belong to the empirical sciences, that they are capable of being falsified by evidence, it is not a scientific proposition. [Joan Robinson 1962, p. 3]

> Popper, more than any other philosopher of science, has had an enormous influence on modern economics. It is not that many economists read Popper. Instead, they read Friedman but Friedman is simply Popper-with-a-twist applied to economics. [Mark Blaug 1978, p. 714]

> I see no reason for denying to the study of the activities and institutions created by scarcity the title of science. It conforms fundamentally to our conception of science in general: that is to say the formation of hypotheses explaining and (possibly) predicting the outcome of the relationships concerned and the testing of such hypotheses by logic and by observation. This process of testing used to be called verification. But, since this way of putting things may involve an overtone of permanence and nonrefutability, it is probably better described, as Karl Popper has taught us, as a search for falsification – those hypotheses which survive the test being regarded as provisionally applicable. [Lionel Robbins 1981, p. 2]

Judging by Blaug's 1978 comments, one gets the impression that most methodologists in economics have adopted Karl Popper's 'philosophy' of science. Judging by Robbins' 1981 comments, one gets the impression that Popper's role is only that of an elocution instructor. I shall argue here that Robbins' view is a better reflection of the state of affairs. So far, Popper's only real accomplishment in economics is the suppression of any open advocacy of Inductivism. Popper also claims to be opposed to both Conventionalism and Instrumentalism, yet both are openly promoted in mainstream neoclassical economics. Judging by Joan

Robinson's comments, it might appear that Popper has made an impression on at least one post-Keynesian theorist but her understanding was also superficial. One reason why Popper has not had any significant impact on the nature of neoclassical methodology is that most economists have obtained their view of Popper by way of the writings of one of his students, Imre Lakatos. For many years most philosophers of science considered Popper to be in direct competition with Thomas Kuhn. As noted above, Kuhn's view of science is quite compatible with that of most methodologists. This is true for Lakatos, as well. Both offer a form of Conventionalism. Moreover, Lakatos endeavored to build a bridge between Kuhn and Popper; and to a great extent he succeeded. But the cost of the reconciliation has been the abandonment of most of the more important aspects of Popper's theory of science.

Testability in mathematical economics

> Popper brings out very clearly that it is the function of a scientific law to 'forbid' some conceivable types of occurrence... A circularity or tautology 'forbids' nothing. It is 'true' whatever occurs, and therefore empirically empty.
>
> Terence Hutchison [1938, p. 126, fn. 52]

> only the smallest fraction of economic writings, theoretical and applied, has been concerned with the derivation of *operationally meaningful* theorems. In part at least this has been the result of the bad methodological preconceptions that economic laws deduced from *a priori* assumptions possessed rigor and validity independently of any empirical human behavior. But only a very few economists have gone so far as this. The majority would have been glad to enunciate meaningful theorems if any had occurred to them. In fact, the literature abounds with false generalization...
>
> By a *meaningful theorem* I mean simply a hypothesis about empirical data which could conceivably be refuted, if only under ideal conditions.
>
> Paul Samuelson [1947/65, pp. 3–4]

While Popper was being shunned by the philosophers of the day, an economics scholar, Terence Hutchison, thought he would take up the challenge in 1938 by arguing that what made scientific economic theories interesting was not that they are verifiable but that they were 'testable'. He made reference to Popper to support this view [Hutchison 1938, p. 48, fn. 19 and p. 49, fn. 35]. Unfortunately, Hutchison did not completely understand what Popper was saying. Moreover, Hutchison's view was pretty much ignored in economics. Instead, anyone writing on methodology at that time continued the Logical Positivist line that verifiability was the true test of a scientific theory.

Despite there being much talk about testability in economics in the 1960s, none of this had to do with Hutchison's path-breaking view of methodology. Instead, the 1940s and 50s were the battle ground for the movement to make economics a mathematical science. As noted before, a popular methodological criticism of mathematical economics was that mathematics could only provide tautologies – namely, statements or theorems that are true by virtue of their logical consistency rather than their empirical content.

It was at the time of Hutchison's launch of testability-directed methodology that Paul Samuelson was beginning to write his Ph.D. thesis which openly promoted the mathematical basis for all economic theory. And, as briefly discussed in Chapter 12, Samuelson directly confronted the critics by saying that his version of mathematical economics could not be dismissed as a bunch of tautologies because he would require economic theorems to be testable and thereby conceivably false. For Samuelson, a testable theorem is 'operationally meaningful' by which he merely meant that it must be 'refutable in principle'. To be refutable in principle, a theorem could not be a tautology. QED.

During the 1950s and early 1960s, there was little discussion of testability in economics and virtually no mention of Popper except by his student, Joseph Agassi [see Klappholz and Agassi 1959]. Instead, almost all of the debate was about Friedman's 1953 defense of Instrumentalism, which to many neoclassical theorists was a methodology that seemed dishonest or simply wrong-headed. Those who wished to promote mathematical economics were dismayed by Friedman's Instrumentalism and set about criticizing it on perceived logical grounds. For the most part, Samuelson [1963] simply made fun of Friedman, trying to eliminate him with ridicule. And it seemed to work for most of us, and in particular, for those of us trained to be mathematical economists.

Testability in abandoned attempts to apply Popper

> We first ask what we mean by science and we then enquire whether or not economics is, or can be, scientific... Very roughly speaking, the scientific approach is to relate questions to evidence...
>   We all know that the natural sciences progress through the development of *theories*... What is a theory and how does one test theories? ... A theory consists of a set of definitions, stating clearly what we mean by various terms, and a set of assumptions about the way in which the world behaves... The implications which are deduced from the assumptions can be tested against actual empirical observations, and we would then conclude either that theory is *refuted* by the facts, or that it is *consistent* with the facts... but it is not possible to conclude that the theory has been *proved correct*...
>   The refutation of a theory should generally be a cause for satisfaction because we learn new, surprising, things through the process of refuting existing theories.
>
> Richard Lipsey [1963, pp. 5, 10–12, 14–15]

At about the same time as Samuelson was putting down Friedman in the annual meetings of the American Economic Association in the early 1960s, Richard Lipsey and Chris Achibald were, to use the words of Achibald, 'building bombs in the basement' at the London School of Economics. They were under the tutelage of none other than Joseph Agassi. At first they thought they would build a new empirically based economics using Popper's theory of science. Like Hutchison before them, they did not quite understand what they were being told. They thought that economics could be made empirical (as opposed to mathematically tautological) by promoting an econometric approach that stressed the need for 'falsifiable' research. Their bomb-construction yielded only one significant work, namely, the first edition of Lipsey's famous textbook where Popper's view was openly promoted. Their project was soon dropped because they found that falsifying econometric propositions was not very easy and sometimes impossible. Popper's view played no role in subsequent editions and thus was soon forgotten. And, both Lipsey and Archibald jumped on the bandwagon of the critics of Popper by promoting their version of Conventionalism.

By the end of the 1960s, Popper's theory of science disappeared from the stage and in its temporary place, Conventionalism became the order of the day. Specifically, the issue became not criticism, but theory-choice and acceptance criteria: the criterion of falsifiability rather than verifiability was now to be the watchword of science. So, when economists of the 1970s and 80s talked about the need for testability and falsifiability of their models and theorems, they were implicitly talking about Samuelson's methodology pronouncements and not Lipsey's weak moment at the beginning of his first edition.

In fact, during the late 1960s and all of the 1970s, hardly anything was said about methodology – it was very difficult to get journal editors to even consider publishing methodology and thus very little was published. The only consistent exception was the last chapter of the various editions of Mark Blaug's history of thought textbook. As early as 1968, Blaug was promoting falsifiability in his history of thought book as a test of true science – but at that time he seemed to be unaware of Popper until the mid-1970s. Unfortunately, Blaug then made the same mistake as Lipsey and Archibald by thinking Popper was promoting falsifiability as the essence of his theory of science. So, Blaug began complaining that economists talk about falsifiability but never practice it. He seems never to have recognized that economists were never trying to fulfill his notion of a so-called Popperian methodology but were instead simply invoking testability and falsifiability as a Conventionalist criterion to choose the best model or theorem in the way recommended by Samuelson – that is, in a way that insulated mathematical economics from the charge of being merely a bunch of tautologies.

Falsificationism in economics

It seems clear to me that Blaug and thereby his followers were misled by Lakatos. They seem to have missed the fact that by the early 1970s (long before Popper died), Lakatos tried to claim the mantle of Popper – and without Lakatos knowing much about science. However, he did know a lot about mathematics. As a result, Lakatos tried to formalize methodology with what he called 'the methodology of scientific research programs'. It is not clear that Lakatos understood Popper's reasons for talking about falsifiability – namely, as a sufficient but not necessary condition for criticism. Lakatos also misled economists by his twisting of Popper's view to overemphasize its growth of knowledge implications. This was unfortunate because such emphasis encouraged historians of economics to follow Blaug's lead and start talking about methodology only in the terms of 'progress' and 'progressive' research strategies that Lakatos promoted. In all of this, Popper was maligned and Lakatos praised.

By 1980, Blaug chose to spin off his final chapter to make a freestanding methodology book. The obvious success of this book challenged the reluctance of other publishers. There soon was a mad scramble to find authors to write books on economic methodology. The editor for one publisher, George Allen and Unwin, took the first step by commissioning me to write the first edition of this book and simultaneously by agreeing (following my recommendation) to publish Bruce Caldwell's Ph.D. thesis. The following two decades have witnessed a very active development of a methodology sub-discipline within economics backed by two or three major publishers. Unfortunately, until quite recently, almost all of the publications in these two decades have tried to turn the clock back to the 1930s problems and questions that continue to interest philosophers rather than address the methodological issues that are of interest to mainstream economists.

Methodology as a sub-discipline without Popper

As a separate sub-discipline of mainstream economics, methodology has shown the developmental signs of youth and adolescence. It would still be floundering in the basement had it not been for the efforts of two leaders of the History of Economics Society, Warren Samuels and Mark Perlman. Together, they encouraged historians of economic thought to make room in their annual meetings for sessions explicitly on methodology. Critics might easily say that this was a big mistake to tie one's dingy to a sinking ship. In the 1960s history of thought was a required course in almost all economics programs – but over the last two decades it has been difficult to find a history of thought course – let alone a required course – in any major economics program. Nevertheless, methodology has found a viable place at least in the published literature if not the curricula.

Over the last two decades at least four camps have developed. The biggest is made up of those methodologists who approach the subject with the interests of the historian of science. This camp spent most of the 1980s exploring how they might apply their understanding of Lakatos to the history of economic thought. As a consequence, there are many articles about 'appraisal' of economic theories and methods. And thus there is much discussion of negative or positive 'heuristics', 'hard cores', 'protective belts' and 'novel facts'. For the most part, this kind of discussion, particularly that concerning the 'hard cores' of research programs, was nothing more than a replacement for the 1970s fascination with Thomas Kuhn's 'paradigms'. All of this Lakatos-inspired methodology literature has at best been a waste of time. At worse, it became a stalking horse for critics of Karl Popper's theory of science. Unfortunately, Lakatos simply did not understand Popper but, nevertheless, these critics were thrilled to have the Lakatos-created cartoon-character of Popper to bash away at. Of particular concern was the false characterization of Popper as a promoter of so-called 'falsificationism', a characterization which unfortunately continues to be promoted in history of economic thought circles by Blaug and his followers.

The fastest growing camp is the least serious. It began with a group who became bored with the grinding that goes on in the Lakatos-inspired methodology literature. To overcome the boredom there is now an eagerness to create and pursue buzz-words and fads [see Boland 1995]. In the mid-1980s, the fads were concerned with finding an alternative philosopher of science – one to quote to create and demonstrate an independence from the 'old' views. In the late 1980s, the new fad was so-called 'recovering practice' which supposedly was directed at understanding how economists practice their trade rather than how they should practice it. But this too became boring. Another group subsequently tried to get everyone interested in deciding between whether the practice of economics is concerned with 'realism' or just a 'social construction' and thus relativist. More recently the fad has been about examining whether or not models are 'mediators' – whatever that means. This too is beginning to bore.

It is difficult to take serious the frequent gathering around the latest fads in order to hold conferences about them. It may make all the eager conference participants feel like they are doing something – something 'new' – but it is still difficult to take seriously any study of methodology that takes a back seat to the immediate social needs of conference participants.

The next camp is driven by the interest of analytical philosophers who still worry about the problems and questions that arose in the 1930s. And they are still licking the wounds inflicted by Popper. Their main hope is to eliminate Popper from the scene. But the most important problem with this camp is that none of them have anything more than an elementary understanding of mainstream economics. While other philosophers are thrilled with each publication from this camp, mainstream economists ignore them completely. After all, it is the concerns of this philosophy camp that Friedman's methodology intentionally addressed; and he provided economists with a reason to ignore the philosophers of the 1930s. Today, it is McCloskey's [1983] emphasis on rhetoric that has replaced Friedman, but the message and purpose is the same, namely, to give reason to ignore this philosophical camp. McCloskey's main argument is that the philosophical camp is concerned only with big-M methodology whereas ordinary economists will be concerned only with small-m methodology.

The fourth camp is very small – although there are signs that it may be growing. This camp is concerned mostly, maybe exclusively, with small-m methodology from a real Popperian perspective. Popper enters the scene simply by viewing every social event, including scientific decisions, as problem solving ploys. The activity of this fourth group is sometimes criticized for being 'always the same' but such criticism may merely reflect a concern for big-M methodology by methodologists who do not understand the ever-changing practice of economics and economic model builders that is the primary domain of the small-m methodologist. This book is a product of this fourth camp.

Testability does not require the practice of falsificationism

From the perspective of this fourth camp, methodology from the beginning was the examination of the reasons why economic model builders assume what they assume. In particular, do economic model builders really think testability is as important as Popper seemed to think? As I noted earlier (p. 202), one particular study – provided in my Ph.D. thesis [Boland 1966, see 1989, chaps. 2 and 3] –

showed that even the simplest Keynesian models of the 1960s are untestable, as they would require more data than is practical or possible. Those model builders who really think they are saying something significant by claiming their models are testable have not fully contemplated what it would take. So, again, if it takes more observations than is possible to perform a refutation in economics, then it is clear that testability is sought only to avoid tautologies and has nothing to do with whatever Lakatos thought Popper said about falsifiability.

What Popper did say was, as a matter of quantificational logic, if you think observations matter, you must recognize that the only decisive observations are those that can be used to falsify a theory. Confirming observations can never be decisive except in trivial situations. Moreover, testing by attempting to falsify someone's theory or explanation is just one of many types of criticism. And, as I have been stressing throughout this book, it is criticism – or more specifically, a critical attitude – that is the hallmark of science. It is not empirical falsifiability as both foes and some friends of Popper seem to think he was saying.

The small-m approach to methodology does not interest philosophers and that's ok, of course. But it does interest economists [cf. Hoover 2001]. Moreover, some methodologists have started talking about the methodology of economic model building and stopped talking about topics such as 'realism', 'progress', 'falsificationism' and similar things that philosophers like to talk about. Today it is becoming clear that methodologists can make a contribution to mainstream economics by helping to sort out and criticize the usual assumptions concerning an economic agent's knowledge and learning. To do this, methodologists will have to give up creating and pursuing methodological fads and instead learn more about modern economic theory so that they can address the needs of practicing economists. For example, methodologists should surely be able to help the mainstream economist to realize that the time has come for him or her to stop assuming that induction is a reliable process of learning. To assume that it is reliable is, after all, to assume a theory of learning that is more than 380 years old and one that was refuted over 200 years ago.

In the next chapter I will endeavor to explain how Popper's theory of science can be understood in a manner that is most useful for neoclassical economic model builders. Obviously, it will be done in a manner that does not call upon the misrepresentations of Popper's theory by the followers of Lakatos.

Part V
PUTTING POPPER
ON THE AGENDA

14 Understanding Popper's Theory of Science

Popper almost alone, and alone in our century, has claimed that criticism belongs not to the *hors d'oeuvre*, but to the main dish.

Joseph Agassi [1968, p. 317]

Eastern thinking is ... far removed from the metacontext of belief, identification, and commitment that one finds in most western philosophies. It is less distant, although still very different, from the *fallibilism* or critical rationalism of Xenophanes – or of Karl Popper... It is precisely language, he insists, that *permits* one to dissociate from, to detach from, one's own positions and hypotheses: to make them into *objects*, not subjective states, not identified with ourselves, which may then be examined... *Unlike* most oriental philosophies, ... Popper searches for a more adequate model or 'vicarious representation' of the world; *like* the oriental, Popper gives no importance to 'right belief,' and searches for a pervasive condition of non-attachment to models and representations generally. For one must detach from, must *objectify,* one's theories in order to improve them. The very asking of the Popperian question – 'Under what conditions would [your] theory be false?' invites a psychological exercise in detachment and objectification, leading one to step outside the point of view shaped by that theory...

In a fallibilist metacontext, ... *How can our intellectual life and institutions be arranged so as to expose our beliefs, conjectures, policies, positions, source of ideas, traditions and the like – whether or not they are justifiable – to maximum criticism, in order to counteract and eliminate as much intellectual error as possible?*

William Bartley [1982, pp. 131–2]

[There is] an impatience which is often to be found in methodological criticisms of economics. This impatience has a variety of targets, such as the 'unnecessarily' slow progress in economics or the futility of much of the work done, and sometimes expresses itself in the complaint that economists often advance hypotheses which appear to be untestable, etc. Our criticism will be based on our methodological point of view, which is that outlined in K. R. Popper's *Logic of Scientific Discovery...* Above all, we contend, that it is important to guard against the illusion that there can exist in any science methodological rules the mere adoption of which will hasten its progress, although it is true that certain methodological dogmas, such as the dogma that only theories pertaining to measurement are significant, or the dogma of inductivism, may certainly retard the progress of science. All one can do is to argue critically about scientific problems.

Kurt Klappholz and Joseph Agassi [1959, pp. 60 and 74]

There are two essential and related considerations without which no clear appreciation of Popper's views can be reached. One is Popper's view of Plato's early 'Socrates', the other is the observation that Popper has strong ties to what is usually called the Austrian School of economics. While any failure to recognize this can cause critics and some friends to misrepresent Popper's theory of science, the primary difficulty is the failure to distinguish between an explanation of science (Popper's theory of science) and prescriptions (Popper's so-called methodology). Popper repeatedly asserts that there is no 'scientific methodology' if one means by this a step-by-step recipe for doing science [see 1961/72, p. 265; 1945/66, vol. 1, p. 285 and 1945/66, vol. 2, p. 363]. What Popper was offering in the 1930s was an alternative explanation to that provided by the analytical philosophers of the day. And Popper's mode of explanation of any actions by individuals (scientists or ordinary people) is to see the action as an attempt to solve a problem. While some actors are explicit in saying they are solving a problem, this is rarely the case. So, Popper conjectures a problem for which the action in question might be seen to be a solution. He calls this the 'problem situation' and it forms an essential part of his mode of explanation that he calls 'situational analysis' [1963/94, p. 166]. Basically, it is important to recognize a simple truism that is the foundation of Popper's mode of explanation: While there may be problems that have no solutions, every solution has at least one problem. Whenever we see Popper discussing the 'Problem of Induction' and the 'demarcation problem', in both cases, Popper is not saying that these are problems that we should always endeavor to solve. Instead, he is saying that we can more clearly understand why the 1930s philosophers viewed science as an enterprise dedicated to producing inductively verified knowledge if we see their pronouncements as solutions to these problems. Popper's alternative theory is that science is an enterprise devoted instead to systematic criticism. And, *if* one thinks Popper's theory is true, then one could make recommendations about how criticism should be practiced but such recommendations are not part of his theory. Moreover, such recommendations should not be considered rules of procedure but only sensible options to keep in mind.

Popper's mode of explanation

Popper's mode of explanation is utilized and demonstrated in Chapters 1 and 2 of this book. There I have offered my explanation of neoclassical economics by claiming that one can understand the various research decisions made by neoclassical theorists as attempts to solve or avoid the problems I conjectured there. The focus of Chapter 2 was the explanatory problem of individualism – can we explain all social events exclusively as consequences of decisions made by individuals. Chapter 1 characterizes the methodology of neoclassical economics as being concerned primarily with the 'Problem of Conventions', which was itself an outcome of the impossibility of ever solving the Problem of Induction.

In his critique of the 1930s philosophers who were convinced that scientific knowledge embodied empirically verified theories, Popper focused on *their* notion that positive evidence matters in science. Popper's argument was that *if* evidence matters it cannot be as a basis for verification but only as a basis for empirical critiques. Again, his reason was simple. Every explanation of an empirical event must include at least one *strictly* universal statement – that is, a statement of the form 'all *X* have property *Y*'. But again, as a matter of simple logic, one could never prove that a strictly universal statement is true if the proof must be inductive – that is, a proof that involves only singular observation statements. However, he notes, strictly universal statements can be refuted by just one (true) singular statement – that is, by a strictly existential statement such as 'there exists at least one *X* that does not have property *Y*'. While this simple matter of logic makes the 1930s philosopher's view of science inherently false, it presents no problem for Popper's theory of science. After all, there is no better example of criticism than the report of any evidence of a falsifying test of a respected theory.

Critics of Popper's theory of science point out that such an empirical refutation must involve the acceptance of conventions such as rules of evidence that are put beyond question. After all, they claim, a refutation is a proof of the falsity of a theory in question. This criticism is fundamentally wrong and totally misses the point of Popper's theory of science. This criticism of Popper presumes that any claim to knowledge must be justified and as such would include knowledge that a refuted theory is false. This presumption, called Justificationism in Chapter 1, is explicitly rejected by Popper. For him, it is not a Conventionalist matter of acceptance but one of prioritization. In its place, Popper's theory of science simply says that everything, every presupposition, every evidentiary convention is open to criticism. While every experimental test may involve background assumptions that are, for the moment, put beyond question for the purpose of the experiment and while the background plays the role of metaphysics in the going research program (as with the assumption of maximization in neoclassical theory) and is thereby put beyond criticism, this is only temporary. Nothing is put completely or permanently beyond criticism as otherwise this would undermine the purpose of the enterprise of science. It would, as he makes clear, restrict the progress of science.

What makes Popper's view of methodology incompatible with Conventionalism is that he rejects Justificationism and its manifestation in the Problem of Induction (unfortunately, he calls his rejection of the Problem of Induction a 'solution' [e.g., 1972, chap. 1]). What makes his view appear to be compatible with Conventionalism is that both deny the logical possibility of inductive proofs. Obviously, to accept a counter-example still requires the acceptance of certain conventional rules of evidence. For Popper, the issue is not this acceptance but only that we are explicit in what we accept for the moment and that the acceptance is only a means to set up one's subsequent criticism. That is, with Conventionalism, acceptance is a truth substitute but for Popper it is a temporary means of focusing on the logic of explanation. Whatever statement or assumption one may temporarily accept without proof for some immediate need is still something that is either true or false – not merely better or worse. I will say more about this below.

Popper's anti-Justificationism

Popper's rejection of the Problem of Induction is based on a specific view which explicitly separates the process of knowing from the object we call knowledge. That is, for Popper we can examine 'knowledge' without the necessity of examining the 'knower' [1972, chap. 3]. All knowledge, in his view, is explanation and, as noted above, explanations must include one or more assertions which are in the form of 'strictly universal statements'. It is here that the impossibility of induction plays a crucial role. Where Conventionalism would say that these considerations would deny truth status for anyone's knowledge, Popper does not. For him, one's knowledge may very well be true, even though we cannot prove that it is true (certainly, not without making additional *a priori* assumptions). Clearly, this is so when it involves unverifiable universal statements.

A corollary of his separation of the question of what is the truth status of one's knowledge from the question of how one knows the truth status of one's knowledge is his separation of epistemology from methodology. Epistemology is about our theories of the nature of knowledge, and methodology is about our theories of learning or of the knowledge acquisition process [Agassi 1969a]. Popper's epistemological position is that all knowledge is essentially theoretical conjecture [1972, chap. 1]. Any empirical conjecture may be true or false – but even if it is true, there is no way we can ever empirically prove that it is true beyond doubt. Moreover, one's inability to prove one's knowledge claim does not prove that it is not true. However, since strictly universal statements logically deny certain specified positive statements (viz., conceivable observations), an observation of an instance of a logically denied statement constitutes a tentative proof of the falsity of one's theory. At minimum, to be consistent, one cannot accept both the theory and its refutation if both are consistent with the same evidence and rules of evidence. And in this manner, since all theories involve universal statements, we can learn by proving that our knowledge is false if we continue to allow some observations to be considered true. But this is now a major departure from the traditional belief in what I have called the inductive learning possibilities function (see Chapter 8). More positive information does not always increase the probability of one's model being true. If we are to learn from experience, it can only be that we learn that some of our theories are false. This, I shall argue, is the essence of what I will call Popper's Socratic theory of learning.

Socratic learning theory

Now, for all I know, Socrates may have been a figment of Plato's imagination. There is, of course, a considerable difference between the Socrates of the early dialogues and the Socrates of the later dialogues [Popper 1945/66, vol. 1, pp. 306-13]. In both versions Socrates spends much of his time asking questions. But there is a major difference. In the early dialogues Socrates is the student asking questions in the process of attempting to learn. In the later dialogues he is the teacher attempting to teach by asking critical and revealing questions. Popper identifies with the early Socrates – that is, with Socrates the student. Moreover, science is engaged in systematic learning and thus, in these terms, scientists are also students.

The best illustration of Socrates-the-student is to be found in the one dialogue which everyone agrees is fictitious – 'Euthyphro'. Let us examine this heuristic dialogue, since it can provide an excellent basis for understanding Popper's theory of learning. The plot of the dialogue is quite simple. Socrates is on his way to the court, where he is to be tried for 'impiety'. Now, Socrates does not understand why he is being charged with impiety – that is to say, given Socrates' understanding of impiety, he is innocent of the charges against him. He encounters his old friend Euthyphro, who is also going to the same court. Euthyphro's business there is that *he* has charged his father with impiety for killing a servant.

It is immediately obvious to Socrates that Euthyphro is an expert on the question of the nature of impiety. Surely no man would take his own father to court for impiety unless he was absolutely sure that he understood what piety and impiety were. The dialogue between Socrates and Euthyphro is carefully staged to illustrate the Socratic approach to learning. Specifically, Socrates attempts to determine where *his own* understanding of piety and impiety has obviously gone wrong. Cynics might say that Socrates was only using Euthyphro to prepare his own defense, but that misses the point, as Socrates is sure that Euthyphro's understanding is correct. So the dialogue consists of Socrates' attempt to reveal his own understanding of piety and impiety to Euthyphro so that it can be *critically* examined by Euthyphro, the expert.

Socrates puts his understanding of piety and impiety on the table for Euthyphro to examine in the same way that we approach a physician when we have an ailment. Piece by piece, each element in Socrates' understanding is put to the test of Euthyphro's expertise. Every time Socrates puts to Euthyphro the question 'Is this correct?' Socrates' understanding survives the test! In the end, nothing is accomplished, as Euthyphro is unable to help by showing where Socrates has gone wrong. But it is the supreme test – since if anyone were going to find something wrong with Socrates' understanding of piety and impiety, Euthyphro would.

For my purposes the point of this dialogue is that Socrates does not learn anything. The only thing that Socrates could learn with the help of his friend Euthyphro is that his understanding is faulty – that is, that there is an error in his understanding. For all of his agreement – that is, his verification of each of the elements in Socrates' understanding – Euthyphro is no help. He could only help by finding an error. Even though Socrates tries not to conceal any element in his understanding, the failure to find a flaw still does not prove that Socrates' understanding of piety and impiety is correct. Surely there is an error somewhere because the fact still stands that Socrates is being charged with impiety and Euthyphro, the expert, is taking his father to court for impiety.

Now Popper's position is that science and the scientist are always in the same predicament as Socrates. We can never prove that our understanding is correct – even when it is. And the only thing we can ever really learn is that our understanding is false – if it actually happens to be false. For this reason, Popper sees science as a *learning* enterprise whose sole objective is to find errors in our understanding. This is why he puts such emphasis on testing, but it must be realized that the only successful test is the refutation of one's theory. This, then, is Popper's Socratic theory of learning: One's understanding is always conjectural but potentially true. The only way one can learn is to find a refutation – to find that one's understanding (i.e., one's theory) is false. The primary evidence that learning has taken place is either the rejection of one's prior theory or an adjustment that recognizes that one's prior theory is false. Seeking to find refutations is the primary purpose of criticism hence Popper considers criticism and a critical attitude to be the center of his theory of learning and hence of science. Science is a social enterprise devoted to learning [cf. Jarvie 2001].

Learning as a process without end

There is a profound perversity in the Socratic learning theory. Given Popper's point that all explanatory theories involve unverifiable universal statements, learning in the more traditional, positive sense (verifying true explanations) is impossible. In this sense, one could never justify one's attempt to learn on the grounds that the ultimate end would be possible. If one can never learn the true theory, why bother? This question is the essence of skepticism. But skepticism is merely an indirect expression of a belief in Justificationism – the view that we are not allowed to claim to know unless we can prove that our knowledge is true [Agassi 1971a]. If one rejects Justificationism, then one is not necessarily led to skepticism. Although we may not be able to prove that our theory (i.e., our knowledge) is true, it does not mean that our theory is not true. Even though we cannot learn in the more positive sense, we can still learn by correcting our errors. Discovering one's errors is definitely a positive step – as long as one does not reserve the idea of a positive step only for a step leading towards a justification or an inductive proof.

For Popper, science is a social institution that is pointing in the right direction even though it is readily admitted that it may never reach the goal at which we might think it is pointing. This is the same situation as that encountered when discussing Austrian economics. Economists from the Austrian School [see Blaug 1980/92, pp. 80–2] do not recommend free-enterprise capitalism because it necessarily reaches an eighteenth-century rationalist's 'best of all possible worlds', a world of long-run equilibrium. On the contrary, as we saw with Hayek (in Chapter 10), to the extent that reaching any long-run equilibrium requires the acquisition of correct knowledge (or the correct expectations) without induction, reaching a long-run equilibrium is never guaranteed. Besides that, what constitutes a long-run equilibrium depends on the exogenous givens, and we all know that they can change faster than the process can ever get us to any long-run equilibrium.

If pushed to justify their faith in free-enterprise capitalism, the Austrians *cannot* say, 'We favor capitalism because, by following it, eventually we reach the "best of all possible worlds" – that is, where everyone is a maximizer and all resources are optimally allocated'. Instead, their justification must involve only an evaluation of the *process* at a specific point in real time. The fundamental Austrian position in this regard is that when individuals are free to choose they are able to exploit (and thereby unintentionally to eliminate) errors in resource allocation. Eliminating error in resource allocation is an improvement for society, just as the Smith-Schumpeter view saw attempting to get ahead as leading to improvements in the overall efficiency of the economic production process. However, unlike the Smith-Schumpeter classical world, which begins with a long-run equilibrium in order to show how greed can thus be virtuous, the Austrians are satisfied with a short-run view.

If one took a survey among neoclassical economists, one would not find very many believers in Austrian economics, but that may only be because today's neoclassical economists require justifications based on the properties of the hypothetical long-run equilibrium. One of the major analytical tools used by neoclassical economists is 'comparative statics', which does nothing but compare alternative long-run equilibria that differ only because there is posited a difference in one or more of the exogenous givens. This difficulty can be extended one more step. As long as neoclassical economists accept only teleological (i.e., goal-directed) justifications, they will never understand Popper's theory of science or his Socratic theory of learning!

False problems raised by Popper and his theory of science

> As we learn from our mistakes our knowledge grows, even though we may never know – that is, know for certain... You will have noticed from this formulation that it is not the accumulation of observations which I have in mind when I speak of the growth of scientific knowledge, but the repeated overthrow of scientific theories and their replacement by better or more satisfactory ones... Thus our criterion of progress or of the potential growth of knowledge, will be the increase of the informative content, or the empirical content, of our theories; and, at the same time, the increase of their testability; and also their explanatory power with respect to (known *and* as yet unknown) evidence.
>
> > Karl Popper [1963/89, pp. vii, 215 and 391]

> I see the problem of knowledge in a way different from that of my predecessors. Security and justification of claims to knowledge are not my problem. Instead, my problem is the growth of knowledge. In which sense can we speak of the growth or the progress of knowledge, and how can we achieve it? ... [T]he commonsense theory is mistaken in different places. It is, essentially, a theory of the genesis of knowledge: the bucket theory is a theory of our acquisition of knowledge – our largely passive acquisition of knowledge – and thus it is also a theory of what I call the *growth of knowledge. But as a theory of the growth of knowledge it is utterly false...*
>
> Accordingly, *the growth of all knowledge consists in the modification of previous knowledge* – either its alteration or its large-scale rejection...
>
> At any rate, one of the things we wish to achieve is to learn something new. According to our schema, progressiveness is one of the things we demand of a good tentative theory: and it is brought out by the critical discussion of it: the theory is progressive if our discussion shows that *it has really made a difference to the problem we wanted to solve;* that is, if the newly emerging problems are different from the old ones.
>
> > Karl Popper [1972, pp. 37, 66, 71 and 288]

Traditional empiricism tries to describe the mind with the help of metaphors, as a *tabula rasa* – something like a well-wiped blackboard or an unexposed photographic plate – to be engraved by observations. This theory, which I have called *'the bucket theory of the mind'*, views the mind as a bucket and the senses as funnels through which the bucket can slowly be filled by observations. The sum total of these observations (or perhaps the ordered or digested sum total) is 'our knowledge'. This view is radically mistaken.

Karl Popper [1983, p. 99]

Rational criticism is indeed the means by which we learn, grow in knowledge, and transcend ourselves.

Karl Popper [1983, p. 27]

As I noted earlier, it is very important to keep in mind that Popper's theory of science is an explanation of why scientists do what they do, and it is not a prescription for how they should go about their business. Unfortunately, it is all too easy to take Popper's theory for granted and then use it to make recommendations – Popper was not immune from this possibility. Popper's mode of explanation is particularly troublesome. That is, he explains all human events as implicit decisions to solve problems that Popper conjectures to be facing the decision-makers. Again, these alleged problems are almost always his conjectures – and it is all too tempting to go a step further and presume that they are universal problems that must be solved. Again, Popper was not immune from this possibility.

One must be careful with this criticism of Popper the man, however. He always saw himself as being engaged in a debate – originally, it was with the philosophers at the University of Vienna. With his critical debate procedure, he always tried to talk in terms of his opponents'. This has led many of his critics and some of his friends to mistakenly attribute the views of his opponents to him. The most obvious example of this is the pervasive attribution of 'falsificationism' to Popper as if he was recommending that scientists should exclusively pursue falsifications – the hole instead of the donut. Again, this is not Popper's view. Popper's view is that in science criticism matters. Testing in order to refute is just one of many possible types of criticism and it is not necessarily an essential type.

The demarcation problem

Early in Popper's career he tried to impress the leaders of the 'Vienna Circle', a leading Logical Positivist school of analytical philosophy in the 1920s and 30s. His method of doing this was to offer challenging solutions to their problems. They were unimpressed. One of his tactics was to argue that they wanted to solve what he called the 'demarcation problem'. According to his story, the Logical Positivists claimed that science was distinguished from philosophy on the basis of the *verifiability* of scientific theories, which entails the view that empirical evidence is significant only when it contributes to verifications. Moreover, philosophy is supposedly not something that is empirically verifiable. Popper argued that, as a simple matter of logic, the Logical Positivists had it all wrong: empirical evidence *is* significant, but only for refutations. Thus *if* science were to be distinguished, (i.e., 'demarcated'), from philosophy, as a matter of logic, it would be only in terms of the *falsifiability* of scientific theories. For those of us who have approached methodology from the perspective of economics and without any prior commitment to analytical philosophy, all this seems rather silly. But perhaps I am being too wise after the fact.

If one does not get involved with the older Logical Positivist views of methodology, then the so-called Demarcation Problem is at best uninteresting. Popper misleads us when he seems to be saying merely that our choice is between falsifiable theories and metaphysics [cf. Bartley 1968; 1982]. Contrarily, metaphysics is a matter of choice and not a matter of logic [Agassi 1971b]. Some theories which may appear to be tautologies may be transformed into non-tautological statements [Watkins 1957]. Again, a circular argument need not be a tautology [Boland 1992a, chap. 12]. Moreover, some theories which are falsifiable may also be false [Wisdom 1963].

'Degrees of corroboration'

In another place Popper creates an intellectual fog with his 'degrees of corroboration'. Presumably this is his effort to win over proponents of Conventionalism – namely, those who accept notions such as degrees of confirmation. In Popper's view [1934/59, chap. 10], a theory is 'corroborated' whenever it passes a test by not being refuted. The greater the likelihood of being refuted, the greater the 'degree of corroboration'. In a sense, corroboration is just a fancy name for unintended confirmation – but this is Popper's point. If we are being critical, we do not set out to corroborate a theory; we set out to refute it in order to test our understanding. To placate those who feel uncomfortable about not having a positive reason for testing theory (or their fear of looking for the hole instead of the donut), he offers them an unintended reward for their efforts. But if one really takes the Socratic theory of learning seriously, no such reward is necessary. What is worse, for Popper's purposes, is that it is too easy to incorporate 'degrees of corroboration' as just another (sophisticated) Conventionalist criterion of acceptability. Theories that are more corroborated are alleged to be somehow superior to those which are less [cf. Hattiangadi 1978] – but this is so only in the eyes of someone adopting a Conventionalist stance.

The growth of knowledge

Another unnecessary dispute which Popper inflames is the question of what constitutes the growth of knowledge. According to Popper's epistemology, knowledge consists exclusively of theories. Thus if knowledge is to grow, we must be able to compare theories on that basis. So Popper [e.g., 1963/89, pp. 240–2] would have us believe that we are better off whenever (1) a new theory can explain everything that any rejected old theory explains, and (2) a new theory explains more and thus is capable of a higher degree of corroboration (because by explaining more it runs a higher risk of being refuted when tested). Some followers of Popper are led to believe that when a new theory is offered that is better by these criteria we are supposed to drop the old, inferior theory. But if the old theory has never been refuted, why must it be dropped? The old theory may be true even though the new theory is considered superior by the Conventionalist criterion of the 'degrees of corroboration'. As long as we are comparing unrefuted theories, if they cannot be verified, then we are simply not in any position to choose! If we do, then we risk conceding that Conventionalism wins. A careful reading of Popper [particularly, 1963/89, p. 242] will show that he just claims that meeting conditions such as (1) and (2) only yields a 'potential step forward', one which is still subject to test. His 'potential step forward' is deemed to be progress only because testability is increased and thus the *potential* for learning is improved. If the test leads us to reject the new theory, we have learned and hence made progress – nothing more.

It is understandable that historians of economic thought might like to talk about the growth of knowledge over time; but I think the notion of knowledge growth begs too many questions. Moreover, the notion of a growth of knowledge presumes the existence of a (quantitative) measure of knowledge. No such measure can exist. Besides, while it may be consistent with what I will call the 'bucket theory of knowledge', it would solve no sensible problem except to be able to talk about the growth of knowledge. As I will suggest in Chapter 16, it makes more sense to see learning as a matter of improving knowledge (which involves Socratic learning and possible adjustments). That is, knowledge is more like health that one can improve than wealth that one can have more of.

Sometimes, Popper refers to 'scientific growth' rather than growth of knowledge. Scientific growth is not obviously a quantitative issue but one can draw an analogy with thermodynamics – perhaps, along the lines I suggested in Chapter 10. Specifically, the '2nd law of thermodynamics' – the so-called Entropy Law [see Georgescu-Roegen 1971] – says in effect that one cannot construct a perpetual motion machine. Energy is always being used up. To represent the notion of used-up energy, the imaginary entity called entropy was invented. So, the '2nd Law' merely says that entropy is always increasing no matter what we are doing. With this in mind as well as Popper's and Socrates' idea that learning means refuting knowledge, one could easily say that the pile of refuted theories increases as science grows [see Agassi 2002, p. 109, fn. 4]. This, I submit, is exactly what Popper means by the growth of science – and if one wishes to stretch this further, it may also be what he means by the growth of knowledge, but this is not as clear.

'Neo-Popperians': Conventionalist pseudo-Popper

> Methodological falsificationism is a brand of conventionalism…
>
> Imre Lakatos [1970, p. 104]

A false image of Popper's theory of science was deliberately created by Lakatos with his selfish efforts to usurp Popper's place in the history of philosophy. The primary vehicle for this effort was the creation of something he called 'falsificationism'– he sometimes qualified this with the adjective 'meth-odological'. As noted earlier, Popper rejected the notion of falsificationism. His reason was simply that 'critical rationalism' which he promoted had nothing to do with a method for doing science of any kind – but instead, it is the name he often gave for his theory of science. Unfortunately, most economic methodologists learned about Popper by reading Lakatos. This began primarily with Blaug's 1975 foray into a Lakatosian critique of Thomas Kuhn followed in 1980 with his methodology book that explicitly promoted 'Popperian falsificationism' for the study of economics. Over the following two decades, there were numerous articles criticizing Blaug's promotion of so-called Popperian falsificationism. Too often, the critics fail to make it clear that they are criticizing Blaug rather than Popper.

Falsifiability as a Conventionalist criterion

Popper's discussion of a falsifiability criterion was offered as a logically valid alternative means of solving the Demarcation Problem that he conjectured to be the problem the Vienna Circle was trying to solve with 'Logical Positivism'. At root, the Vienna Circle was promoting a verifiability criterion as a means of preventing 'metaphysical statements'. Unfortunately, despite Popper's intentions, his falsifiability criterion is all too easily incorporated into the list of acceptable Conventionalist criteria [see Boland 1989, chap. 4]. Again and again I have pointed out, no matter how well a theory fares by any Conventionalist criterion (which does not include truth or falsity), there is nothing to connect the success of the theory in those terms with the actual truth or falsity of the theory. So what is accomplished by requiring that all 'scientific' theories be falsifiable? It does preclude tautologies as Paul Samuelson obviously understood in the 1940s, but despite this criterion's origins, it still does not preclude metaphysics [Agassi 1971b] – and this is despite what some 1930s philosophers claimed.

The most important assumptions in neoclassical economics, such as the maximization hypothesis, may be unfalsifiable even when they are true. Although the maximization hypothesis is not a tautology, it is usually unfalsifiable because neoclassical economists put it beyond question [see Boland 1981b; 1997, chap. 6]. Similarly, the most important assumptions in Marxist theory are unfalsifiable. Almost every Marxist model presumes the existence of a class struggle or an exogenously given rate of capitalist accumulation [see Hammes and Boland 1984]. Neither of these assumptions is ever put to the test. Both are just assumed to be obviously true – just as the neoclassical maximization assumption is considered to be obviously true. If one were to believe in a Conventionalist implementation of the falsifiability criterion, there would virtually be no acceptable social theory, since all explanatory theories involve at least one key assumption which is put beyond refutation or criticism [Agassi 1965].

Popper and the 'new heterodoxy'

Blaug identifies Popper's theory of science as the 'watershed between old and new views of the philosophy of science' [1980/92, p. 4]. The new heterodoxy, according to Blaug, is the Conventionalism of Kuhn's or Lakatos' compromised version of Popper's view. How one conceives of a 'watershed' transition from the Conventionalism of the Logical Positivists to the Conventionalism of Kuhn which passes through Popper's anti-Conventionalism is difficult to understand. The 'new heterodoxy' is nothing but the 'old heterodoxy' dressed up in clothes designed by Lakatos. The 'watershed' has yet to be crossed. Nowhere do we find Popper's Socratic view of learning represented in either neoclassical methodology or neoclassical theory. Without any doubt, Socrates did not submit to the conventional wisdom of authorities he faced in the court. Socrates considered his view of his situation to be true even though the votes were not in its favor. To the extent that Blaug's views represent the state of the methodology of mainstream neoclassical economics, Popper's impact on economics seems, to me, to be only cosmetic.

Popper vs. 'falsificationism'

Students of Popper from the 1950s are dismayed by the identification of Popper with the 'can' of falsificationism that Lakatos tried to tie on Popper's 'tail'. Popper and his students have over and over claimed that his theory of science is that science is, in effect, critical debate; Popper repeatedly calls his view Critical Rationalism. As noted above, Popper denied that his view of science is anything like the falsificationism that Lakatos promoted. Nevertheless, Mark Blaug and his many followers continue to characterize Popper's theory of science as falsificationism. Many critics of Popper willingly accept the view that Popper is advocating falsificationism. For example, the anti-Popper philosopher Daniel Hausman says 'Popper's relevant views concerning falsificationism as a methodology or a policy are unfounded and unacceptable' [1988, p. 65]. Several economic methodologists criticize 'Popperian falsificationism' yet never seem to make clear that they are not criticizing Popper [e.g., Caldwell 1982/94, 1991a and Hands 1993, 2001]. These methodologists seem unwilling to separate their views of Popper from falsificationism. Sometimes, they even accuse Popper of being inconsistent or claim there must be an incompatibility or 'tension' between his alleged advocacy of falsificationism and his critical rationalist approach to social science, which he calls 'situational analysis' [see Caldwell 1994, p. 137 and Hands 1985b, 2001, p. 283]. One can see the existence of a tension in Popper's view only by mistakenly thinking that Popper must lay claim to falsificationism. Once Popper's denial of falsificationism is truly accepted, the alleged tension or inconsistency disappears.

Rather than merely advocating an alternative Conventionalist philosophy of science, Popper thought he was extending Einstein's view – which was that science is never stable but always in a state of constant revolution. And Popper's reason for this was that science was a social enterprise of coordinated criticism rather than coordinated agreement [Jarvie 2001]. Practicing what he preached, Popper pounded his fists on the doors of the Logical Positivists at the University of Vienna trying to convince them that they were going down the wrong path. Their path involved a logic of probabilities where the 'best' theory is the one that can be shown to be the most probable theory given the positive evidence made available by inductivist scientists. Popper argued that this would not be very interesting science and instead scientific theories are interesting because they appear at first to be the least probable explanations of positive evidence.

It might seem strange for someone who is advocating that we take Popper's theory of science more seriously than it has been up to now in economics, but I think it is time for practicing methodologists to stop talking about Popper. It is all right for them to criticize Popper, but this is something for philosophers to worry about. Today, there surely are more important things for economic methodologists to do. They might begin by putting Popper on the agenda of neoclassical economics – hopefully along the lines that I will try to demonstrate in the next four chapters.

15 Situational Analysis and Neoclassical Explanation

In the few places where Popper directly refers to economics, he is almost never discussing his falsificationist approach to natural science. Instead, economics is discussed in the context of his 'situational analysis' or 'situational logic' approach to historical and social explanation. Of course *if* 'situational analysis' were entirely consistent with Popper's falsificationist philosophy of social science, then the current characterization of Popper by economic methodologists would be entirely appropriate. Regrettably though, this is not the case. Most philosophers who have addressed this issue, including Popper himself, have implied that situational analysis produces explanations which are entirely unique to social science and less than adequate when judged by strict falsificationist standards.

The possibility of Popper having a nonfalsificationist view of economic method raises a number of interesting questions. Exactly what is the relationship between economics and situational analysis? Will a detailed study of situational analysis provide additional insights into the methodological questions of economics which would be unavailable through falsificationist spectacles? What questions does such a potential dualism raise regarding methodological monism, the view ostensibly supported by Popper, that the method of social science and the method of natural science should not differ in significant ways? And finally, what does Popper really advise about practicing the science of economics?

Wade Hands [1985b, p. 84]

The fact is that Popper knew little about social science and even less about economics.

Mark Blaug [1985, p. 287]

There is some justification for Blaug's complaint. Popper only infrequently provided examples of economic reasoning, and when he did, they usually were somewhat naive.

Bruce Caldwell [1991a, p. 21, fn. 5]

Popper recommends a [Situational Analysis] approach to the social sciences that seems to be inconsistent with falsificationism, but that inconsistency can be mitigated by accepting the critical rationalist reading of Popper's overall philosophy. Until the publication of *The Myth of the Framework* there simply was not enough discussion of [Situational Analysis] in Popper's writings to settle this debate; critical rationalism seemed more consistent with [Situational Analysis], but it was not entirely clear what Popper meant by [Situational Analysis]..., and most economists who supported a Popperian position did so because they endorsed falsificationism... So the debate seemed fairly inconclusive until now; now we have the full text of Popper's main written discussion of [Situational Analysis]..., and it is also a text that is heavily laced with economics and written for an economic audience. So what does it say? Does chapter eight of *The Myth of the Framework* help settle this debate or not?

The answer is yes, and the result does not look very good for the falsificationist position... All in all the discussion in chapter eight comes down quite squarely on the side of critical rationalism.

Wade Hands [1996, pp. 319–20]

Until quite recently many economic methodologists (i.e., particularly, those who began their careers in the late 1970s) were of the opinion that Karl Popper was misguided about economics. Those less bent on criticizing Popper merely claimed that Popper never said much about economics. Of course, many of these methodologists, being misled by Imre Lakatos (by way of Mark Blaug), thought the only way in which Popper could have said something would be only if it was about the falsifiability of economics. This false identification of Popper with so-called 'falsificationism' (by friends and foes alike) has begun to break down. This breakdown has been fostered by both Bruce Caldwell [1991a] and Wade Hands [1996, 2001]. All of the angst came to a head with the 1994 publication of Popper's 1963 lecture to Harvard's department of economics.

Many of us began our appreciation of Popper with our reading of the *Open Society*. I remember thinking about how easy it was to understand since it seemed to be just a generalization of neoclassical economics in terms of both methodological individualism and situational analysis. While today it might be easy to complain that basing one's understanding of Popper on neoclassical economics leads to a narrow and useless appreciation of Popper, this too is misleading. The problem is not neoclassical economics but neoclassical economists. After all, clearly Popper himself thought the best way to teach economists about his views concerning methodology was to emphasize that his views can easily be understood as a generalization of neoclassical economics [e.g., Popper 1963/94].

In this chapter I will eventually explain how to start putting Popper on the agenda of neoclassical economics; but to be careful, I think before launching into this issue, it would be wise to briefly review how to explain neoclassical economic methodology in a manner that separates the nature of neoclassical economics from the practice of some neoclassical economists.

A review of the essentials of neoclassical explanation

There are only two essential principles of neoclassical explanation. One is the methodological individualism discussed in Chapter 2 and the other is the standard assumption discussed in Chapters 3 and 4 that every choice can be *explained* as a rational choice.

As explained in Chapter 2, methodological individualism merely says that only individuals make choices, things do not choose. In effect, methodological individualism merely restricts the list of acceptable exogenous variables. But, as I have stressed, most neoclassical economists go further and adopt psychologistic individualism and thereby choose to limit the list to only Nature-given constraints (which includes Nature-given psychological states of individuals). I have also stressed, however, that such an extreme limitation is unnecessary.

As explained in Chapter 3, rational choice is usually characterized as an instance of constrained maximization. While many critics of neoclassical economics are quick to focus on the realism of such things as utility maximization, it is easy to be misled by such criticism. That is, too much is being read into the notion of utility maximization, particularly whenever utility maximization is thought to be a psychological process. The relationship between the notion of rational choice and utility maximization is almost mundane – 'rational' choice always means that one can specify a set of reasons from which one can logically deduce the choice in question (i.e., the choice being explained). Neoclassical economists, as opposed to classical economists, chose to represent rational choice with the calculus notion of constrained maximization. Once the theorist has specified an objective function to be maximized and the constraints facing the decision-maker, the implicit claim is that *anyone* facing those constraints and maximizing according to that objective function will make the same (unique) choice. It is important to keep in mind that it is the theorist who specifies both the objective function and the constraints and hence the veracity of an explanation is exclusively determined by this specification and not by the assumption of maximization. If an explanation turns out to be false, the neoclassical economist will always question the specification of either the constraints or the objective function – never will the assumptions of maximization or rationality be put into question.

The possible problems of neoclassical explanation

There are two possible opposing problems with the practice of neoclassical economists. One concerns the success orientation of most neoclassical economists and the other concerns the posited determinants of the constraints.

Neoclassical explanation as Whig history

Several years ago Paul Samuelson [1987] gave a talk to a luncheon meeting of historians of economics and argued in favor of what he called 'Whig history'. His reason for advocating Whig history was that this is what customers want and so, if historians of thought want their sub-discipline to thrive, they should recognize that there is no market for discussions of the trials and tribulations of famous economists. Moreover, every effort should be made to write histories of the thoughts of famous economists in the most up-to-date terms – i.e., from a modern perspective, looking backward. What he was advocating was that we should see the history of economics as *successfully* culminating in the present state of economic theory. Interestingly, later in the same day, Axel Leijonhufvud argued the opposite, that the history of economics should be seen as an expanding tree with many decision forks where the history follows a path involving backtracking after failed decisions. In Whig history, there are no unintended consequences. In Leijonhufvud's backtracking through a decision tree, there is constant evaluation of unintended consequences.

Modern neoclassical economists take Samuelson's perspective to an extreme. Since explanation takes place after the event, that is, after the choice they wish to explain has been made, neoclassical explanations are always instances of Whig history. As such, the neoclassical theorist sees every choice made as a successful choice given the posited objective function and posited constraints. Specifically, the objective function and constraints are identified simply because the choice being explained would be successful. Thus, while superficially a Whig history-type of explanation does resemble a straightforward application of Popper's situational analysis, there is no room for unintended consequences. Moreover, since there is no role for learning in a Whig-history-type of explanation, too many questions are begged about the realism of the explanation. How did the successful decision-maker know all of the relevant constraints? How did the successful consumer know his or her entire utility function without prior testing of all points in the range of the objective function?

Neoclassical explanation as mechanics: A brief review

In the 1940s there was the ongoing debate in neoclassical literature about the realism of assuming that a firm could or would ever try to make the fine measurements necessary to determine if profit maximization is being achieved – even if we could ignore the questions concerning how the firm has acquired the necessary knowledge. As explained in Chapter 3, Armen Alchian [1950] argued, in effect, that this debate missed the point. It does not matter whether or not the firm is a deliberate, conscious maximizer – the realism of the maximization assumption is irrelevant. Again, his reason was that in a long-run equilibrium, only profit maximizers can survive and this is regardless of whether they are *deliberately* maximizing or just maximizing by accident. This, he claims, is just a straightforward application of Darwinian evolution.

Alchian's clever ploy is merely an instance of the more general character of neoclassical long-run equilibrium-based explanations that presume psychologistic individualism: the presumption that the only constraints are those exogenous variables given by Nature. As explained in Chapter 7, if all exogenous variables are nature-given, then the nature of the ultimate long-run equilibrium is a matter of mere mechanics – much in the spirit of the eighteenth-century rationalism. This means that a neoclassical theorist can build a model of the logic of the situation facing all decision-makers and then, by means of simple calculus, calculate the ultimate equilibrium.

If the equilibrium is to be an explanation of long-run prices, etc., then the equilibrium must be unique. But, this then begs a question concerning the autonomy of the individual that is the essential characteristic of methodological individualism. If the ultimate equilibrium is predetermined by the mechanics of all of the Nature given exogenous variables, what is the role of the individual? What if individuals make mistakes?

Compounding this problem of mechanics is the tendency to address the issue of how decision-makers acquire the knowledge needed to assure the successful achievement of maximization by making learning a mechanical affair. Specifically, neoclassical theorists usually take Inductivism for granted and thus presume that there is a logic of induction which allows one to reach true knowledge after obtaining a finite set of observations of Nature. In this sense, learning is also assumed to be a mechanical exercise such that all people making the same observations will (within acceptable mechanical tolerances) reach the same conclusions. This is the basis for the 1970s neoclassical school of Rational Expectations. But, of course, there is no logic of induction that could ever provide the needed mechanical means of learning.

Overcoming the problem of neoclassical explanation

The neoclassical predisposition to mechanical exercises is the most significant problem plaguing neoclassical explanation methodology. So, with the above review in mind, I will endeavor to show how the methodological problem of mechanical explanations can be overcome and at the same time make room for Popper on the agenda. There are two crucial decisions made by neoclassical economists that turn economics away from the appreciation of situational analysis that Popper wished to teach them. Both concern the key question raised by Hayek sixty-five years ago: How do all decision-makers know what they need to know in order for there to be a stable equilibrium that would coordinate the actions of autonomous individuals?

Post hoc success vs. the learning process: Each decision is a test of one's knowledge

The answer to this question is that they cannot know *a priori*. Instead, they must test their knowledge with every decision they make. That is, the theorist must abandon the success orientation discussed above and see that thereby *decision-making is a process not an event*. Note well though, abandoning success orientation does not preclude so-called rational decision-making. Moreover, the process of testing one's knowledge is also a matter of situational logic, one with many opportunities for unintended consequences that will have to be dealt with when making the next decision.

Methodological individualism with macrofoundations: Avoid presuming psychologistic individualism is the only individualism

Avoiding success orientation is somewhat less important than avoiding the narrow, extreme form of methodological individualism which turns neoclassical explanations into mechanical exercises. Of course, the extreme form is simply psychologistic individualism. Again, the problem is that psychologistic individualism requires that any non-individualist, non-natural variables must be explained. While an individual decision-maker may face given prices, the individual's decisions are not explained until those given prices are also explained. Obviously, such a requirement means that the complete explanation of any one individual's decisions is not obtained until one explains the general equilibrium of all individuals who have influence on the prices. Only in a state of long-run, general equilibrium is it possible to satisfy the requirements of psychologistic individualism where all constraints facing individuals are explained as epiphenomena, that is, explained as consequences of successful decisions made by all other individuals in the economy.

A less ambitious form of neoclassical explanation would recognize that, in the mind of the decision-maker, there are non-individualist, non-natural variables and constraints. Thus, any explanation of the logic of the situation must also specify how the individual views the logic of the situation that he or she faces. As suggested in Chapter 9, it is virtually impossible to conceive of a decision-maker who is not facing or including macroeconomic variables in the logic of their situation. For example, to what extent does the current (or expected!) inflation rate influence one's decision to rent or buy a house? Or does the current rate of unemployment affect one's employment or wage decisions? Again, including macrofoundations in one's microeconomics violates neither Popper's situational analysis nor his version of methodological individualism: institutional individualism.

The major problem with neoclassical economics today is not something inherent in neoclassical economics but instead a limitation caused by methodological decisions made by neoclassical economists who want to think of a world where governments cannot change the course of an economy except in a detrimental way. In other words, if there is a problem with neoclassical economics today, it is due to the ideology of some neoclassical economists and not due to the essential nature of neoclassical economics itself.

Adjusting the neoclassical hidden agenda

In the next three chapters I will endeavor to demonstrate how to put Popper's *epistemology* – that is, his theory of knowledge – to work by building more realistic models of neoclassical economics. Contrary to the views of many philosophers and methodologists, Popper has no methodology, but he does have a specific theory of knowledge that can be applied to neoclassical economics [viz., Popper 1972, chap. 3]. For the remainder of this chapter, I just need to explain in more general terms how to put Popper's epistemology on the agenda of neoclassical economics and how it can be used to deal with the questions of dynamics that have plagued neoclassical economics for decades. But to do so, it must be recognized that epistemology is not enough and so I will draw on the well-known views of other scholars to put together a complete package – I will call this package the Popper-Hayek program.

Eliminating the first item on the neoclassical agenda

If one is so inclined, including Popper's epistemological perspective is conceptually rather easy. The key to Popper's epistemology is the rejection of the Problem of Induction – and its short-run stand-in, the Problem of Conventions. If we eliminate the need for authoritarianism, then there is no need to deal with the classic Problem of Induction. This means that we can also cease taking such things as the inductive learning possibilities function for granted. For example, we might wish to recognize that some observations or additional bits of information actually refute our knowledge rather than increase its probability of being true. Instead we can focus on neoclassical model building as a systematic attempt to learn by our theoretical mistakes and thereby emphasize the role of criticism and disagreement in the development of neoclassical economics. Similarly, the presumed need to solve the short-run Problem of Conventions erroneously presumes a need of acceptance and agreement. As long as one's contribution is criticizable, anything should be allowed to be considered. There is no theoretical reason why we should choose between competitors – particularly since some of them may still not have been subjected to tests. What is more important, from the perspective of Popper's epistemology, is our understanding of the problems that anyone's contribution is intended to solve, as well as the alternative ways the problems may be solved. For the purposes of learning, rather than looking for the one correct or acceptable solution, it is more important that we continue to look for more and more alternative solutions.

Generalizing the second item on the agenda

Continuing along the lines of considering the implications of any attempt to include Popper's epistemology among the items on the hidden agenda, let us now examine the second item, methodological individualism. If we reject the need either to deal with or to solve the Problem of Induction or the Problem of Conventions, then there is no need to adopt the extreme form of methodological individualism that is based on an unsupported presumption of psychologism. What this means for methodology is that individuals are not to be identified with their psychological states. Rather than taking individuals' psychological states as irreducible givens, we can attempt to explain their psychological states. This does not necessarily rule out individualism. Individuals still make all of the decisions. The concern here is only with the basis of their decision-making. What I will argue below is that a major ingredient in every decision is the theories held to be true by the decision-maker and that in the absence of an inductive logic such theories cannot be reduced to the given nature of the physical world. Why any individual might consider a particular theory to be true may or may not be at issue. It all depends on the problems that the individual is or is conjectured to be trying to solve.

Dealing with the knowledge basis of decision-making

By following Popper's rejection of the Problem of Induction – and with it, his rejection of Inductivism and Conventionalism – the door is open for the neoclassical economist to attempt to explain the knowledge basis of decision-making. By dropping the presumption that permits only psychological states and natural givens, the way is clear for the recognition that in order to explain the process of decision-making, the methodology of the decision-maker needs to play an essential role. What a particular decision-maker's methodology actually is depends on the problem-situation facing the decision-maker including the decision-maker's epistemology – that is, his or her theory of knowledge. To a great extent the decision-maker's methodology (as distinguished from epistemology) depends on the decision-maker's *theory* of that problem-situation. There is no reason why anyone should expect any decision-maker to hold a true theory of their problem-situation, nor is there any reason why all decision-makers should employ the same methodological and epistemological perspectives. The focus of these considerations will ultimately be concerned with how individual decision-makers deal with the discovery of evidence that contradicts the theories which they thought were true in the process of making their decisions. That is, the focus will ultimately be the endogenous dynamics discussed in Chapter 10.

Real-time individualism in the short run

Discussing arbitrary changes in the research agenda of neoclassical economics is really not very interesting unless we can see how the new agenda affects the nature of any neoclassical theory. The one research topic where Popper's situational analysis as well as his epistemology can play a dramatic role concerns the appropriate short-run setting for neoclassical economics. As explained in Chapter 10, the usual treatment of time in neoclassical explanatory models has been inadequate. Specifically, the dynamics of the usual neoclassical models based on Inductivism and Conventionalism are exogenous and hence unexplained. I wish to show here that by dropping Inductivism and Conventionalism and instead relying on Popper's views of knowledge and learning, the way is open to the development of real-time explanations in neoclassical theory. To be neoclassical all that is required is that we retain methodological individualism – that is, the view that only individuals make decisions – as well as situational analysis – that is, rational decision-making. However, it should be stressed that Popper's situational analysis focuses on rational decision-*making* and not on rational decision-*makers*.

The general problem of explaining change (dynamics) in the context of rational decision-making is that the decision-maker's knowledge (of the givens) is hopelessly static – as John Hicks [1976, p. 136; 1979] observed. Although Hicks appreciated the problem, he missed the source of the difficulty. It is not that our knowledge itself is static, but rather that the traditional *views of knowledge* assert that knowledge is static. I shall argue that there is not necessarily a problem with rational decision-making, except when its logical basis presumes that the individual's knowledge (of the givens), or its acquisition, is exogenously given.

Traditionally we are required to choose between the two views of knowledge that I have identified with the first item on the hidden agenda: On the one hand, Inductivism, which asserts that knowledge is only the facts collected up to a certain point in time; on the other hand, Conventionalism, which considers knowledge to be only the latest, accepted theory (of the facts) at a certain point in time. Both views make knowledge static because it is exogenously given at any point in time.

To emphasize my advocated viewpoint of knowledge in the short-run setting, let me review the essentials of the discussion in Chapter 1 of these two views of knowledge and what they mean for the explanation of neoclassical dynamics. What is salient in both of the traditional views or theories of knowledge is that an empirical statement or a theory is considered knowledge only to the extent that it is supported by the facts. These traditional views differ only in regard to what is meant by 'supported by the facts', or what constitutes 'the facts'. With Inductivism, factual support is alleged to be direct and logically complete. However, with Conventionalism, all knowledge can be considered an accepted system of catalogues used to file or 'capture' the available facts and thus knowledge is only 'better' or 'worse' rather than 'true' or 'false'.

As explained in Chapter 1, both views are based on the common belief in Justificationism, that is, the doctrine that a theory is not truly knowledge unless it is justified (i.e., proven true). A first step toward solving the problem of explaining dynamics in the short run is the recognition that Justificationism is false (not only because it is unjustified itself). Below I will argue that by rejecting Justificationism, that is, by separating the truth status of a statement from the proof or the provability of its truth status, the way is clear to resolving the dilemma discussed in Chapter 10 of having to choose between dynamic explanations and explanations of dynamics.

A basis for an individualist explanation of dynamics

To solve the problem of explaining dynamics I begin by formulating a non-psychologistic, individualist research agenda based on the epistemology of Popper and a modified version of the methodological individualism of Hayek. This is what I am calling the Popper-Hayek program for explaining any rational dynamic process. For the purpose of discussion let me itemize the essential parts of this proposed agenda.

- *Anti-Justificationism*: First, all knowledge is presumed to be essentially theoretical, hence conjectural; second, it is possibly true, although we cannot prove its truth status beyond doubt [Popper 1972, chap. 3].
- *Anti-psychologism*: It is presumed that everyone's knowledge is potentially objective [Popper 1972, chap. 1].
- *Rational decision-making*: It is presumed that what one does at any point in time depends on one's knowledge *at that time* and the logic of the situation in which that knowledge is used [Hayek 1937/48; Hicks 1973, 1979].
- *Situational dynamics*: It is presumed that one's behavioral changes can result from changes in one's knowledge as well as from intended or unintended changes in one's situation [Hayek 1937/48; Shackle 1972].

It should be pointed out that this approach to solving the problem of explaining dynamics within a short-run individualist framework requires the rejection of Hayek's inductivist epistemology and its replacement with Popper's concept of objective knowledge. The latter requires the rejection of psychologism. The first step is to specify one or more actors, in the past or present, who have been causing or contributing to the change in question, and the *theories they held at the time of their actions*. Next, we must specify the unintended consequences of their actions, entailing conjectures about why their theories were *false*. Note that the falsity of the theories may be unknown to the actors at the time; in fact, it is by means of these unintended consequences that actors in question may learn that their knowledge is false. In short, this framework asserts that economics *in time* is a sequence of unintended consequences of acting on the basis of (unknowingly) false theories [cf. Hicks 1965, p. 184; 1979]. (Note that this is not an application of Instrumentalism, since the truth status may still matter.) Let us more closely examine the elements of this Popper-Hayek individualist program.

Objective theoretical knowledge

Discussing epistemology, the theory of the nature of knowledge, is quite difficult because knowledge itself is usually given a rather lofty status. Nevertheless, it cannot be avoided. I think it is important to recognize a simple separation between the truth status of someone's knowledge (i.e., whether it is actually true or false) and the role that knowledge plays in his or her decision-making process – that is, to provide a sufficient and logically consistent explanation of the world he or she faces. Of course, at the very minimum, knowledge must be logically consistent if it is to be able to provide a true explanation of something. This is so even though the logical consistency of any explanation does not imply its truth. Nevertheless, it is the consistency of a decision-maker's knowledge which plays the major role in our explanation of his or her behavior. The truth of his or her knowledge is much more difficult to ascertain. But, more important, the truth of his or her knowledge is not always necessary for a successful action on his or her part. It should be noted that separating the truth status from the role of knowledge does not mean that theories or knowledge cannot be true; and it definitely does not mean that all theories are false [e.g., Solow 1956], since that is a self-contradiction. On the contrary, what I am simply asserting is that a theory can be true even though its truth status is usually unknown to us.

By saying that knowledge is essentially theoretical I am emphasizing that the truth status of anyone's knowledge is always conjectural (i.e., not completely justified) and that it is potentially objective. By 'potentially objective' I mean only that by its logical nature it is capable of at least being stated in words or in other repeatable forms to the extent that it is the knowledge of the real world [Popper 1972, pp. 106ff.]. It could be argued that the potential objectivity of any decision-maker's knowledge makes possible Samuelson's so-called 'operationally meaningful' explanation of anyone's behavior.

In the view I am advocating here, since all knowledge is theoretical, anyone's knowledge can be put on the table for everyone to see. The view that knowledge is potentially objective stands in opposition to the implications of the more common view identified above as psychologism. Psychologism presumes that knowing is either a natural given, directly provable by induction, or a mysterious psychological process. While rejecting induction precludes the former, the latter makes one's knowledge private or subjective [Popper 1972, pp. 1-7]. A corollary of psychologism is that one can never explain someone else's knowledge in the absence of induction. Either way, the proposed view requires at least a rejection of psychologism.

The common psychologistic view of knowledge may only be saying that one cannot guarantee a *true* explanation of someone else's knowledge. This reading of psychologism explains why anyone might think that it is impossible to explain someone else's knowledge. If this reading is correct, then psychologism is merely another variant of the Justificationism rejected earlier. In the remainder of this chapter when I refer to someone's knowledge I will not be referring to his or her inherently private views but rather to his or her (objective) explanations or theories of the behavior and nature of the world around him or her.

The role of knowledge

Hayek and others have recognized that the individual decision-maker must have knowledge of the givens or constraints if these are to play an active role in the decision process. If this view is correct, the individual's knowledge must also play an active role in any explanation of his or her behavior. This prescription is not novel. Since late in the nineteenth century most social scientists have adopted a methodology in which the actor is presumed to be 'rational' concerning his or her given situation. This is evident in much of the formal social theory of the late nineteenth century, which often presumes a fixed frame of reference, such as an 'ideal-type' decision-maker, whose behavior is based either on the presumed possibility of perfect knowledge or on the presumption of a fool-proof method of acquiring perfect knowledge. In this old epistemology the behavior of an actual individual is explained by noting to what extent, or why, his or her behavior is not ideal or perfectly rational. However, it should be recognized that for the purposes of explaining behavior, the decision-maker's epistemology is essentially static. If we are to find a way to explain the dynamics, it will have to involve the decision-maker's view of methodology – perhaps along the lines suggested in Chapter 10.

Ideal-type methodology was discussed in Chapter 5. There it was noted that one source of an individual's deviance from the ideal stems from the so-called imperfections in his or her knowledge of the givens. The imperfections of one's knowledge might result, of course, from the fact that in real time an inductively rational acquisition of knowledge is always inadequate. With regard to explaining rational dynamic processes, we may wish to give the imperfections a systematic and prominent role, but this is possible only to the extent that the methodology (based on that knowledge) itself plays a role. Perhaps the only complaint one might have regarding the ideal-type methodology is that it actually neutralizes the role of the actor's methodology by presuming that there is some ('scientific') method of acquisition which will always give him or her the true knowledge of the givens. Such a method is essential to the definition of the ideal type. If such a method is presumed to apply, any deviance from the ideal can only result from the actor's 'irrationality'. Note that the use of the 1970s Rational Expectations Hypothesis avoids this escape clause by arguing that apparent imperfections are actually quite rational! And recall that evolutionary game theorists use imperfect knowledge as a means of assuring variety in a population in order to be able to talk about a distribution of various types in a population evolving. Except for a few 'apriorists' (e.g., Ludwig von Mises), using the ideal-type methodology usually implies a reliance on inductive logic to provide the rational method of acquisition. With the prior rejection of Inductivism, one would thus have at least rejected any reliance on ideal-type methodology with regard to the knowledge of the individual decision-maker.

Here I am arguing that the question of the truth status of an actor's knowledge (i.e., whether it is actually true or actually false) is a separate question from why the actor thinks or believes his or her knowledge is true. In particular, the truth status of any actor's knowledge is usually independent of the method of its acquisition. An actor's theory of something can be true regardless of how he or she came to hold that theory to explain numerous observations; he or she could have dreamt it. Any method of acquisition may succeed or fail. In my view, this separation of status and method is important because the truth status of the actor's knowledge and the method of acquisition play different roles in any ongoing decision process.

By now, Hayek's view [1945/48] of the essential role of knowledge seems to be widely accepted – but more care still needs to be taken to avoid taking Inductivism for granted. For example, Hayek's use of the word 'acquisition' was consistent with an inductivist theory of learning, namely, one in which learning involves collecting facts (e.g., observing 'gray elephants') and then inductively leaping to the conclusion that some general proposition about them is true (e.g., the statement 'All elephants are gray'). Such general propositions or theories are said to have been 'acquired'. I do not wish to limit the concepts of learning or acquiring to exercises in inductive logic, since, as argued above, such learning requires an unreal (infinite) amount of time. The actual (real-time) discovery of refuting evidence that shows one's current theory to be false is also a form of learning – namely, Socratic learning. This form of learning (i.e., having one's knowledge refuted) is most important in the proposed program for explaining dynamic processes in the short run. The status of an actor's knowledge may give a reason for change, but it does not tell us what the change will be. However, knowing the actor's learning methodology may provide a clue to what change he or she may attempt to effect [Boland and Newman 1979]. In the next three chapters I will try to show how the Popper-Hayek program can be used to bring the neoclassical research program up to speed with Popper's theory of science.

Part VI
APPLIED METHODOLOGY FOR ECONOMIC MODEL BUILDING

16 Knowledge and Learning in Economic Models

In traditional general equilibrium theory an economy is described by the preferences and endowments of agents and by the available technological knowhow. But we need also to know something about agents' expectations and beliefs, leave alone their information and the institutions in which they operate... As game theorists have found, even rather orthodox, hyper-rational and 'hyper-informed' agents can give rise to many equilibria. There are, in spite of numerous attempts, no decisive ways of choosing between them so that even this approach does not escape the 'anything can happen'. This alerts one to the obvious fact that the process of learning and adjusting – indeed history – will need to be brought into the story. But processes themselves will need to be invoked in the account of equilibrium. For instance, if a process never reveals a certain kind of information, then the equilibrium associated with it cannot have actions and states depending on such information.

Frank Hahn [1994, pp. 252–3]

It is clear that, if we want to make the assertion that, under certain conditions, people will approach [a state of equilibrium], we must explain by what process they will acquire the necessary knowledge. Of course, any assumption about the actual acquisition of knowledge in the course of this process will ... be of a hypothetical character.

... the assumptions or hypotheses, which we have to introduce when we want to explain the social processes, concern the relation of the thought of an individual to the outside world, the question to what extent and how his knowledge corresponds to the external facts. And the hypotheses must necessarily run in terms of assertions about causal connections, about how experience creates knowledge.

Fredrich Hayek [1937/48, pp. 46–7]

Although Hayek long ago called for a recognition of the necessity of including knowledge and its acquisition explicitly in our explanations of economic decision-making, little significant progress has been made. And if methodologists today were not so interested in the big-M methodology questions that are of interest to philosophers but instead would focus on the one area of economic model building where methodology is directly relevant, perhaps more could be accomplished. That is, if we choose to abide by methodological individualism we must focus on the decision process of the individual. Every decision must involve the decision-maker's knowledge and learning and thus must involve some sort of small-m methodology. How does the individual know the nature of the situation he or she faces? How does the individual learn from disappointed expectations?

One can, of course, find many models today that include assumptions about learning and knowledge. Unfortunately, virtually every such model adopts directly or indirectly the view of knowledge and learning that was proposed 380 years ago by Francis Bacon and subsequently refuted more than 200 years ago by David Hume – namely, the inductivist theory of knowledge and learning discussed in Chapter 1. In this chapter I will try to outline what I think one needs to understand before one attempts to model knowledge and learning in economics. I will explain how we can go beyond both Inductivism in particular as well as its compromised form in Conventionalism and still address the need to recognize knowledge and learning in neoclassical economics.

Applying the Popper-Hayek Program to knowledge recognition in models of neoclassical economics

Before addressing how the Popper-Hayek Program might be implemented in neoclassical model building, let us review the contents of the toolbox that the program provides. From Chapter 1 we have the distinctions between Inductivism, Conventionalism and Instrumentalism. These distinctions will be important simply because they all are attempts to deal with the perceived need to satisfy Justificationism. From Chapter 2 we have the distinction between the narrow version of methodological individualism (viz., psychologistic individualism) and the more general version, institutional individualism. This distinction is important because when psychologism is taken for granted it thereby presumes that methodological individualism is not satisfied unless the individual is reduced to an exogenously given psychological entity. Such a presumption is a major obstacle to developing a realistic neoclassical economics or at least one that can deal with the real world. From Chapter 10 we have the important observation [from Hayek 1933/39] that in neoclassical economics the only way to explain dynamics is to see it as a response to failed maximization. In Chapter 15, I called this 'situational dynamics'. From Chapter 14 we have the Socratic theory of learning, namely, that one learns by discovering errors in one's understanding. I expressed the significance of this view of learning by distinguishing between two views of knowledge: quantitative vs. qualitative. Specifically, I suggested that we should consider knowledge to be like health rather than wealth and thus learning is a matter of improving one's knowledge rather than increasing one's knowledge. From Chapter 15 we also have a brief mention of an important distinction not often discussed – namely, the distinction between methodology and epistemology. At this point, it will be helpful to expand on this distinction.

Methodology vs. epistemology: An important distinction

This distinction is important but little appreciated and sometimes not even recognized. Many people (particularly, European academics) mistakenly use the terms interchangeably. The confusion is a by-product of taking Inductivism for granted. According to Inductivism, the method of learning (or justifying one's knowledge) is to collect facts (i.e., singular statements of singular observations) and thereby acquire knowledge. But the knowledge acquired is nothing more than the collection of observations. Thus whether we ask the epistemological question, 'what is knowledge?' or we ask the methodological question, 'how do you know?', the answer is the same: the list of all of the observations. Instrumentalism differs only to the extent that the list is not of observations but of successful explanations or predictions using the claimed knowledge. Conventionalism requires a different form of answer although it still requires the same answer for both questions. In this case, the answer would be that knowledge is the analytical proof that shows that one's knowledge is the best available given the current conventions. The proof is both one's knowledge and a demonstration of how it is the best available and thus how one currently knows.

Popper's epistemology, which I will be using here, is different. For this view, knowledge is theories, explanations, arguments, etc. The source of such knowledge imparts no status whatsoever. The 'how do you know?' question is irrelevant as it is a question that is only of interest to someone who wishes to proceed with Justificationism. That is, this question is really a request for a justification. In its place, the relevant question is 'how does one learn?'. Note, it is not 'how do you learn that your knowledge is true?' as this invites some form of Justificationism. Instead, from Popper's Socratic perspective, learning is, as noted before, a matter of improvement of knowledge rather than its acquisition. It is certainly not a quantitative issue.

Methodology vs. epistemology: Against the 'bucket theory of knowledge'

According to the 380-year-old Inductivist theory of knowledge, one *acquires* knowledge by making observations or, more generally, knowledge is accumulated experience. In other words, knowledge is nothing more than a summary of past observations or experience. Following Popper, I call this the 'bucket theory of knowledge' on the grounds that the more observations one makes (or observations of others one accepts), the more knowledge one has. According to the bucket theory of knowledge, not only is one's knowledge merely the contents of one's bucket but one learns only by adding more to the contents of one's bucket.

The strongest version of the bucket theory of knowledge is based obviously on a belief in the possibility of inductive logic and proofs – the Inductivism discussed in Chapter 1. According to Inductivism, the quality of one's knowledge is a direct consequence of the quality of one's observations. Obviously, scientific observations lead to scientific knowledge. The key notion is that if your claim to knowledge is false then you must have made a mistake in your observations. Perhaps you were biased or not clear-headed. Specifically, according to Inductivism, if your claim to knowledge is true you should be able to prove that it is true using *only* the observations made to date.

A weaker version of the bucket theory of knowledge is found in economics today: an explicit bucket-theory-based assumption concerning learning, viz., so-called 'Bayesian learning' which on the surface seems to be at variance with

Inductivism. Specifically, it is assumed that one does not simply collect observations and then induce some *a posteriori* true proposition. Instead, in the simplest form of the assumption, one begins with an *a priori* proposition and then collects observations that increase one's so-called 'subjective probability' which represents a measure of one's belief that the proposition is true. It could be argued that since Bayesian learning requires an *a priori* proposition to begin with, one's knowledge is thus not based only on observations. Critics counter that basing knowledge on Bayesian learning is merely 'sophisticated Inductivism' since *learning* is still invested only in the *process* of collecting observations. Moreover, it could be claimed that in the limit, if the proposition is true, the collected observations will constitute an inductive proof. But the sole purpose of invoking Bayesian learning is to avoid considering knowledge to be true but only the best that can be justified with the available information or observations. As such, the presumption of Bayesian learning is just another instance of presuming that every decision-maker is like the Conventionalist consumer I discussed in Chapter 10.

Still, some people might claim just that when one is making observations one is learning but this claim is simply uninformative. Actually, Inductivism is more informative since, according to the 380-year-old theory of knowledge, one learns *only* by experience. That is, one's claim to knowledge must be based only on experience. But here lies the problem. This theory of knowledge is itself a claim to knowledge – namely, this theory is itself our knowledge about how we acquire knowledge. Is this knowledge about knowledge acquisition based only on experience? To be consistent, it must be. But this unfortunately leads to an infinite regress. Where does one get one's knowledge about one's knowledge about one's knowledge acquisition? And so on.

Does the possibility of an infinite regress mean therefore that people cannot make claims to knowledge? If one thinks that any knowledge claim must always be provable by experience, then one will be left to suffer the cul-de-sac of 'skepticism' – namely, the belief that humans cannot know since they cannot prove their knowledge is true. A common alternative to skepticism is, of course, Conventionalism since it recommends a retreat from any claims to knowledge other than what can be shown to be consistent with the conventions accepted by the scientific community.

This retreat to conventional 'truth' is prompted by an unwillingness to give up the bucket theory of knowledge – that is, an unwillingness to give up the notion that knowledge is nothing more than a sophisticated way of cataloguing or summarizing observations. The bucket theory of knowledge is false and we should reject it. One way to reject it is to recognize two things. First one's knowledge is always a theory and second that any non-tautological theory can be false. Said another way, one's knowledge can be true even though one cannot prove that it is true.

The most prevalent problem with the bucket theory of knowledge is that it limits our view of learning. Hayek's notion of learning as 'knowledge acquisition' is characteristic. According to the bucket theory of knowledge, knowledge acquisition would simply mean that one has added to the contents of one's bucket. More technically, if one thinks that knowledge is achieved only by providing a proof of one's knowledge claim and one only accepts inductive proof (i.e., the proof must consist only of observation reports), the foundation of one's knowledge is only the collection of observation reports. At this point one might think that I should be talking about information rather than either mere observations or grand knowledge claims. To do so, however, would usually be misleading. The term 'information' is ambiguously used in economics. Sometimes it means merely a collection of observations and at other times it means something more like knowledge. The ambiguity is merely a consequence of confusing knowledge with its inductive support. In other words, inductive learning is simultaneously the creation of knowledge and the inductive proof of the truth of one's knowledge claim. Inductive learning is *nothing more than* contributing to the inductive proof.

Learning without the bucket theory of knowledge

It might obviously be asked, how can we conceive of an alternative theory of knowledge and learning? The alternative that I wish to discuss further in this chapter is, of course, the one offered by Popper. As I said above, its chief characteristic is that it disentangles methodology from epistemology, learning from knowledge. Specifically, knowledge is claimed to be manifested in one's theories. Learning is manifested in one's attempts to critically test one's own knowledge claims. Most important, one learns only when one *refutes* one's prior knowledge claim!

For an application example, consider again the textbook theory of the consumer discussed in Chapter 8. Traditionally, the consumer is assumed to know *a priori* his or her utility function as expressed by an indifference curve map over all conceivable choice bundles – and any demand decision is merely a logical consequence of the consumer's use of that known function to calculate which bundle would provide the highest level of utility. Some theorists may think they are making this *a priori* knowledge assumption plausible by their assuming also that the number of conceivable bundles is small and finite – perhaps along the lines of game theory as discussed in Chapter 4. Restricting choice to a small finite set of options might be acceptable if one is only explaining the behavior of one individual consumer in isolation. But limiting *ad hoc* every individual to a decision situation involving a small finite set of options raises questions concerning the usefulness of the explanation with regard to the responsiveness of the individual to changes in prices, that is, with regard to the individual's market behavior. (For more about explanations of consumer choices over restricted sets, see Boland [1986a, Chapter 5].) As suggested in Chapter 8, a plausible alternative is to assume that the consumer *conjectures* an indifference map and with each consumption choice is testing whether or not the current view concerning which point of choice is truly the one which maximizes utility – this is an easy test since if another choice increases utility then the previous point was not a maximum. In other words, one learns by discovering that one's prior knowledge was false.

As noted above, in one sense we have here a quality vs. quantity distinction – namely, improving health vs. increasing wealth. Clearly, using the bucket theory, knowledge can always be viewed as a quantity and thus amenable to quantitative treatment and neoclassical economic analysis. This possibility is evident in Stigler's famous 1961 article (which I discussed in Chapter 8). His basic notion is that the greater the quantity of observations, the smaller the standard deviation of the estimated mean. At best, Stigler's view of knowledge is limited to just one type of knowledge, namely, knowledge of the true value of one variable. Assumptions about how one learns about the true shape of one's indifference map would seem to be more complicated. Nevertheless, rejecting the bucket theory does not necessitate rejecting Stigler's analysis, *per se*. However, it does beg the question about what we assume concerning how a decision-maker interprets the quantity of information. Moreover, keep in mind that here we are always talking about explanatory knowledge – not the vocabulary knowledge of a language for which quantity and quality might be interchangeable.

The key point to be made here is that knowledge is always theoretical, always conjectural and thus always susceptible to being false. If one considers learning to be a process of improving rather than increasing knowledge, then one will be in a position to better appreciate Popper's alternative view of knowledge. His view says, in effect, that no matter how many observations one has made to date, the next observation may refute one's knowledge claim. Moreover, unlike the bucket theory where every observation makes a positive contribution to one's knowledge, Popper's alternative – like that of Socrates – says learning is always a negative experience, namely, one of refuting prior claims.

Towards including realistic learning in economic models

Whether all this matters depends directly on the model one is trying to build. In this section I wish to present some diagnostic questions that can be used to determine when the issues discussed here can matter. For each question, I will try to indicate what I think should have been learned from what I have presented in the first fifteen chapters of this book.

Does learning matter?

The keystone for building models where learning matters is the rejection of the bucket theory of knowledge in favor of Popper's Socratic theory of knowledge. That is, we must reject any theory that equates learning with the accumulation of data and instead adopt the view that learning is error correction. If we adopt this Socratic view, the first step is to recognize that every individual decision-maker holds one or more theories about the various elements of the decision situation faced. Moreover, and most important, these theories are possibly false.

To adopt the view that knowledge is manifested in theories is not as demanding as might first seem. Today, almost everyone can accept the notion that decision-making is a process rather than an instantaneous event and thus every decision involves expectations formation. Expectations are nothing more than theoretical conjectures. At minimum, what Popper's Socratic view does is to extend the notion of theoretical conjectures to all of the knowledge requirements of decision-making.

Recalling the example from Chapter 8, extending the notion of theoretical conjectures to all knowledge requirements means that the consumer is not assumed to know *a priori* what his or her true utility function is. Instead the consumer is assumed to conjecture what he or she would expect to be his or her reaction to consuming a particular bundle or to switching from one particular bundle to another. By positing that a consumer has a particular type of utility function we, as model builders, are in effect merely assuming that the *consumer* conjectures that such a utility function is what would be confirmed if he or she had the time to try out all of the infinity of possible bundles. While the bucket theory would see the consumer to be accumulating data with each purchased bundle to confirm the *a priori* conjecture, such a view of learning is incapable of dealing with refuting data. Since the Socratic view explicitly considers refuting data as potential learning opportunities, how the decision-maker deals with refuting data has to be made an essential part of the explanation of the decision-maker's behavior that we are modeling. Just recognizing that a consumer might have a particular theory of his or her preferences is not enough. As explained in Chapter 10, how a decision-maker deals with refutations also depends on the decision-maker's theory of knowledge and learning.

What role do probabilities play in the decision-maker's learning process?

Note that so far in this chapter nothing has been said about the common notions of 'uncertainty', 'risk' or 'probabilities' that I discussed at the beginning of Chapter 8. It might simply be that the typical introduction of any of these common notions is a direct consequence of the model builder's attempt to avoid giving up the bucket theory and yet still be recognizing the fallibility of a decision-maker's knowledge or expectations. But, the issue missing in any model based on the bucket theory is that there is still no way to deal with refuting data. By fuzzing up the issue with probability-based notions of fallible knowledge, model builders are inadvertently making explicit learning recognition virtually impossible. Specifically, if people learn by discovering and correcting their errors, probability notions make learning arbitrary or at least make it very difficult to know when one has made an error. I stress here that the problem is not with probability notions *per se* but with the bucket theory of knowledge that model builders seem unwilling to abandon.

The Socratic view of knowledge and learning does not preclude the use of probability notions. It does, however, require that the model builder be explicit about how the decision-maker incorporates probability notions in his or her decision-making process. For example, what kind of evidence would cause the decision-maker to determine that his or her knowledge of the situation is in error? What theory does the decision-maker hold concerning data handling? Does the decision-maker really think one can answer non-stochastic questions with statistical analysis?

Does the model involve decision errors?

Once one recognizes the fallibility of all knowledge, particularly knowledge necessary for the process of decision-making, one must also recognize the necessity of addressing the possibility of decision errors. To address the possibility of decision errors one must first deal with how the decision-maker becomes aware of an error and then deal with how the decision-maker responds. This task is made much easier if we recognize that at least some decision-makers are aware of the fallibility of their knowledge and thus they treat every decision as a test of their knowledge. In the case of a consumer, the consumer is never certain that the choice made is the one which maximizes utility. Again, the strategy employed by the consumer will depend on the theories held by the consumer. In the simplest case discussed in Chapter 8, the consumer may assume his or her indifference map is convex to the origin as in Figure 3.2 and further that his or her choice has no effect on the price. In this case, the consumer merely searches along the budget line by first trying out two widely spaced points and then tests the theory by buying a point midway between them. If the consumer's theory is correct, the third point will likely be better than the first two. In such a sequence of trial and error, the consumer can narrow the choice down to the one which according to the convexity assumption would be the utility-maximizing bundle. If the consumer's theory is false (either the map is not strictly convex as in Figure 8.4 or prices are not fixed), the consumer may not be able to narrow the choice in this way. In the case of such a failure to maximize, the consumer would have to determine the source of the error. Such a determination is beyond the textbook theory of the consumer. Obviously, if the consumer thinks his or her behavior has an effect on the given prices, then a much more complicated decision strategy would have to be involved.

Modeling error awareness can also be easy or difficult. The easy case occurs in the trial and error sequence when the consumer finds that the third point is not preferred to the first two. Similarly, going to the market expecting one price level and finding the price is different involves direct awareness of an error. Knowing what is the source of the error is a more difficult question. Clower's ignorant monopolist which I will discuss in the next chapter represents a problem for error awareness. Specifically, if the market is cleared for the expected prices, there is no additional information available to indicate that the assumptions made by the decision-maker are false and thus that maximization is not actually being achieved. The extent to which a decision-maker must make assumptions prior to participating in a market leaves the question of error awareness rather troublesome. And again, the textbook theory is not very helpful.

17 Individualism and Social Knowledge

Information has ... both public and private aspects. There are more and more examples of firms whose primary value is the possession of an informational advantage. This points to what I think will be an increasing issue in the analysis of industrial organization. The private property essential to the firm is eroded by the public access to the information which is part of that property.

Kenneth Arrow [1994, p. 8]

As noted in Chapter 9, many game theorists see a direct connection between evolution and social learning. While some game theorists are interested only in the question of how all individual players learn to play the same equilibrium strategy whenever there are multiple equilibria possible, evolutionary game theorists seem to go further. If all individuals in equilibrium models possessed the same knowledge (as in the case of the assumption of 'common knowledge of rationality' discussed in Chapter 4), then equilibrium models would seem plausible although it does beg the question of how that knowledge was 'acquired' or better, why do they have the same knowledge. If one presumes that induction is possible, then perhaps whenever everyone faces the same facts they will induce the same knowledge. But, as I have repeatedly stressed, there is no inductive logic and thus no means of assuring such unanimity.

While some game theorists may see evolution as a means of selecting among multiple equilibria, evolutionary theorists see evolution in a very contrary context. Specifically, recall from Chapters 9 and 10, evolution is also a means of understanding the dynamics of a competitive market system. That is, the market is a means of selecting between competing agents who offer different products or services. Rather than a concern for explaining unanimity, evolutionary economics (and evolutionary game theory that utilizes genetic algorithms) is mostly about recognizing variety within a population – bounded rationality is sometimes invoked to justify the lack of unanimity regarding knowledge acquisition. And those theorists, following some mathematical biologists, may even allow the possibility that an equilibrium can be reached where there is no unanimity but instead many different types of individuals interacting in a stable equilibrium system. In this case, it is not clear whether all individuals need have the same knowledge. However we go about this, the impossibility of unanimity being produced by induction, or similarly by the presumption of bounded rationality, raises the question of how all individuals could ever acquire the same knowledge as required for the usual equilibrium model. One way to overcome this question is simply to posit the existence of a social knowledge that is shared by all individuals. But, this would raise the question of how all individuals could ever acquire the same knowledge as required for the usual equilibrium model. Moreover, where does this social knowledge reside? How do individuals go about sharing the knowledge?

Knowledge without a knower: Who possesses knowledge?

Once it is recognized that one's knowledge is no more than a theory which one claims (or presumes) to be true, it might seem that this involves only a minor theoretical adjustment. After all, it is not much of a change to substitute one's theory for one's bucket. However, the difference is more than minor. At minimum, rejecting the bucket theory of knowledge precludes assuming automatically that knowledge is quantifiable – if for no other reason, without the bucket theory of knowledge, neither more information nor better information would ever mean more knowledge, as there will not necessarily be a monotonically positive relationship between the quantity of observations and the truth status of theory. For example, if one learns by trial and error, what is the benefit or cost of a refuting observation?

Objective knowledge

More importantly, once we recognize that knowledge is embodied in fallible theories which an individual claims to be true, we must then recognize a certain objectivity to the nature of knowledge. Such objective knowledge means that potentially it has an existence separate from the individual who makes the knowledge claims [see Popper 1972, chap. 3]. That is, potentially one can simply write a statement of one's knowledge on the classroom's blackboard (or overhead). But, once the knowledge is explicitly stated, knowledge exists even though whoever wrote it on the board may not even be in the room. As is often done today, we can go even further by saying that knowledge is not knowledge until it is made objective. This is the essence of the Efficient Markets Hypothesis [Fama 1970] and is consistent with Capital Asset Pricing Models [Lintner 1965; Sharpe 1964]. Such a view of knowledge opens the door to an important question. If knowledge is objective (as in the case of the blackboard's contents), who possesses knowledge?

This is the heart of the problem of recognizing social knowledge in both neoclassical economics and evolutionary game theory. Unless knowledge is objective there cannot be any social knowledge. But the corollary is that once we recognize the possibility that knowledge is objective we have thereby recognized that to acquire the knowledge an individual does not need to be the creator of that knowledge nor even someone who claims that the knowledge in question is true. In this sense, one can see that a library is a repository of knowledge without the knowers or at least without the knowledge creators. Each book on the shelf makes knowledge claims but rarely do we have the author of this knowledge standing next to us as we read the book. This separation of knowledge from the knower is essential to the recognition of social knowledge.

Institutions as social knowledge

If we recognize that knowledge can exist separately from the knower then we are in a position to recognize that knowledge can be deposited with something other than an individual. As with the classic question 'when a tree falls and there is no one in the forest, is there any sound?', we can ask whether when everyone leaves the classroom with the knowledge written on the blackboard, is there any knowledge? According to Arrow, 'Information may be supplied socially, but to be used, it has to be absorbed individually' [1994, p. 8]. Does this contradict the notion of separate social knowledge? Unless one is careful, it can.

Before considering this question, let us consider how knowledge can be separate in the sense that it exists beyond the knower both in time and space. When I was a child I was willing to sit on the curb and directly observe how many passing cars had two doors vs. how many had four doors. Few adults would have such patience. Instead, adults rely on institutions to provide such social information. For example, one can search the Internet for a web page for the information or one can go to the library and consult an appropriate reference book on the shelf. Assuming there is such a web page or reference book, it would represent knowledge about the social distribution of two-door cars. As such, the web page or book represents knowledge whether or not the creator of that knowledge is present or even alive. Actually, the library itself is knowledge – namely, about how to solve the problem of making available society's knowledge about specific things without the high cost that would be entailed if everyone had to own a copy of every book ever published. In fact, we have institutions such as the Library of Congress and the British repository libraries that are explicitly created for the purpose of overcoming the need for every library to hold copies of all books ever published. We can go further to say that any human creation (beyond procreation) constitutes knowledge. A bridge over a river manifests knowledge about one way to get from one side to the other without getting wet. A written constitution manifests knowledge about how to organize and change a society.

As discussed in Chapter 6, it could be argued that all social institutions embody social knowledge. In this light, perhaps following Popper's lead, one understands a social institution by seeing it as a solution to a social problem. A written constitution is the obvious example. But it is most important to recognize that institutionalizing social knowledge itself solves an unavoidable social problem. Specifically, as a group we may discover a solution to an important social problem and we may agree among ourselves to conduct our intra-group business according to our discovery. But being based on our common agreement, our solution is limited to our group and our time; again, our solution exists only because we have formed a *consensus* that our discovery is worthy of following. If we think other groups or other generations would benefit from our solution, that is, from our knowledge of how to solve the important social problem that gave rise to our discovery, again, we could try to make our solution *concrete*. Writing the solution on the blackboard is one step in that direction and recording it in class notes might be another. Carving it in stone might be more effective in terms of durability but may not be so effective in terms of sharing with other groups. Durability and sharing (or scope) are also social problems which many groups have tried to solve. On the one hand, we have consensus institutions including brand name products such as Coca Cola or Pepsi and generic products such as cigarettes. That is, marketing is all about attempting to create consensus institutions. If successful, a marketing agent would make its product something that members of a society cannot do without. Doing so involves creating a consensus institution. On the other hand, concrete institutions can be seen to be ways of providing durability and scope to the social knowledge embodied in consensus institutions. So, again, the existence of concrete institutions shows both the existence of social knowledge and its autonomy from individuals, particularly from the individuals who may have created the institutions.

Autonomous institutionalized social knowledge sounds like something that would directly contradict Arrow's requirement that to be useful social knowledge must be 'absorbed individually'. The point to stress is that the source of knowledge is not always important (and perhaps for this reason Arrow does not distinguish between knowledge and information). What is important is that every decision-maker requires knowledge – knowledge of one's aims and knowledge of one's constraints (George Richardson [1959] called these respectively *primary* and *secondary* knowledge). Of course, any one of the constraints is a limitation on the decision-maker's knowledge. Specifically, how does the decision-maker acquire or absorb the social knowledge embodied in the institutions which form all or part of the constraints? The education system is a social institution that might be seen to have as its primary purpose to be the vehicle that makes citizens absorb and appreciate the knowledge embodied in society's institutions. Perhaps, by the individual's being limited by his or her knowledge of the constraining institutions' embodied social knowledge, Arrow is led to say that social knowledge must be 'absorbed individually' while at the same time recognizing that the social knowledge is deposited in the institutions. But, does this merely say we must abide by psychologistic individualism?

To summarize so far: If we wish to meaningfully incorporate social knowledge in an individualist view of the economy, we need to do the following. First, we should avoid restricting individualism to the narrow and static methodology of reductive, psychologistic individualism. Second, we should avoid being constrained by the simple-minded bucket theory of knowledge and in particular its long-refuted inductivist version. Third, we should give up the notion that knowledge is not knowledge unless an individual possesses the knowledge. Doing all of this allows us to recognize that social knowledge can exist independent of an individual knower. And finally, and most importantly, we should recognize that all knowledge, whether absorbed by an individual or embodied in a social institution, can be false. How individuals are assumed to deal with their needed, but possibly false, knowledge must be a central feature of any economic model that purports to involve learning.

Applications of individualism and social knowledge fundamentals

There are two major aspects of modern economic thinking that depend on how the fundamentals of knowledge and methodological individualism are dealt with. First, there is the repressed anxiety concerning the problem of microfoundations. And second, there is the question, if prices are social phenomena, does their information content depend on the existence of *unexplained* social institutions?

Micro vs. macrofoundations

Concerning the issue of microfoundations, not much more has to be said other than to note how it is a necessary manifestation of psychologistic individualism. This was central in the discussion of Chapter 9 where it was argued that if psychologistic individualism is actually rejected in favor of the more general methodological individualism, so as to make knowledge and learning a meaningful part of economic models, then there would not seem to be any need to reduce macro economic models to micro models. So, what problem is thought to be solved by those theorists who dare to advocate such a reduction?

Some theorists see no problem that would require microfoundations. Instead, following on from the discussion in Chapter 9, it could easily be argued that theorists such as Richardson [1959] and Arrow [1986, 1994] are in effect arguing for macrofoundations of microeconomics. Clearly the demand for macrofoundations would be silly if we were to continue assuming that economic explanations must satisfy the narrow dictates of psychologistic individualism. It might even be asked whether the demand for macrofoundations is some sort of neo-Marxian 'Holism'. It does not have to be, so as long as we are satisfied with the more liberal requirements of methodological individualism. It is one of the persistent fallacies of methodology that by not endorsing psychologistic individualism one must be endorsing holism. Holism is simply the view that wholes (such as Nations, Clans, Tribes, or Social Classes) determine how individuals in society behave. For example, you may think you are making a free choice but you may be naively unaware that your tastes are determined by your social position. For the most part, it can be argued, most people in the same social position behave the same way and thus make the same kind of choices. But the demand for macrofoundations does not necessarily make this holist type of argument.

Macrofoundations in a general methodological-individualist context only intends to recognize that any individual's decision-making relies on knowledge of macro variables. The existence of a market system itself is a social phenomenon that is more than the behavior of one individual. Even a price is a social phenomenon since its value depends on the behavior of all other individuals in the market. That a decision-maker (e.g., a labor negotiator) does to any extent base his or her demand for a wage-rate on the current level of the Consumer Price Index indicates that macro variables matter in micro economics. Hayek [1937/48] argued in effect that when setting out to buy two or more goods, a decision-maker ought to consider not only the prices of the goods but also their availability before deciding which store to go to first [see Boland

1986a, chap. 7]. Availability depends on decisions made by other consumers and thus on social constraints. For example, consider a consumer buying meat and bread in real time, that is, someone who has to decide whether to go to the butcher first and the baker second or the reverse. In real time, the consumer cannot be in two places at the same time. If one thinks it is likely that there will be a shortage of bread that day (perhaps based on expectations concerning what other demanders will do), then it would be wise to go to the baker before going to the butcher. The necessity of making such a decision obviously raises again the question of how an individual acquires the needed social knowledge concerning availability.

Prices as social institutions: assumptions and expectations

Hayek [1945/48] was a strong advocate of recognizing that market prices are conveyors of social knowledge. Clearly when the market price is rising it would be wise for individual producers to recognize that it means that demanders want more of the good. It is in this sense that Hayek sees prices as social knowledge. But to appreciate a role for such social knowledge it is important to be aware of the dynamic aspect of Hayek's viewpoint. The key point, as in the question of availability, is that the decision-maker must be seen to be making decisions in a sequence of steps rather than as a singular static event. The first step is the one where knowledge matters. The last step is where learning matters.

Using Hayek's terms, the first step involves forming a 'plan'. That is, one decides what the price is expected to be before going to the market to sell one's produce. Based on the expected price, one decides how much to produce – the 'how much' is usually assumed to be the amount which would maximize profit. The next step is to go to the market with the consequences of one's prior decision, that is, with one's plan. The last step depends on the outcome of one's trip to the market. If one's expectations were correct, then one will sell all that was produced (and this would be the case even if the price was underestimated). If one overestimated the market clearing price, then one will be left with unsold goods. How does one interpret such socially provided information? That is, how does one learn from such refuted expectations? To answer this question, the bucket theory is absolutely useless.

How does the producer interpret refuted expectations? Interestingly, Robert Clower [1959] presented a simple model that dealt explicitly with this question. He posited a monopolist behaving as Hayek seems to suggest with the minor exception that the monopolist instead of forming an expectation of a simple market price, forms an expectation as to the elasticity of the market demand curve (in effect, an expectation of the monopolist's expected marginal revenue). Clower refers to the monopolist as 'an ignorant monopolist', that is, one who does not know the market's true demand curve. Clower has his monopolist making an *a priori* assumption that the demand curve faced is linear when in fact the true demand curve is not. As a consequence of this false assumption, the monopolist mistakenly interprets each subsequent failed expectation as evidence that a shift in the linear demand curve has taken place. Assuming a stable configuration of cost and demand curves, the firm can easily reach an 'equilibrium' where the expected marginal revenue is not the true marginal revenue and hence the firm is not truly maximizing profit [see further, Boland 1997, chap. 14].

The point of this reference is that Clower's ignorant monopolist tries to learn from the available disequililbrium information socially provided by the market but to do so, the information needs to be interpreted and such interpretation depends on the assumptions made by the decision-maker. Moreover, what is also recognized is that the decision-maker must have some way of dealing with disappointed expectations concerning price or elasticity and thus must be equipped to deal with such errors. In other words, information from a disequilibrium market needs to be interpreted and such an interpretation depends on fallible assumptions. Contrary to what our usual behavioral assumption would have us believe, Clower demonstrated that if the monopolist's assumptions are false, then there is no reason to think that the firm is truly maximizing *even in equilibrium*. Moreover, the monopolist's market is in a state of equilibrium since the firm thinks it is maximizing profit and thus it has no reason to change its supply quantity.

Prices as social institutions: presumed social signals

The question to consider at this stage is whether the price written on a price tag conveys sufficient information or whether we need also to make assumptions about the social knowledge conveyed by the price tag. A related consideration is whether the social knowledge embodied in the market institution matters when going to the market.

To illustrate the problem at hand, let me recount a situation I witnessed at a local camera store several years ago. A fellow, who said he recently arrived from Central Europe, was attempting to purchase a camera at a typical Canadian camera store. He said he would buy the camera if the salesman would also include free rolls of film and a few other things. The salesman said, 'Sir, we do not do that here'. My interpretation of this event is that the customer was behaving as he would have back in his Central European culture and thus treated the price on the price tag as a starting price in a bargaining situation. The salesman, on the other hand, was acting in a typical Canadian way by assuming that the price tag provides the only price, no bargaining. To me, this raises an important question. Is the price tag *sufficient* information (as Hayek might claim for a single market), or must we take into account the sociology of the market, too? Judging by the failed market transaction that I witnessed, it would seem that social knowledge matters if one wants to buy a camera in Canada.

Do objects of choice contain social knowledge?

It is common to think that when a consumer buys an object, say a suit of clothes, that the object has no intrinsic value. The only value to be obtained lies in the eyes of the buyer – namely, the amount of utility to be obtained. Whether one's choice is solely a matter of personal utility would seem to depend on whether or not there is any social significance in that choice. For example, consider a consumer choosing between two similar objects – say a gray pin-striped suit and a dark blue pin-striped suit. If the consumer is a lawyer, perhaps the best choice is the dark blue pin-striped that other lawyers typically wear. If the consumer is a banker, the gray pin-stripe might be more socially acceptable.

Thorstein Veblen long ago raised the issue of the social content of objects of choice. In Veblen's terms it was a question of ostentatious consumer behavior. But the point is that ostentatious consumption depends heavily on social context – an audience. When one buys a Mercedes-Benz rather than a humble Volkswagen, usually the consumer is trying to send a message such as 'see, I am so rich I can afford to buy a Mercedes-Benz'. Whether this is the received message depends on the cultural norms of the audience. If this were in a small village in a third-world country, people might be impressed just that the consumer could buy an automobile, even a humble Volkswagen would do. In a wealthy suburban neighborhood, buying a mere Mercedes-Benz may have the opposite effect than was intended – why not a Rolls Royce?

Veblen's observations point to a dilemma that occurs whenever social knowledge plays an important role in the individual's choices. Is the social significance of an object of choice intrinsic to the good or a matter incorporated in the individual's private utility function?

It might be thought that a consideration of ostentatious consumption merely calls into question the nature of a consumer's utility function. Whether one buys a Mercedes-Benz, Volkswagen or Rolls Royce is already part of the definition of the goods over which the utility function establishes preferences. However, if an object of choice is thought to signal other members of society, then even the definition of the object (and implicitly the nature of the utility function) depends on the notions held by *other* members of society. Rather than implicitly investing the private utility function with the social attributes of objects of choice, it might be thought that from the perspective of the individual decision-maker, given the society in which the choice is being made, the social significance of the object of choice is intrinsic to the good. Either way, it can easily be argued that objects of choice have a social dimension that seems to be ignored in textbook economics. This is so even when one thinks the consumer is making a private choice.

Does the individual require private knowledge?

Given the above observations and despite what Hayek wished to promote, it is not clear that purely private knowledge is possible. In a way, an individual's utility function is significantly influenced by society and society's norms. And in this sense, it is inconceivable that one could ever expect to fulfill the requirements of reductive, psychologistic individualism.

If the social dimension of an individual's knowledge is to be recognized, how should we go about modeling this? There is no formula answer to this question. All that can be said is that we should avoid presuming that a state of equilibrium is an *unintended* consequence of individuals privately maximizing. Society matters in every individual's decision and, to be realistic, we should endeavor to make sure our models incorporate the social dimension of an individual's decision-making. So long as psychologistic individualism and the bucket theory of knowledge are rejected, there is no reason to think neoclassical economics is excluded from such a concern for realism.

18 Obstacles to Building Realistic Models

The most important methodological issue in economics has been and persists to be over what is called the 'realism' of theories and their 'assumptions'. Profit maximization, perfect information, transitive preferences, diminishing returns, rational expectations, perfectly competitive markets, givenness of tastes, technology and institutional framework, non-gendered agents – these and many other ideas have been assumed by some economists and questioned by others.

Uskali Mäki (1994, p. 236]

Discussing 'realism' has been a growth industry lately. Where once we might have heard philosophers argue over realism vs. idealism or vs. instrumentalism, over the last decade or so the discussion has been concerned with various types of realism. According to methodologists such as Uskali Mäki [1992] and Tony Lawson [1994], there are many types: critical, commonsense, empirical, ontological, scientific, scholastic, social, structural, transcendental, transfactual, etc. It is not clear that everyone understands the need for all these distinctions. Those readers with a Popperian background have always taken 'critical realism' for granted. One would think any concern for critical realism is either an obvious necessity or it is mere rhetoric. For the purposes of 'small-m' methodologists, the question of critical realism concerns only the methodology of model building in economics. Basically, the main question is: do the model's assumptions truly represent reality, that is, represent the real, objective world?

In this chapter I will try to draw together much of what has been presented so far and, in particular, I am going to apply the methodological concerns of Popper's critical realism to two aspects of the methodology of model building. To begin, I will criticize some of the common excuses given for accepting less than desirable realism in economic models, drawing on the discussion of the previous chapters. Then, I will briefly discuss various small-m methodological obstacles to obtaining realistic economic models.

Excuses for accepting unrealistic models

There is … always the possibility and the temptation of proving all sorts of theorems which have no empirical relevance whatsoever... [I]t is a forward step when theorems ... are no longer merely asserted, but actually proved. Yet the ultimate criterion is whether what the theorem asserts is what is found in reality. One cannot help but be reminded of Hans Christian Andersen's story of the Emperor's clothes.

Oskar Morgenstern [1972, pp. 1164–5]

not all well-articulated models will be equally useful... The more dimensions on which the model mimics the answers actual economies give to simple questions, the more we trust its answers to harder questions. This is the sense in which more 'realism' in a model is clearly preferred to less.

Robert Lucas [1980, pp. 696–7]

It is not always clear what economic model builders think they are doing. Today more than ever it would seem that they are less interested in whether their models represent observable reality and more interested in whether their models are novel applications of the latest fad in model building methodology. If you press economic theorists today about the unrealism of some of their assumptions, you will usually be told in effect that 'absolute' truth is unattainable and thus methodological demands for realism will not be appreciated. It would seem that Richard Lester has lost the battle discussed in Chapter 3. It always appears to be counter-productive to ask economists whether they thought their opinion of the unattainableness of 'absolute' truth is itself absolutely true. But one should still ask why they think we should not expect their models to be absolutely true.

Excuses for stopping short of the pursuit of absolute realism are based on Conventionalism which, of course, declares that theories are neither true nor false but only better or worse. Accordingly, theories are most often considered mere filing systems or catalogues to be used to describe observed data. And so, theories are not intended to be realistic representations of the world that generates the data.

The only philosophical problem that Conventionalism ever needs to consider is the problem of 'theory choice'. The Conventionalist excuse merely presumes that we must fulfill the requirements of Justificationism while still overcoming the Problem of Induction. Thus, it is claimed that for someone to say a theory is absolutely true it must be possible to prove its truth status. Moreover, it is presumed that the only acceptable proof must be based solely on indisputable facts, that is, all proofs need to be inductive. But as is widely accepted today, there are no indisputable facts, only theory-laden facts – every proof involves theoretical assumptions which in turn would have to be proven. Thus, at best, one's proof would be circular and, at worse, it would lead to an infinite regress.

Conventionalism is then a denial of realism. In the place of realism, we can find Conventionalism in several forms – two of them were discussed in Chapter 12. There was the optimistic form which I called 'approximationism' and the defeatist form that turns out to be difficult to distinguish from Instrumentalism. In this chapter, I will examine a third, pessimistic form which some philosophers call 'relativism'. Each of these can be seen to provide convenient excuses for accepting unrealistic representative economic models.

Approximationism vs. realism

Approximationism is the most common form of Conventionalism. It seems to appeal to commonsense. It simply says that while we might like our assumptions to be true, that is, realistic, as a practical matter true representative models would be too complex and thus intractable. Instrumentalism as found in Friedman's 1953 essay agrees with this starting point but departs by immediately accepting simple and obviously false assumptions so as to push on with dealing with practical problems on the grounds that for practical problems theories do not need to be true. The obvious supporting example for Instrumentalism is engineering which never claims to deal with true assumptions yet addresses practical problems. Engineering does so in a simple manner, it employs safety factors and recognizes degrees of measurement tolerance. Conventionalism, however, is interested in more than immediate practical problems. For this reason, the criteria to be used in the problem of theory choice are central.

According to Conventionalism, science is distinguished from engineering because science transcends immediate practical problems by being concerned with general understanding. In the hands of mathematical economists this has led to the view that the more general a model is, the better the model. General equilibrium theory is the obvious example. Rather than explain one product's price, we should develop models that apply to the explanation of all prices. In the extreme, the most general models have minimal indications that they are about economics.

Everyday economics does not go to such extremes. Instead, while every model needs assumptions, there is no need to be any more general than the problem at hand requires. For example, while two-dimensional diagrams might not be an adequate basis for a general proof, they can adequately represent the essential notions of economics. Specifically, consider 2×2×2 models where an Edgeworth-Bowley box can be used to describe all of the necessary conditions for general equilibrium. In the equilibrium between any two people consuming two different goods, their Marginal Rates of Substitution (i.e., the slopes of their 'iso-utility' curves shown within the Edgeworth-Bowley box which has the quantities of the two goods as its dimensions – see Figure 3.3) must equal the ratio of the prices of those two goods. Similarly, in an equilibrium between any two factors used to produce those two goods, the Marginal Rate of Technical Substitution (i.e., the slopes of so-called 'iso-output' curves shown similarly within an Edgeworth-Bowley box which has instead the available labor and capital as its dimensions) must equal the ratio of the respective factor prices. Although most textbooks fail to mention it, a necessary condition for any given income distribution can also be shown in an equilibrium Edgeworth-Bowley box such as Figure 3.3.

Apart from the assertion that two-dimensional diagrams adequately approximate the conditions of general equilibrium, there are numerous other assumptions that are claimed to approximate the reality that textbook models claim to represent. Before examining some that might be no more problematic than two-dimensional diagrams, I will add some brief comments on the pessimistic form of Conventionalism that has been gaining ground in recent years.

Relativism vs. realism

The most recent challenge to realism comes from those who are advocating a more pessimistic view of the Conventionalist problem of theory choice. According to this pessimistic Conventionalism, since any choice could never be proven absolutely, one should not try to choose just one all-purpose theory, model or even paradigm. At best, it is claimed that any choice will always be relative to the basic criteria approved in one's cultural environment. The code words for this view in economic methodology are 'rhetoric' and 'pluralism'. Rhetoric is the extreme form of pessimistic Conventionalism and pluralism is the mild form.

Pluralism is also the leading feel-good form of pessimistic Conventionalism. It says that since we cannot ever (inductively) prove that our chosen theory is the true theory, we must be tolerant of others who have chosen other theories. Thus, this mild form is not an outright ban of theory choice, but only recognition that we should limit our claims for our choice to those which would appeal to someone who accepts our Conventionalist criteria of choice. Moreover, it is all too easy to see that one's acceptance of particular criteria cannot be justified beyond their consistency relationship to the chosen theory. While philosophers worry a lot about the circularity of this form of pessimistic Conventionalism, economists and some methodologists just take it for granted. And since they take it for granted, they are easy targets for proponents of the extreme form of pessimistic Conventionalism.

Rhetoric technically is concerned with how one goes about convincing an audience that one's proposition is true or otherwise correct. The eighteenth-century philosophers' advocating logic as the only acceptable means of convincing an audience is merely one example of rhetoric but not one that is discussed by the rhetoric of economics advocates today. Today, even eighteenth-century rationalism is the subject of criticism and ridicule by pessimistic followers of Conventionalism. By whose standards of rationality are we able to convince an audience? Well, obviously, only by the standards or conventions accepted by the audience. This will obviously be different for different audiences. Standards of rationality are considered relative since they are alleged to be culturally dependent. An argument that might convince someone educated in a Marxist environment is not likely to be convincing in a meeting of neoclassical economists and vice versa. Understanding and exploring the relativity of rhetoric is the celebrated cause promoted by the advocates of the rhetoric of economics such as Dierdre McCloskey and Arjo Klamer. For such relativists, there is no absolute reality; reality is only in the eyes of the beholder. Thus, given their understanding of both optimistic and defeatist Conventionalism, advocates of the rhetoric of economics have much fun ridiculing those methodologists who would ever claim to have Conventionalist criteria that might be considered universal.

At best, the published disputes between pluralists and advocates of the rhetoric of economics are mere family disputes. Both reject realism. Both advocate some form of relativism. Both violate their own principles by asserting that theirs is the true methodology – even though, of course, rhetoric is claimed to be an alternative to methodology (this is merely a typical expression of a family dispute). Both say that it is illegitimate to argue about the truth status of the basic or fundamental assumptions of neoclassical economics. So, as the philosopher Joseph Agassi [1992] has pointed out, arguing over basic, fundamental principles is universally forbidden by relativists, particularly, feel-good relativists.

Obstacles to representative realism

Realism in mainstream economics is concerned with the realism of assumptions used in building economic models. Those advocating rhetoric of economics will usually ridicule the mainstream interest in model building so there is no need to discuss them further. In the remainder of this chapter I will discuss four obstacles to building realistic representative models in economics. These four obstacles lie at the foundation of neoclassical economics and thus are not likely to have been the subject of critical consideration by model builders who rely on some form of Conventionalism to provide their guiding methodological principles. Remember, according to Conventionalist principles, we are told that we should not argue over the truth of one's theory or model since ultimately one would have to prove that one's basic principles are true. And since such proofs could only ultimately succeed inductively, that is when they are shown to be based on indisputable facts, as noted above, this is precluded by the recognition of theory-laden facts.

The four obstacles I will discuss are (1) the usual presumption of an inductive basis for knowledge assumptions in economic models, (2) the inconsistency between any explanation of the process of reaching an equilibrium and the conditions necessary for equilibrium, (3) the inconsistency between a model's assumptions and the ideas being modeled and (4) confusing unrealistic mathematical assumptions with objects in the real world.

Inductive basis for knowledge assumptions

A persistent, theoretical key question of realism was first addressed in Chapter 8: How does the consumer know he or she is maximizing utility? What knowledge is required to prove one is maximizing utility? Obviously, one must know the prices and one's income. Since these are both objective and easily calculated, it is easy to assume the consumer knows them. But, what about the utility function? The utility function is supposed to tell us how many 'utils' an individual would obtain for *any* bundle of goods that might be consumed. 'Any' bundle means that the utility function is able to report on an infinity of conceivable bundles. How does the individual know the 'utils' provided by each of an infinity of bundles given that infinity is an impossible quantity? That is, no living person could ever directly consider in real time an infinity of bundles. So just how do the individuals know their utility functions? This problem was indirectly addressed more than fifty years ago under the name of the integrability problem [Samuelson 1950a]. Even if one could quiz an individual about the Marginal Rate of Substitution (*MRS*) for each of a finite set of bundles involving three or more goods, one could never deduce the utility function (or equivalent indifference map) that would yield that set of observations. Moreover, as can be seen in Chapter 8, it is not even clear that the individual knows the *MRS* for any one point let alone all of the infinity of points.

The more general problem is the one discussed in Chapter 14, namely that when in doubt, theorists, realizing that one must make assumptions about needed knowledge on the part of the individual decision-makers, simply assume that the individual's knowledge is acquired inductively. That is, the individual is presumed to acquire the needed knowledge simply by making observations and inducing the general principles embodied in that knowledge. How does the individual know his or her inductive knowledge is true? Inductive proofs require an infinity of observations, a clear impossibility. Or they require that the observations were made instantaneously, that is, infinitely fast. Either way, people cannot acquire their needed knowledge inductively. Any theory that presumes so cannot be considered a mere approximation since realistically it is an impossibility.

In Chapters 8 and 16, I suggested that neoclassical economists could construct more realistic models simply by dropping the presumption that all individuals know their preferences and instead assume that they try to learn their preferences by trial and error. Taking this approach to explaining consumer behavior would have the advantage of not only avoiding the false presumption of inductive learning but it would also avoid the problems of realism that are fostered by having to invoke the questionable and unrealistic notions of infinity and an infinitesimal – both of which are impossible entities and thus must at least be considered possibly unrealistic entities [for more on this obstacle, see Boland 1986a, chap. 5].

Disequilibrium process vs. equilibrium attainment

Many critics of neoclassical economics might see these observations as criticisms of equilibrium economics. In one sense, this will be true since any market equilibrium implies simultaneous maximization by all demanders and all suppliers. The demand curve is the locus of price-quantity combinations at which all the demanders would be maximizing. That is, the quantity demanded in the market is the sum of the quantities demanded by each maximizing individual for the given price. The supply curve is defined in a similar way. Thus, if demand does not equal supply at the going price, either one or more of the demanders is not maximizing, or one or more of the suppliers (or both).

With this in mind, Arrow's famous 1959 article asked a simple question: who sets the given price? And, if at that going price demand and supply are not equal, who changes the price? That is, just what is our theory of price adjustment?

It would be tempting to ask who knows that demand and supply are not equal. But, by considering the discussion of Chapter 7, this question is easy to answer when we keep in mind the definitions of demand and supply curves. If the price is above the market clearing price then supply quantity will exceed the demand quantity. This would mean that at least one supplier is not able to maximize profit at the going price. So in this sense, we can easily explain who knows that there is a disequilibrium. Moreover, we also know who will offer to change the price, namely, the non-maximizing supplier. The non-maximizing supplier tries to compete with other suppliers by offering to sell for a lesser price (thereby inducing some buyer to switch suppliers). So long as the price is still above the market-clearing price, such competitive behavior will continue to cause the price to fall. The price-adjustment behavior stops when the market-clearing price is reached. But a question remains, how does the non-maximizing supplier know by how much to lower the price? And worse, the definitions of demand and supply curves are based on the notion of decision-makers as price takers. We have an inconsistency here between the behavior of demanders and suppliers when the market clears – that is, where everyone can be a price-taking maximizer – and when the market is not clearing – that is, when at least one ceases to be a price taker and instead chooses to offer a price other than the given price.

One suggestion Arrow makes is to recognize that the theory of a monopolist has the monopolist deciding what the price is. At first blush, it sounds a lot like a theory of price adjustment. But, what is this theory? The price-setting monopolist would set the price where the corresponding marginal revenue equals marginal cost. This means that by not being a perfect competitor, this firm faces a downward sloping demand curve which in turn means that marginal revenue is always less than the price. Thus, as was shown in Figure 7.4, the price set by the monopolist is never the one where price equals marginal cost – as would be the case with the perfectly competitive (i.e., price-taking) profit maximizer.

The result of this is a simple dichotomy. If the market clears, and thus everyone is facing the market-clearing price, all firms can be perfect competitors. But if the market is not clearing, we have to have a non-perfectly competitive theory of the prices. This is a clear inconsistency. If equilibrium requires one theory and disequilibrium requires another, then we cannot have just one theory to explain prices. Moreover, these two theories are inconsistent. In equilibrium, everyone sets the price at the marginal cost but in disequilibrium, the price is set where marginal cost equals a marginal revenue that is not equal to the price.

Again, the notion that our simple assumption that the market is determining the price in a competitive manner is an adequate approximation will not do if it involves, as I am arguing, an inherent contradiction. But another question might be raised if we choose to explain all price behavior with one price adjustment theory, the monopolist. There would be no problem if we were also to assume that the monopolists have sufficient knowledge about the demand curves facing them. However, if, as is more likely, they are ignorant about their demand curves, then we cannot be guaranteed that the resulting equilibrium is the one where everyone is maximizing. This is the problem of the 'ignorant monopolist' discussed in Chapter 17. To repeat, Clower showed that an ignorant monopolist must make assumptions about the demand curve and there are no obvious assumptions to make. He then showed that, even with plausible assumptions, if they are false we can be led to a market equilibrium where the monopolist may think he or she is maximizing profit, but actually is not maximizing profit and possibly not so by a wide margin. In this case, in the ignorant monopolist's market, market clearance does not imply universal maximization. So, even Arrow's optimistic approach to price adjustment seems to lack promise. And again, this is not just a matter of approximation but a broader question of how the monopolistic price adjuster could be assumed to have acquired true knowledge. In any case, as Clower's ignorant monopolist demonstrates, there is no reason to think that the monopolist's deviation from the true maximizing output is a mere matter of acceptable approximation.

Inconsistent model assumptions

The econometrics theorist David Hendry has for several years pointed out problems that he thinks econometric model builders cause by ignoring inconsistencies between the modeling assumptions they make and the econometric theorems they apply. His complaints have to do with the technical mathematical forms of the models constructed. Here I wish to consider some less technical contradictions that are even more fundamental. Consider again how some theorists model how people deal with information when facing uncertainties – specifically, so-called Bayesian learning that was discussed in Chapter 8. One can even find econometricians advocating the use of the Bayesian learning viewpoint to motivate how econometrics should deal with new information or data [e.g., Leamer 1983; Poirier 1988]. As data are collected, the probability of the truth status changes in accordance with Bayes's theorem. While it is obviously possible to build plausible models based on Bayes's theorem, the question never considered is whether this theorem is consistent with the principles of logic that are used to prove or establish other aspects of the models. Without going into more detail about the nature of Bayes's theorem than I did in Chapter 8, it is enough just to note that it presumes that the truth status of any proposition is a probability. That is, the truth status is alleged to be between 0 and 1 and rarely is it either 0 or 1.

Bayes's theorem would have us violate the essential axiom of excluded middle (discussed in Chapter 12). That is, attaching any value other than 0 or 1 as the statement's truth status would put a value that says the statement is neither true nor false. Now, this is not necessarily a problem so long as one is willing to avoid indirect proofs. Who among the Bayesian econometricians is willing to show that absolutely none of the mathematical theorems used in econometric theory employs an indirect proof? One suspects that even if they could, which is a very doubtful possibility, there still remain all the problems surrounding the common use of infinity and infinitesimals which are both, by definition, impossible. The question here however is whether this is merely a matter of approximation.

Clearly, one cannot approximate the axioms of logic. The 1989 Nobel prize-winner Trygve Haavelmo [1944] made this point almost sixty years ago. In his day (and for some, even today) it was thought that one could use probabilities with values of between 0 and 1 in place of absolute true or false truth status such that the conclusions reached in a logical argument would simply inherit the same values. As explained in Chapter 12, such is not the case. If all of the assumptions of a model are said to be 'true' with a probability of 0.5, any logically valid conclusion will usually carry a probability much below 0.5. For this reason, Haavelmo advocated that econometricians should give up on the hope that they could begin by building probabilistic algebraic models to estimate the values of the coefficients of the corresponding exact model and then substitute the estimated values into the exact (algebraic) model to finish deducing (by means of *modus ponens*) various propositions about the economy. Instead, he said that one needs to enter the world of probabilistic models and never leave. While I agree with his warning concerning the misuse of logic, I do not think the recommendation to remain within the world of probabilistic models avoids the unrealism of probability-based explanations.

Unrealistic mathematical objects

Some non-probabilistic models are also open to question when it comes to the question of realism. Here I wish to discuss two mathematical objects that are problematic even though few economists seem aware of this. One is the ubiquitous Lagrange multiplier and the other is the Keynesian marginal propensity to consume. I will discuss the marginal propensity to consume only because it is an obvious example although it is not the only example.

To begin, let me clearly define what I mean by the Lagrange multiplier. Consider the problem of maximizing utility given prices, budget (*B*) and a given utility function, U(*X, Y*) – that is, a standard problem of constrained maximization. Supposedly, the problem here is that the consumer needs to juggle two different evaluations as was implicit in the discussion of Figure 3.2. On the one hand, a consumer must evaluate choices in terms of his or her utility implications – that is, the utility value which is indicated by the given utility function, U(*X, Y*). On the other hand, he or she must evaluate the cost implications of differing choices – that is, comparing the total cost, $P_x X + P_y Y$ with the available budget, *B*. Clever mathematicians will point out that one can deal with these two different evaluations simultaneously by creating a Lagrange multiplier. Specifically, the two separate evaluations can be combined into a variable V that represents the value of a single function to be maximized, V(*X, Y*) as follows:

$$V = V(X, Y) = U(X, Y) + \lambda(B - P_x X - P_y Y)$$

Note that this requires the introduction of a new variable, the Lagrange multiplier λ. The role of this variable is solely to translate differing dimensions of the two evaluations. The function U(*X, Y*) is measured in units of utility, so-called 'utils'. The budget and the expenditures are both measured in monetary units. Thus the primary role of the λ is to translate monetary units into utils so that we are not adding apples and oranges. The point here is that the λ is an artifact of the mathematics of creating the combined function and nothing more.

Unfortunately, many model builders lose sight of the artificiality of the Lagrange multiplier. Instead they wish to interpret the λ as the 'marginal utility of money'. This is amazing since money is not an argument in the utility function, U(*X, Y*). Only consumable goods *X* and *Y* are. Is this merely a matter of approximation? It is not obvious how it could be. Either *B* is an argument in the utility function or it is not. This is clearly not a matter of approximation.

Let us turn to a more elementary issue. Consider a simple-minded Keynesian consumption function, $C = \alpha + \beta Y$. It is commonplace to call β the marginal propensity to consume as if it is a natural parameter characterizing the real world of consumers. Is this an object in the real world? Or, is this merely an artifact of the assumption that consumption *C* is a *linear* function of income *Y*? From a realist's perspective, it does not necessarily correspond to anything in the real world. Consider what we would face had we assumed a quadratic rather than a linear function, namely, had we assumed that $C = \alpha + \beta Y + \gamma Y^2$. Now there is no single parameter representing the 'marginal propensity to consume'. Instead, the marginal propensity to consume is $\beta + 2\gamma Y$ and thus not a natural constant as implied by the notion of the textbook's marginal propensity to consume. Again, the difference between $\beta + 2\gamma Y$ and β is not a matter of approximation.

Reading real-world significance into artifacts of arbitrary mathematical assumptions is not uncommon. Nevertheless, representable realism demands that the parameters of models should represent autonomous real world, phenomena. That is, the phenomena come first and the model second, not the other way around. Of course, one could be claiming that there is a constant real world marginal propensity to consume, but just how would one test for this? For that matter, how do we even know that the other parameter, α, is a constant? Put another way; is the assumption of linearity a matter of mathematical convenience or an empirical assertion about the nature of the real world? One suspects that it is the former – or worse, merely an Instrumentalist tool.

Concluding lessons

As I mentioned earlier, realism was never seen as a problem for the followers of Popper's view of methodology. But, in the 1980s one could find historians of economic thought exhorting us to 'put more realism in our models'. The philosopher Ian Hacking was often called upon as an authority to support this exhortation. Given Popper's long-standing advocacy of critical realism, such exhortation was shocking. For one reason, it made realism a commodity that one could simply pour into our models. For another, it seemed to be saying we are all dummies incapable of seeing that the solution to all of our problems is simply to use more realism. More important, it seems that what we really needed was to kowtow to someone's favorite philosopher. Either way many followers of Popper found such exhortations to be offensive. Nevertheless, realism is important, as I have explained in this chapter.

Realism, however, directly conflicts with every form of Conventionalist methodology that is advocated today. Those methodologists who are currently advocating some form of philosophical realism need to examine why they are doing so. Is it because realism is seen to be a useful avenue to criticize mainstream economics? Perhaps it is, but one must be careful to not advocate that mainstream economics needs more realism while simultaneously arguing for alternative methodological principles which are provided only by some form of Conventionalism or Instrumentalism.

Epilogue

Problem-oriented methodology: Towards a Popperian 'small-m' methodology of economics

> To abandon neoclassical theory is to abandon economics as a science.
> Douglass C. North [1978, p. 974]

> Do not presume, one of the thieves was damned; do not despair, one of the thieves was saved.
> St Augustine

When the first edition of this book was published in 1982, the economic methodology literature was fairly thin. There were a few collections of methodology essays [e.g., Krupp 1966; Machlup 1963; 1978]; there was a slim 1978 volume by Stanley Wong that discussed the methodology of Samuelson's revealed preference analysis. Wong's book is significant for being the first methodology book employing an openly Popperian approach. Specifically, Wong reconstructed the history of revealed preference analysis by seeing it as a progression of differing problems that Samuelson endeavored to solve. Then there followed a 1979 textbook on economic methodology by Ian Stewart which still is used today by many undergraduate teachers but it has never been considered a major contribution to the sub-discipline of economic methodology. The year 1980 brought forth two books. The most prominent was Mark Blaug's very successful book that was a spin-off of his successful history of thought textbook. The other was Homa Katouzian's book on methodology with special emphasis on ideology. Even though Katouzian explicitly dealt with Popper's theory of science without confusing it with the views of Lakatos, the book did not get much of a following. Perhaps it was because its sympathetic views of Marxian economics were viewed as out-of-date or because its criticisms of neoclassical economics failed to satisfy neoclassical economists.

In 1982 Bruce Caldwell published his very successful history of economic methodology. In that book he promoted a view of methodology that he called 'methodological pluralism'. Interestingly, methodological pluralism seems to constitute a view of methodology that is compatible with what I was arguing at the end of my first edition. In this chapter I wish to critically examine this supposed compatibility as well as some other views that are neither compatible with what I argued nor with Caldwell's 'pluralism'. Before doing this, I will begin by revisiting the concluding chapter of the first edition. Since that chapter was written in 1981, I have taken the opportunity here to make some editorial changes that correct a couple errors and to bring some references up to date with what has been argued so far in this second edition.

The view from my 1981 Popperian perspective

Despite frequent comments by methodologists over the last two decades that Popper's theory of science is a guiding light for economists, the fact is that neoclassical economics is still founded on a methodology consisting of Conventionalism mixed with bits of overt Instrumentalism and inadvertent Inductivism. So far, with the exception of Wong's 1978 book and the first edition of this book, Popper's contribution has been limited to only an improvement in the methodological jargon. Where Popper sees science as an enterprise built upon systematic criticism, our profession's reliance on Conventionalism to deal with the Problem of Induction has always put a high value on agreement, that is, on having our views accepted by our colleagues. Given that there is no formal inductive logic, everyone seems to think that a theory can be considered successful only if it has been included somewhere in the accepted view of economics.

The common presumption that there should be one accepted view is immediately open to question. Yet it is a presumption that is at the core of virtually every methodological dispute. The traditional view is that in order to discover the true nature of the economy we must first have the one correct method for analyzing the economy. As the tradition goes, famous physicists such as Newton or Einstein were successful only because they used the correct 'scientific method'. The companion tradition says that anyone who is not successful must be using an 'unscientific method'.

These traditional views are so well entrenched that it may be difficult for me to convince any reader that there may be something wrong here. Nevertheless, that was the task I set out to do in the last chapter of the first edition. I argued that the traditional view is misleading on two counts. First, it presumes there is only one correct method for all of science; and second, it reflects an even more fundamental item on the hidden agenda of every science that would require 'authoritative support' for anyone's explanation of anything of scientific interest.

Regardless of the wisdom or foolishness of anyone's concern for whether or not economics is a science, there is an overriding concern that whatever the outcome of an examination of our methods of analysis, we should at least agree on some general principles of analysis. The reason is simple. Economics is not a one-person affair these days. Improvements in our understanding of the workings of an economy depend on the combined efforts of many individuals. But we must be careful here. No matter how necessary common agreements may be, there are still some dangers of putting too much emphasis on them. (Remember how Hans Christian Andersen demonstrated those dangers in his story of 'The Emperor's New Clothes' in which the common, agreed upon view was definitely wrong.)

The primary reason for putting too much emphasis on common agreement is the frequent plea that the economic problems of society need urgent solutions. Sympathy with this urgency puts the academic economist in an awkward position. On the one hand, if we all could agree on general principles, less time would be wasted in arguing about fundamentals and more time would be available for finding good solutions to our pressing problems. On the other hand, good solutions may require new principles better suited to contemporary conditions. In effect, we always face a choice between immediate returns, which may be limited by the current understanding, and long-term benefits that might follow from a new or improved understanding. The choice is never easy – but I think we still must not presume the existence of universally acceptable criteria.

The traditional view of methods

Is there a method of analysis somewhere which, if we always used it, would ensure that we would never make a mistake? Indeed, it would be nice should there ever be such a method, but unfortunately there is not. We need not despair, though. Popper – and Socrates long before – told us that we learn by discovering our mistakes; all we can hope is that our mistakes do not cause too much damage. As I discussed in the first edition and again in this second edition, there was a time when many people thought there was a foolproof and objective method by which individuals could avoid mistakes by being extremely careful in the collection of 'facts' and, above all, by not passionately 'jumping to conclusions' before all the facts were collected.

Today, being a scientist is not such a personal matter. Rather, it is a matter of being part of a scientific community. Membership in a scientific community is governed by two factors: one's credentials and the acceptance of one's methods. The appropriate credentials are rather obvious – one needs a graduate degree or two. But one's education is not enough unless it involves being trained in the use of the accepted methods. Just what are the appropriate credentials or the accepted methods is not always obvious, since they can vary from one generation to the next or from one discipline to the next.

In many cases it is not easy to tell whether the latest accepted methods are not just the latest fad – but I will now leave this critical note aside. It is important to recognize that what may be considered '*the* scientific method' today may tomorrow be considered very inadequate and thus may be replaced by another 'accepted' method. Some scientists would consider the method supposedly followed in Newton's time rather silly or naive today. Yet no one is willing to dismiss Newton's theories merely because his methods may be a bit suspect today. In retrospect, it would seem that the significance of one's theories may be judged separately from the acceptability of one's methods.

Notwithstanding this historical perspective, every scientific community operates day to day as if there were one and only one acceptable method of analysis. It is this fact that we must face. If you want to play an immediate role in the development of modern economics, you must learn how to use the currently accepted method. Paradoxically, even attempts to change the accepted method must proceed according to the currently accepted method.

Authoritarianism and the hidden agenda of science

Apart from the obvious paradox, the problem of pulling oneself up by one's bootstraps that may trouble anyone who wishes to change the currently accepted method of analysis, there are other problems that should concern us. Although it is difficult for educated people to admit, the reliance on credentials and accepted methods as a means of discriminating significant from insignificant theories carries with it a more serious problem. It is the problem of inadvertently advocating authoritarianism.

The primary item on the hidden agenda (i.e., dealing with the Problem of Induction) is the view that if anyone wishes to be 'scientific', he or she must imitate the methods of physics or some other 'hard' science. It is as if physicists had a monopoly in clear thinking. Nevertheless, one must be careful to avoid overreacting. Economics and most of the natural sciences have many things in common. Logic, mathematics and statistics are pretty much the same regardless of where they are used. And many of the apparent differences turn out, upon close examination, to be merely terminological, reflecting only differences in professional jargon. But there is no reason why physics methodology should carry any authority in economics analysis.

The view that there is one and only one acceptable method of analysis implies that a theory created according to the accepted method has some authority over other possible theories. Despite our years of education, which were supposedly directed at teaching us to think for ourselves, we are supposed to surrender our judgment to the authority of the accepted scientific method or the current scientific community. It is unlikely that I could convince everyone that there is no authority implied by anyone's theory being deemed scientific. This is because I will be asked to specify the authority upon which I have based such a claim! The best one can hope for is that everyone will become aware of the hidden agenda involved in any enterprise. It is still pointless to try to solve the problem of authoritarianism in a book such as this on methodology. Instead, it should be enough just to call attention to its role in the hidden agenda peculiar to methodology discussions in economics.

Methodological agreement

Although there is considerable personal recognition given to individuals in science (for example, Nobel prizes), most of the everyday business of doing economic analysis relies on the cooperation and combined efforts of many people. The publication of articles and books would not be possible without some common intellectual framework, paradigm, or research program. All introductory textbooks are written to introduce students to that which is common to all members of the given scientific community. But apart from giving textbook writers a job, a common agreement is necessary for the coordination of a large community's research efforts. Those familiar with the current research program will know which problems are on the agenda, and most important, which research methods are considered acceptable.

The need for agreement

The necessity of commonly agreed upon research principles is most evident when the scientific community faces problems needing urgent solutions. Many of the current research tools in economics were developed during the urgencies of World War II. Of course, the development of the tools was facilitated by large government grants. But what the grants did was to focus the research and to force a minimum amount of agreement on principles. When there is an agreement over research principles and problems, it is possible for everyone to avoid endless arguments over which problems need solving and which tools should be used. Thus one expects research to be more productive when there is widespread agreement and very little disagreement. But such expectations can be misleading.

The dangers of forced agreement

Very often an argument in favor of the urgency of a problem may be only a disguised attempt to deflect a potential argument over basic principles. For obvious reasons, once one has spent many years of toil obtaining the necessary training in currently accepted research principles, one is not going to welcome a change to new and different techniques. This is very often the reason why methodology itself is not accorded priority on the research agenda, as it tends to focus criticism on currently accepted research principles.

One does not usually have to argue for the urgency of a problem when it is really urgent. Thus it is usually easy to spot such false arguments. Nevertheless, the dangers or costs of misrepresenting the urgency of a problem can be far-reaching. To the extent that any science progresses in Socratic learning terms, by improving its fundamental principles and theories, any diversion of research from fundamental theoretical problems in favor of short-term, immediate, practical problems may lead to extensive long-term costs.

Just as it is a mistake to think that there is one and only one scientific method for all problems and for all time, it is a mistake to think our understanding of the economy today will be adequate for everything in the future. It is thus in the scientific community's interest to allocate some research efforts or funds to the critical study of basic research methods.

The false choice problem

The primary source of disputes over criteria such as simplicity, generality or falsifiability is the Conventionalist's choice problem itself. It is a false problem. That is to say, nothing much is accomplished by solving that problem. I realize that very many philosophers think it is an important problem, but I argued to the contrary. Specifically, as I argued in the first edition, when it comes to problems that require a choice between theories, those problems are usually the problems that involve Instrumentalism. But of course, this may seem to blunt a judgment so let me again take things one step at a time. Disputes over the choice of the best methodology (e.g., between Inductivism, Conventionalism, Pragmatism or Instrumentalism) presuppose that there is one correct, all-purpose methodology. The presumption is wrong. The best methodology for today depends on the problems that concern us today. Different problems sometimes require different methods. This leads to a similar problem concerning choice criteria. There need not be an all-purpose criterion.

Is there an all-purpose criterion?

There need not be one all-purpose methodology in the usual authoritarian sense – instead, there are many different methodologies, each of which contains prescriptive or proscriptive criteria that are appropriate only for specific sets of problems. Every given methodology has its limitations and may not be appropriate for other problems.

Conventionalism is designed to deal with the shortcomings of our not having a direct solution to the Problem of Induction. Specifically, versions of Conventionalism can be used to provide a philosophical perspective when writing textbooks or when writing about the history of a given science. For example, Paul Samuelson uses his form of Conventionalism to explain the history of Demand Theory. From his perspective, we can see how Demand Theory has changed over time, each change representing an improvement in generality ([1938, p. 61], see the quotation on page 20). From his perspective, the history of Demand Theory has culminated in the 'generalized law of demand' [Hicks 1959, p. 139], which is a mathematical relationship between the slope of the demand curve and the nature of consumers' preferences (for Samuelson [1953, p. 2] it is called the 'Fundamental Theorem' and his *Foundations* [1947/65, p. 111] refers to the 'general demand functions'). According to this version of Conventionalism, then, the ultimate criterion for choosing among competitors is generality.

Judging by the current form of published articles in most leading journals, many economists agree with the mathematics-oriented Conventionalism along the lines I discussed in Chapter 12 of this edition – others see the mathematics orientation of modern economic theory as merely the source of useful instruments. The prescribed methodological objective of these writers is to increase the generality of economic analysis or the generality of the scope of the produced instruments. Formal mathematics is recognized as the means of providing the most general form of any given theory or instrument. Surely there are some limitations to formal mathematical analysis? Open any leading economics journal and you will find rather complicated arguments concerning such questions as the analytic tractability of a given instrument, its logical coherence, its success at providing a means of equilibrium selection, etc. It is all too easy to argue that little of the content of such journals has any direct relevance to practical questions of policy.

Few policy-oriented followers of the Instrumentalism of Friedman's 1953 essay would find anything useful in the leading analytical theory journals. Most of modern economic theory is so general that it is virtually impossible to apply it to practical situations. For example, the 'Generalized Law of Demand' basically says almost anything is possible. The old-fashioned 'Law of Demand' [Marshall 1920/49, p. 84] said that only downward-sloping demand curves were possible. This is not a trivial matter for those economists interested in making policy judgments based on a calculation of consumer surplus. Such a calculation requires a downward-sloping demand curve.

Generalized economic models have so many variables that it would take forever to collect all the information just to apply them to simple cases. For a very elementary example, consider $Q = a + bP$, the typical textbook's first-degree (i.e., linear) demand function – between a single good's price (P) and the quantity demanded (Q) – has only two parameters, its slope (b) and its intercept (a). Just raising its generality to $Q = a + bP + cP^2$ by saying it is a second-degree (i.e., quadratic) demand function between the same two variables adds another parameter (c) and thus increasing the degree increases the number of extra parameters that will have to be measured.

The linear model is very special and very simple. The non-linear model allows for the linear model as a special case (e.g., when $c = 0$) but it also allows for many other cases (i.e., when c is negative and when c is positive). In this sense the non-linear model is more general. But we can see why general models can easily get out of hand. We can allow for more and more types of cases but only by introducing more and more parameters.

These considerations show both sides. We can see why Instrumentalism puts a premium on simplicity rather than generality. And we can see why Conventionalism finds generality superior to simplicity. From the Conventionalist standpoint, increased generality allows for a larger filing cabinet; and the bigger the filing cabinet, the 'better' the theory. For Instrumentalism, the benefits of increased generality may not always justify the extra costs.

Is there an all-purpose methodology?

These considerations also show us why Conventionalism and Instrumentalism can be at such odds whenever anyone thinks there is one and only one correct methodology. Except for very special occasions, surely both views cannot simultaneously be correct. Moreover, they do not seem to address the same problems. On the one hand, Instrumentalism's desire for simplicity is appropriate whenever we are faced with immediate, short-run, practical problems which preclude measuring a large number of parameters. On the other hand, short-run practical success may not be very durable because parameters have a tendency to change quite often. For longer-run problems, perhaps Conventionalism's generality is more appropriate.

The fundamental choice problem

Perhaps economists will persist in limiting methodological considerations to either Instrumentalism or Conventionalism (or maybe something in between such as fideistic Pragmatism), but once one accepts that these competing methodologies have their respective places, one has reached the position where it seems that most methodological disputes in economics are rather empty on their own terms. If there is a dispute between adherents of Conventionalism (such as Paul Samuelson or Gerard Debreu and their followers) and adherents of Instrumentalism (such as Milton Friedman or Robert Lucas and their followers), it is only about specifying what are the most important problems facing economists today. (But for some mathematics-oriented game theorists such as Robert Aumann, there is no dispute since today they advocate both positions – see Chapter 4.)

Objectives come first

Before economists argue about what is the 'best' methodology (and note that the use of the term 'best' may have already predisposed the argument in favor of Conventionalism), they should reach some agreement about their objectives. If they do not, then their arguments will likely be at cross-purposes. But as I have just warned, one must be careful to avoid posing the choice problem so that only one method can win the debate.

Very often when economists think their methodology is the final word on the one true, all-purpose methodology they tend to search only for those problems that can be solved by their methods. Such an approach is not necessarily wrong, but from the perspective of the study of methodology it can be very misleading. When reading books or articles written by Conventionalist methodologists, one will find that the problems of 'scientific' interest are those problems for which one is supposed to choose the 'best' alternative theory (or model) from a list of competitors. Conversely, when reading Instrumentalist views of methodology, one will find that the truly scientific problems are those dealing with immediate practical problems and thus one should choose the most 'useful' method for dealing with those problems. Of course, the method that is most 'useful' is Instrumentalism itself. Thus one can see that in these cases, objectives do not come first. For these writers there is one fundamental choice problem in methodology: the arbitrary prior choice of one's all-purpose methodology.

Problem-dependent methodology

Once one accepts my argument here that there is no universal, all-purpose methodology, then most discussions of methodology become uninteresting because they are too biased. The celebrated dispute between Friedman and Samuelson is a case in point. Without some way of independently determining what the really interesting problems are, there will never be a way to resolve the dispute – perhaps this is why we see few methodological disputes openly argued today! Instead of an all-purpose methodology there are really many possible methodologies. Each one is appropriate for a limited list of problems. If at present practical problems are most interesting, then Instrumentalism is appropriate. If catalogue choice problems are the most pressing, then perhaps Conventionalism is the appropriate methodology. If learning for learning's sake is an important consideration, then perhaps Popper's methodology, which emphasizes problems, criticism and, above all, disagreement, is a more appropriate perspective.

The role of methodology

In the first edition of this book I was satisfied to finish by noting that throughout the book, I was stressing a significant role for both the Popper-Socrates theory of learning and the related problem-dependent methodology of this chapter in any neoclassical program for explaining individual decision-making. I also welcomed critics who might argue that in stressing one view of methodology I was in effect violating my own caution to avoid seeking an all-purpose methodology. I argued that I was not, for the following reasons: (1) I have *not* argued that a problem-dependent methodology is the 'best' methodology, but rather, that it is the only available methodology which is consistent with a realistic short-run neoclassical theory – that is, with one in which individuals are assumed to be making decisions in real time; (2) conversely, not much will be gained by considering the Popper-Hayek program of explanation if one does not wish to consider such research topics as real-time dynamic neoclassical models, 'expectational errors' or disequilibrium models of macroeconomics. But in the intervening two decades since the publication of the first edition, other views have been expressed, which might be seen as more informative – to which I now turn.

The view of methodology after 1981

> The most significant contribution of the growth of knowledge philosophers was the demonstration that the quest for a single, universal, prescriptive scientific methodology is quixotic.
>
> Bruce Caldwell [1982/94, p. 244]

> If economic methodologists now agree that positivism can no longer provide the philosophical underpinnings for our understanding of economics as a science, it is also at this point that the general consensus ends. No single vision of what should replace positivism has emerged in philosophy, and similarly a diversity of approaches to methodological questions exists today in economics... Blaug believes that one methodology is better than all of its rivals, however, and that methodology is Popper's falsificationism. He is careful to acknowledge that there may be some problems in applying falsificationism in economics. Blaug nonetheless concludes that the profession would be improved if economists would make their theories more testable and if falsifications were taken more seriously...
>
> Boland [1970b and 1982] asserts that all attempts to solve the unsolvable 'problem of conventions' are fruitless. Therefore, economists who argue that any particular set of conventions (e.g., predictive adequacy plus generality, realism plus elegance) is the best are simply wasting time; they are pursuing an uninteresting question... Boland ultimately embraces a form of pluralism, arguing that it is 'folly' to search for an 'all-purpose methodology'. His position is a variant of Popper's critical rationalism. Criticizable theories should be considered not for the purpose of choosing among them but in order

to understand both the problems the theorist is attempting to solve and the alternative ways that a problem may be set up.

In *Beyond Positivism* I argue for (a rather vaguely defined) methodological pluralism.

> Bruce Caldwell [1984b, pp. 196–7 and 200]

Note ... that pluralism is a *meta-methodological* position. It offers no specific methodological advice to economists. Indeed, what economists do is taken as given by the pluralist... Pluralist methodologists do not embrace a particular tradition; their goal is the evaluation of all traditions. In a sense, pluralist methodologists attempt to practice *value-free evaluations*: Their assessments are critical, but they do not presuppose some ultimate universal grounds for criticism... Methodological pluralism makes no epistemological claims; it is not grounded in any theory of truth...

The goals of pluralism *are* modest. Methodologists are not set up as experts offering advice to economists on how to do their science. Methodologists do not try to solve the demarcation problem, or the theory choice problem, or the problem of truth. Rather, methodologists try, together with their colleagues in the history, sociology, and rhetoric of science, to enable us to reach a better understanding of the science of economics.

> Bruce Caldwell [1988, pp. 240–1 and 243]

I have elsewhere described in greater detail some suggestions for how to do methodological work, a meta-methodological program which I originally called methodological pluralism but which is probably better dubbed critical pluralism.

> Bruce Caldwell [1990, p. 65]

I have advocated *critical pluralism* on a number of occasions... There are some important differences between my approach and Popper's position. I am much more interested in developing a coherent methodological position for economics, for example, so have been less concerned with strictly epistemological matters. Critical pluralism deemphasizes demarcation and encourages novelty. It encourages new programs, looking ever forward to the day when they can be subjected to critical scrutiny.

> Bruce Caldwell [1991a, p. 27, fn. 7]

During the decade that followed the publication of the first edition of this book, methodology discussion in economics was filled with the discussion of just three topics: economic rhetoric [McCloskey 1983, 1984, 1985, 1988a, 1988b; Caldwell and Coats 1984; Backhouse 1992]; the pseudo-Popperian 'falsificationism' that was created by Lakatos and promoted by Blaug [Hands 1984, 1985a, 1985b, 1988, 1990a, 1990b; Caldwell 1984a, 1990, 1991b; Blaug 1985, 1990, 1991 and 1992] and methodological pluralism [Caldwell 1982/94, 1984b, 1985, 1986, 1988, 1989, 1990, 1991a]. The decade of the 1990s was less focused but there were some promising signs that I will discuss below.

Beating the drums for Lakatos or rhetoric

What ... is to be gained from analysing research programmes using the Lakatosian devices of heuristics, hard core and protective belt? Two answers suggest themselves. (1) ... the effect of Lakatosian methodology has been to direct economists towards detailed studies of episodes in the history of economic thought, and away from making broad, under-researched, generalizations about research programmes in economics. (2) Lakatos's concepts have provided a set of questions that can form a useful starting point in analysing historical episodes.

Roger Backhouse [1994b, p. 186]

Science is writing with intent, the intent to persuade other scientists, such as economic scientists. The study of such writing with intent has been called since the Greeks 'rhetoric'. Until the seventeenth century it was the core of education in the West and down to the present it remains, often unrecognized, the core of humanistic learning. A science like economics should be read skillfully, and if so the reading needs a rhetoric, the more explicit the better. The choice is between an implicit and naive rhetoric or an explicit and learned one, the naive rhetoric of significance tests, say, or the learned rhetoric that knows what it is arguing and why.

Donald McCloskey [1994, p. 320]

Enough was said in Chapters 13 and 14 about how Blaug has misled many of his followers about Popper's theory of science by confusing it with Lakatos' self-serving distortion of it. One can still understand why historians of economic thought [e.g., Backhouse 1994b; Weintraub 1985, 1988] might find the views of Lakatos interesting since he provided an easily accessible framework for discussions of how various research programs develop over time – such as neoclassical economics or general equilibrium theory or that attributed to John Maynard Keynes. All that I am stressing is that no matter how loudly they beat this drum, it still has nothing to do with Popper. Both Wade Hands [1993, 2001] and Bruce Caldwell [1991a] have tried to convince Blaug and his followers but to date none of them have been convinced to give it up.

McCloskey has been more successful. The idea that economists engage in rhetoric is difficult to deny. To go further and claim that economics is nothing but rhetoric is more problematic. Nevertheless, references to McCloskey's plea for the recognition of economic rhetoric are common outside of the sub-discipline of economic methodology. Where in the past one could find references to Friedman's famous 1953 methodology essay, today these references have been replaced by references to McCloskey's 1983 essay. The reason for the replacement is simple. Friedman's essay was, if nothing else, a clever means of deflecting the demands of the 1930s analytical philosophers who inspired critics of neoclassical economics to easily point out that neoclassical economics has not been verified and hence could not be considered scientific. Thus, Friedman's essay has always been popular with neoclassical economists who need some authority to explain why it is reasonable to ignore what philosopher's prescribe. McCloskey's essay is thus merely an up-to-date and sophisticated version of Friedman's essay. The target is the same, namely, the Logical Positivists of the 1930s. And if the truth is told, the promotion of economic rhetoric is merely beating a dead horse (see further the last chapter of Boland [1989]).

Methodological pluralism vs. problem-dependent methodology

we do not stick to one method or another, we do not require ourselves to start only with physics or only with psychology or social anthropology, only with empirical findings on the smallest scale, or only with grand-scale metaphysics proper. We try in all directions ... because we are ignorant and so have no preferred direction. This hypothesis opposes practically everything written in the field of methodology. Most philosophers who write on scientific method recommend one or another set of different rules; and most of them also observe – erroneously I think – that only one of the different sets of rules is properly applied...

For my part, I am a trifle biased against the extreme empiricist method, both on account of its pathological tangibilism or concretism, and on account of its finding merit in disorder; and so I think it is of extremely narrow applicability. When in a metaphysical mood I always look for guiding principles, for regulative ideas of all sorts, and when in a skeptical mood I advocate pluralism and let the better party win.

Joseph Agassi [1977, pp. 67–8]

Throughout the 1980s, Caldwell frequently promoted what he seemed to think was a *new* view of economic methodology. As he said, it is a *meta-methodology* – that is, a view that critically assesses ordinary methodological views of economics. It is predicated on the notion that there are many different views of methodology to compare and evaluate. What I have called 'problem-oriented methodology' is also predicated on the notion that there are many different views of methodology and thus one can understand why we might be talking about the same thing. But, we are not – although there is obvious over-lap.

In his 1991 advocacy of what he now calls critical pluralism, Caldwell [1991a] claims that it differs from Popper's – presumably to lay claim that something new is being offered. But, given that Caldwell's pluralism explicitly rejects or 'deemphasizes demarcation' and no longer sees a need to solve the Conventionalist 'theory choice problem', it is difficult to see how pluralism differs from Popper's theory of science. Pluralism does differ from Blaug's favored 'falsificationism' but Popper also rejected 'falsificationism'. Where a doubt might be raised – by any claim that methodological or critical pluralism is finally in line with Popper's critical rationalism – is when Caldwell claims that pluralism 'makes no epistemological claims; it is not grounded in any theory of truth'. If by this Caldwell means that he has no theory of knowledge, then it is not clear what critical pluralism is about. And if by 'not grounded in any theory of truth' he means to say that the truth status of one's theories does not matter, then it is difficult to distinguish his pluralism from Conventionalism or Instrumentalism.

The difference between my 'problem-dependent methodology' and Caldwell's 'critical pluralism' is found by considering what he meant by 'meta-methodology'. In effect, the critical pluralist puts on a judge's robe and rises up to be above the fray in order to evaluate and pass judgment – but, of course, the judgment must be 'value-free'. And, of course, one could always ask whether an evaluation at the lofty meta level requires a single universal criterion. If it does, then we are no better off than we were before critical pluralism was invoked.

My problem-dependent methodology goes in the other direction. The interesting problems are not the lofty ones that philosophers of science struggle with but the low-level problems addressed each time a theorist or model builder introduces a new assumption. For example, when evolutionary economics makes use of the assumption of imperfect knowledge (e.g., bounded rationality) in its explanation of the behavior of firms, what problem does this assumption solve?

As argued in Chapter 9, assuming imperfect knowledge allows the model builder to deal with a world where there is a variety of types of firms and thereby raising the possibility of discussing changes in the distribution of the types in an evolutionary manner. Had there been perfect knowledge, there would be no reason for the variety of types since every firm would know the best way to conduct business and all firms would have the same knowledge. The issue here is not whether the model builders are making the best assumption but whether my conjectured problem explains why the assumption of imperfect knowledge is made.

A similar low-level assumption concerning methodology was discussed when asking why mathematical economists such as Paul Samuelson were so concerned that their models and assumptions were falsifiable. As noted in Chapter 12, their concern for falsifiability or testability was not to satisfy philosophers but to avoid the problem recognized by methodology-oriented critics who complained that mathematics produces tautologies. Tautologies are not falsifiable (or even conceivably false) thus requiring falsifiability successfully solves the problem by sidestepping the complaint. Again, my conjectured problem explains both why falsifiability is such a popular methodological requirement among mathematical model builders and why Karl Popper's theory of science was never the concern of Samuelson and his followers.

These examples illustrate how 'small-m' methodology can proceed. On the one hand, it is difficult to see how it could be used to answer 'big-M' methodology questions that interest philosophers and hence it is not difficult to see why they show no interest in problem-dependent methodology. On the other hand, it is easy to see how philosophers might find Caldwell's critical pluralism to be a means of promoting some form of relativism or even rhetoric. However, Caldwell [1988] addresses this possibility and offers his counter argument. Whether he was successful at preventing this relativist interpretation of critical pluralism remains to be seen. And since Caldwell has not contributed much to the discussion of economic methodology since his 1994 article about Popper's theory of science, and since nobody else seems to be interested in promoting critical pluralism, I guess we may never know.

Pluralism vs. 'critical pluralism'

There is, today, considerable discussion of pluralism in economics but this should not be confused with Caldwell's 'critical pluralism' or with my problem-dependent methodology. Pluralism in economics is promoted by so-called heterodox economists – such as institutionalists, Marxists, post-Keynesians and self-labeled 'critical realists'. Pluralism in these cases is advocated solely to urge making room in mainstream economics for such heterodox promotions [e.g., see Salanti and Serepanti 1997; Steuer 1998].

As Caldwell stresses, his view of pluralism is at the level of meta-methodology and that it is intended to encourage many views of methodology so long as they are subjected to criticism. Non-critical meta-methodology is more common. After all, Friedman's famous 1953 methodology essay is nothing but an application of Instrumentalism as a defense of Instrumentalism. In one sense,

Friedman's essay demonstrates that at least his version of Instrumentalism passes the consistency test of a self-reference. But, of course, Friedman would never promote his form of Instrumentalism without its being consistent at the meta-methodology level where the issue of self-reference is put to test. This is merely meta-methodology as self-justification and thus it is hardly an example of critical pluralism.

The critical use of meta-methodology does not always avoid the fundamental choice problem I mentioned earlier in this chapter. For example, if methodologists were to criticize my problem-dependent methodology as not being accepted today, they would be employing Conventionalism at the meta level. That is, stressing *acceptance* as a test of anyone's view of methodology is always an exercise in Conventionalist methodology. But worse, if we were to convene a meeting of Conventionalists and took a vote on the acceptability of any view of methodology, even when the vote is unanimous there is always the possibility that they are unanimously wrong. Moreover, if acceptance were to be the only relevant criterion to critically assess a view of methodology, then Friedman's Instrumentalism will win at the sub-meta-methodology level (for examples of the practice of Instrumentalism, refer back to the discussion in Chapters 4 and 5). In any case, there is little sign of anyone eagerly adopting Caldwell's meta-methodology to engage in a critical assessment of anyone's methodology today. Too bad. We could all benefit from critical assessments but they are best when they are not just a means of promoting one's own view of methodology.

The hope of small-m methodology

Perhaps the lack of interest in critical pluralism is due to the relativist interpretation that sees critical pluralism as addressing big-M methodology questions and that big-M methodology is losing its appeal among economic methodologists. If recent efforts of Kevin Hoover [2001] and the conferences organized by Backhouse and Salanti [2001] are any indication, we may be finally on the road to addressing the problems of small-m methodology.

Conjecturing problems is, of course, a straightforward application of Popper's situational analysis. And as with all conjectures, they are always open to criticism. And unlike big-M methodology where there are only a very few problems to consider, the domain of small-m methodology is very large. In this book I have taken the opportunity to demonstrate some small-m methodological analysis – in particular, those topics that interest me involving assumptions made by model builders who see the need to address the neoclassical decision-maker's knowledge and learning methodology. Obviously, when it comes to assumptions concerning the neoclassical decision-maker's knowledge and learning there is a place for a problem-oriented methodology that can make a good use of Popper's theory of science.

Bibliography

Agassi, J. [1960] Methodological individualism, *British Journal of Sociology, 11*, 244–70

Agassi, J. [1963] *Towards an Historiography of Science, History and Theory, Beiheft 2* (The Hague: Mouton)

Agassi, J. [1965] The nature of scientific problems and their roots in metaphysics, in M. Bunge (ed.), *The Critical Approach to Science and Philosophy* (New York: Collier-Macmillan)

Agassi, J. [1966a] Sensationalism *Mind, 75*, 1–24

Agassi, J. [1966b] The mystery of the ravens: discussion, *Philosophy of Science, 33*, 395–402

Agassi, J. [1968] Science in flux: footnotes to Popper, in R. Cohen and M. Wartofsky (eds), *Boston Studies in the Philosophy of Science, 3* (New York: Humanities Press), 293–323

Agassi, J. [1969a] The novelty of Popper's philosophy of science, *International Philosophical Quarterly, 8*, 442–63

Agassi, J. [1969b] Unity and diversity in science, in R. Cohen and M. Wartofsky (eds), *Boston Studies in the Philosophy of Science, 4* (New York: Humanities Press), 463–522

Agassi, J. [1971a] The standard misinterpretation of skepticism, *Philosophical Studies, 22*, 49–50

Agassi, J. [1971b] Tautology and testability in economics, *Philosophy of Social Sciences, 1*, 49–63

Agassi, J. [1975] Institutional individualism, *British Journal of Sociology, 26*, 144–55

Agassi, J. [1977] *Towards a Rational Philosophical Anthropology* (The Hague: Martinus Nijhoff)

Agassi, J. [1985] *Technology: Philosophical and Social Aspects* (Dordrecht: Reidel)

Agassi, J. [1987] Theories of rationality, in J. Agassi and I. Jarvie (eds), *Rationality: The Critical View* (Boston: Martinus Nijhoff Publishers), 249–63

Agassi, J. [1992] False prophecy versus true quest: a modest challenge to contemporary relativists, *Philosophy of Social Science, 22*, 285–312

Agassi, J. [2002] A touch of malice, *Philosophy of the Social Sciences, 32*, 107–19

Akerlof, G. [2002] Behavioral macroeconomics and macroeconomic behavior, *American Economic Review, 92*, 411–33

Albert, H. [1979/99] The economic tradition: economics as a research program for social science, in H. Albert, *Between Social Science, Religion and Politics: Essays in Critical Rationalism* (Amsterdam: Rodopi), 91–114

Albert, M. [2001] Bayesian learning and expectations formation, in D. Corfield and J. Williamson (eds), *Foundations of Bayesianism* (Boston: Kluwer), 341–62

Alchian, A. [1950] Uncertainty, evolution and economic theory, *Journal of Political Economy, 58,* 211–21

Archibald, G. [1961] Chamberlin versus Chicago, *Review of Economic Studies, 29,* 1–28

Arrow, K. [1951/63] *Social Choice and Individual Values* (New York: John Wiley)

Arrow, K. [1959] Towards a theory of price adjustment, in M. Abramovitz (ed.), *Allocation of Economic Resources* (Stanford: Stanford Univ. Press)

Arrow, K. [1969/83] The organization of economic activity: issues pertinent to the choice of market versus nonmarket allocation, in *Collected Papers of Kenneth Arrow: General Equilibrium, volume 2* (Oxford: Blackwell), 133–55

Arrow, K. [1974] *The Limits of Organization* (New York: Norton)

Arrow, K. [1979/84] The property rights doctrine and demand revelation under incomplete information, in *Collected Papers of Kenneth Arrow: The Economics of Information, volume 4* (Oxford: Blackwell), 216–32

Arrow, K. [1986] Rationality of self and others in an economic system, *Journal of Business, 59 (supplement),* s385–99

Arrow, K. [1994] Methodological individualism and social knowledge, *American Economic Review, Proceedings, 84,* 1–9

Arrow, K. and Debreu, G. [1954] Existence of an equilibrium for a competitive economy, *Econometrica, 22,* 265–90

Aumann, R. [1985] What is game theory trying to accomplish?, in K. Arrow and S. Honkapohja (eds), *Frontiers of Economics* (Oxford: Basil Blackwell), 28–76

Aumann, R. [1987] Game theory, in *The New Palgrave: A Dictionary of Economic Theory and Doctrine,* 460–82

Aumann, R. [1995] Backward induction and common knowledge of rationality, *Games and Economic Behavior, 8,* 6–19

Aumann, R. [1996] Reply to Binmore, *Games and Economic Behavior, 17,* 138–46

Backhouse, R. [1992] The constructivist critique of economic methodology, *Methodus, 4,* 65–82

Backhouse, R. (ed.) [1994a] *New Directions in Economic Methodology* (London: Routledge)

Backhouse, R. [1994b] The Lakatosian legacy in economic methodology, in Backhouse [1994a], 173–91

Backhouse, R. and Salanti, A. (eds) [2001] *Macroeconomics and the Real World, volume 2: Keynesian Economics, Unemployment and Policy* (Oxford: Oxford Univ. Press)

Bartley, W. [1968] Theories of demarcation between science and metaphysics, in I. Lakatos and A. Musgrave (eds), *Problems in the Philosophy of Science* (Amsterdam: North Holland), 40–64

Bartley, W. [1982] The philosophy of Karl Popper: Part III, rationality, criticism, and logic, *Philosophia, 11,* 121–221

Becker, G. [1965] A theory of the allocation of time, *Economic Journal, 75,* 493–517

Bennett, R. [1981] An empirical test of some post-Keynesian income distribution theories, Ph.D. Thesis, Simon Fraser University

Bicchieri, C. [1993] *Rationality and Coordination* (Cambridge: Cambridge Univ. Press)

Binmore, K. [1995] Foreword to Weibull [1995], x–xi

Binmore, K. [1997] Rationality and backward induction, *Journal of Economic Methodology, 4,* 23–41

Blaug, M. [1968] *Economic Theory in Retrospect, 2nd edn* (Homewood: Irwin)

Blaug, M. [1975] Kuhn versus Lakatos, or paradigms versus research programmes in the history of economics, *History of Political Economy, 7*, 399–433

Blaug, M. [1978] *Economic Theory in Retrospect, 3rd edn* (Cambridge: Cambridge Univ. Press)

Blaug, M. [1980/92] *The Methodology of Economics, 2nd edn* (Cambridge: Cambridge Univ. Press)

Blaug, M. [1985] Comment on D. Hands, 'Karl Popper and economic methodology: a new look', *Economics and Philosophy, 1*, 286–8

Blaug, M. [1990] Reply to D. Wade Hands' 'Second thoughts on "Second Thoughts"': reconsidering the Lakatosian progress of *The General Theory*', *Review of Political Economy, 2*, 102–4

Blaug, M. [1991] Second thoughts on the Keynesian revolution, *History of Political Economy, 23*, 171–92

Blaug, M. [1992] Comment on D.W. Hands' 'Falsification, situational analysis, and scientific programmes: the Popperian tradition in economic methodology', in de Marchi [1992] 55–9

Blaug, M. [1994] Why I am not a constructivist: confessions of an unrepentant Popperian, in Backhouse [1994a], 109–36

Blaug, M. [1997] *Economic Theory in Retrospect, 5th edn* (Cambridge: Cambridge Univ. Press)

Blaug, M. and de Marchi, N. (eds) [1991] *Appraising Modern Economics: Studies in the Methodology of Scientific Research Programmes* (Aldershot, England: Edward Elgar)

Böhm-Bawerk, E. [1889] *Positive Theory of Capital*, trans. W. Smart (New York: Stechert)

Boland, L. [1966] On the methodology of economic model building, Ph.D. thesis, University of Illinois, Urbana, Ill.

Boland, L. [1968] The identification problem and the validity of economic models, *South African Journal of Economics, 36*, 236–40

Boland, L. [1969] Economic understanding and understanding economics, *South African Journal of Economics, 37*, 144–60

Boland, L. [1970a] Axiomatic analysis and economic understanding, *Australian Economic Papers, 9*, 62–75

Boland, L. [1970b] Conventionalism and economic theory, *Philosophy of Science, 37*, 239–48

Boland, L. [1974] Lexicographic orderings, multiple criteria, and 'ad hocery', *Australian Economic Papers, 13*, 152–7

Boland, L. [1975] Uninformative economic models, *Atlantic Economic Journal, 3*, 27–32

Boland, L. [1977a] Testability in economic science, *South African Journal of Economics, 45*, 93–105

Boland, L. [1977b] Testability, time and equilibrium stability, *Atlantic Economic Journal, 5*, 39–47

Boland, L. [1977c] Model specifications and stochasticism in economic methodology, *South African Journal of Economics, 45*, 182–9

Boland, L. [1978] Time in economics vs. economics in time: the 'Hayek Problem', *Canadian Journal of Economics, 11*, 240–62

Boland, L. [1979a] A critique of Friedman's critics, *Journal of Economic Literature, 17*, 503–22

Boland, L. [1979b] Knowledge and the role of institutions in economic theory, *Journal of Economic Issues, 8*, 957–72

Boland, L. [1980] Friedman's methodology vs. conventional empiricism: a reply to Rotwein, *Journal of Economic Literature, 18*, 1555–7

Boland, L. [1981a] Satisficing in methodology: a reply to Rendigs Fels, *Journal of Economic Literature, 19*, 84–6

Boland, L. [1981b] On the futility of criticizing the neoclassical maximization hypothesis, *American Economic Review, 71*, 1031–6

Boland, L. [1982] *The Foundations of Economic Method* (London: Geo. Allen & Unwin)

Boland, L. [1986a] *Methodology for a New Microeconomics* (Boston: Allen & Unwin)

Boland, L. [1986b] Methodology and the individual decision-maker, in I. Kirzner (ed.), *Subjectivism, Intelligibility and Economic Understanding* (New York: New York Univ. Press), 30–8

Boland, L. [1988] Individualist economics without psychology, in P. Earl (ed.), *Psychological Economics: Development, Tensions, Prospects* (Boston: Kluwer), 163–8

Boland, L. [1989] *The Methodology of Economic Model Building: Methodology after Samuelson* (London: Routledge)

Boland, L. [1990] The methodology of Marshall's 'Principle of Continuity', *Economie Appliquée, 43*, 145-59

Boland, L. [1992a] *The Principles of Economics: Some Lies My Teachers Told Me* (London: Routledge)

Boland, L. [1992b] Understanding the Popperian legacy in economics, *Research in the History of Economic Thought and Methodology, 9*, 273–84

Boland, L. [1995] Style vs. substance in economic methodology, in R. Cohen and N. Laor (eds) *Critical Rationalism The Social Sciences and the Humanities, Boston Studies in the Philosophy of Science, 162* (Boston: Kluwer), 115–28

Boland, L. [1997] *Critical Economic Methodology: A Personal Odyssey* (London: Routledge)

Boland, L. [2000] On methodology of 'the economics of ...' literature, *Research in the History of Economic Thought and Methodology, 18-A*, 129–35

Boland, L. [2001] Towards a useful methodology discipline, *Journal of Economic Methodology, 8*, 3–10

Boland, L. and Newman, G. [1979] On the role of knowledge in economic theory, *Australian Economic Papers, 18*, 71–80

Caldwell, B. [1980] Critique of Friedman's methodological instrumentalism, *Southern Economic Journal, 47*, 366–74

Caldwell, B. [1980] Positivist philosophy of science and the methodology of economics, *Journal of Economic Issues, 14*, 53–76

Caldwell, B. [1982/94] *Beyond Positivism* (London: Routledge)

Caldwell, B. [1984a] Some problems with falsificationism in economics, *Philosophy of Social Science, 14*, 489–95

Caldwell, B. [1984b] Economic methodology in a postpositivist era, *Research in the History of Economic Thought and Methodology, 2*, 195–205

Caldwell, B. [1985] Some reflections on *Beyond Positivism, Journal of Economic Issues, 19*, 187–94

Caldwell, B. [1986] Towards a broader conception of criticism, *History of Political Economy, 18*, 675–81

Caldwell, B. [1988] The case for pluralism, in de Marchi [1988], 231–44

Caldwell, B. [1989] The trend of methodological thinking, *Ricerche Economiche, 18*, 8–20

Caldwell, B. [1990] Does methodology matter? How should it be practiced? *Finnish Economic Papers, 3*, 64–71

Caldwell, B. [1991a] Clarifying Popper, *Journal of Economic Literature, 29*, 1–33

Caldwell, B. [1991b] The methodology of scientific research programmes in economics: criticisms and conjectures, in G. Shaw (ed.), *Essays in Honour of Mark Blaug*, (Aldershot: Edward Elgar), 95–107

Caldwell, B. [1994] Two proposals for the recovery of economic practice, in Backhouse [1994a], 137–53

Caldwell, B. and Coats, A.W. [1984] The rhetoric of economists: a comment on McCloskey, *Journal of Economic Literature, 22*, 575–8

Camerer, C. [1997] Progress in behavioral game theory, *Journal of Economic Perspectives, 11*, 167–88

Chamberlin, E. [1934] *The Theory of Monopolistic Competition* (Cambridge, Mass.: Harvard Univ. Press)

Chiang, A. [1984] *Fundamental Methods of Mathematical Economics, 3rd edn* (New York: McGraw-Hill)

Chipman, J., Hurwicz, L., Richter, M. and Sonnenschein, H. [1971] *Preferences, Utility and Demand* (New York: Harcourt Brace)

Clower, R. [1959] Some theory of an ignorant monopolist, *Economic Journal, 69*, 705–16

Clower, R. [1965] The Keynesian counterrevolution: a theoretical appraisal, in F. Hahn and F. Brechling (eds), *The Theory of Interest Rates* (London: Macmillan), 103–25

Clower, R. and Leijonhufvud, A. [1973] Say's principle, what it means and doesn't mean, *Intermountain Economic Review, 4*, 1–16

Coase, R. [1937] The nature of the firm, *Economica, 4 (NS)*, 386–405

Coase, R. [1960] Problem of social costs, *Journal of Law and Economics, 3*, 1–44

Coddington, A. [1979] Friedman's contribution to methodological controversy, *British Review of Economic Issues*, 1–13

Dantzig, G. [1949/51] Maximization of a linear function of variables subject to linear inequalities, in Koopmans [1951], 339–47

Dantzig, G. [1951] A proof of the equivalence of the programming problem and the game problem, in Koopmans [1951], 330–5

Davidson, P. [1972] *Money and the Real World* (New York: Wiley)

Davidson, P. [1981] Post Keynesian economics: solving the crisis in economic theory, in D. Bell and I. Kristol (eds), *The Crisis in Economic Theory* (New York: Basic Books), 151–73

Davidson, P. [1991] Is probability theory relevant for uncertainty?: a post Keynesian perspective, *Journal of Economic Perspectives, 5*, 129–43

Debreu, G. [1959] *Theory of Value* (New York: Wiley)

Debreu, G. [1991] The mathematization of economic theory, *American Economic Review, 81*, 1–7

DeVany, A. [1976] Uncertainty, waiting time and capacity utilization: a stochastic theory of product quality, *Journal of Political Economy, 84*, 523–41

Dorfman, R., Samuelson, P. and Solow, R. [1958] *Linear Programming and Economic Analysis* (New York: McGraw-Hill)

Duhem, P. [1906/62] *The Aim and Structure of Physical Theory* (New York: Atheneum)

Earl, P. (ed.) [1988] *Psychological Economics: Development, Tensions, Prospects* (Boston: Kluwer)

Eddington, A. [1928] *The Nature of the Physical World* (Cambridge: Cambridge Univ. Press)

Einstein, A. [1936/50] Physics and reality, *Out of My Later Years* (New York: Wisdom Library), 58–94

Einstein, A. and Infeld, L. [1938/61] *The Evolution of Physics: The Growth of Ideas from Early Concepts to Relativity and Quanta* (New York: Simon & Schuster)

Fama, E. [1970] Efficient capital markets: a review of theory and empirical work, *Journal of Finance, 25*, 383–417

Friedman, M. [1953] Methodology of positive economics, in *Essays in Positive Economics* (Chicago: Univ. of Chicago Press), 3–43

Friedman, M. [1978] Correspondence dated 14 April

Frisch, R. [1926/71] On a problem of pure economics, in Chipman, *et al.* [1971], 386–423

Frisch, R. [1936] On a notion of equilibrium and disequilibrium, *Review of Economic Studies, 3*, 100–5

Gellner, E. [1959/68] *Words and Things* (Harmondsworth, Middlesex: Penguin Books)

Georgescu-Roegen, N. [1971] *The Entropy Law and the Economic Process* (Cambridge, Mass.: Harvard Univ. Press)

Gordon, D. and Hynes, A. [1970] On the theory of price dynamics, in E. Phelps, *et al.* [1970], 369–93

Gordon, S. [1991] *The History and Philosophy of Social Science* (London: Routledge)

Haavelmo, T. [1944] Probability approach to econometrics, *Econometrica, 12, Supplement*, 1–115

Hahn, F. [1973] *On the Notion of Equilibrium in Economics* (Cambridge: Cambridge Univ. Press)

Hahn, F. [1994] An intellectual retrospect, *Banca Nazionale Del Lavoro Quarterly Review, 48*, 245–58

Hammes, D. [1985] Prices, information and explanation in neoclassical economic theory, Ph.D. Thesis, Simon Fraser University

Hammes, D. and Boland, L. [1984] Neoclassical vs. classical economic models, *Philosophy of the Social Sciences, 14*, 107–113

Hammond, J.D. [1993] An interview with Milton Friedman on methodology, in B. Caldwell (ed.), *The Philosophy and Methodology of Economics, volume 1* (Aldershot: Edward Elgar), 216–38

Hands, D.W. [1979] The methodology of economic research programmes (review of Latsis, *Method and Appraisal in Economics*), *Philosophy of the Social Sciences, 9*, 293–303

Hands, D.W. [1984a] Blaug's economic methodology, *Philosophy of the Social Sciences, 14*, 115–25

Hands, D.W. [1984b] The role of crucial counterexamples in the growth of economic knowledge: two case studies in the recent history of economic thought, *History of Political Economy, 16*, 59–67

Hands, D.W. [1985a] Second thoughts on Lakatos, *History of Political Economy, 17*, 1–16

Hands, D.W. [1985b] Karl Popper and economic methodology, *Economics and Philosophy, 1*, 83–99

Hands, D.W. [1988] Ad hocness in economics and the Popperian tradition, in de Marchi [1988], 121–37

Hands, D. W. [1990a] Second thoughts on 'Second Thoughts': reconsidering the Lakatosian progress of *The General Theory, Review of Political Economy, 2*, 69–81

Hands, D.W. [1990b] Thirteen theses on progress in economic methodology, *Finnish Economic Papers, 3*, 72–6

Hands, D.W. [1992a] Falsification, situational analysis, and scientific research programs: the Popperian tradition in economic methodology, in de Marchi [1992], 19–53

Hands, D.W. [1992b] Reply, in de Marchi [1992], 61–3

Hands, D.W. [1993] *Testing, Rationality, and Progress: Essays on the Popperian Tradition in Economic Methodology* (Lanham: Rowman & Littlefield)

Hands, D.W. [1996] Karl Popper on the myth of the framework: lukewarm Popperians +1, unrepentant Popperians –1 (review of Popper [1994]), *Journal of Economic Methodology, 3*, 317–22

Hands, D.W. [2001] *Reflection without Rules: Economic Methodology and Contemporary Science Theory*, (Cambridge: Cambridge Univ. Press)

Hanson, N. [1965] *Patterns of Discovery* (Cambridge: Cambridge Univ. Press)

Hargreaves Heap, S. and Varoufakis, Y. [1995] *Game Theory: A Critical Introduction* (London: Routledge)

Harsanyi, J. [1967-68] Games with incomplete information played by Bayesian players, *Management Science, 14*, 159–82, 320–34, 486–502

Hattiangadi, J.N. [1978] Structure of problems, *Philosophy of the Social Sciences, 8*, 345–65

Hausman, D. [1988] An appraisal of Popperian methodology, in de Marchi [1988], 65–85

Hausman, D. [1992] *The Inexact and Separate Science of Economics* (New York: Cambridge Univ. Press)

Hayek, F. [1933/39] Price expectations, monetary disturbances and malinvestments, in *Profits, Interest and Investments* (London: Routledge)

Hayek, F. [1937/48] Economics and knowledge, *Economica*, 4 (NS), 33–54, reprinted in Hayek [48], 33–56

Hayek, F. [1945/48] The uses of knowledge in society, *American Economic Review, 35*, 519–30, reprinted in Hayek [1948], 77–91

Hayek, F. [1948] *Individualism and Economic Order* (Chicago: University of Chicago Press)

Hempel, C. [1966] *Foundations of Natural Science* (Englewood Cliffs: Prentice-Hall)

Hendry, D. [1997] The role of econometrics in scientific economics, in A. d'Autume and J. Cartelier (eds), *Is Economics Becoming a Hard Science?* (Cheltenham: Elgar), 165–86

Hennart, Jean-François, Anderson, E. and Anderson, Erin (1993), Countertrade and the minimization of transaction costs: an empirical examination, *Journal of Law, Economics and Organization, 9*, 290–313

Hey, J. [1981] *Economics in Disequilibrium* (Oxford: Martin Robertson)

Hicks, J. [1937] Mr. Keynes and the classics: a suggested interpretation, *Econometrica*, 5, 147–59

Hicks, J. [1939/46] *Value and Capital, 2nd edn* (Oxford: Clarendon Press)

Hicks, J. [1959] *A Revision of Demand Theory* (Oxford: Clarendon Press)

Hicks, J. [1965] *Capital and Growth* (Oxford: Oxford Univ. Press)

Hicks, J. [1973] The Austrian theory of capital and its rebirth in modern economics, in J. Hicks and W. Weber (eds), *Carl Menger and the Austrian School of Economics* (Oxford: Oxford Univ. Press), 190–206

Hicks, J. [1976] Some questions of time *in* economics, in A. Tang, F. Westfield and J. Worley (eds), *Evolution, Welfare and Time in Economics* (Toronto: Heath), 135–51

Hicks, J. [1979] *Causality in Economics* (Oxford: Blackwell)

Hicks, J. and Allen, R. [1934] A reconsideration of the theory of value, *Economica, 1 (NS)*, 54–76 and 196–219

Hirsch, A. and de Marchi, N. [1990] *Milton Friedman: Economics in Theory and Practice* (Ann Arbor: Univ. of Michigan Press)

Hirshleifer, J. and Riley, J. [1979] The analytics of uncertainty and information: an expositional survey, *Journal of Economic Literature, 17*, 1375–421

Hodgson, G. [1988] *Economics and Institutions: A Manifesto for a Modern Institutional Economics* (Philadelphia: Univ. of Pennsylvania Press)

Hodgson, G. [1993] *Economics and Evolution: Bringing Life Back into Economics* (Cambridge: Polity Press)

Hodgson, G. [1997] The evolutionary and non-Darwinian economics of Joseph Schumpeter, *Journal of Evolutionary Economics, 7*, 131–45

Hodgson, G. [1998] The approach of institutional economics, *Journal of Economic Literature, 36*, 166–92

Hodgson, G. [1999] *Evolution and Institutions: On Evolutionary Economics and the Evolution of Economics* (Cheltenham: Edward Elgar)

Hollis, M. and Nell, E. [1975] *Rational Economic Man* (Cambridge: Cambridge Univ. Press)

Hollis, M. and Sugden, R. [1993] Rationality in action, *Mind, 102*, 1–35

Hoover, K. [2001] *The Methodology of Empirical Macroeconomics* (Cambridge: Cambridge Univ. Press)

Hughes, R.I.G. [1981] Quantum logic, *Scientific American, 245*, 202–13

Hume, D. [1739] *Treatise on Human Nature*

Hutchison, T. [1938] *The Significance and Basic Postulates of Economic Theory* (London: Macmillan)

Hutchison, T. [1988] The case for falsification, in de Marchi [1988], 169–81

Jarvie, I. [1964] *The Revolution in Anthropology* (London: Routledge & Kegan Paul)

Jarvie, I. [2001] *The Republic of Science: The Emergence of Popper's Social View of Science 1935-1945* (Amsterdam: Rodopi)

Kahneman, D. and Tversky, A. [1979] Prospect theory: an analysis of decision under risk, *Econometrica, 47*, 263–91

Keynes, J.M. [1936] *General Theory of Employment, Interest and Money* (New York: Harcourt, Brace & World)

Keynes, J.M. [1937] The general theory of employment, *Quarterly Journal of Economics, 51*, 209–23

Keynes, J.M. [1939] Professor Tinbergens's method, *Economic Journal, 49*, 558–68

Keynes, J.N. [1917] *The Scope and Method of Political Economy, 4th edn* (London: Macmillan)

Klappholz, K. and Agassi, J. [1959] Methodological prescriptions in economics, *Economica, 26 (NS)*, 60–74

Klein, L. [1946] Remarks on the theory of aggregation, *Econometrica, 14*, 303–12

Knight, F. [1921] *Risk, Uncertainty and Profit* (Chicago: Univ. of Chicago Press)

Koopmans, T. [1951] *Activity Analysis of Production and Allocation* (New York: Wiley)

Koopmans, T. [1957] *Three Essays on the State of Economic Science* (New York: McGraw-Hill)

Koopmans, T. [1979] Economics among the sciences, *American Economic Review, 69*, 1–13

Kreps, D. [1990] *Game Theory and Economic Modelling* (Oxford: Clarendon Press)

Krupp, S. [1966] *The Structure of Economic Science: Essays on Methodology* (Englewood Cliffs: Prentice-Hall)

Kuhn, T. [1962/70] *The Structure of Scientific Revolutions, 2nd edn* (Chicago: Chicago Univ. Press)

Kuhn, T. [1971] Notes on Lakatos, in R. Buck and R. Cohen (eds), *Boston Studies in the Philosophy of Science, 8* (Dordrecht: Reidel), 135–46

Kydland, F. and Prescott, E. [1991] The econometrics of the general equilibrium approach to business cycles, *Scandinavian Journal of Economics, 93,* 161–78

Kydland, F. and Prescott, E. [1996] The computational experiment: an econometric tool, *Journal of Economic Perspectives, 10,* 69–85

Laibson, D. [1997] Golden eggs and hyperbolic discounting, *Quarterly Journal of Economics, 111,* 443–77

Lakatos, I. [1970] Falsification and the methodology of scientific research programmes, in I. Lakatos and A. Musgrave (eds), *Criticism and the Growth of Knowledge* (Cambridge: Cambridge Univ. Press), 91–196

Lakatos, I. [1971] History of science and its rational reconstructions, in R. Buck and R. Cohen (eds), *Boston Studies in the Philosophy of Science, 8* (Dordrecht: Reidel), 91–136

Lancaster, K. [1966] A new approach to consumer theory, *Journal of Political Economy, 74,* 132–57

Latsis, S. [1972] Situational determinism in economics, *British Journal for the Philosophy of Science, 23,* 207–45

Latsis, S. [1976] *Methodology and Appraisal in Economics* (Cambridge: Cambridge Univ. Press)

Laue, M. von [1950] *History of Physics* (New York: Academic Press)

Lawson, T. [1988] Probability and uncertainty in economic analysis, *Journal of Post Keynesian Economics, 11,* 38–65

Lawson, T, [1994] A realist theory for economics, in Backhouse [1994a], 257–85

Lawson, T. [1997] *Economics and Reality* (London: Routledge)

Leamer, E. [1983] Let's take the con out of econometrics, *American Economic Review, 73,* 31-43

Leibenstein, H. [1979] A branch of economics is missing: micro-micro theory, *Journal of Economic Literature, 17,* 477–502

Leijonhufvud, A. [1976] Schools, 'revolutions' and research programmes in economic theory, in Latsis [1976], 65–108

Leontief, W. [1947] Introduction to the theory of the internal structure of functional relationships, *Econometrica, 15,* 361–73

Leontief, W. [1971] Theoretical assumptions and nonobserved facts, *American Economic Review, 61,* 74–81

Lester, R. [1946] Shortcomings of marginal analysis for wage-employment problems, *American Economic Review, 36,* 63–82

Lester, R. [1947] Marginalism, minimum wages, and labor markets, *American Economic Review, 37,* 135–48

Lindley, D. [1987] Thomas Bayes (1702-1761), *The New Palgrave: A Dictionary of Economic Theory and Doctrine,* 205–6

Lintner, J. [1965] The valuation of risky assets and the selection of risky investments in stock portfolios and capital budgets, *Review of Economics and Statistics, 47,* 13–37

Lipsey, R. [1963] *An Introduction to Positive Economics, 1st edn* (London: Weidenfeld & Nicolson)

Lipsey, R. [1966] *An Introduction to Positive Economics, 2nd edn* (London: Weidenfeld & Nicolson)

Lipsey, R. [1983] *An Introduction to Positive Economics, 6th edn* (London: Weidenfeld & Nicolson)

Loasby, B. [1993] Institutional stability and change in science and the economy, in U. Mäki, B. Gustafsson and C. Knudsen (eds), *Rationality, Institutions and Economic Methodology* (London: Routledge), 203–21.

Lucas, R. [1980] Methods and problems in business cycle theory, *Journal of Money, Credit and Banking, 12*, 696–715

Lucas, R. [1987] *Models of Business Cycles* (Oxford: Blackwell)

Lucas, R. and Sargent, T. [1978] After Keynesian macroeconometrics, in *After the Phillips Curve*, Federal Reserve Bank of Boston, Conference Series No. 19, 49–72

Machina, M. [1987] Choice under uncertainty: problems solved and unsolved, *Journal of Economic Perspectives, 1*, 121–54

Machlup, F. [1946] Marginalism analysis and empirical research, *American Economic Review, 36*, 519–54

Machlup, F. [1947] Rejoinder to an antimarginalist, *American Economic Review, 37*, 148–54

Machlup, F. [1951] Schumpeter's economic methodology, *The Review of Economics and Statistics, 33*, 145–51

Machlup, F. [1955] The problem of verification in economics, *Southern Economic Journal, 22*, 1–21

Machlup, F. [1963] *Essays on Economic Semantics* (Englewood Cliffs, NJ: Prentice-Hall)

Machlup, F. [1978] *Methodology of Economics and Other Social Sciences* (New York: Academic Press)

Mäki, U. [1990] Methodology of economics: Complaints and guidelines, *Finnish Economic Papers, 3*, 77–84

Mäki, U. [1992] Social conditioning of economics, in Neil de Marchi [1992], 65–104

Mäki, U. [1994] Reorienting the assumptions issue, in Backhouse [1994a], 236–56

Mäki, U. [1995] Diagnosing McCloskey, *Journal of Economic Literature, 33*, 1300–18

Malinvaud, E. [1966] *Statistical Methods of Econometrics* (Chicago: Rand-McNally)

de Marchi, N. (ed.) [1988] *The Popperian Legacy in Economics* (Cambridge: Cambridge Univ. Press)

de Marchi, N. (ed.) [1992] *Post-Popperian Methodology of Economics: Recovering Practice* (Boston: Kluwer)

Marschak, J. [1953] Economic measurements for policy and prediction, in Hood and Koopmans [1953], 1–26

Marshall, A. [1920/49] *Principles of Economics, 8th edn* (London: Macmillan)

Maslow, A. [1954] *Motivation and Personality* (New York: Harper & Row)

Matthews, R.C.O. [1986] The economics of institutions and the sources of growth, *The Economic Journal, 96*, 903–18

Maynard Smith, J. [1970] Time in the evolutionary process, *Studium Generale, 23*, 266–72

Maynard Smith, J. [1982] *Evolution and the Theory of Games* (Cambridge: Cambridge Univ. Press)

McCloskey, D. [1983] The rhetoric of economics, *Journal of Economic Literature, 21*, 481–517

McCloskey, D. [1984] Reply to Caldwell and Coats, *Journal of Economic Literature, 22*, 579–80

McCloskey, D. [1985] *The Rhetoric of Economics* (Madison: Univ. of Wisconsin Press)

McCloskey, D. [1988a] Thick and thin methodologies in the history of economic thought, in de Marchi [1988] 245–57

McCloskey, D. [1988b] The Consequences of rhetoric, in A. Klamer, D. McCloskey and R. Solow (eds), *The Consequences of Economic Rhetoric* (Cambridge, England: Cambridge Univ. Press), 280–93

McCloskey, D. [1988c] Two replies and a dialogue on the rhetoric of economics, *Economics and Philosophy, 4*, 150–66.

McCloskey, D. [1989] Why I am no longer a positivist, *Review of Social Economy, 47*, 225–38

McCloskey, D. [1994] How to do rhetorical analysis and why, in Backhouse [1994a], 319–42

McShea, D.W. [1996] Metazoan complexity and evolution: is there a trend?, *Evolution, 50*, 477–92

Miller, D. [1994] *Critical Rationalism: A Restatement and Defense* (Chicago: Open Court)

Miller, D. [2002] Induction: a problem solved, in J.M. Böhm, H. Holweg and C. Hoock (eds), *Karl Poppers kritischer Rationalismus heute* (Tübingen: Mohr Siebeck), 81–106

Mirowski, P. [1989] *More Heat than Light: Economics as Social Physics, Physics as Nature's Economics* (Cambridge: Cambridge Univ. Press)

Morgan, M. and Morrison, M. [1999] *Models as Mediators: Perspective on Natural and Social Science* (Cambridge: Cambridge Univ. Press)

Morgenstern, O. [1972] Thirteen critical points in contemporary economic theory: an interpretation, *Journal of Economic Literature, 10*, 1163–89

Muth, J. [1961] Rational expectations and the theory of price movements, *Econometrica, 29*, 315–35

Nash, J. [1951] Non-cooperative games, *Annals of Mathematics, 54*, 286–95

Nelson, R. and Winter, S. [1973] Toward an evolutionary theory of economic capabilities, *American Economic Review, 63*, 440–9

Nelson, R. and Winter, S. [1974] Neoclassical vs. evolutionary theories of economic growth: critique and prospectus, *Economic Journal, 84*, 886–905

Nelson, R. and Winter, S. [1982] *An Evolutionary Theory of Economic Change* (London: Harvard Univ. Press)

Nerlove, M. [1972] Lags in economic behavior, *Econometrica, 40*, 221–51

Neumann, J. von [1928] Zur Theorie der Gessellshaftspiele, *Mathematische Annalen*, 295–320

Neumann, J. von [1937/45] A model of general equilibrium, *Review of Economic Studies, 13*, 1–9

Neumann, J. von and Morgenstern, O. [1944] *Theory of Games and Economic Behavior*, (Princeton, N.J.: Princeton Univ. Press)

Newman, G. [1972] Institutional choices and the theory of consumer behaviour, unpublished MA thesis, Simon Fraser University

Newman, G. [1976] An institutional perspective on information, *International Social Science Journal, 28*, 466–92

Newman, G. [1981] Individualism and the theory of short-run aggregate economic coordination, Ph.D. Thesis, Simon Fraser University

Newton, I. [1704/1952] *Optics* (Chicago: University of Chicago Press)

North, D. [1978] Structure and performance: the task of economic history, *Journal of Economic Literature, 16*, 963–78

North, D. [1991] Institutions, *Journal of Economic Perspectives, 5*, 97–112

Oi, Walter Y. [1983] Heterogeneous firms and the organization of production, *Economic Inquiry, 21*, 143–71

Okun, A. [1980] Rational-expectations-with-misperceptions as a theory of the business cycle, *Journal of Money, Credit and Banking, 12*, 817–25

Pareto, V. [1935/63] *The Mind and Society* (New York: Dover Publications)

Pesendorfer, W. [1995] Design innovation and fashion cycles, *American Economic Review, 85*, 771–92

Phelps, E. *et al.* [1970] *Microeconomic Foundations of Employment and Inflation Theory* (New York: Norton)

Pirsig, R. [1974] *Zen and the Art of Motorcycle Maintenance* (New York: Bantam)

Pirsig, R. [1991] *Lila: An Inquiry into Morals* (New York: Bantam Books)

Poincaré, H. [1905/52] *Science and Hypothesis* (New York: Dover)

Poirier, D. [1988] Frequentist and subjectivist perspectives on the problem of model building in economics, *Journal of Economic Perspectives, 2*, 121–70

Popper, K. [1934/59] *Logic of Scientific Discovery* (New York: Science Editions)

Popper, K. [1944/61] *Poverty of Historicism* (New York: Harper & Row)

Popper, K. [1945/66] *The Open Society and its Enemies, 2 vols, 5th edn* (New York: Harper & Row)

Popper, K. [1961/72] Evolution and the tree of knowledge, reprinted in Popper [1972], 256–84

Popper, K. [1963/89] *Conjectures and Refutations: The Growth of Scientific Knowledge* (London: Routledge)

Popper, K. [1963/94] Models, instruments and truth: the status of the rationality principle in the social sciences, in Popper [1994], 154–84

Popper, K. [1972] *Objective Knowledge* (Oxford: Oxford Univ. Press)

Popper, K. [1983] *Realism and the Aim of Science* (London: Routledge)

Popper, K. [1994] *The Myth of the Framework: In Defense of Science and Rationality* (London: Routledge)

Pringle, J. [1951] On the parallel between learning and evolution, *Behaviour, 3*, 90–110.

Quine, W. [1965] *Elementary Logic, rev. edn* (New York: Harper & Row)

Ramsey, F. [1926/31] Truth and probability, in R.B. Braithwaite (ed.), *Foundations of Mathematics and Other Logical Essays* (London: Routledge and Kegan Paul), 156–98 [1931]

Richardson, G. [1959] Equilibrium, expectations and information, *Economic Journal, 69*, 225–37

Robbins, L. [1981] Economics and political economy, *American Economic Review, Proceedings, 71*, 1–10

Robinson, J. [1933] *The Economics of Imperfect Competition* (London: Macmillan)

Robinson, J. [1962] *Economic Philosophy* (London: C.A. Watts)

Robinson, J. [1967] *Economics: An Awkward Corner* (New York: Pantheon)

Robinson, J. [1974] History versus equilibrium, *Thames Papers in Political Economy*

Robson, A. [2001] The biological basis of economic behavior, *Journal of Economic Literature, 39*, 11–33

Roth, A. [1996] Comments on Tversky's 'Rational theory and constructive choice', in K. Arrow, E. Colombatto, M. Perlman, and C. Schmidt (eds), *The Rational Foundations of Economic Behavior* (New York: Macmillan), 198–202

Rotwein, E. [1959] On 'The methodology of positive economics', *Quarterly Journal of Economics, 73*, 554–75

Rotwein, E. [1980] Friedman's critics: a critic's reply to Boland, *Journal of Economic Literature, 18*, 1553–5

Rubinstein, A. [1991] Comments on the interpretation of game theory, *Econometrica, 59*, 909–24

Runde, J. [1998] Clarifying Frank Knight's discussion of the meaning of risk and uncertainty, *Cambridge Journal of Economics, 22*, 39–46

Russell, B. [1945] *A History of Western Philosophy* (New York: Simon & Schuster)

Rutherford, M. [1997] American institutionalism and the history of economics, *Journal of the History of Economic Thought, 19*, 178–95

Rutherford, M. [2001] Institutionalism: then and now, *Journal of Economic Perspectives, 15*, 173–94

Sainsbury, R. [1995] *Paradoxes* (Cambridge: Cambridge Univ. Press)

Salanti, A. [1989] 'Internal' criticism in economic theory: are they really conclusive?, *Economic Notes, 19*, 1–14

Salanti, A. and Serepanti, E. (eds) [1997] *Pluralism in Economics*, (Aldershot and Lyme, NH: Edward Elgar)

Samuelson, L. [1997] *Evolutionary Games and Equilibrium Selection* (London: MIT Press)

Samuelson, P. [1938] A note on the pure theory of consumer behavior, *Economica, 5 (NS)*, 61–71

Samuelson, P. [1947/65] *Foundations of Economic Analysis* (New York: Atheneum)

Samuelson, P. [1948] Consumption theory in terms of revealed preference, *Economica, 15 (NS)*, 243–53

Samuelson, P. [1950a] The problem of integrability in utility theory, *Economica, 17 (NS)*, 355–85

Samuelson, P. [1950b] Valuation of real national income, *Oxford Economic Papers, 2 (NS)*, 1–29

Samuelson, P. [1952] Economic theory and mathematics: an appraisal, *American Economic Review, 42*, 56–66

Samuelson, P. [1953] Consumption theorems in terms of overcompensation rather than indifference comparisons, *Economica, 20 (NS)*, 1–9

Samuelson, P. [1963] Problems of methodology: discussion, *American Economic Review, Proceedings, 53*, 231–6

Samuelson, P. [1963/66] Modern economic realities and individualism, in J. Stiglitz (ed.) *The Collected Scientific Papers of Paul Samuelson* (Cambridge, Mass.: MIT Press), 1407–18

Samuelson, P. [1964] Theory and realism: a reply, *American Economic Review, 54*, 736–9

Samuelson, P. [1965] Professor Samuelson on theory and realism: reply, *American Economic Review, 55*, 1164–72

Samuelson, P. [1967] Monopolistic competition revolution, in R. Kuenne (ed.), *Monopolistic Competition Theory: Studies in Impact* (New York: Wiley)

Samuelson, P. [1972] The consumer does benefit from feasible price stability, *Quarterly Journal of Economics, 86*, 476–93

Samuelson, P. [1987] Out of the closet: a program for the whig history of economic science, *H.E.S. Bulletin, 9*, 51–60

Samuelson, P. [1998] How *Foundations* came to be, *Journal of Economic Literature, 36*, 1375–86

Samuelson, P., Nordhaus, W. and McCallum, J. [1988] *Economics* (Toronto: McGraw-Hill Ryerson)

Savage, L.J. [1954] *The Foundations of Statistics* (New York: Wiley)

Schumpeter, J. [1909] On the concept of social value, *Quarterly Journal of Economics, 23*, 213–32

Schumpeter, J. [1928] The instability of capitalism, *Economic Journal, 38*, 361–86

Schumpeter, J. [1942/50] *Capitalism, Socialism and Democracy, 3rd edn* (New York: Harper & Row)

Scitovsky, T. [1976] *Joyless Economy* (Oxford: Oxford Univ. Press)

Shackle, G. [1972] *Epistemics and Economics* (Cambridge: Cambridge Univ. Press)

Shackle, G. [1973] *An Economic Querist* (Cambridge: Cambridge Univ. Press)

Sharpe, W. [1964] Capital asset prices: a theory of market equilibrium under conditions of risk, *The Journal of Finance, 19*, 425–42

Simon, H. [1955] A behavioral model of rational choice, *Quarterly Journal of Economics, 69*, 99–118

Simon, H. [1963] Problems of methodology: discussion, *American Economic Review, Proceedings, 53*, 229–31

Simon, H. [1979] Rational decision-making in business organizations, *American Economic Review, 69*, 493–513

Simon, H. [1986] Rationality in psychology and economics, *Journal of Business, 59*, s209–24

Smith V. K. [1969] The identification problem and the validity of economic models: a comment, *South African Journal of Economics, 37*, 81

Smith, V.L. [1989] Theory, experiment and economics, *Journal of Economic Perspectives, 3*, 151–69

Solow, R. [1956] A contribution to the theory of economic growth, *Quarterly Journal of Economics, 70*, 65–94

Solow, R. [1979] Alternative approaches to macroeconomic theory: a partial view, *Canadian Journal of Economics, 12*, 339–54

Sraffa, P. [1926] The laws of returns under competitive conditions, *Economic Journal, 38*, 535–550

Steuer, M. [1998] Review of Salanti, A. and Screpanti, E. (eds) [1997], *Economic Journal, 108*, 1926–30

Stewart, I. [1979] *Reasoning and Method in Economics* (London: McGraw-Hill)

Stigler, G. [1961] The economics of information, *Journal of Political Economy, 69*, 213–25

Stigler, G. [1963] Archibald vs. Chicago, *Review of Economic Studies, 30*, 63–4

Stigler, G. and Becker, G. [1977] De gustibus non est disputandum, *American Economic Review, 67*, 76–90

Tarascio, V. and Caldwell, B. [1979] Theory choice in economics: philosophy and practice, *Journal of Economic Issues, 13*, 983–1006

Taylor, P. and Jonker, L. [1978] Evolutionary stable strategies and game dynamics, *Mathematical Biosciences, 40*, 145–56

Vajda, S. [1956] *The Theory of Games and Linear Programming* (London: Methuen & Co.)

Wald, A. [1936/51] On some systems of equations of mathematical economics, *Econometrica, 19*, 368–403

Watkins, J. [1957] Between analytic and empirical, *Philosophy, 32*, 112–31

Weibull, J. [1995] *Evolutionary Game Theory* (London: MIT Press)

Weibull, J. [1998] What have we learned from evolutionary game theory so far? Research Institute of Industrial Economics working paper 487, 1–29

Weintraub, E.R. [1977] The microfoundations of macroeconomics: a critical survey, *Journal of Economic Literature, 15*, 1–23

Weintraub, E.R. [1979] *Microfoundations* (Cambridge: Cambridge Univ. Press)

Weintraub, E.R. [1985] *General Equilibrium Analysis: Studies in Appraisal,* (Cambridge: Cambridge Univ. Press)

Weintraub, E.R. [1988] The neo-Walrasian program is empirically progressive, in de Marchi [1988], 213–27

Weirich, P. [1998] *Equilibrium and Rationality: Game Theory Revised by Decision Rules*, (Cambridge: Cambridge Univ. Press)

Weisskopf, W. [1979] The method is the ideology: from a Newtonian to a Heisenbergian paradigm in economics, *Journal of Economic Issues, 13*, 869–84

Williamson, O. [1981] The Modern Corporation: Origins, Evolution, Attributes, *Journal of Economic Literature, 19*, 1537–68

Williamson, O. [1985] *The Economic Institutions of Capitalism: Firms, Markets, Relational Contracting* (London: Collier Macmillan Publishers)

Winter, S. [1964] Economics 'natural selection' and the theory of the firm, *Yale Economic Essays, 4*, 225–72

Winter, S. [1971] Satisficing, selection and the innovating remnant, *Quarterly Journal of Economics, 85*, 237–61

Wisdom, J. [1963] The refutability of 'irrefutable' laws, *British Journal for the Philosophy of Science, 13*, 303–6

Wong, S. [1973] The 'F-twist' and the methodology of Paul Samuelson, *American Economic Review, 63*, 312–25

Wong, S. [1978] *The Foundations of Paul Samuelson's Revealed Preference Theory* (London: Routledge & Kegan Paul)

Name Index

Subject Index

Printed in the United States
by Baker & Taylor Publisher Services